The New Sabin

Entries 11226-13513

The New Sabin;
Books Described by Joseph Sabin and His
Successors, Now Described Again on the
Basis of Examination of Originals,
and Fully Indexed by Title, Subject,
Joint Authors, and Institutions and Agencies

by

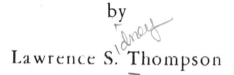

Lawrence S. Thompson

Entries 11226-13513

Volume V

The Whitston Publishing Company
Troy, New York
1978

PREFACE

A milestone has been passed with this volume of *The New Sabin*. The cumulative author-title-subject-secondary entry index, including all titles in the first five volumes, provides many avenues of access to a significant, although as yet uneven, collection of Americana. As the set grows, and as each fifth volume is accompanied by a cumulative index, an increasingly larger collection of Americana will be available through many approaches. At present there are many gaps in the coverage of Americana in this first cumulative index. With the indexes projected for the tenth, fifteenth, and each subsequent fifth volume, students on all levels will find detail in *The New Sabin* represented in no other single guide to the historical literature of this hemisphere.

The cumulative indexes will necessarily have many of the deficiencies (as well as advantages) of the traditional library catalog, since this work is based on catalog cards prepared for various microform collections which include titles in the original Sabin and others which fall within its scope. There are certain entries which contain a very large number of references, apparently unwieldy, yet representing mini-bibliographies of basic works in broad fields (*e.g.,* history of individual states and regions). On the other hand, many subject and secondary entries have been added to those Library of Congress cards which were used in order to provide analysis in depth, on the basis of actual examination of the texts described here. Original cataloging was quite generous in assigning subject and secondary entries, with a view to their inclusion in this index. In general, the policy has been to provide an index which will gradually become a massive historical encyclopedia of America.

The fifth volume of *The New Sabin* contains titles taken directly from Sabin's *Dictionary*. Just as in the first four volumes, all titles recorded here are in print in microform. Titles in this volume have been issued by the Lost Cause Press, Louisville. Many of these microforms were copied from originals in the Library of Congress, and notation of made-up series of bound pamphlets (*e.g.,* Duane, Wolcott, Hazard, Miscellaneous) has been retained in our entries.

Lawrence S. Thompson
Lexington, Kentucky
May, 1978

To James Bennett Childs

1896-1977

11226 The American laborer, devoted to the cause of protection
to home industry, embracing the arguments, reports and
speeches of the ablest civilians of the United States
in favor of the policy of protection to American labor,
with the statistics of production in the United States
... v. 1; Apr. 1842-Mar. 1843. New York, Greeley &
McElrath, 1843.
    1 p.l., 381, [1] p.   24 cm.   monthly.
    Horace Greeley, editor.

11227 The answer at large to Mr. P-tt's speech. London,
Printed for W. Nicoll, 1766.
    22 p.   19 1/2 cm.

11228 Army and Navy chronicle. v. 1-13, no. 18 (no. 1-383);
Jan. 3, 1835-May 21, 1842. Washington, T. Barnard
[etc.]
    13 v. in 12.   illus.   26cm. (v. 1: 29 cm.)
weekly.
    Publication suspended Jan. 14-Aug. 1841?
    Vol. 1, no. 1 preceded by a specimen number dated
June 30, 1834.
    Called "new series" beginning with v. 2.
    Edited by B. Homans.
    Superseded by the Army and Navy chronicle and
scientific repository in Jan. 1843.

11229 [Atwater, Caleb] 1778-1867.
    Mysteries of Washington city, during several months
of the session of the 28th Congress. By a citizen of
Ohio. Washington, D. C., Printed by G. A. Sage, 1844.
    xi, 218 p., 1 l.   16 1/2 cm.

11230 [Ayres de Casal, Manuel] b. 1754?
    Corografia brazilica, ou, Relação historico-geo-
grafica do reino do Brazil, composta c dedicada a Sua
Magestade fidelissima por hum presbitero secular do
gram priorado do Crato... Rio de Janeiro, Impressão
regia, 1817.
    2 v.   22 cm.

11231   Backman, Daniel And.
        ... Om nyttan som kunnat tilfalla wårt kjäre fäder-
        nesland af des nybygge i America, fordom Nya Sverige
        kalladt... under Herr Pehr Kalms inseende, til all-
        mänt ompröfwande och förswarande den 13. julii, 1754.
        i Åbo... för magister wärdighetens ärhållande... Åbo,
        Jacob Merckel, 1754.
            16 p.   22 cm.

11232   Barlow, Joel, 1754-1812.
            The political writings of Joel Barlow - Containing -
        Advice to the privileged orders. Letter to the Nation-
        al convention. Letter to the people of Piedmont. The
        conspiracy of kings. A new ed. cor. New York, Printed
        by Mott & Lyon, at their printing office, no. 71,
        Barclay street, and sold by them at their store, no.
        70, Vesey-street, 1796.
            xvi, [17]-258 p.   17 1/2 cm.

11233   Barnes, William H[oratio]
            History of the Thirty-ninth Congress of the United
        States. By William H. Barnes... Indianapolis, Ind.,
        Macauley & company, 1867.
            613 p.   front. (port.)   23 1/2 cm.

11234   Barnum, Phineas Taylor, 1810-1891.
            The humbugs of the world. An account of humbugs,
        delusions, impositions, quackeries, deceits and
        deceivers generally, in all ages. By P. T. Barnum...
        New York, Carleton, 1866.
            x, [11]-424 p.   19 1/2 cm.

11235   Barré de Saint-Venant, Jean, 1737-1810.
            Des colonies modernes sous la zone torride, et
        particulièrement de celle de Saint-Domingue; ouvrage
        dans lequel on découvre les causes de leurs malheurs,
        et où l'on développe les véritables principes du
        gouvernement qui leur convient; les moyens économiques
        de... rendre le sort des nègres préférable à celui
        d'aucun peuple de l'Europe. Par m. Barré Saint-
        Venant... Paris, Brochot père et compagnie, an X
        (1802)
            1 p.l., xvi, 516 p.   fold. tab.   20 cm.

11236 Barrington, Shute, bp. of Durham, 1734-1826.
       The political life of Wiliam Wildman, viscount
       Barrington, comp. from original papers by his brother,
       Shute, bishop of Durham. London, Printed by W. Bulmer
       and co., 1815.
       2 p.l., ii, 207, [4] p.   front. (port.)
       25 1/2 x 27 cm.

11237 Barrow, Sir John, bart., 1764-1848.
       An auto-biographical memoir of Sir John Barrow,
       bart., late of the Admiralty; including reflections,
       observations, and reminiscences, at home and abroad,
       from early life to advanced age. London, J. Murray,
       1847.
       xi, 515 p.   front. (port.)   22 1/2 cm.

11238 Barrow, Sir John, bart., 1764-1848.
       Voyages of discovery and research within the Arctic
       regions, from the year 1818 to the present time:
       under the command of the several naval officers em-
       ployed by sea and land in search of a North-west
       passage from the Atlantic to the Pacific: with two
       attempts to reach the North pole. Abridged and
       arranged from the official narratives, with occasional
       remarks. By Sir John Barrow... London, J. Murray,
       1846.
       xiv, 530 p.   front. (port.) 2 maps (1 fold.)
       22 1/2 cm.

11239 [Barry, Henry] 1750-1822.
       The general, attacked by a subaltern; or, The
       structures on The friendly address examined, and a
       refutation of its principles attempted. Addressed
       to the people of America... Boston, printed;
       New York, re-printed, by James Rivington [1775]
       11 p.   20 cm.
       A reply to Charles Lee's "Strictures on a pamphlet,
       entitled, a 'Friendly address to all reasonable
       Americans' [by Thomas Bradbury Chandler]"

11240 Barton, David, 1783-1837.
       Speech of Mr. D. Barton, of Missouri; delivered in
       the Senate of the United States, February 9th, 1830,
       in the debate which arose upon Mr. Foot's resolution
       relative to the public lands. 2d ed. Washington,
       The National journal, 1830.
       36 p.   23 1/2 cm.

11241   Barton, William Paul Crillon, 1786-1856.
            Hints for naval officers cruising in the West
        Indies. By William P. C. Barton, M. D. Philadelphia,
        E. Littel; Boston, Carter & Hendee [etc., etc.] 1830.
            222 p.   15 cm.

11242   Bartram, John, 1699-1777.
            Observations on the inhabitants, climate, soil,
        rivers, productions, animals, and other matters
        worthy of notice. Made by Mr. John Bartram, in his
        travels from Pensilvania to Onondago, Oswego and the
        Lake Ontario, in Canada. To which is annex'd, a
        curious account of the cataracts at Niagara. By Mr.
        Peter Kalm... London, Printed for J. Whiston and
        B. White, 1751.
            1 p.l., viii, [9]-94 p.   front. (fold. plan.)
        21 cm.

11243   The battle of Fort Sumter and first victory of the
        southern troops, April 13th, 1861. Full accounts of
        the bombardment, with sketches of the scenes, inci-
        dents, etc. Comp. chiefly from the detailed reports
        of the Charleston press. Pub. by request. Charleston,
        Steam-power presses of Evans & Cogswell, 1861.
            35 p.   front. (fold. map)   22 1/2 cm.

11244   Baxter, William.
            Pea Ridge and Prairie Grove; or, Scenes and inci-
        dents of the war in Arkansas... Cincinnati, Poe &
        Hitchcock, 1864.
            262 p.   19 cm.

11245   Beck, Lewis Caleb, 1798-1853.
            Botany of the northern and middle states; or, A
        description of the plants found in the United States,
        north of Virginia, arranged according to the natural
        system. With a synopsis of the genera according to
        the Linnaean system - a sketch of the rudiments of
        botany, and a glossary of terms. By Lewis C. Beck,
        M. D. Albany, Printed by Webster and Skinners, 1833.
            2 p.l., v-lv, 471 p.   19 cm.

11246   Beecher, Lyman, 1775-1863.
            Letters of the Rev. Dr. Beecher and Rev. Mr.
        Nettleton, on the "new measures" in conducting re-
        vivals of religion. With a review of a sermon, by
        Novanglus... Published at the request of several

4

gentlemen of the city of New York. New York,
G. & C. Carvill, 1828.
viii, [9]-104 p.   21 1/2 cm.
"Review. A sermon preached in the Presbyterian
church, Troy, March 4, 1827, by the Rev. Charles G.
Finney": p. 44-80.

11247 Beecher, Lyman, 1775-1863.
Six sermons on the nature, occasions, signs, evils,
and remedy of intemperance. By Lyman Beecher, D. D.
New York, American tract society [c1827]
104 p.   15 1/2 cm.

11248 Belfast, Ireland.
Ireland and America, via Galway. Memorial to the
Right Hon. Lord John Russell, from the Town council,
Harbour commissioners, and Chamber of commerce of
Belfast, and statement in support thereof by the
deputation from these bodies. London, J. Madden,
1852.
16 p.   21 cm.
Petitioning an Irish transatlantic packet station.

11249 Bell, Benjamin, 1752-1836.
A sermon preached at Steuben April 1013. In which
are shewn the evil effects of war, and when it may
be lawful and expedient to go to war. By Rev. Benjamin Bell, A. M. Sangerfield [N. Y.] J. Tenny,
printer, 1814.
84, [2] p.   16 1/2 cm.

11250 Bell, John, 1797-1869.
An address, delivered before the Alumni society of
the University of Nashville, October 3, 1843, by the
Hon. John Bell, A. M. With an appendix, containing
a catalogue of the alumni and certain proceedings of
the Society. Nashville, W. F. Bang & co., printers,
1844.
42 p.   22 1/2 cm.

11251 Bellamy, George Anne, 1731?-1788.
An apology for the life of George Anne Bellamy,
late of Covent-Garden theatre. Written by herself.
To which is annexed, her original letter to John
Calcraft... The 4th ed. ... London, Printed for the
author, and sold by J. Bell, 1786.
5 v.   fronts.   17 1/2 cm.

"Supposed to have been arranged and transcribed by Alexander Bicknell." - Dict. nat. biog.

11252   Belsham, Thomas, 1750-1829.
Memoirs of the late Reverend Theophilus Lindsey, M. A., including a brief analysis of his works; together with anecdotes and letters of eminent persons, his friends and correspondents; also a general view of the progress of the Unitarian doctrine in England and America. By Thomas Belsham... 2d ed., cor. London, Printed for R. Hunter, 1820.
xvi, 423 p.   23 cm.

11253   Bentham, Jeremy, 1748-1832.
Papers relative to codification and public instruction; including correspondence with the Russian emperor, and divers constituted authorities in the American United States. Pub. by Jeremy Bentham. London, Printed by J. M'Creery [etc.] 1817.
2 p.l., 171 p.   22 cm.

11254   Bentom, Clark.
A statement of facts and law, relative to the prosecution of the Rev. Clark Bentom, Protestant missionary from the London missionary society, for the assumption of the office of a dissenting minister of the gospel in Quebec, by the King's attorney general of Lower Canada... Troy, Printed for the author by O. Penniman & co., 1804.
32 p.   20 cm.

11255   [Benton, Thomas Hart] 1782-1858.
Historical and legal examination of that part of the decision of the Supreme court of the United States in the Dred Scott case, which declares the unconstitutionality of the Missouri compromise act and the self-extension of the Constitution to territories, carrying slavery along with it. With an appendix, containing: I. The debates in the Senate in March, 1849, between Mr. Webster and Mr. Calhoun, on the legislative extension of the Constitution to territories, as contained in vol. II. ch. CLXXXII of the "Thirty years' view." II. The inside view of the southern sentiment, in relation to the Wilmot proviso, as seen in vol. II. ch. CLXVIII of the "Thirty years' view." III. Review of President Pierce's annual message to Congress of December, 1856, so far as it

relates to the abrogation of the Missouri compromise
act and the classification of parties... By the
author of the "Thirty years' view." New York, D.
Appleton and company, 1857.
    4, [3]-193 p.   24 cm.

11256 Berkeley, George, bp. of Cloyne, 1685-1753.
    A word to the wise; or, An exhortation to the Roman
Catholic clergy of Ireland. By George Berkeley, D.D.,
bishop of Cloyne... Dublin, Printed by G. Faulkner,
1752.
    (In A collection of tracts and treatises illustrative
of the natural history, antiquities, and the political
and social state of Ireland. Dublin, 1860-61. 23 cm.
v. 2, p. [205]-224)

11257 Bernard, David, 1798-1876.
    Light on masonry: a collection of all the most
important documents on the subject of speculative
free masonry: embracing the reports of the Western
committees in relation to the abduction of William
Morgan... with all the degrees of the order conferred
in a master's lodge, as written by Captain William
Morgan... By Elder David Bernard... Utica, W.
Williams, printer, 1829.
    x, [2], [13]-506, 54, [1] p.   front. (port.) pl.
18 cm.

11258 Bernard, Sir Francis, bart., 1712?-1779.
    Select letters on the trade and government of
America; and the Principles of law and polity, applied
to the American colonies. Written by Governor Bernard, at Boston, in the years 1763, 4, 5, 6, 7, and 8.
Now first published: to which are added The petition
of the assembly of Massachuset's bay against the
governor, his answer thereto, and the order of the
king in Council thereon. London, Printed for T.
Payne, 1774.
    1 p.l., vii, 130 p.   23 1/2 cm.

11259 Berredo, Bernardo Pereira de, d. 1748.
    Annaes historicos do estado do Maranhão, em que
se da' noticia do seu descobrimento, e tudo o mais
que nelle tem succedido desde o anno em que foy des-
cuberto até o de 1718: offerecidos ao augustissimo
monarca D. João v. nosso senhor. Escritos por Bernardo Pereira de Berredo... Segunda edição. Maranhão,

Typographia Maranhense, 1849.
xxv, 655, xi p.   20 1/2 cm.

11260   Berriman, William.
A sermon preach'd before the honourable Trustees
for establishing the colony of Georgia in America,
and the associates of the late Rev. Dr. Bray; at their
anniversary meeting, March 15, 1738-9. In the parish
church of St. Bridget, alias St. Bride, in Fleetstreet,
London. By William Berriman... London, J. Carter,
1739.
24 p.   22 cm.

11261   Biart, Lucien, 1828-1897.
La terre chaude; scènes de moeurs mexicaines,
par Lucien Biart... Paris, E. Jung-Treuttel [1862]
2 p.l., iii, 327 p., 1 l.   17 1/2 cm.

11262   Biddle, Richard, 1796-1847.
Speech of Mr. Biddle, on the bill to authorize
the issue of treasury notes. Delivered in the House
of representatives, May 15, 1838. Washington, 1838.
19 p.   23 1/2 cm.

11263   Bigelow, John, 1817-1911.
Les États-Unis d'Amérique en 1863; leur histoire
politique, leurs ressources minéralogiques, agri-
coles, industrielles et commerciales, et la part pour
laquelle ils ont contribué à la richesse et à la
civilisation du monde entier, par John Bigelow...
Paris, L. Hachette et c^{ie}, 1863.
3 p.l., [iii]-xxiv, 551 p.   fold. tab.   22 cm.

11264   Bigelow, John Flavel, 1818-1884.
The hand of God in American history. A discourse
delivered in the Baptist church, Keeseville, N. Y.,
July 7, 1861; also before the United literary
societies of New Hampton institution, Fairfax, Vt.,
July 15, 1861. By Rev. John F. Bigelow... Burlington, W. H. & C. A. Hoyt & co., printers, 1861.
42 p.   23 1/2 cm.

11265   Biggs, William.
The military history of Europe, &c. from the commencement of the war with Spain in 1739, to the
treaty of Aix-la-Chapelle in 1748; containing all
the transactions of that war both by sea and land;

also comprehending a concise and impartial history
of the rebellion in Scotland. By William Biggs...
London, Printed for R. Baldwin [etc.] 1755.
    4 p.l., 411 (i.e. 439), [9] p.   3 fold. tab.
20 1/2 cm.
    Paging irregular: nos. 305-332 repeated.

11266 Bigland, John, 1750-1832.
    Letters on the study and use of ancient and modern
history: containing observations and reflections on
the causes and consequences of those events which
have produced conspicuous changes in the aspect of
the world, and the general state of human affairs.
By John Bigland... Philadelphia, Printed for W. W.
Woodward, 1806.
    xvi, 17-536 p.   18 1/2 cm.

11267 Bill, Ledyard, 1836-1907, comp.
    Pen-pictures of the war. Lyrics, incidents, and
sketches of the rebellion; comprising a choice selection of pieces by our best poets, also, current and
well authenticated anecdotes and incidents of the
war. Together with a full account of many of the
great battles, also, a complete historical record of
all events, both civil and military, from the commencement of the rebellion. Comp. by Ledyard Bill.
New York, 1864.
    x, [11]-344 p.   front.   20 1/2 cm.

11268 Billerica, Mass.
    Celebration of the two hundredth anniversary of
the incorporation of Billerica, Massachusetts,
May 29th, 1855; including the proceedings of the
committee, address, poem, and other exercises of
the occasion. With an appendix... Lowell, S. J.
Varney, 1855.
    152 p.   23 cm.

11269 Bingham, John Armor, 1815-1900.
    Argument of John A. Bingham... before the Senate
of the United States sitting for the trial of Andrew
Johnson, president of the United States, impeached
of high crimes and misdemeanors, May 4, 5 and 6,
1868. Washington, F. & J. Rives & G. A. Bailey,
1868.
    59 p.   23 cm.

11270 [Binney, Horace] 1780-1875.
　　　An inquiry into the formation of Washington's
　　Farewell address... Philadelphia, Parry & McMillan,
　　1859.
　　　vii, [9]-250 p.　　23 1/2 cm.

11271 [Binney, Horace] 1780-1875.
　　　The leaders of the old bar of Philadelphia...
　　Philadelphia, Printed by C. Sherman & son, 1859.
　　　v, [7]-120 p.　　22 1/2 cm.

11272 Binney, Horace, 1780-1875.
　　　The privilege of the writ of habeas corpus under
　　the Constitution. Philadelphia, T. B. Pugh, 1862.
　　　2 v.　　19 cm.
　　　Part 2 published by J. Campbell.

11273 [Birch, James H　　　] 1804-1878.
　　　Letters to the President of the United States
　　exposing the official malversations of the commis-
　　sioner of the General land office and of the secretary
　　of the Interior as shown in Senate committee report,
　　no. 289.　Saint Joseph, Mo., F. M. Posegate & co.,
　　printers, 1858.
　　　cover-title, 39, [1] p.　　22 cm.

11274 Bird, Francis William, 1809-1894.
　　　The last agony of the great bore.　2d ed.　By F. W.
　　Bird...　Boston, E. P. Dutton & co., 1868.
　　　96 p.　　23 cm.
　　　Relating to the Hoosac tunnel.

11275 Bird, Francis William, 1809-1894.
　　　The road to ruin; or, The decline and fall of the
　　Hoosac tunnel... By F. W. Bird.　Boston, Wright &
　　Potter, printers, 1862.
　　　46 p.　　23 1/2 cm.

11276 Birdseye, George W　　　1844-
　　　... Woman and the war.　A poem, by George W.
　　Birdseye...　New York, J. Dickson, book and job
　　printer, 1865.
　　　22, [2] p.　　18 1/2 cm.

11277 Bishop, John Soast, 1834-1915.
　　　A concise history of the war, designed to accompany
　　Perrine's new war map of the southern states, with an

introduction and statistical appendix, comp. from
authentic sources. By Lt. Col. John S. Bishop.
Indianapolis, C. O. Perrine [c1864]
   1 p.l., v-x, 11-213, vi [i.e., v] p.   fold. map.
15 cm.

11278   Bishop, Judson Wade, 1831-1917.
        History of Fillmore county, Minnesota, with an
   outline of her resources, advantages, and the inducements she offers to those seeking homes in the west.
   By J. W. Bishop, C. E.   Chatfield, Minn., Holley &
   Brown, printers, 1858.
        40 p.   front. (fold. map)   21 1/2 cm.

11279   Bishop, Samuel G
        Eulogium on the death of George Washington.   By
   Samuel G. Bishop.   Roxbury [Bradstreet press]   Priv.
   print. for W. Elliot Woodward, 1866.
        1 p.l., iv, 15 p.   27 1/2 cm.

11280   Blair, Montgomery, 1813-1883.
        Letter of Hon. Montgomery Blair, postmaster general,
   to the meeting held at the Cooper institute, New
   York, March 6, 1862.   Washington, Printed at the
   Congressional globe office, 1862.
        8 p.   23 1/2 cm.
        On slavery.

11281   Blake, Francis, 1774-1817.
        An examination of the constitutionality of the
   embargo laws; comprising a view of the arguments on
   that question before the Honorable John Davis,
   esquire, judge of the District Court for Massachusetts,
   in the case of the United States vs. brigantine
   William, tried and determined at Salem (Mass.)
   September term, 1808.   To which is added, The opinion
   pronounced by the court on the constitutional question,
   arising in the trial of the case.   Worcester, Printed
   by Goulding and Stow, 1808.
        61 p.   25 cm.

11282   Blake, William Phipps, 1826-1910.
        Annotated catalogue of the principal mineral
   species hitherto recognized in California, and the
   adjoining states and territories; being a report
   to the California State board of agriculture, by
   William P. Blake, geologist of the California State

11

board of agriculture... Sacramento, Printed for
the author, 1866.
31, [1] p.   23 1/2 cm.

11283 Blake, William Phipps, 1826-1910.
Report of a geological reconnaissance in California:
made in connection with the expedition to survey
routes in California, to connect with the surveys of
routes for a railroad from the Mississippi River to
the Pacific Ocean, under the command of Lieut. R. S.
Williamson, Corps Top. Eng'rs, in 1853. By William
P. Blake... With an appendix, containing descriptions
of portions of the collection, by Prof. Louis Agassiz,
Aug. A. Gould, M. D., Prof. J. W. Bailey, T. A. Conrad,
Prof. John Torrey, Prof. Geo. C. Schaeffer, J. D.
Easter, Ph. D. New York, London, H. Baillière [etc.,
etc.] 1858.
xvi p., 1 l., 370 p., 1 l., xiii p.   illus.,
36 pl. (incl. front., part col.) iv col. maps (1
fold.) diagrs. (part fold.)   30 1/2 x 24 cm.

11284 Blatchford, John, 1762(ca.)-1794(ca.)
The narrative of John Blatchford, detailing his
sufferings in the revolutionary war, while a prisoner
with the British. As related by himself. With an
introduction and notes, by Charles I. Bushnell.
New York, Priv. print., 1865.
2 p.l., [iii]-vl, [7]-127 p.   front. (port.)
pl.   24 cm.
Includes a reprint of original t.p.: Narrative
of remarkable occurences in the life of John Blatchford, of Cape Ann, commonwealth of Massachusetts,
containing, his treatment in Nova Scotia - the West
Indies - Great Britain - France, and the East Indies,
as a prisoner in the late war. Taken from his own
mouth. New London, Printed by T. Green, 1788.
Also issued as no. 3 of v. 2 of Bushnell's Crumbs
for antiquarians, New York, 1864-1866.

11285 Bliss, Leonard, 1811-1842.
The history of Rehoboth, Bristol county, Massachusetts; comprising a history of the present towns
of Rehoboth, Seekonk, and Pawtucket, from their
settlement to the present time; together with
sketches of Attleborough, Cumberland, and a part of
Swansey and Barrington, to the time that they were
severally separated from the original town. By

12

Leonard Bliss, jr. ... Boston, Otis, Broaders,
and company, 1836.
v, 294 p., 1 l.   23 1/2 cm.

11286 Bliss, Sylvester.
A geography of New England: being a descriptive
key, to accompany the "Outline map of New England"
... Boston, J. P. Jewett & co., 1847.
96 p.   15 cm.

11287 Blodget, Lorin, 1823-1901.
On the climatic conditions of the summer of 1853,
most directly affecting its sanatary character (a
report to the secretary of the Smithsonian institution, Washington) By Lorin Blodget... New York,
Holman, Gray & co., printers, 1853.
23 p.   23 cm.
From the New York journal of medicine.

11288 [Blodget, Samuel] 1757-1814.
Thoughts on the increasing wealth and national
economy of the United States of America. City of
Washington, Printed by Way and Groff, North E street,
near the Post-office, 1801.
vi, [7]-40 p.   fold. tab.   22 1/2 cm.
The preface, addressed "To the people of America",
is signed "Observator".
"The first book printed in the city of Washington."
- A. R. Spofford.

11289 Blois, John T
Gazetteer of the state of Michigan, in three parts
... with a succinct history of the state, from the
earliest period to the present time... with an
appendix, containing the usual statistical tables
and a directory for emigrants, &c. By John T. Blois.
Detroit, S. L. Rood & co.; New York, Robinson,
Pratt & co., 1838.
xi, [13]-418 p.   18 1/2 cm.

11290 Blood, Henry Ames, 1838-1901?
The history of Temple, N. H. By Henry Ames
Blood... Boston, Printed by G. C. Rand & Avery,
1860.
v, [2] p., 1 l., [3]-352 p.   front., plates,
ports.   23 cm.

11291   Blood, William.
        A mission to the Indians of Orialla, South America.
        To which is added, a narrative of the destruction,
        by fire, of "The Amazon". With reflections, by the
        Rev. William Blood, one of the survivors. With six
        illustrations. London, Partridge and Oakey [1853]
           1 p.l., x, 190 p.   front. (port.) 6 pl.   18 cm.

11292   [Bloodgood, Simeon De Witt] 1799-1866.
        An Englishman's sketch-book; or, Letters from New
        York... New York, G. and C. Carvill, 1828.
           2 p.l., [iii]-iv, [7]-195, [1] p.   20 cm.

11293   Bloodgood, Simeon De Witt, 1799-1866.
        A treatise on roads, their history, character, and
        utility; being the substance of two lectures deli-
        vered before the Young men's association of the city
        of Albany. By S. De Witt Bloodgood. Albany, O.
        Steele, 1838.
           vi, [7]-227, [1] p.   20 cm.
        "Laws of New York. Highways and bridges":
        p. 175-210.
        "Turnpike corporations": p. 211-227.

11294   The bloody week! Riot, murder & arson, containing a
        full account of this wholesale outrage on life and
        property, accurately prepared from official sources,
        by eye witnesses, with portraits of "Andrews," the
        leader and "Rosa," his Eleventh street mistress...
        New York, Coutant & Baker [1863]
           cover-title, 32 p.   23 cm.

11295   Bloor, Alfred Janson, d. 1917.
        Letters from the Army of the Potomac, written
        during the month of May, 1864, to several of the
        supply correspondents of the U. S. sanitary commis-
        sion, by Alfred J. Bloor, assistant secretary.
        Washington, D. C., McGill & Witherow, printers, 1864.
           67 p.   25 cm.

11296   Blount, William, 1749-1800, defendant.
        Proceedings on the impeachment of William Blount,
        a senator of the United States from the state of
        Tennessee, for high crimes and misdemeanors. Phila-
        delphia, Printed by Joseph Gales, 1799.
           102 p.   23 cm.

11297   Blow, Henry Taylor, 1817-1875.
            Speech of Hon. Henry T. Blow, of Mo., in reply to
        the charges of Hon. F. P. Blair and the postmaster
        general. Delivered in the House of representatives,
        Tuesday, February 23, 1864. [Washington, McGill &
        Witherow, printers, 1864]
            16 p.   24 cm.

11298   Blundell, Bezer.
            The contributions of John Lewis Peyton to the his-
        tory of Virginia and of the civil war in America,
        1861-65. Reviewed by B. Blundell... London, J.
        Wilson, 1868.
            46 p.   20 1/2 cm.

11299   Blunt, Joseph, 1792-1860.
            A historical sketch of the formation of the confe-
        deracy, particularly with reference to the provincial
        limits and the jurisdiction of the general government
        over Indian tribes and the public territory. By
        Joseph Blunt. New York, G. and C. Carvill, 1825.
            6, 116 p.   21 cm.

11300   Blyth, Joseph.
            An oration, on the death of General George Washing-
        ton, delivered at the chapel of All Saint's parish,
        on the 22d of February, 1800, at the desire of the
        officers and privates of Capt. Ward's company, and
        published by their request. By Doctor Joseph Blyth.
        Georgetown, S. C., Printed by John Burd, 1800.
            22 p.   19 cm.

11301   Boardman, George Dana, 1828-1903.
            Addresses delivered in the meeting-house of the
        First Baptist church of Philadelphia, April 14th,
        16th, and 19th, 1865, by the Reverend George Dana
        Boardman, pastor. [Philadelphia, Sherman & co.,
        printers, 1865]
            cover-title, 64 p.   23 cm.
            Each address has special t.-p.
            Contents. - An address in commemoration of the
        re-establishment of the national flag at Fort Sumter
        ... - Death, the law of life. A discourse deli-
        vered on the Sunday morning after the murder of
        President Lincoln... - An address in commemoration
        of Abraham Lincoln...

11302   Boardman, George Nye, 1825-1915.
         The death of President Lincoln. A sermon, preached
         in the Presbyterian church, Binghamton, Sabbath
         morning, April 16, 1865, by George N. Boardman...
         Binghamton, N. Y., F. N. Chase, printer, 1865.
         16 p.   22 cm.

11303   Boardman, Henry Augustus, 1808-1880.
         The American union: a discourse delivered on
         Thursday, December 12, 1850, the day of the annual
         thanksgiving in Pennsylvania, and repeated on Thurs-
         day, December 19, in the Tenth Presbyterian church,
         Philadelphia. By Henry A. Boardman, D. D.   Phila-
         delphia, Lippincott, Grambo and co., successors to
         Grigg, Elliot & co., 1851.
         iv, [5]-56 p.   24 cm.

11304   Boardman, Henry Augustus, 1808-1880.
         A discourse on the life and character of Daniel
         Webster. By H. A. Boardman, D. D. Philadelphia,
         J. M. Wilson, 1852.
         64 p.   22 cm.

11305   Boardman, Henry Augustus, 1808-1880.
         The federal judiciary. A Thanksgiving discourse,
         by Henry A. Boardman, D. D. Philadelphia, W. S. &
         A. Martien, 1862.
         54 p.   23 cm.

11306   Boardman, Henry Augustus, 1808-1880.
         Healing and salvation for our country from God
         alone. A sermon preached in the Tenth Presbyterian
         church, Philadelphia, on Thanksgiving day, Nov. 24,
         1864. By Henry A. Boardman, D. D. Philadelphia,
         W. S. & A. Martien, 1864.
         24 p.   22 1/2 cm.

11307   Boardman, Henry Augustus, 1808-1880.
         The importance of religion to the legal profession:
         with some remarks on the character of the late
         Charles Chauncey, esq. A discourse delivered on
         Sunday evening, September 30th, and repeated on
         Sunday evening, October 14th, 1849, in the Tenth
         Presbyterian church, Philadelphia. By Henry A.
         Boardman, D. D. Philadelphia, W. S. Martien, 1849.
         40 p.   23 cm.

11308   Boardman, Henry Augustus, 1808-1880.
        The low value set upon human life in the United
        States: a discourse delivered on Thanksgiving-day,
        November 24th, 1853, by H. A. Boardman, D. D.
        Philadelphia, J. M. Wilson, 1853.
        32 p.   22 1/2 cm.

11309   Boardman, Henry Augustus, 1808-1880.
        The new doctrine of intervention, tried by the
        teachings of Washington: an address delivered in
        the Tenth Presbyterian church, Philadelphia... the
        23d and 24th of February, 1852. By H. A. Boardman,
        D. D.   Philadelphia, Lippincott, Grambo and co.,
        1852.
        63 p.   22 1/2 cm.

11310   Boardman, Henry Augustus, 1808-1880.
        The peace we need, and how to secure it. A sermon
        preached in the Tenth Presbyterian church, Philadel-
        phia, on the day of national humiliation, June 1,
        1865. By Henry A. Boardman, D. D.   Philadelphia,
        J. S. Claxton, successor to W. S. & A. Martien, 1865.
        32 p.   23 cm.

11311   Boardman, Henry Augustus, 1808-1880.
        The peace-makers. A sermon preached in the Tenth
        Presbyterian church, Philadelphia, on Sunday,
        April 9, 1865, appointed by the governor of Penn-
        sylvania as a day of thanksgiving for the recent
        victories of the national forces in Virginia. By
        Henry A. Boardman, D. D.   Philadelphia, J. S. Clax-
        ton, successor to W. S. & A. Martien, 1865.
        31 p.   23 cm.

11312   Boardman, Henry Augustus, 1808-1880.
        The sovereignty of God, the sure and only stay of
        the Christian patriot in our national troubles. A
        sermon preached in the Tenth Presbyterian church,
        Philadelphia, Sept. 14, and in the West Spruce street
        church, September 28, 1862. By Henry A. Boardman,
        D. D.   Philadelphia, W. S. & A. Martien, 1862.
        31 p.   22 1/2 cm.

11313   Boardman, Henry Augustus, 1808-1880.
        What Christianity demands of us at the present
        crisis: a sermon preached on Thanksgiving day,
        Nov. 29, 1860. By Henry A. Boardman, D. D.   Phila-

17

delphia, J. B. Lippincott & co., 1860.
28 p.   23 1/2 cm.

11314 Bockett, Elias.
A poem to the memory of Aquila Rose: who died at
Philadelphia, August the 22d, 1723. aetat. 28. By
Elias Bockett. London, printed. Philadelphia, re-
printed at the new printing office [on B. Franklin's
press]
(In Rose, Aquila. Poems on several occasions.
Philadelphia, 1740. 18 1/2 cm, p. [45]-51)

11315 Boddily, John, 1755-1802.
A sermon delivered at Newburyport, on the 22d
February, 1800. Newburyport, Printed by E. M. Blunt,
1800.
15 p.   23 cm.

11316 [Boesnier,   ]
Le Mexique conquis... Paris, Desaint & Saillant
[etc., etc.] 1752.
2 v. in 1.   2 fold. maps.   17 cm.

11317 Bogart, David Schuyler, 1770-1839.
The voice of gratitude. A discourse, delivered on
the 22d of November, 1804; being the anniversary
Thanksgiving in the Presbyterian church at Southampton   on Long-island. By David S. Bogart, A. M.
Sag Harbor [N. Y.] Printed by Alden Spooner, 1805.
24 p.   23 cm.

11318 [Bogart, William Henry] 1810-1888.
Who goes there? or, Men and events. By "Sentinel"
[pseud.] ... New York, Carleton, 1866.
2 p.l., [vii]-viii p., 1 l., 11-288 p.   19 cm.

11319 Bogen, Frederick W
The German in America, or Advice and instruction
for German emigrants in the United States of America.
Also, a reader for beginners in the English and
German languages. By F. W. Bogen... 2d ed.
Boston, B. H. Greene; New York, Koch & co. [etc.]
1851.
177 p.   16 cm.
Added t.-p. in German.
German and English on opposite pages.
Contents. - General remarks. - The Constitution of

the United States. - Sketch of the life of Washington. - Sketch of the life of Franklin.

11320 ... The Bohemian. [no. 1] Richmond, Va., G. W. Gary,
printer [1863]
cover-title, 40 p.   23 cm.
At head of title: Christmas, 1863...
No more published.

11321 Bohun, Edmund, 1645-1699.
The diary and autobiography of Edmund Bohun, esq.
With an introductory memoir, notes, and illustrations,
by S. Wilton Rix. Beccles [Eng.] Priv. print. by
R. Crisp, 1853.
1 p.l., xxxiv p., 1 l., [2], 148 p.   front.,
illus., plates, 2 facsim., fold. geneal. tab.
29 cm.

11322 The boiler explosion of the Martin boiler on board the
U. S. "double-ender" Chenango. The coroner's in-
quest, a full report of the testimony, the charge
of Dr. Norris to the jury, and the two verdicts.
New York, J. A. Gray & Green, printers, 1864.
141 p.   22 1/2 cm.

11323 [Boimare, A   L   ]
Notes bibliographiques et raisonnées sur les prin-
cipaux ouvrages publiés sur la Floride et l'ancienne
Louisiane, depuis leur découverte jusqu'à l'époque
actuelle. Accompagnées de trois cartes, de Guillaume
Delisle, publiées en 1703 et 1712. [Paris, 1855]
cover-title, 60, [2] p.   30 cm.

11324 Boislecomte, André Olivier Ernest Sain de, b. 1799.
De la crise américaine et de celle des nationalités
en Europe par M. Sain de Boislecomte, ancien ministre
de la République Francaise en Italie et aux États-
Unis. Paris, E. Maillet, 1862.
2 p.l., 155 p.   22 cm.

11325 Boker, George Henry, 1823-1890.
Poems of the war, by George H. Boker. Boston,
Ticknor and Fields, 1864.
vi, [7]-202 p.   18 1/2 cm.

11326 Boker, George Henry, 1823-1890.
The Second Louisiana. May 27th, 1863. By George

19

H. Boker. [n.p., 1863?]
1 l.   21 1/2 cm.

11327 Bokum, Hermann, 1807-1878, ed.
    The stranger's gift. A Christmas and New York's
    present. Ed. by Hermann Bokum... Boston, Light and
    Horton, 1836.
      103 p.   front.   19 1/2 cm.
      Contents. - Dedication. - Introduction. - The arri-
    val. - The American Germans. - The American Dutch. -
    The environs of the Mohawk. - New England. - The
    German emigrant. - The stranger's hope. - Conclusion.

11328 Bokum, Herman, 1807-1878.
    The testimony of a refugee from east Tennessee.
    By Hermann Bokum... Philadelphia, Printed for gra-
    tuitous distribution, 1863.
      24 p.   22 cm.

11329 Bokum, Hermann, 1807-1878.
    Wanderings north and south, by Hermann Bokum...
    Philadelphia, King & Baird, printers, 1864.
      2 p.l., 73 p.   22 1/2 cm.
      The first article was published previously as a
    pamphlet under title: Testimony of a refugee from
    East Tennessee.
      Contents. - A refugee's testimony. - Sketches of
    East Tennessee life. - Life and death of a Christian
    soldier[Charles Crary] - The Turner's Lane hospital.

11330 Bollaert, William, 1807-1876.
    Antiquarian, ethnological, and other researches
    in New Granada, Equador, Peru and Chili, with obser-
    vations on the pre-Incarial, Incarial, and other
    monuments of Peruvian nations. By William Bollaert
    ... London, Trübner & co., 1860.
      1 p.l., 279 p.   17 pl. (incl. front.) map.
    23 cm.

11331 [Bollan, William] d. 1776.
    The ancient right of the English nation to the
    American fishery; and its various dimunutions; exam-
    ined and stated. With a map of the lands, islands,
    gulph, seas, and fishing banks comprising the whole.
    Humbly inscribed to the sincere friends of the
    British naval empire... London, Printed and sold

by S. Baker, 1764.
1 p.l., 105 p.   front. (fold. map)
27 x 21 1/2 cm.

11332 [Bollan, William] d. 1776.
Coloniae anglicanae illustratae; or, The acquest
of dominion, and the plantation of colonies made by
the English in America, with the rights of the colonists, examined, stated, and illustrated. Pt. I...
London, S. Baker, 1762.
3 p.l., [v]-viii, 141, [1] p.   28 cm.

11333 [Bollan, William] d. 1776.
Continued corruption, standing armies, and popular
discontents considered; and the establishment of the
English colonies in America, with various subsequent
proceedings, and the present contests, examined with
intent to promote their cordial and perpetual union
with their mother-country, for their mutual honour,
comfort, strength, and safety... London, Printed by
J. Almon, 1768.
82 p.   pl.   27 x 21 1/2 cm.

11334 [Bollan, William] d. 1776.
The free Britons memorial, to all the freeholders,
citizens and burgesses, who elect the members of the
British Parliament, presented in order to the effectual defence of their injured right of election...
London, Printed for J. Williams, 1769.
2 p.l., 35 p.   26 cm.

11335 [Bollan, William] d. 1776.
The freedom of speech and writing upon public
affairs considered; with an historical view... London,
S. Baker, 1766.
1 p.l., 160 p.   28 x 22 1/2 cm.

11336 [Bollan, William] d. 1776.
The importance and advantage of Cape Breton, truly
stated and impartially considered. With proper
maps... London, Printed for J. and P. Knapton,
1746.
vi, [2], 156 p.   2 fold. maps.   20 cm.
Attributed by Brit. mus. Catalogue to Sir William
Pepperrell.
The descriptive part is taken from Charlevoix's
Histoire et description générale de la Nouvelle

France. The maps bear titles: "Map of the island
of Cape Breton as laid down by the Sieur Bellin,
1746" and "A map of North America as far as relates
to the English settlements, taken from the Sieur
Bellin, 1746."

11337 Bolles, James Aaron, 1810-1894.
The Episcopal church defended: with an examination
into the claims of Methodist episcopacy; in a series
of letters addressed to the Rev. Allen Steele, with
his replies. By James A. Bolles... Batavia, N. Y.,
Printed by F. Follett [1843]
199 p.   19 cm.

11338 Bolles, John Augustus, 1809-1878.
Genealogy of the Bolles family in America. By
John A. Bolles. Boston, H. W. Dutton & son, 1865.
2 p.l., viii, 63 p.   30 x 23 1/2 cm.

11339 Bolles, John Augustus, 1809-1878.
An oration, delivered before the inhabitants of
Winchester, Mass. July 4, 1860. By John A. Bolles.
Boston, Press of T. R. Marvin & son, 1860.
19 p.   21 cm.

11340 Bolles, Lucius, 1779-1884.
A discourse, delivered before the members of the
Salem female charitable society, September 27, 1810.
Being their tenth anniversary. By Lucius Bolles...
Salem, Printed by Thomas C. Cushing, 1810.
16 p.   24 cm.

11341 Bollmann, Erick, 1769-1821.
A letter to Thomas Brand... on the practicability
and propriety of a resumption of specie payments...
By Erick Bollmann, M. D. Re-pub. from the London
ed. Philadelphia, M. Thomas; New York, J. Haly and
C. Thomas, 1819.
2 p.l., 76 p.   22 cm.

11342 Bollmann, Erick, 1796-1821.
Plan of an improved system of the money-concerns
of the Union. By Erick Bollmann, M. D. Philadelphia,
Printed for the author, William Fry, printer, Walnut,
near Fifth street, 1816.
vi p., 1 l., 52 p.   23 cm.

11343 [Boloix, Pablo]
Sucinta noticia del ramo de la cera en la isla de
Cuba, a fines de marzo del año de 1815. Habana,
Arazoza y Soler [1815]
10 p.   29 1/2 cm.
Published under the auspices of the Real sociedad
patriotica de la Habana.

11344 Bolton, E[dward] C[hichester]
The confederation of British North America. By
E. C. Bolton and H. H. Webber... London, Chapman &
Hall, 1866.
4 p.l., 149 p.   fold. maps.   20 1/2 cm.

11345 Bolton, Robert, 1814-1877.
A guide to New Rochelle and its vicinity. New
York, Printed by A. Hanford, 1842.
67 p.   front.   16 cm.

11346 Bolton, Robert, 1814-1877.
A history of the county of Westchester, from its
first settlement to the present time. By Robert
Bolton, jr. New York, Printed by A. S. Gould, 1848.
2 v.   front. (port.) illus., plates, maps
(partly fold.) fold. geneal. tables.   22 cm.
Appendix (p. 499-557): Pedigrees of the families
of the county of Westchester.

11347 Bombardement de Valparaiso (documents officiels)
suivi du Combat du Callao. 2. éd., corr. et augm.
Paris, Imprimerie Vallée, 1866.
vi, 182 p.   23 cm.
Introduction signed: F.
Combat du Callao; rapport officiel du commodore
américain Rodgers: p. 175-181.

11348 Bona, Félix de, 1821?-1889.
Cuba, Santo Domingo y Puerto-Rico. Historia y
estado actual de Santo Domingo, su reincorporacion
y ventajas ó inconvenientes segun se adopte ó no
una política liberal para su gobierno, para el de las
demás Antillas y para nuestras relaciones interna-
cionales. - Estado actual político y económico de
Cuba y Puerto-Rico. - Urgente necesidad y conveniencia
de liberalizar su administracion. - Observaciones á
la doctrina emitida en el Senado sobre política
ultramarina y poblacion de Cuba por los generales

23

duque de Tetuan y marqués de la Habana en su contes-
tacion al marqués de O'Gavan. Con un apéndice en
que se insertan el discurso en el Senado de dicho
marqués de O'Gavan y del Lord Russell en 1850, ambos
sobre reforma de la politica ultramarina. Por Félix
de Bona... Madrid, Impr. de M. Galiano, 1861.
   2 p.l., 155, [1] p.   21 1/2 cm.
With this is bound: Cunha Reis, M. B. da. Memoria
general; ó sea, Resumen de las razones justificativas
del proyecto de inmigracion de brazos libres africanos.
Madrid, 1861.

11349 Bonaparte, Charles Lucien Jules Laurent, prince de
      Canino, 1803-1857.
     A geographical and comparative list of the birds of
Europe and North America. By Charles Lucien Bonaparte, prince of Musignano. London, J. Van Voorst,
1838.
   1 p.l., [v]-vii, 67, [1] p.   21 1/2 cm.

11350 Bond, Alvan, 1793-1882.
     A discourse on the life and character of Dea.
Joseph Otis, delivered in the Second Congregational
church, Norwich, Conn., March 19, 1854. With an
appendix by the pastor, Alvan Bond... Norwich,
A. Stark, printer, 1855.
   75 p.   17 cm.

11351 Bond, Alvan, 1793-1882.
     A historical discourse, delivered at the hundredth
anniversary of the organization of the Second Congregational church, Norwich, Conn., July 24, 1860.
With an appendix. By Alvan Bond, D. D. Norwich,
Manning, Platt & co., printers, 1860.
   64 p.   fold. plan.   23 cm.

11352 Bond, John Wesley, 1825-1903.
     Minnesota and its resources, to which are appended
campfire sketches or notes of a trip from St. Paul
to Pembina and Selkirk settlement on the Red River
of the North... New York, Redfield, 1853.
   364 p.   illus.   20 cm.

11353 Bond, John Wesley, 1825-1903.
     Minnesota and its resources; to which are appended
Campfire sketches, or, Notes of a trip from St. Paul
to Pembina and Selkirk settlement on the Red River

of the North. By J. Wesley Bond. Chicago, Keen &
Lee; Philadelphia, C. Desilver, 1856.
    1 p.l., 412 p.   front., plates, fold. map.
18 cm.
    "Prince Rupert's Land - The Hudson Bay and Northwest
company - The Esquimaux, Montagnes, Crees, Sauteux,
Sioux, Assiniboins, etc." (by the Rev. G. A. Belcourt;
tr. from the French by Mrs. Letitia May): p. [335]-
358.

11354 Bond, William Cranch, 1789-1859.
    History and description of the Astronomical obser-
vatory of Harvard college. By William Cranch Bond...
Cambridge, Metcalf and company, printers to the University, 1856.
    3 p.l., cxci p.   illus., plans.   29 1/2 x
24 1/2 cm. (Added t.-p.: Annals of the Astronomical
observatory of Harvard college. vol. I, pt. I)

11355 Bond, William Key, d. 1864.
    Speech of Mr. Bond, of Ohio, on the treasury note
bill. Delivered in the House of representatives,
March 18, 1840. [Washington? 1840]
    31 p.   24 cm.

11356 Bond, William Key, d. 1864.
    Speech of Mr. Bond, of Ohio, upon the resolution
to correct abuses in the public expenditures, and to
separate the government from the press. Delivered
in the House of representatives, April, 1838.
[Washington, 1838]
    16 p.   26 cm.

11357 Bondage a moral institution, sanctioned by the Scriptures of the Old and New Testaments, and the preaching
and practice of the Saviour and his apostles. By a
southern farmer... Macon, Printed by Griffin & Purse,
1837.
    78 p.   22 cm.

11358 Bonduel, Florimond J
    Souvenir d'une mission indienne. Nakam et son fils
Nigabianong; ou, L'enfant perdu; précédé d'une notice
historique, et dédié aux élèves des collèges et des
pensionnats de la Belgique. Par le R. P. Fl. J.
Bonduel... Tournai, Typ. de J. Casterman et fils,
1855.

44 p.   front. (port.) plates, double map,
music.   24 cm.

11359 Bone, John Herbert A   1830-1906.
       Petroleum, and petroleum wells... With a complete
       guide book and description of the oil regions of
       Pennsylvania, West Virginia and Ohio. By J. H. A.
       Bone. New York, American news company; Philadelphia,
       J. B. Lippincott & co., 1865.
       95 p.   17 cm.

11360 Bonneau, Alexandre, 1820-
       Haïti; ses progrès, son avenir; avec un précis
       historique sur ses constitutions, le texte de la
       constitution actuellement en vigueur, et une biblio-
       graphie d'Haïti. Par Alexandre Bonneau. Paris,
       E. Dentu, 1862.
       176 p.   24 cm.

11361 Bonnefoux, L
       Extracts from a treatise on the Constitution of
       the United States, by L. Bonnefoux... New York,
       W. C. Bryant & co., printers, 1863.
       32 p.   22 cm.
       "These articles are detached numbers (nos. 7 and 8)
       from a 'Treatise on the Constitution of the United
       States', which is intended to be published." - p. [3]

11362 Bonner, John, 1828-1899.
       A child's history of the United States. By John
       Bonner... New York, Harper & brothers, 1855.
       2 v.   17 1/2 cm.

11363 Bonnet, Stede, d. 1718, defendant.
       The tryals of Major Stede Bonnet, and other pirates,
       viz. Robert Tucker, Edward Robinson, Neal Paterson
       [and others] ... Who were all condemn'd for piracy.
       As also the tryals of Thomas Nichols, Rowland Sharp,
       Jonathan Clarke, and Thomas Gerrat, for piracy, who
       were acquitted. At the admiralty sessions held at
       Charles-town, in the province of South Carolina, on
       Tuesday the 28th of October, 1718, and by several
       adjournments continued to Wednesday the 12th of Novem-
       ber, following. To which is prefix'd, an account of
       the taking of the said Major Bonnet, and the rest of
       the pirates. London, Printed for B. Cowse, 1719.
       vi, 50 p.   35 1/2 cm.

11364 [Bonneville, Zacharie de Pazzi de] supposed author.
De l'Amérique et des Américains, ou Observations
curieuses du philosophe La Douceur, qui a parcouru
cet hémisphere pendant la dernière guerre, en faisant
le noble métier de tuer des hommes sans les manger.
Berlin, S. Pitra, 1771.
2 p.l., [3]-80 p.   19 cm.
Also attributed to Pierre Poivre, Pernety, and
various other writers.
Attacks the theories of de Pauw's "Recherches philo-
sophiques sur les Américains", Berlin, 1768-1770.

11365 Bonnycastle, Sir Richard Henry, 1791-1847.
The Canadas in 1841. By Sir Richard H. Bonnycastle
... London, H. Colburn, 1841.
2 v.   fronts., illus., fold. map.   21 cm.

11366 Bonnycastle, Sir Richard Henry, 1791-1847.
Newfoundland in 1842: a sequel to "The Canadas in
1841". By Sir Richard Henry Bonnycastle... London,
H. Colburn, 1842.
2 v.   fronts. (v. 2: port.) pl., fold. map.
18 1/2 cm.
"List of works hitherto published on Newfoundland":
p. [336]-344.
Contents. - I. Political and general history of
Newfoundland. Natural history. Physical history. -
II. Physical history (contin.) Moral history. Poli-
tical economy. Modern geography and topography. -
Appendix.

11367 Bonnycastle, Sir Richard Henry, 1791-1847.
Spanish America; or, A descriptive, historical,
and geographical account of the dominions of Spain
in the Western hemisphere, continental and insular;
illustrated by a map of Spanish North America, and
the West-India islands; a map of Spanish South America,
and an engraving, representing the comparative alti-
tudes of the mountains in those regions. By R. H.
Bonnycastle... London, Longman, Hurst, Rees, Orme,
and Brown, 1818.
2 v.   fold. fronts. (v. 1, map) fold. map,
tables.   23 cm.
"List of works on, or relating to, Spanish America
...": v. 2, p. [305]-310.

11368   Bonynge, Francis.
        The future wealth of America: being a glance at
the resources of the United States and the commercial
and agricultural advantages of cultivating tea,
coffee, and indigo, the date, mango, jack, leechee,
guava, and orange trees, etc. With a review of the
China trade. By Francis Bonynge... New York,
Author, 1852.
        xii, [13]-242 p.   19 cm.

11369   The book of bubbles; a contribution to the New York
        fair in aid of the Sanitary commission. New York,
        Endicott & co., 1864.
            1 p.l., iv p., 68 pl.   16 x 24 1/2 cm.
        Nonsense verses with illustrations.

11370   The book of peace; a collection of essays on war and
        peace. Boston, G. C. Beckwith; Philadelphia,
        Perkins and Purves [etc., etc.] 1845.
            3 p.l., 606 p.   19 1/2 cm.
        Sixty-four tracts, compiled and edited by George C.
        Beckwith, corresponding secretary of the American
        peace society. Each tract is separately as well as
        consecutively paged.

11371   A book of the continuation of forreign passages. That
        is, of the peace made between this common-wealth, &
        that of the United Provinces of the Netherlands, with
        all the articles of that peace. Apr. 5, 1654. And
        the articles of peace, friendship and entercourse
        agreed between England and Sweden, in a treaty at
        Upsall. May 9, 1654. As also the substance of the
        articles of the treaty of peace betwixt England and
        France. Given at White Hall the 20 of Novemb: 1655...
        Moreover, an attempt on the island of Jamaica, and
        taking the town of St. Jago de la Viga... May 10,
        1655... With a true narrative of the late successe
        ... of the fleet of this common-wealth... against
        the King of Spains West India fleet... 1656...
        London, Printed by M. S. for T. Jenner, 1657.
            1 p.l., 61 p. illus. (incl. ports., map)
        18 1/2 x 14 1/2 cm.

11372   Boole, William H
        Antidote to Rev. H. J. Van Dyke's pro-slavery dis-
course, by Rev. Wm. H. Boole. "American slavery has
no foundation in the Scriptures." Delivered in the

M. E. church, Mount Vernon, New York, on Sunday,
January 13, 1861. New York, E. Jones & co.,
printers, 1861.
   34 p.   23 cm.

11373 The Boot on the other leg; or, Loyalty above party.
      Philadelphia, 1863.
        16 p.   22 cm.
      Includes extracts from The olive branch, by Mathew
      Carey.
      "Support of the Union," reprint from the New York
      times: p. [2]-[3] of cover.

11374 Booth, Mary Louise, 1831-1889, comp. and tr.
      New and complete clock and watchmakers' manual...
      Comp. from the French. With an appendix containing
      a history of clock and watchmaking in America. By
      M. L. Booth... New York, J. Wiley, 1860.
        xvii, 288 p.   VI (i.e. 12) fold. pl.   20 cm.
      Based on Magnier's revised and enlarged edition of
      Le Normand and Janvier's "Manuel de l'horloger". -
      cf. Pref.

11375 Booth, Robert Russell.
      Personal forgiveness and public justice. A sermon
      preached in the Mercer street Presbyterian church,
      New York, April 23, 1865, by the pastor, Robert
      Russell Booth... New York, A. D. F. Randolph, 1865.
        23 p.   23 cm.
      "Published by request of the Young men's association
      of the church."

11376 Booth, Sherman M
      Justice essential to national prosperity. Address
      delivered before the National equal suffrage asso-
      ciation, by Sherman M. Booth... at the Union league
      hall, Washington, D. C., June 6, 1866. Published by
      the Association. Washington, D. C., Chronicle steam
      print, 1866.
        12 p.   23 cm.

11377 Borden, Nathaniel B   1801-1865.
      Address of Hon. Nathaniel B. Borden, mayor of the
      city of Fall River, at the last regular meeting of
      the Board of aldermen, for municipal year, ending
      with April, 1858. Fall River, W. S. Robertson,
      printer, 1858.

18 p.   22 1/2 cm.

11378   The border ruffian code in Kansas.   [New York, Tribune
         office, 1856]
            15, [1] p. incl. map.   23 cm.
            Republican campaign document.

11379   Borland, Solon, 1808-1864.
            Speech of Hon. Solon Borland, of Arkansas, against
         the Collins line of steamers, and against special
         legislation - the doctrine of protection - and all
         monopolies.   Delivered in the Senate of the United
         States, May 12 and 17, 1852... Washington, Printed
         at the Congressional globe office, 1852.
            24 p.   23 cm.

11380   Borrett, George Tuthill.
            Out West: a series of letters from Canada and the
         United States.   By George Tuthill Borrett...   London,
         Groombridge and sons, 1866.
            2 p.l., 294 p.   19 1/2 cm.

11381   Bory de Saint-Vincent, Jean Baptiste Geneviève Marcellin,
         baron, 1778-1846.
            Essais sur les isles Fortunées et l'antique Atlan-
         tide, ou, Précis de l'histoire générale de l'archipel
         des Canaries, par J. B. G. M. Bory de St. Vincent...
         Paris, Baudouin, an XI [1803]
            3 p.l., 522, [2] p.   7 pl. (part fold.)   3 fold.
         maps.   28 1/2 cm.

11382   Bosch, Gerardus-Balthasar, 1794-1839.
            Reizen in West Indië, en door een gedeelte van
         Zuid- en Noord-Amerika; door G. B. Bosch...   Utrecht,
         N. van der Monde, 1829-43.
            3 v.   20 1/2 cm.
            Vol. 3 edited by Leonard Eduard Bosch.

11383   Bosch-Spencer, [Guillaume] H[enri] 1802-1873.
            Commerce de la côte occidentale de l'Amérique
         du Sud.   Statistique commerciale du Chili, de la
         Bolivie, du Pérou, de l'Equateur, de la Nouvelle-
         Grenade, de l'Amérique Centrale et du Mexique...
         Par M. H. Bosch-Spencer...   Bruxelles, Impr. de D.
         Raes, 1848.
            xxvii, xxi, 421, [1] p. incl. tables (partly fold.)
         and atlas of 1 p.l., 17 fold. pl.   24 1/2 cm.

11384   Bossi, Bartolomé, 1812-1891.
        Viage pintoresco por los rios Paraná, Paraguay,
S^n Lorenzo, Cuyabá y el Arino tributario del grande
Amazonas; con la descripcion de la provincia de Mato
Grosso bajo su aspecto fisico, geografico, mineralo-
jico y sus producciones naturales, por el C. Bartolomé
Bossi. Paris, Dupray de la Mahérie, 1863.
        xi, 153 p., 1 l. incl. front., illus.   plates,
ports., map.   27 cm.

11385   Boston.
        An appeal to the world; or, A vindication of the
town of Boston, from many false and malicious aspersions contained in certain letters and memorials,
written by Governor Bernard, General Gage, Commodore
Hood, the commissioners of the American Board of
customs, and others, and by them respectively transmitted to the British ministry.   Pub. by order of the
town.   Boston, Printed by Edes and Gill; and London,
Reprinted for J. Almon, 1770.
        2 p.l., 3-58 p.   21 cm.
        "The general belief is that the author of this de-
fence was Samuel Adams... though it has been ascribed
to William Cooper, to James Otis, and to Otis and
Adams combined." - Winsor, Narr. and crit. his., v. 6,
1888, p. 84.
        The letters referred to were published at Boston in
1769, and reprinted in London under title: Letters to
the ministry from Governor Bernard, General Gage, and
Commodore Hood.   And also memorials... from the commissioners of the customs...

11386   The Bostonian prophet.   An heroi-comico-serious-
        parodical-Pindaric ode, in imitation of the bard.
        With notes critical, satirical, and eplanatory by
        the editor...   London, Printed for C. Etherington,
        1779.
        1 p.l., [5]-12, [xiii]-xiv p.   27 x 21 cm.

11387   Bostwick, David, 1721-1763.
        A fair and rational vindication of the right of
infants to the ordinance of baptism: being the substance of several discourses from Acts ii. 39. Containing I. The Scripture ground, on which the rights
of infants to baptism is founded.   II. The evidence
by which it is supported.   And, III. A solution of the
most material objections. By David Bostwick, A. M.,
late minister of the Presbyterian church, in the city

31

of New York... New York printed; London, re-printed
for Edward and Charles Dilly, 1765.
viii, [9]-54 p.   20 1/2 cm.

11388   Bostwick, Henry, 1787-1836 or 7.
Lectures upon portions of history, with historical
outlines for the use of schools, comp. from the
printed charts and unpublished manuscripts of the
late Henry Bostwick... New York, Printed by H.
Ludwig, 1838.
iv, 24, 154 p., 1 l.   tab.   23 1/2 cm.
Includes: An epitome of ancient geography. An
outline of history from the creation to 3500 A.M.
A continuation of the outline from 3500 to the time
of Augustus. A chronological index of the most important events from A.M. 3250 to 4004. A further
continuation of the outline, &c., to the reign of
Charlemagne, A.D. 800. A chronological index from
the birth of Christ to the reign of Charlemagne.
Fragments of history of Spain, Gaul, Italy, after the
time of Charlemagne. A table of European sovereigns
from 800 to the present time.

11389   Boteler, Alexander Robinson, 1815-1892.
Speech of Hon. Alexander R. Boteler, of Virginia,
on the organization of the House. Delivered in the
House of representatives January 25, 1860. Washington,
W. H. Moore, printer, 1860.
16 p.   24 1/2 cm.
Contains also "An incident of 1775", a poem by
Mrs. L. H. Sigourney, and "A bee line for Boston",
by a daughter of Virginia, E. E. S.

11390   Botta, Carlo Giuseppe Guglielmo, 1766-1837.
History of the war of the independence of the
United States of America. Written by Charles Botta.
Tr. from the Italian, by George Alexander Otis...
Philadelphia, Printed for the translator, Lydia R.
Bailey, printer, 1820-21.
3 v.   21 1/2 cm.

11391   Botts, John Minor, 1802-1869.
The great rebellion; its secret history, rise,
progress, and disastrous failure. By John Minor Botts,
of Virginia. The political life of the author vindicated... New York, Harper & brothers, 1866.
xxviii, [29]-402 p. incl. front. (port.)   19 cm.

11392　Boturini Benaducci, Lorenzo, 1702-1751.
　　　　　Idea de una nueva historia general de la America
　　　Septentrional.　Fundada sobre material copioso de
　　　figuras, symbolos, caratères, y geroglificos, can-
　　　tares, y manuscritos de autores indios, ultimamente
　　　descubiertos.　Dedicala al rey n^{tro} señor en su Real,
　　　y supremo consejo de las Indias el cavallero Lorenzo
　　　Boturini Benaduci, señor de la Torre, y de Hono.
　　　Con licencia.　En Madrid, En la imprenta de Juan de
　　　Zúñiga, 1746.
　　　　　20 p.l., 167 p., 1 l., [6], 96 p.　　front., port.
　　　20 1/2 cm.

11393　Boucarut, Alcide, b. 1825.
　　　　　... Manuel de la navigation dans le Rio de la Plata,
　　　d'après les documents nautiques les plus récents,
　　　recueillis et mis en ordre par A. Boucarut...　Paris,
　　　Impr. de P. Dupont, 1857.
　　　　　120 p.　　24 cm.

11394　Bouchacourt, Charles.
　　　　　Notice industrielle sur la Californie, par m. Ch.
　　　Bouchacourt...　Paris, F. Mathias; Lyon, C. Savy,
　　　jeune, 1849.
　　　　　72 p.　　22 cm.

11395　Boucher, Jonathan, 1738-1804.
　　　　　A view of the causes and consequences of the American
　　　revolution; in thirteen discourses, preached in North
　　　America between the years 1763 and 1775; with an his-
　　　torical preface...　London, Printed for G. G. & J.
　　　Robinson, 1797.
　　　　　4 p.l., xciv p., 1 l., 596 p.　　21 1/2 cm.

11396　Boucher de la Bruère,　　　fils.
　　　　　Le Canada sous la domination anglaise.　(Analyse
　　　historique)　Par Boucher de la Bruère, fils.　St. Hya-
　　　cinthe, Imprimé par Lussier et frères, 1863.
　　　　　80 p.　　22 cm.

11397　Bouchot, Auguste.
　　　　　Histoire du Portugal et de ses colonies, par
　　　Auguste Bouchot...　Paris, L. Hachette et c.^{ie}, 1854.
　　　　　1 p.l., xvi, 432, [3] p.　　illus., 2 maps, 2 plans.
　　　18 1/2 cm.　[Histoire universelle, publiée... sous
　　　la direction de V. Duruy]

11398   Boudinot, Elias, d. 1839.
        An address to the whites. Delivered in the First
        Presbyterian church, on the 26th of May, 1826. By
        Elias Boudinot, a Cherokee Indian. Philadelphia,
        Printed by W. F. Geddes, 1826.
        16 p.   21 cm.

11399   Boudinot, Elias, d. 1839.
        Letters and other papers relating to Cherokee
        affairs; being in reply to sundry publications
        authorized by John Ross. By E. Boudinot, formerly
        editor of the Cherokee Phoenix. Athens, Printed at
        the office of the "Southern banner", 1837.
        66 p.   19 1/2 cm.

11400   [Boudinot, Elias] 1740-1821.
        A memoir of the Rev. William Tennent, minister of
        Freehold, Monmouth county, N. J., first published
        in the Evangelical magazine... Springfield [N. J.]
        G. W. Callender [1822]
        67 p.   15 cm.

11401   Boudinot, Elias, 1740-1821.
        An oration, delivered at Elizabeth-town, New
        Jersey, agreeably to a resolution of the state Society
        of Cincinnati, on the Fourth of July, 1793. Being
        the seventeenth anniversary of the independence of
        America. By Elias Boudinot... Elizabeth-town,
        Printed by Shepard Kollock, 1793.
        iv, [5]-32 p.   19 1/2 x 16 cm.

11402   Boudinot, Elias, 1740-1821.
        A star in the West; or, A humble attempt to dis-
        cover the long lost ten tribes of Israel, preparatory
        to their return to their beloved city, Jerusalem.
        By Elias Boudinot... Trenton, N. J., Published by
        D. Fenton, S. Hutchinson and J. Dunham. George Sher-
        man, Printer. 1816.
        iv, xxi, [23]-312 p.   20 1/2 cm.

11403   Bouguer, Pierre, 1698-1758.
        La figure de la terre, déterminée par les obser-
        vations de messieurs Bouguer & de la Condamine, de
        l'Académie royale des sciences, envoyés par ordre du
        roy au Pérou, pour observer aux environs de l'équateur.
        Avec une relation abregée de ce voyage qui contient
        la description du pays dans lequel les opérations ont

été faites. Paris, C. A. Jombert, 1749.
cx, 394 p.   diagr.   26 cm.

11404   Bouillé, René, marquis de, 1802-1882.
Essai sur la vie du marquis de Bouillé (François-
Claude-Amour) ... par son petit-fils René de Bouillé
... Paris, Amyot, 1853.
vii, 472 p.   21 1/2 cm.

11405   Bouis, Amédée Théodore.
Biographie du général Andrew Jackson, ancien
président des Etats-Unis, par Amédée Théod. Bouis,
citoyen de la Louisiane... Paris, Impr. de H.
Fournier et c^e, 1842.
31 p.   front. (port.)   24 cm.

11406   [Boulanger, Nicolas Antoine] 1722-1759.
The origin and progress of despotism. In the
Oriental, and other empires of Africa, Europe, and
America... Amsterdam, Printed, 1764.
1 p.l., 285 p.   19 cm.
"This theologico-political research is calculated
for an introduction and key to Montesquieu's Spirit
of laws."
John Wilkes was probably the translator of this
English version of Boulanger's Recherches sur l'origine
du despotisme oriental; having printed a French edition
of this work at his private press, London, in 1763.
cf. Dict. nat. biog., v. 61, p. 249.

11407   Boulter, Hugh, abp. of Armagh, 1672-1742.
A sermon preached before the incorporated Society
for the propagation of the gospel in foreign parts;
at their anniversary meeting in the parish-church of
St. Mary-le-Bow; on Friday, the 16th of February,
1721 [i.e. 1722] By the Right Reverend Father in
God, Hugh, lord bishop of Bristol. London, Printed
by J. Downing, 1722.
61, [3] p.   20 cm.
Includes "An abstract of the Proceedings of the
Society for the propagation of the gospel in foreign
parts, from... February, 1720 [i.e. 1721] to...
February, 1721 [i.e. 1722]" (p. 35-48), "List of
the Society's missionaries, catechists, and school-
masters", and "List of the members".

11408   [Bourdon, Louis Gabriel] 1741-1795.
     Voyage d'Amérique. Dialogue en vers, entre
l'auteur et l'abbé ***. A Londres; et se trouve à
Paris, chez Pichard, 1786.
     156 p.   16 1/2 cm.

11409   Bourne, Benjamin Franklin.
     The captive in Patagonia; or, Life among the
giants. A personal narrative. By Benjamin Franklin
Bourne... Boston, Gould and Lincoln, 1853.
     1 p.l., [xix]-xxiv, [25]-233 p. incl. plates.
front.   19 1/2 cm.

11410   Bourne, Edward E[merson]
     An address on the character of the colony founded
by George Popham, at the mouth of the Kennebec river
Aug. 19, (o.s.) 1607. Delivered in Bath, on the
two hundred and fifty-seventh anniversary of that
event... Portland [Me.] Print. by B. Thurston, 1864.
     60 p.   20 cm.

11411   [Bourne, George] 1780-1845.
     The picture of Quebec and its vicinity. 2d ed.,
rev. and cor. Quebec, P. and W. Ruthven, 1831.
     3 p.l., [5]-134, [3] p., 1 l.   front., 14 illus.
on 7 pl., fold. map.   14 1/2 cm.

11412   Bourne, Henry Richard Fox, 1837-1909.
     English seamen under the Tudors, by H. R. Fox
Bourne. London, R. Bentley, 1868.
     2 v.   maps.   21 cm.

11413   Bourne, William Oland.
     Poems of the republic. By Wm. Oland Bourne, A. M.
A contribution to the Metropolitan fair, New York,
by Edward O. Jenkins. [New York, E. O. Jenkins,
printer] 1864.
     48 p.   19 1/2 cm.

11414   Bouton, Jacques, 1592-1658.
     Relation de l'establissement des Francois depvis
l'an 1635. En l'isle de la Martinique, l'vne des
Antilles de l'Amerique. Des moeurs des sauuages,
de la situation, & des autres singularitez de l'isle.
Par le p. Iacqves Bovton, de la Compagnie de Iesvs.
A Paris, Chez S. Cramoisy, 1640.

4 p.l., 141 p.   17 cm.
The oldest known account of Martinique. cf. Sabin,
Bibl. amer.

11415 Bouton, John Bell, 1830-1902.
A memoir of General Louis Bell, late col. of the
fourth N. H. regiment, who fell at the assault on
Fort Fisher, N. C., January 15th, 1865. By John Bell
Bouton... New York [Priv. print.] 1865.
53 p.   23 cm.
Read before the N. H. historical society, Sept.
14th, 1865. Published by request.

11416 Bouton, Nathaniel, 1799-1878.
The fathers of the New Hampshire ministry. An
historical discourse, preached before the General
association of New Hampshire, at its annual meeting
in Manchester, August 22, 1848. By Nathaniel Bouton...
Concord, Printed by A. McFarland, 1848.
43 p.   21 1/2 cm.

11417 Bouton, Nathaniel, 1799-1878.
The history of Concord, from its first grant in
1725, to the organization of the city government
in 1853, with a history of the ancient Penacooks.
The whole interspersed with numerous interesting
incidents and anecdotes, down to the present period,
1855; embellished with maps; with portraits of distinguished citizens, and views of ancient and modern
residences... By Nathaniel Bouton... Concord [N. H.]
B. W. Sanborn, 1856.
2 p.l., 786 p.   front., illus., plates, ports.,
fold. map, plans, fold. facsim.   23 1/2 cm.

11418 Bouton, Nathaniel, 1799-1878.
The history of education in New Hampshire. A discourse, delivered before the New Hampshire historical
society, at their annual meeting in Concord, June 12,
1833. By Nathaniel Bouton... Concord, Marsh, Capen
and Lyon, 1833.
36 p.   23 1/2 cm.

11419 Bouton, Nathaniel, 1799-1878, comp. and ed.
Provincial papers. Documents and records relating
to the province of New Hampshire, from the earliest
period of its settlement: 1623-[1776]   Pub. by
authority of the legislature of New Hampshire...

Comp. and ed. by Nathaniel Bouton... Concord, G. E.
Jenks, state printer [etc., etc.] 1867-73.
7 v.   23 1/2 cm.   [New Hampshire. Provincial
and state papers, v. 1-7]

11420   Bouton, Nathaniel, 1799-1878.
The responsibilities of rulers. A sermon, delivered at Concord, June 5, 1828, before the constituted
authorities of the state of New Hampshire. By
Nathaniel Bouton... Concord, Printed by H. E. Moore,
1828.
31 p.   21 1/2 cm.

11421   Boutwell, George Sewall, 1818-1905.
Address of Governor Boutwell at the dedication of
the monument to the memory of Capt. Wadsworth, at
Sudbury, Mass., Nov. 23, 1852. (From the Boston
traveller of Nov. 24) [Boston? 1852?]
8 p.   25 cm.

11422   Boutwell, George Sewall, 1818-1905.
The tax-payer's manual; containing the entire
internal revenue laws, with the decisions and rulings
of the commissioner, tables of taxation, exemption,
stamp-duties, &c., and a complete alphabetical index.
Prepared by Hon. George S. Boutwell... Boston,
Little, Brown and company, 1865.
2 p.l., 197 p.   24 cm.

11423   Bouvet de Cressé, Auguste Jean Baptiste, 1772-1839, ed.
Histoire de la catastrophe de Saint-Domingue,
avec la correspondance des généraux Leclerc, (beau-
frère de Bonaparte), Henry-Christophe (depuis roi
d'Haïti), Hardy, Vilton, etc., certifiée conforme
aux originaux déposés aux archives, par le lieutenant
général Rouanez jeune, secrétaire d'État, publiées
par A. J. B. Bouvet de Cressé... Paris, Librairie
de Peytieux, 1824.
2 p.l., vii, 156 p.   21 cm.

11424   Bouvet de Cressé, Auguste Jean Baptiste, 1772-1839.
Histoire de la marine de tous les peuples depuis
la plus haute antiquité jusqu'à nos jours. Par
A. J. B. Bouvet de Cressé... Paris, A. André, 1824.
2 v.   20 1/2 cm.

11425   Bouvier, John, 1787-1851.
         A law dictionary, adapted to the Constitution and
         laws of the United States of America, and of the
         several states of the American union; with references
         to the civil and other systems of foreign law. By
         John Bouvier... Philadelphia, T. and J. W. Johnson,
         1839.
            2 v.   24 1/2 cm.
            "Appendix. A dictionary of the Norman or Old French
         language. By Robert Kelham...": v. 2, p. [509]-628.

11426   Bowditch, Henry Ingersoll, 1808-1892.
         An address on the life and character of James
         Deane, M. D., of Greenfield, Mass., by Henry I. Bow-
         ditch, M. D., August 4, 1858. Greenfield, H. D.
         Mirick & co., printers, 1858.
            45 p.   24 cm.

11427   Bowditch, Henry Ingersoll, 1808-1892.
         A brief plea for an ambulance system for the army
         of the United States, as drawn from the extra suffer-
         ings of the late Lieut. Bowditch and a wounded com-
         rade. By Henry I. Bowditch... Boston, Ticknor and
         Fields, 1863.
            20 p.   21 1/2 cm.

11428   .Bowditch, Henry Ingersoll, 1808-1892.
         Consumption in New England; or, Locality one of
         its chief causes. An address delivered before the
         Massachusetts medical society, by Henry I. Bowditch,
         M. D. Boston, Ticknor & Fields, 1862.
            vi, [5]-104 p.   maps (partly fold.)   24 cm.

11429   Bowditch, Henry Ingersoll, 1808-1892.
         Memoir of Amos Twitchell, M. D., with an appendix,
         containing his addresses, etc. By Henry I. Bowditch,
         M. D. Boston, Printed by J. Wilson and son, 1851.
            v p., 1 1., 212 p.   front. (port.)   19 1/2 cm.

11430   [Bowditch, Henry Ingersoll] 1808-1892.
         Memorial [of Nathaniel Bowditch, lieutenant, First
         Massachusetts cavalry, 1839-1863] ... Boston, Priv.
         print. by J. Wilson & son, 1865.
            vi p., 1 1., 134 p.   port.   24 x 19 cm.

11431   Bowditch, Nathaniel, 1773-1838.
         Directions for sailing into the harbours of Salem,

Marblehead, Beverly, and Manchester. By Nathaniel
Bowditch... Printed by Edmund M. Blunt, Newburyport,
1806.
    v, [6]-30 p.   21 1/2 cm.

11432   Bowditch, N[athaniel] I[ngersoll] 1805-1861.
    The ether controversy. Vindication of the hospital
report of 1848. By N. I. Bowditch. Boston, Printed
by J. Wilson, 1848.
    32 p.   24 cm.
    Written in reply to "A defence of Dr. [Charles T.]
Jackson's claims to the discovery of etherization,"
which appeared shortly after the publication of the
Report of the trustees of the Massachusetts general
hospital, Jan. 26, 1848.

11433   Bowditch, Nathaniel Ingersoll, 1805-1861.
    A history of the Massachusetts general hospital.
By N. I. Bowditch... Not published. Boston,
Printed by J. Wilson & son, 1851.
    xi, 442 p., 1 l.   front., pl., 2 port.   23 cm.

11434   Bowditch, Nathaniel Ingersoll, 1805-1861.
    Memoir of Nathaniel Bowditch, by his son Nathaniel
Ingersoll Bowditch. Originally prefixed to the
fourth volume of the Mécanique céleste. 2d ed.
Boston, C. C. Little and J. Brown, 1840.
    172 p.   2 port. (incl. front.)   28 1/2 x
23 1/2 cm.

11435   Bowditch, Nathaniel Ingersoll, 1805-1861.
    Suffolk surnames. By N. I. Bowditch... 2d ed.,
enl. Boston, Ticknor & Fields, 1858.
    xv, 383 p.   24 cm.

11436   [Bowditch, Nathaniel Ingersoll] 1805-1861.
    Wharf property; or, The law of flats; being remarks
before the Judiciary committee of the Senate of
Massachusetts, April 14, 1852. Boston, Printed by
J. Wilson & son, 1852.
    40 p.   diagrs.   22 cm.

11437   [Bowditch, William Ingersoll] 1819-1909.
    God or our country. Review of the Rev. Dr. Putnam's
discourse, delivered on Fast day, entitled God and
our country... Boston, I. R. Butts, 1847.
    23 p.   23 1/2 cm.

11438 Bowditch, William Ingersoll, 1819-1909.
          The rendition of Anthony Burns. By William I.
       Bowditch. Boston, R. F. Wallcut, 1854.
          40 p.   23 cm.

11439 Bowditch, William Ingersoll, 1819-1909.
          Slavery and the Constitution. By William I. Bow-
       ditch. Boston, R. F. Wallcut, 1849.
          2 p.l., 156 p.   24 cm.

11440 Bowdler, Thomas, 1754-1825.
          A short view of the life and character of Lieuten-
       ant-General Villettes, late lieutenant-governor
       and commander of the forces in Jamaica. To which
       are added, letters written during a journey from
       Calais to Geneva, and St. Bernard in the year 1814.
       By Thomas Bowdler... With an appendix containing a
       few original letters and anecdotes of the late Madame
       Elizabeth de France... Bath, Printed by R. Cruttwell,
       1815.
          2 p.l., 159 p.   front. (port.)   20 1/2 cm.
       Bound with this is A postscript to The letters
       written in France in 1814. By Thos. Bowdler...
       Bath, Printed by R. Cruttwell, 1815 (40 p.)

11441 Bowdoin port-folio... Conducted by the undergraduates
       of Bowdoin college. [v. 1]; Apr.-Dec. 1839. Bruns-
       wick, J. Griffin [1839]
          4 p.l., 248 p.   23 1/2 cm.   monthly.
       No number issued for May 1839.
       No more published?

11442 Bowen, Abel, 1790-1850.
          Bowen's picture of Boston, or The citizen's and
       stranger's guide to the metropolis of Massachusetts,
       and its environs. To which is prefixed the annals
       of Boston... 2d ed. enl. and improved. Boston,
       Lilly, Wait & co. [etc.] 1833.
          7 p.l., [9]-316 p.   illus., plates, fold. maps.
       15 cm.

11443 Bowen, Benjamin B   1819-1905.
          A blind man's offering: by B. B. Bowen... Boston,
       The author, 1847.
          viii, [9]-432 p.   front. (port.)   20 cm.
       "The fairy waltz" (music): p. 430-432.

41

11444   Bowen, Eli, b. 1824.
        Coal and coal oil; or, The geology of the earth.
Being a popular description of minerals and mineral
combustibles. By Eli Bowen... Philadelphia, T. B.
Peterson & brothers [c1865]
      iv, 3-494 p.   19 cm.
      First edition issued under title: Physical history
of the earth.
      "Second edition."

11445   Bowen, Francis, 1811-1890.
        Documents of the constitution of England and
America, from Magna charta to the federal Constitution
of 1789. Comp. and ed., with notes, by Francis Bowen
... Cambridge, Mass., J. Bartlett, 1854.
      vii, [1], 142 p.   22 cm.

11446   Bowen, Francis, 1811-1890.
        The principles of political economy applied to
the condition, the resources, and the institutions
of the American people. By Francis Bowen... Boston,
Little, Brown, and company, 1856.
      xxv, 546 p.   23 1/2 cm.

11447   Bowen, Henry L   1810-1865.
        Memoir of Tristam Burges; with selections from his
speeches and occasional writings. By Henry L. Bowen.
Providence, Marshall, Brown & company; Philadelphia,
W. Marshall & company, 1835.
      xii, [13]-404 p.   23 cm.
      Speeches: p. [193]-404.

11448   Bowen, Nathaniel, 1779-1839.
        A discourse, delivered at the request of the
American revolution society, before that society,
and the state Society of the Cincinnati, on the death
of Gen. Christopher Gadsden, September 10, 1805.
By Nathaniel Bowen... Published by the request of
the two societies. Charleston, Printed by W. P.
Young [1805]
      21 p.   19 cm.

11449   Bowen, Noel Hill, d. 1872.
        An historical sketch of the isle of Orleans, being
a paper read before the Literary and historical
society of Quebec, on Wednesday evening, the 4th
of April, 1860; by N. H. Bowen... Quebec, Printed at

the "Mercury" newspaper office, 1860.
40 p.   21 1/2 cm.

11450   Bowker, J
Wreck-elections of a busy life; designed by J.
Bowker. Hartford, Conn., Kellogg & Bulkeley, c1867.
2 p.l., 20 pl.   24 x 31 cm.
Caricatures and verses parodying Horace Greeley's
"Recollections of a busy life," published in the New
York ledger.

11451   Bowles, Charles S   P   ed.
... Report of Charles S. P. Bowles, foreign agent
of the United States sanitary commission, upon the
International congress of Geneva, for the amelioration
of the condition of the sick and wounded soldiers of
armies in the field, convened at Geneva, 8th August,
1864. London, Printed by R. Clay, son, and Taylor
[1864?]
67, [1] p.   23 1/2 cm.

11452   Bowling, William King, 1808-1885.
Historical address to the graduating class of 1868,
in the Medical department of the University of Nashville. By W. K. Bowling... Nashville, W. H. F. Ligon,
pr., 1868.
31 p.   21 1/2 cm.
On cover: 2d edition.

11453   Bowling, William King, 1808-1885.
Lecture introductory to the second course in the
Medical department of the University of Nashville,
delivered at the Odd fellow's hall, Nov. 1st, 1852,
by appointment of the Faculty of medicine. By W. K.
Bowling... Nashville, Tenn., J. T. S. Fall, book and
job pr., 1852.
23 p.   24 cm.

11454   Bowman, Samuel Millard, 1815-1885.
Sherman and his campaigns: a military biography.
By Col. S. M. Bowman and Lt. Col. R. B. Irwin. New
York, C. B. Richardson; Cincinnati, C. F. Vent &
co. [etc., etc.] 1865.
512 p.   front., port., maps.   19 cm.

11455   Boyd, Belle, 1844-1900.
Belle Boyd in camp and prison, written by herself.

With an introduction, by George Augusta [!] Sala.
New York, Blelock & company, 1865.
1 p.l., [5]-464 p.   18 1/2 cm.
"Lieutenant Hardinge's journal": p. 341-456.

11456   Boyd, Hugh, 1746-1794.
Miscellaneous works of Hugh Boyd, the author of
the letters of Junius. With an account of his life
and writings by Lawrence Dundas Campbell. London,
T. Cadell and W. Davies, 1800.
2 v.   22 cm.
Contents. - v. 1. Life. Political essays: The Free-
holder, a series of letters addressed to the electors
of the county of Antrim. Democraticus, a series of
letters, originally printed in the Publick advertiser,
1779. The Whig, a series of letters published in the
London courant, 1779-80. Genuine abstracts from two
speeches of the late Earl of Chatham. Miscellaneous
poems. - v. 2. Embassy to Candy. The Indian observer,
1793-94.

11457   Boyd, John.
The vision, and other poems, in blank verse, by
John Boyd, a man of colour. Pub. for the author's
benefit, and prefaced by some preliminary observations, by C. R. Nesbitt... Exeter, Printed by R. J.
Trewman; London, Longman and co., 1834.
xix, 23, [1] p.   18 1/2 cm.

11458   [Boyd, John Parker] 1764-1830.
Documents and facts, relative to military events,
during the late war. [n.p., 1816]
28 p.   21 cm.
Defending the author's generalship.

11459   [Boyd, Samuel Stillman] 1807-1867.
Considerations on the appointment of a justice of
the Supreme court of the United States, respectfully
addressed to the President and Senate. By Juris-
consult. [n.p.] 1852.
14 p.   23 cm.

11460   Boyd, William, d. 1800.
An oration, on the death of Mr. John Russell,
senior sophister, at Harvard university. Delivered
November 25, in the college chapel; by William Boyd.
Boston, Printed by John W. Folsom, for the author,

1795.
18 p.   22 cm.

11461   Boyle, Frederick, b. 1841.
A ride across a continent: a personal narrative
of wanderings through Nicaragua and Costa Rica.
By Frederick Boyle... London, R. Bentley, 1868.
2 v.   fronts., plates.   19 1/2 cm.

11462   Boyle, Henry.
The chronology of the eighteenth and nineteenth
centuries; comprehending every important transaction,
from the year 1700, to the close of the year 1825.
By Henry Boyle... London, Sherwood, Gilbert, and
Piper, 1826.
iv, 688 p.   22 cm.

11463   Boyle, Robert, 1627-1691.
General heads for the natural history of a country,
great or small; drawn out for the use of travellers
and navigators. Imparted by the late Honourable
Robert Boyle, esq. ... To which is added, other
directions for navigators, &c. with particular observations of the most noted countries in the world:
by another hand. London, Printed for J. Taylor,
1692.
2 p.l., 138, [2] p.   15 cm.

11464   Boylston, Thomas, 1720?-1798.
The will of Thomas Boylston, esq., late of London.
[Boston? 181-]
16 p.   24 cm.
Contains an introduction and letters to the select-
men of Boston, by Ward Nicholas Boylston.

11465   Boylston, Zabdiel, 1679-1766.
An historical account of the small-pox inoculated
in New England, upon all sorts of persons, whites,
blacks, and of all ages and constitutions. With some
account of the nature of the infection in the natural
and inoculated way, and their different effects on
human bodies. With some short directions to the
unexperienced in this method of practice. Humbly
dedicated to Her Royal Highness the Princess of Wales,
by Zabdiel Boylston, physician. London, S. Chandler,
1726.
1 p.l., iv, viii, 62 p.   23 cm.

11466   Boynton, Charles Brandon, 1806-1883.
        English and French neutrality and the Anglo-French
alliance, in their relations to the United States &
Russia, including an account of the leading policy
of France and of England for the last two hundred
years - the origin and aims of the alliance - the
meaning of the Crimean war - and the reason of the
hostile attitude of these two powers towards the
United States, and of the movement on Mexico, with a
statement of the general resources - the army and
navy of England and France - Russia and America -
showing the present strength and probable future of
these four powers. By Rev. C. B. Boynton, D. D.
Cincinnati, Chicago, C. F. Vent & co., 1864.
        576 p.   23 cm.

11467   Boynton, Charles Brandon, 1806-1883.
        The four great powers: England, France, Russia,
and America; their policy, resources, and probable
future. A revision with important modifications of
... "English and French neutrality." By Rev. C. B.
Boynton... Cincinnati, Chicago [etc.] C. F. Vent &
co., 1866.
        4 p., 1 l., [vii]-x, [11]-520 p.   23 cm.

11468   [Boynton, Charles Brandon] 1806-1883, comp.
        History of the Great western sanitary fair.
Cincinnati, C. F. Vent & co. [1864]
        xxx, 31-578 p. incl. front. (port.)   24 cm.

11469   Boynton, Charles Brandon, 1806-1883.
        The history of the navy during the rebellion.
By Charles B. Boynton... New York, D. Appleton &
co., 1867-68.
        2 v.   front., illus., plates (part col.) port.,
maps.   23 1/2 cm.

11470   Boynton, Edward Carlisle, 1824-1893.
        History of West Point, and its military importance
during the American revolution: and the origin and
progress of the United States military academy. By
Captain Edward C. Boynton... New York, D. Van Nostrand [etc., etc.] 1863.
        xviii p., 1 l., [9]-408 p.   fold. front., illus.,
plates (1 col.) maps, fold. plans, facsim.   24 cm.

11471　The boys and girls stories of the war... Richmond,
　　　　West & Johnston [1863?]
　　　　　　　cover-title, 32 p.　　illus.　　11 1/2 cm.
　　　　　　　Contents. - Story of a refugee. - The mountain
　　　　guide. - Commodore Foote and Colonel Small. - The
　　　　lost kite. - The brave editor.

11472　Bozman, John Leeds, 1757-1823.
　　　　　　　The history of Maryland, from its first settlement,
　　　　in 1633, to the restoration, in 1660, with a copious
　　　　introduction, and notes and illustrations. By John
　　　　Leeds Bozman. Baltimore, J. Lucas & E. K. Deaver,
　　　　1837.
　　　　　　　2 v.　　23 cm.

11473　Brace, Charles Loring, 1826-1890.
　　　　　　　The best method of disposing of our pauper and
　　　　vagrant children. [By] C. L. Brace, secretary of
　　　　Children's aid society. New York, Wynkoop, Hallen-
　　　　beck & Thomas, printers, 1859.
　　　　　　　36 p.　　22 1/2 cm.
　　　　　　　"Appendix. Letters from gentlemen in the West,
　　　　on the work of the Children's aid society": p. 19-36.

11474　Brackenridge, Henry Marie, 1786-1871.
　　　　　　　Early discoveries by Spaniards in New Mexico:
　　　　containing an account of the castles of Cibola, and
　　　　the present appearance of their ruins. By H. M.
　　　　Brackenridge... Pittsburgh, H. Miner & co., 1857.
　　　　　　　48 p.　　23 cm.

11475　Brackenridge, Henry Marie, 1786-1871.
　　　　　　　History of the late war, between the United States
　　　　and Great Britain. Containing a minute account of
　　　　the various military and naval operations... By
　　　　H. M. Brackenridge, esq. 2d ed., rev. and cor.
　　　　Baltimore, J. Cushing, 1817.
　　　　　　　xxiv, [25]-363 p.　　front., 4 pl.　　18 cm.

11476　Brackenridge, Henry Marie, 1786-1871.
　　　　　　　History of the western insurrection in western
　　　　Pennsylvania, commonly called the whiskey insurrect-
　　　　ion. 1794. By H. M. Brackenridge... Pittsburgh,
　　　　Printed by W. S. Haven, 1859.
　　　　　　　xiv, [15]-336 p.　　22 1/2 cm.

11477   Brackenridge, Henry Marie, 1786-1871
... Mexican letters written during the progress
of the late war between the United States and Mexico,
by B. H. M. Brackenridge: now collected and republished, with notes and corrections, to be completed
in two numbers... [no. 1] Washington, Printed by
R. A. Waters, 1850.
85 p.   22 1/2 cm.

11478   [Brackenridge, Henry Marie] 1786-1871.
North American pamphlet on South American affairs.
(In The Pamphleteer. London, 1818. 22 1/2 cm.
v. 13, p. [35]-83)

11479   [Brackenridge, Henry Marie] 1786-1871.
South America; a letter on the present state of
that country, to James Monroe, president of the United
States. By an American... Washington, Printed and
published, at the office of the National register...
October 15, 1817.
52 p.   21 cm.

11480   Brackenridge, Henry Marie, 1786-1871.
Speeches on the Jew bill, in the House of delegates
of Maryland, by H. M. Brackenridge, Col. W. G. D.
Worthington, and John S. Tyson, esquire. Together
with an argument on the chancery powers, and an
eulogy on Thomas Jefferson and John Adams, &c.,
by H. M. Brackenridge. Philadelphia, J. Dobson
(agent) 1829.
2 p.l., 236 p.   24 1/2 cm.
"Western antiquities, communicated in a letter to
Thomas Jefferson, by H. M. Brackenridge": p. [192]-
205.
"Letter on the culture of live oak, to the secretary
of the navy, by H. M. Brackenridge": p. [206]-225.
"Report [prepared by H. M. Brackenridge] adopted
by the City council of Baltimore, on the subject of
the defence, &c.": p. [226]-236.

11481   [Brackenridge, Hugh Henry] 1748-1816.
The battle of Bunkers-hill. A dramatic piece,
in five acts, in heroic measure. By a gentleman of
Maryland... Philadelphia, Printed and sold by Robert
Bell, in Third-Street, 1776.
4 p.l., [5]-49 (i.e. 51) p.   front.   21 1/2 cm.
The numbers 31-32 are repeated in paging.

Frontispiece, "The death of Warren," engraved by Norman.
"The drama appears to have been actually represented on the stage." - Sabin, Bibl. amer.

11482 [Brackenridge, Hugh Henry] 1748-1816.
The death of General Montgomery, in storming the city of Quebec. A tragedy. With an ode, in honour of the Pennsylvania militia, and the small band of regular Continental troops, who sustained the campaign, in the depth of winter, January, 1777, and repulsed the British forces from the banks of the Delaware. By the author of a dramatic piece, on the battle of Bunker's-hill. To which are added, Elegiac pieces, commemorative of distinguished characters. By different gentlemen... Philadelphia, Printed and sold by Robert Bell, in Third-Street, next door to St. Paul's Church, 1777.
6 p.l., [9]-79, [2] p.   front.   21 1/2 cm.
On the verso of the first prelim. leaf an explanation is given of the frontispiece "The death of Montgomery" by Norman, who had already engraved the frontispiece "The death of Warren" for the author's "The battle of Bunkers-hill", Phila., R. Bell, 1776, which is "said to be the earliest known specimen of engraving in British America by a native artist". - Sabin, Bibl. amer.

11483 Brackenridge, Hugh Henry, 1748-1816.
An eulogium of the brave men who have fallen in the contest with Great-Britain: delivered on Monday, July 5, 1779. Before a numerous and respectable assembly of citizens and foreigners, in the German Calvinist church, Philadelphia. By Hugh M. [!] Brackenridge, A. M. ... Philadelphia, Printed by F. Bailey, in Market-street [1779]
25 p.   23 x 17 1/2 cm.

11484 Brackenridge, Hugh Henry, 1748-1816.
Incidents of the insurrection in the western parts of Pennsylvania, in the year 1794. By Hugh H. Brackenridge. Philadelphia, Printed and sold by John M'Culloch, no. 1, North Third-street, 1795.
3 v. in 1.   21 x 12 cm.

11485 Brackett, Edward Augustus, 1818-1908.
Twilight hours: or, Leisure moments of an artist.

By E. A. Brackett... Boston, Printed by Freeman and Bolles, 1845.
viii p., 1 l., [11]-95 p.   18 1/2 cm.

11486   Brackett, Joseph Warren, 1775-1826.
The ghost of law, or, Anarchy and despotism.
A poem, delivered before the Phi Beta Kappa, Dartmouth college, at their anniversary, August 23, 1803.
By J. Warren Brackett... Hanover [N. H.] Printed by Moses Davis, 1803.
24 p.   19 1/2 cm.

11487   Bradburn, George, 1806-1880.
A statement, by George Bradburn, of his connection with the "True Democrat", and John C. Vaughan.
Cleveland, The author, 1853.
20 p.   23 cm.

11488   Bradbury, Charles, 1798-1864.
History of Kennebunk port, from its first discovery by Bartholomew Gosnold, May 14, 1602, to A. D. 1837.
By Charles Bradbury. Kennebunk, Printed by J. K. Remich, 1837.
301 p.   front.   18 1/2 cm.
"Brief notices of the earlier settlers": p. 223-287.

11489   Bradbury, James Ware, 1802-1901.
Removals and appointments to office. Speech of Hon. J. W. Bradbury, of Maine, in the Senate of the United States, April 23, 1850. [Washington, Printed at the Congressional globe office, 1850]
16 p.   23 cm.

11490   Bradbury, James Ware, 1802-1901.
Speech of Hon. James W. Bradbury. Of Maine, on the bill providing for the payment of claims for French spoliations previous to the year 1800. Delivered in the Senate of the United States, April 15, 1852. Washington, Gideon & co., printers, 1852.
20 p.   22 cm.

11491   Bradford, Alden, 1765-1843.
Complete and authentic history of the battle of Bunker Hill, June 17, 1775; derived from the best authorities. By Alden Bradford, esq. Boston,

J. N. Bradley & co. [1825]
13, [1] p.   illus.   25 cm.

11492 Bradford, Alden, 1765-1843.
An eulogy, in commemoration of the "sublime virtues"
of General George Washington, late president of the
United States, who died December 14th, 1799; pronounced in Wiscasset, February 22d, 1800. Agreeable
to the recommendation of Congress. By Alden Bradford
... Wiscasset [Me.] Printed by Henry Hoskins, 1800.
16 p.   23 1/2 cm.

11493 Bradford, Alden, 1765-1843.
History of Massachusetts... By Alden Bradford...
Boston, Richardson and Lord [etc.] 1822-29.
3 v.   22 cm. (v. 3: 25 cm.)
Vol. 2 pub. by Wells and Lilly; v. 3 by the author.
Contents. - [v. I] From 1764, to July, 1775. -
[v. 2] From July, 1775, to the year 1789 (inclusive)
- [v. 3] From the year 1790, to 1820.

11494 Bradford, Alden, 1765-1843.
History of the federal government, for fifty years:
from March, 1789, to March, 1839. By Alden Bradford
... Boston, S. G. Simpkins, 1840.
viii, [9]-480 p.   22 1/2 cm.

11495 Bradford, Alden, 1765-1843.
Memoir of the life and writings of Rev. Jonathan
Mayhew, D. D., pastor of the West church and society
in Boston, from June, 1747, to July, 1766. By Alden
Bradford... Boston, C. C. Little & co., 1838.
iv, 484 p.   front. (port.)   24 cm.

11496 Bradford, Alden, 1765-1843.
New England chronology; from the discovery of the
country, by Cabot, in 1497, to 1800. By Alden Bradford... Boston, S. G. Simpkins, 1843.
202 p.   18 1/2 cm.
Contents. - New England chronology [1350-1816] -
Addenda [1556-1820]

11497 Bradford, Alden, 1765-1843.
A sermon delivered before the Congregational society
at Thomaston, (Maine) November 2, 1806; being the
Lord's day after the interment of the Hon. Henry
Knox, who died, October 25th, aetat. 56 years. By

51

Alden Bradford... [Wiscasset, Me.] Printed by
Babson & Russt [!] [1806]
16 p.   21 1/2 cm.

11498   Bradford, Alexander Warfield, 1815-1867.
American antiquities and researches into the origin
and history of the red race. By Alexander W. Bradford. New York, Dayton and Saxton; Boston, Saxton
and Pierce, 1841.
435 p.   22 cm.

11499   Bradford, Alexander Warfield, 1815-1867.
An oration delivered at Portchester, in the town
of Rye, county of Westchester, on the fourth day of
July, 1865, by Alexander W. Bradford... New York,
Bradstreet press, 1866.
42 p.   25 cm.

11500   Bradford, Ebenezer, 1746-1801.
The nature and manner of giving thanks to God,
illustrated. A sermon, delivered on the day of the
national thanksgiving February 19, 1795. By Ebenezer
Bradford, A. M., pastor of the First Church in
Rowley... Boston, From the Chronicle-press, by Adams
& Larkin, 1795.
23 p.   21 1/2 cm.
[Theological pamphlets, v. 61, no. 13]

11501   Bradford, Ebenezer, 1746-1801.
The nature of humiliation, fasting and prayer
explained. A sermon, delivered on the day of public
humiliation and prayer in the commonwealth of Massachusetts, April 2, 1795: with an appendix, in answer
to Dr. Tappan's remarks on his thanksgiving sermon,
dated February 19, 1795. By Ebenezer Bradford...
Published by desire. Boston, Printed by Adams &
Larkin, 1795.
40 p.   23 1/2 cm.

11502   Bradford, Ephraim Putnam, 1776-1845.
A sermon, preached at Concord, before His excellency
Samuel Bell, governor, the honourable Council, and the
two houses, composing the legislature of the state
of New Hampshire, June 7, 1821. By Ephraim P. Bradford, minister of the Presbyterian society, New
Boston. Concord, Printed by Hill & Moore, 1821.
27 p.   21 1/2 cm.

[Theological pamphlets, v. 42, no. 3]
Printed by order of the New Hampshire General court.

11503 Bradford, George W   1796-1883.
Historical and biographical address, delivered
before the Cortland county medical society, at the
fiftieth anniversary meeting, August 10, 1858. By
Geo. W. Bradford... Published at the request of the
society. Homer [N. Y.] J. R. Dixon, printer, 1858.
27 p.   22 cm.

11504 Bradford, Moses, 1765-1838.
A sermon, delivered at Concord, before His Excellency the Governor, the honorable Council, and both
branches of the legislature of the state of New
Hampshire, June 4th, A. D. 1812. By Moses Bradford,
A. M., pastor of the church in Francestown. Concord,
Printed by I. and W. R. Hill, for the General court,
1812.
26 p.   24 cm.

11505 Bradford, S[amuel] D[exter]
Letters to the Honorable William M. Meredith,
secretary of the Treasury, on his recent Treasury
report. The injurious effects of protective and
prohibitory duties, and the advantages of free
trade... By S. D. Bradford... Boston, Printed by
Beals & Greene, 1850.
36 p.   22 cm.
Pub. in the Boston post, February 4th, 5th, 6th,
7th and 8th, 1850.

11506 Bradford, William John Alden, 1791-1858.
Notes on the Northwest, or valley of the upper
Mississippi... By Wm. J. A. Bradford. New York,
Wiley and Putnam, 1846.
vi p., 1 1., 302 p.   19 1/2 cm.

11507 Brainerd, C   N
My diary: or, Three weeks on the wing. A peep at
the great west... New York, Egbert, Boirne & co.,
printers, 1868.
45 p.   23 1/2 cm.

11508 Breazeale, J   W   M
Life as it is; or, Matters and things in general:
containing, amongst other things, historical sketches

of the exploration and first settlement of the state
of Tennessee; manners and customs of the inhabitants;
their wars with the Indians; battle of King's Mountain; history of the Harps (two noted murderers)
a satirical burlesque on the practice of electioneer-
ing; legislative, judicial and ecclesiastical incidents; descriptions of natural curiosities; a collection
of anecdotes, &c., by J. W. M. Breazeale. Knoxville,
Printed by J. Williams, 1842.
   2 p.l., [15]-256 p.   19 cm.

11509 Breen, Henry Hegart.
    St. Lucia: historical, statistical, and descriptive.
By Henry H. Breen, esq. (Thirteen years a resident
in the island)   London, Longman, Brown, Green, and
Longmans, 1844.
   xvi, 423, [1] p.   21 cm.

11510 Brerewood, Edward, 1565?-1613.
    Enquiries touching the diversity of languages and
religions, through the chief parts of the world.
Written by Edw. Brerewood... London, Printed for
Samuel Mearne, John Martyn, and Henry Herringman,
1674.
   16 p.l., 252 p., 2 l.   17 1/2 cm.

11511 Brett, William Henry, 1818-1886.
    Indian missions in Guiana. By the Rev. W. H.
Brett... London, G. Bell, 1851.
   ix, [1], 301 p.   front., 9 pl., map.   18 cm.

11512 Brewerton, George Douglas, 1820-1901.
    The war in Kansas. A rough trip to the border,
among new homes and a strange people. By G. Douglas
Brewerton... New York, Derby & Jackson; Cincinnati,
H. W. Derby, 1856.
   xii, [13]-400 p.   front. (port.) plates.
18 1/2 cm.

11513 Brice, James R
    History of the revolutionary war... brief account
of the captivity and cruel sufferings of Captain
Deitz, and John and Robert Brice... who were taken
prisoners of war by the British Indians and Tories.
Now first published over said Robert Brice's own
signature, the horrible massacre of the Deitz family,
in Bern, Albany co., seventy-one years ago. Brief

account of an attempt... to defraud said Robert
Brice out of his property. Testimony of ex-Governor
Wm. H. Seward, proving James R. Brice perfectly
innocent of perjury, with which he was charged in
March, 1834... Affidavits of astonishing cures of
dropsy, by Jas. R. Brice... In three vols. - To be
continued. - vol. I. By James R. Brice... Albany,
Printed for the author, 1851.
    48 p.   24 1/2 cm.
    No more published?
    "The captive boys of Rensselaerville - John and
Robert Brice" (p. [3]-10) was written by Josiah
Priest and first published in his "Stories of the
revolution", Albany, 1836.

11514 Briceño, Mariano de.
    Memoir justificatory of the government of Venezuela
on the Isla de Aves question, presented to His Excellency the secretary of state of the United States,
by the envoy extraordinary and minister plenipotentiary of Venezuela, Doctor Mariano de Briceño.
Washington, F. H. Sage, printer, 1858.
    22 p.   21 cm.

11515 Brickell, John, 1710?-1745.
    The natural history of North Carolina. With an
account of the trade, manners, and customs of the
Christian and Indian inhabitants. Illustrated with
copper-plates, whereon are curiously engraved the
map of the country, several strange beasts, birds,
fishes, snakes, insects, trees, and plants, &c.
By John Brickell, M. D. ... Dublin, printed by
James Carson... From the author, 1737. [Raleigh,
Reprinted by authority of the Trustees of the public
libraries, 1911]
    2 p.l., xiv, 417, [1] p.   front. (fold. map)
plates.   23 cm.
    Introductory note signed: J. Bryan Grimes.
    An almost verbal transcript of Lawson's History of
Carolina. cf. North American review, v. 23,
p. 288-289.

11516 Bridge, Josiah, 1739-1801.
    A sermon preached before His Excellency John
Hancock, esq., governour; His Honor Benjamin Lincoln,
esq., lieutenant-governour; the honourable the Council,
Senate and House of representatives, of the common-

wealth of Massachusetts, May 27, 1789. Being the
day of general election. By Josiah Bridge, A. M.,
pastor of the church in East-Sudbury. Boston,
Printed by Adams & Nourse, printers to the Honourable
General court, 1789.
    54 p.   21 cm.

11517 A brief and impartial review of the state of Britain,
at the commencement of the session of 1783; humbly
addressed to the right honourable and honourable
the Lords and Commons of Great Britain... The second
edition corrected. London, Printed for J. Debrett,
1783.
    2 p.l., 75 p.   20 1/2 cm.

11518 A brief and true narrative of the hostile conduct
of the barbarous natives towards the Dutch nation.
Tr. by E. B. O'Callaghan. Albany, J. Munsell, 1863.
    48 p.   26 cm.
    "The paper of which the following is a translation
is to be found in vol. VI of the original Dutch mss.
in the secretary's office, Albany, N. Y. It consists
of a petition dated 31st October, 1655, one copy of
which was addressed to the States general of the
United Netherlands; another to the Burgomasters and
Common council of the city of Amsterdam, and a third
to the directors of the West India company, Chamber
at Amsterdam." - Introd.

11519 A brief examination of the plan and conduct of the
northern expedition in America, in 1777. And of
the surrender of the army under the command of Lieutenant-General Burgoyne. London, Printed for T. Hook-
ham, 1779.
    52 p.   21 cm.
    General Burgoyne's letter to Lord George Germaine:
p. [29]-52.

11520 Briggs, Charles Frederick, 1804-1877.
    ... The story of the telegraph, and a history of
the great Atlantic cable; a complete record of the
inception, progress, and final success of that under-
taking. A general history of land and oceanic tele-
graphs. Descriptions of telegraphic apparatus, and
biographical sketches of the principal persons connected with the great work. By Charles F. Briggs
and Augustus Maverick... New York, Rudd & Carleton,

1858.
   255 p.   front. (port.)   illus., fold. map.
19 cm.

11521 Brissot, Jean-Pierre, 1754-1793, called Brissot de
      Warville.
      A critical examination of the marquis de Châtellux's
      travels, in North America, in a letter addressed to
      the marquis; principally intended as a refutation of
      his opinions concerning the Quakers, the negroes,
      the people, and mankind. Translated from the French
      of J. P. Brissot de Warville, with additions and
      corrections of the author... Philadelphia, Printed
      by Joseph James, in Chestnut-street, 1788.
      1 p.l., 89 p.   22 cm.

11522 Brissot, Jean-Pierre, 1754-1793, called Brissot de
      Warville.
      Mémoires de Brissot... sur ses contemporains, et
      la révolution française. Pub. par son fils; avec
      des notes and des éclaircissements historiques, par
      M. F. de Montrol... Paris, Ladvocat, 1830.
      2 v.   20 1/2 cm.

11523 The British sailor's discovery; or, The Spanish pre-
      tensions confuted. Containing a short history of
      the discoveries and conquests of Spain in America,
      with a particular account of the illegal and un-
      christian means they made use of to establish their
      settlements there: proving that the sovereign sole
      dominion, claimed by the Crown of Spain to the West-
      Indies, is founded upon an unjustifiable possession;
      whilst the rights and possessions of the British sub-
      jects in those parts are both agreeable to the law
      of nations, and principles of Christianity. That
      America was discovered and planted by the ancient
      Britons 300 years before Columbus conducted the
      Spaniards thither... Also the declaration of war
      against Spain by Oliver Cromwell, in 1655, translated
      from the Latin original... London, Printed for
      T. Cooper, 1739.
      2 p.l., 72 p.   20 cm.

11524 British temperance emigration society and saving fund.
      Description of the Wisconsin territory and some of
      the states and territories adjoining to it in the
      western parts of the United States of America. 2d ed.,

enlarged. Published by the committee of the British
temperance emigration society and saving fund.
Robert Gorst, secretary. Liverpool, Printed by
G. Cutler, 1844.
    48 p.   17 1/2 cm.   (On cover: The emigrant's
instructer on Wisconsin and the western states of
America)

11525 Brito, Paulo José Miguel de, d. 1832.
    Memoria politica sobre a capitania de Santa Catha-
rina, escripta no Rio de Janeiro em o anno de 1816.
Por Paulo Joze Miguel de Brito... correspondente da
Academia real das sciencias. Lisboa, Typ. da mesma
academia, 1829.
    2 p.l., xii, 181, [2] p.   2 fold. maps, fold.
plan, fold. tables.   21 cm.

11526 Broad, Amos, defendant.
    The trial of Amos Broad and his wife, on three
several indictments for assaulting and beating Betty,
a slave, and her little female child Sarah, aged
three years. Had at the Court of special sessions
of the peace, held in and for the city and county of
New York, at the City-hall, of the said city, on
Tuesday, the 28th day of February, 1809. Present,
the Hon. Pierre C. Van Wyck, recorder. Peter Mesier
and James Drake, esquires, aldermen. To which is
added, the motion of counsel in Mr. Broad's behalf,
to mitigate the imprisonment of his person, and impose
a fine – and the reply of Mr. Sampson. Also, the
prayer or invocation of Mr. Broad, to the court, for
mercy – and the address of His Honor, the recorder,
on passing sentence on the defendants. New York,
Printed by Henry C. Southwick, no. 2, Wall-street,
1809.
    31 p.   20 1/2 cm.

11527 The Broadway. A London magazine of society and politics.
[v. 1] Sept. 1867-Aug. 1868; new ser., v. 1-4;
Sept. 1868-July 1870; new ser., v. 1-5, Aug. 1870-
Dec. 1872. London and New York, G. Routledge and
sons [1867-72]
    10 v. in 9.   plates.   21-22 1/2 cm.   monthly.
    Title varies: Sept. 1867-Aug. 1868, The Broadway
annual, a miscellany of original literature in poetry
and prose. Sept. 1868-July 1870, The Broadway, a
London magazine. Aug. 1870-Dec. 1872, The Broadway,

a London magazine of society and politics.

11528 Brockett, Linus Pierpont, 1820-1893.
Woman's work in the civil war: a record of
heroism, patriotism and patience. By L. P. Brockett
... and Mrs. Mary C. Vaughan. With an introduction,
by Henry W. Bellows... Illustrated with sixteen
steel engravings. Philadelphia, Pa. [etc.] Zeigler,
McCurdy & co.; Boston, Mass., R. H. Curran, 1867.
3 p.l., 5-799 p.   15 port. (incl. front.)
22 1/2 cm.

11529 Brodhead, John Romeyn, 1814-1873.
An address, delivered before the New York His-
torical Society, at its fortieth anniversary, 20th
November, 1844; by John Romeyn Brodhead... New York,
Press of the New York Historical Society, 1844.
51 p.   22 cm.

11530 Broeck, Matheus van den.
Journael, ofte historiaelse beschrijvinge van
Matheus vanden Broeck. Van 't geen hy selfs ghesien
ende waerachtigh gebeurtis, wegen 't begin ende
revolte van de Portugese in Brasiel, als mede de con-
ditio en het overgaen van de forten aldaer, Amstel-
redam, G. van Goedesbergen, 1651.
2 p.l., 40 p.   2 fold. pl., fold. map.   20 cm.

11531 Bromley, Walter.
An appeal to the virtue and good sense of the
inhabitants of Great Britain, &c. in behalf of the
Indians of North America. By Walter Bromley...
Halifax, Printed by E. Ward, 1820.
57, [1] p.   19 cm.

11532 Bromme, Traugott, 1802-1866.
Reise durch die Florida's, von St. Augustine durch
die halbinsel nach Pensacola. (Aus Bromme's Reisen
besonders abgedruckt)... Baltimore, Md., C. Scheld
und co., 1837.
5 p.l., [3]-80 p.   19 1/2 cm.

11533 Bromwell, William Jeremy, 1834-1874.
History of immigration to the United States,
exhibiting the number, sex, age, occupation, and
country of birth, of passengers arriving... by sea
from foreign countries, from September 30, 1819 to

December 31, 1855; compiled entirely from official
data: with an introductory review of the progress
and extent of immigration to the United States prior
to 1819, and an appendix, containing the naturalization
and passenger laws of the United States... By
William J. Bromwell... New York, Redfield, 1856.
1 p.l., [11]-225 p.   22 1/2 cm.

11534   Bronson, Henry, 1804-1893.
         Biographical notice of Prof. William Tully, M. D.
By Henry Bronson... [New Haven? 1861?]
         cover-title, 7 p.   23 1/2 cm.

11535   Bronson, Henry, 1804-1893.
         A historical account of Connecticut currency,
continental money, and the finances of the revolution.
By Henry Bronson, M. D. Read November 30th, 1863,
and afterward.
         (In New Haven colony historical society, New Haven,
Conn. Papers of the New Haven colony historical
society, New Haven, 1865. 23 1/2 cm. vol. I,
192 p.)

11536   Brook, Benjamin, 1776-1848.
         The lives of the Puritans: containing a biogra-
phical account of those divines who distinguished
themselves in the cause of religious liberty, from
the reformation under Queen Elizabeth, to the Act
of uniformity in 1662. By Benjamin Brook...
London, Printed for J. Black, 1813.
         3 v.   22 cm.

11537   Brooke, Francis Taliaferro, 1763-1851.
         A narrative of my life; for my family. By Francis
T. Brooke... Richmond, Printed for the writer [by]
Macfarlane & Fergusson] 1849.
         90 p.   16 1/2 cm.
         Includes a narrative of the author's service in
Harrison's regiment of Continental artillery, 1780-
1783.

11538   Brooke, John T
         Short notes on the Dred Scott case. By J. T.
Brooke... Cincinnati, Moore, Wilstach, Keys & co.,
printers, 1861.
         29 p.   23 cm.

11539 Brooklyn, N. Y.
      A law to revise and amend the several acts relating
to the city of Brooklyn; adopted in convention,
assembled in pursuance of an act of the legislature,
passed May 10, 1847. Brooklyn, Lees & Foulkes,
printers, 1848.
      viii, [5]-72 p.   21 1/2 cm.

11540 Brooklyn, N. Y. Ordinances, etc.
      Laws and ordinances of the city of Brooklyn, toge-
ther with such general laws of the state as affect
the city in its corporate capacity. Comp. and pub.
by order of the Common council. New York, Bergen &
Tripp, printers, 1865.
      iv, 394, 20, xvii p.   23 cm.
Preface signed by the compiler, Henry McCloskey.

11541 The Brooklyn city and Kings county record: a budget
of general information; with a map of the city,
an almanac, and an appendix, containing the new
city charter. Compiled... by William H. Smith.
Brooklyn, W. H. Smith, 1855.
      216, 71 p.   front. (fold. map)   19 1/2 cm.

11542 Brooklyn city library.
      Act of incorporation, by-laws and Catalogue of
the Brooklyn city library. Brooklyn, A. Spooner &
son, printers, 1840.
      80 p.   21 cm.

11543 [Brooks, Charles Timothy] 1813-1883.
      The controversy touching the old stone mill,
in the town of Newport, Rhode-Island. With remarks,
introductory and conclusive. Newport, C. E. Ham-
mett, jr., 1851.
      91, [1] p. incl. 1 illus., pl.   front.   18 cm.

11544 [Broom, Walter William]
      Abraham Lincoln's character. Sketched by English
travellers. [Brooklyn? 1865]
      [4] p.   23 cm.

11545 Brother Jonathan's wife: a lecture... By a retired
editor... Philadelphia, A. Peirce, 1842.
      16 p.   25 cm.

11546　Brotherhead, William.
　　　　Autographi-holographiani.　By Wm. Brotherhead.
　　　Philadelphia, 1857.
　　　　19 p.　　34 x 27 cm.
　　　　Caption title:　A visit to F. J. Dreer's collection
　　　of autographs.

11547　Brougham and Vaux, Henry Peter Brougham, 1st baron,
　　　　1778-1868.
　　　　... Political philosophy.　By Henry, Lord Brougham.
　　　Third ed. [pts. I and II, 1853]　Second ed. [pt. III,
　　　1849]　London, H. Bohn, 1853, 1849.
　　　　3 v.　　23 cm.
　　　　At head of title:　Under the superintendence of
　　　the Society for the Diffusion of Useful Knowledge.
　　　　Contents. - pt. I. Principles of government.
　　　Monarchical government. - pt. II. Of aristocracy.
　　　Aristocratic governments. - pt. III. Of democracy.
　　　Mixed monarchy.

11548　Brougham and Vaux, Henry Peter Brougham, 1st baron,
　　　　1778-1868.
　　　　The speech of Henry Brougham, esq., M. P., in the
　　　House of commons, on Tuesday, the 16th of June,
　　　1812.　Upon the present state of commerce and manu-
　　　factures; from a report taken in short hand.　London,
　　　Longman, Hurst, Rees, Orme, and Brown [etc.] 1812.
　　　　2 p.l., 59 p.　　22 1/2 cm.

11549　Broughton, Thomas.
　　　　The speech of Rev. Sir Thomas Broughton, Bart.
　　　at the meeting held at Stafford, the 29th of February
　　　last, for the purpose of addressing the king on the
　　　present state of public affairs.　London, John S.
　　　Stockdale, 1784.
　　　　21 p.　　20 1/2 cm.

11550　Brown, Aaron Venable, 1795-1859.
　　　　Address of Ex-Gov. Aaron V. Brown, before the
　　　Democratic association of Nashville, June 24, 1856.
　　　Nashville, Printed by G. C. Torbett and company,
　　　1856.
　　　　22 p.　　22 cm.

11551　Brown, Aaron V[enable] 1795-1859.
　　　　Agricultural address of ex-Gov. Aaron V. Brown,
　　　at Knoxville, Tenn., October, 1854.　Nashville,

J. F. Morgan, printer [1855]
18 p.   22 1/2 cm.   [With his Speeches, congressional and political, and other writings. Nashville, 1854]
-- -- Agricultural address delivered at Knoxville,
Tenn., October, 1854. (In his Speeches, congressional
and political, and other writings. Nashville, Tenn.,
1854-[55?]   21 1/2 cm.   p. [660]-672)

11552   Brown, Albert Gallatin, 1813-1880.
Letter of Albert G. Brown, to his constituents.
[Washington, Printed at the Congressional globe office,
1850]
8 p.   23 cm.

11553   Brown, Alexander Enos, d. 1865.
Address delivered before the American Whig and
Cliosophic societies of the College of New Jersey,
June 23d, 1846. By Alexander E. Brown. Princeton,
Printed by J. T. Robinson, 1846.
30 p.   21 cm.

11554   Brown, Andrew, 1748-1813.
A letter concerning family history. By Andrew
Brown. [n.p.] 1812.
12 p.   21 1/2 x 17 1/2 cm.

11555   [Brown, Charles Brockden] 1771-1810.
An address to the Congress of the United States,
on the utility and justice of restrictions upon
foreign commerce. With reflections on foreign
trade in general, and the future prospects of
America. Philadelphia, Published by C. & A. Conrad
& co., Chesnut-street, John Binns, printer, 1809.
vii (i.e. viii), 97 (i.e. 95) p.   22 cm.
[Miscellaneous pamphlets, v. 67, no. 2]

11556   Brown, David Paul, 1795-1872.
The forum: or, Forty years full practice at the
Philadelphia bar. By David Paul Brown... Philadelphia, R. H. Small, 1856.
2 v.   facsims.   23 cm.

11557   Brown, Francis, 1784-1820.
A sermon, delivered July 23, 1812, on occasion of
the state fast, appointed in consequence of the
declaration of war against Great Britain. By Francis

Brown... Portland [Me.] Hyde, Lord and co. [from the Gazette press] 1812.
　32 p.　22 1/2 cm.

11558　Brown, Frederick Thomas, 1822-1893.
　An address delivered in the Central Presbyterian church, Chicago, July 4th, 1865, by the pastor, Rev. Frederick T. Brown, D. D.　Chicago, Jameson & Morse, printers, 1865.
　24 p.　22 cm.

11559　Brown, Frederick Thomas, 1822-1893.
　A sermon: giving thanks for Union victories, preached in Bridge street Presbyterian church, Georgetown, D. C., August 6th, 1863, by the pastor, Frederick T. Brown.　Pub. by request of (and by) the congregation.　Washington, H. Polkinhorn, printer, 1863.
　1 p.l., 15 p.　22 cm.

11560　Brown, George William, 1812-1891.
　The origin and growth of civil liberty in Maryland. A discourse delivered by Geo. Wm. Brown, before the Maryland historical society, Baltimore, April 12, 1850, being the fifth annual address to that association.　Baltimore, J. D. Toy, 1850.
　40 p.　23 cm.

11561　Brown, Henry, 1789-1849.
　The history of Illinois, from its first discovery and settlement to the present time.　By Henry Brown ... New York, J. Winchester, 1844.
　x, 492 p.　fold. map.　22 1/2 cm.

11562　Brown, Henry, 1789-1849.
　A narrative of the anti-masonick excitement, in the western part of the state of New York, during the years 1826, '7, '8, and a part of 1829.　By Henry Brown... Batavia, N. Y., Printed by Adams & M'Cleary, 1829.
　4 p.l., 244 p.　18 cm.
On the abduction of William Morgan.

11563　Brown, Isaac Van Arsdale, 1784-1861.
　Biography of the Rev. Robert Finley, D. D. of Basking Ridge, N. J.　2d ed., enl. with an account of his agency as the author of the American coloni-

zation society; also a sketch of the slave trade;
a view of our national policy and that of Great
Britain towards Liberia and Africa. With an appendix.
By Rev. Isaac V. Brown, A. M. Philadelphia, J. W.
Moore, 1857.
  xii, [13]-336 p.   19 cm.
First pub. New Brunswick, 1819, with title:
Memoirs of the Rev. Robert Finley.

11564 Brown, Isaac Van Arsdale, 1784-1861.
  A historical vindication of the abrogation of the
plan of union by the Presbyterian church in the
United States of America. By the Rev. Isaac V.
Brown... Philadelphia, W. S. and A. Martien, 1855.
  vi, [7]-325 p.   23 1/2 cm.
On cover: Old school Presbyterianism vindicated.

11565 Brown, Isaac Van Arsdale, 1784-1861.
  Memoirs of the Rev. Robert Finley, D. D., late
pastor of the Presbyterian congregation at Basking
Ridge, New Jersey, and president of Franklin college,
located at Athens, in the state of Georgia. With
brief sketches of some of his contemporaries, and
numerous notes. By the Rev. Isaac V. Brown, A. M.
New Brunswick, Terhune & Letson, 1819.
  viii, [9]-370 p., 1 l.   front. (port.)
21 1/2 cm.

11566 Brown, John, 1722-1787.
  The Christian, the student, and pastor, exempli-
fied; in the lives of Mess. James Frazer, James
Hogg, Thomas Halyburton, in Scotland; Owen Stockton,
Matthew Henry, Philip Doddridge, in England; Thomas
Shepherd, Cotton Mather, and Jonathan Edwards, in
America. By John Brown... Edinburgh, Printed by
and for G. Als[ton] 1781.
  iv, 295, [1] p.   17 1/2 cm.

11567 Brown, John Mathias, 1745-1838.
  A brief sketch of the first settlement of the
county of Schoharie, by the Germans: being an answer
to a circular letter, addressed to the author, by
"The historical and philosophical society of the
state of New York." By John M. Brown. Schoharie
[N. Y.] Printed for the author, by L. Cuthbert,
1823.
  23 p.   23 1/2 cm.

11568   Brown, Jonathan, M. D.
        The history and present condition of St. Domingo.
        By J. Brown... Philadelphia, W. Marshall and co.,
        1837.
        2 v.   18 cm.

11569   Brown, Leonard, 1837-1914.
        Poems of the prairies. [By] Leonard Brown...
        New ed. Des Moines, Redhead and Wellsbager, 1868.
        x, [2] p., 1 l., [15]-186 p.   18 1/2 cm.

11570   [Brown, Peter] 1784-1863.
        The fame and glory of England vindicated; being
        an answer to "The glory and shame of England" [by
        C. Edwards Lester]... By Libertas... New York &
        London, Wiley and Putnam, 1842.
        iv, [5]-306 p.   19 cm.

11571   [Brown, Mrs. Rebecca (Warren)]
        Stories about General Warren, in relation to the
        fifth of March massacre, and the battle of Bunker
        Hill. By a lady of Boston. Boston, J. Loring, 1835.
        112 p. incl. pl.   15 1/2 cm.
        "Oration, delivered in Boston, March 6, 1775, by
        Dr. Joseph Warren, in commemoration of the evening
        of the fifth of March, 1770": p. [90]-112.

11572   Brown, Samuel, 1768-1805.
        A treatise on the nature, origin and progress of
        the yellow fever, with observations on its treatment;
        comprising an account of the disease, in several of
        the capitals of the United States: but more parti-
        cularly as it has prevailed in Boston. By Samuel
        Brown... Boston, Printed by Manning & Loring, 1800.
        viii, [9]-112 p.   22 1/2 cm.

11573   Brown, Samuel Gilman, 1813-1885.
        An address delivered before the Society of the
        alumni of Dartmouth college, at their first triennial
        meeting, July 25, 1855. By Samuel Gilman Brown.
        With an account of the proceedings of the society.
        Published by request. Concord, N. H., Press of
        McFarland & Jenks, 1856.
        69 p.   24 cm.

11574   Brown, Samuel R   1775-1817.
        An authentic history of the second war for inde-

pendence: comprising details of the military and
naval operations, from the commencement to the close
of the recent war; enriched with numerous geographical
and biographical notes. By Samuel R. Brown...
Auburn [N. Y.] Pub. by J. G. Hathaway, Kellogg &
Beardslee, printers, 1815.
2 v.   17 1/2 cm.

11575   Brown, Samuel R   1775-1817.
Views of the campaigns of the north-western army,
&c. Comprising, sketches of the campaigns of
Generals Hull and Harrison, a minute and interesting
account of the naval conflict on Lake Erie, military
anecdotes, abuses in the army, plan of a military
settlement, view of the lake coast from Sandusky to
Detroit. By Samuel R. Brown... Troy, N. Y.,
Printed by F. Adancourt, 1814.
156 p.   19 cm.

11576   Browne, John Ross, 1817-1875.
Etchings of a whaling cruise, with notes of a
sojourn on the island of Zanzibar. To which is
appended a brief history of the whale fishery...
By J. Ross Browne... New York, Harper & brothers,
1846.
xiii p., 1 l., 580 p.   front., illus., plates.
23 1/2 cm.

11577   Browne, Nathaniel Borodaille, 1819-1875.
An address delivered before the Union league in
the 24th ward of the city of Philadelphia, at its
opening celebration, May 9, 1863, by N. B. Browne,
esq. ... Philadelphia, The League, 1863.
16 p.   22 1/2 cm.

11578   Browne, Patrick, 1720?-1790.
The civil and natural history of Jamaica. In three
parts. Containing, I. An accurate description of
that island... with a brief account of its former
and present state, government, revenues, produce,
and trade. II. A history of the natural productions
... native fossils... III. An account of the nature
of climates in general, and their different effects
upon the human body... By Patrick Browne, M. D.
London, Printed for the author, and sold by T. Osborne
and J. Shipton, 1756.

2 p.l., viii, 503, [2] p.   49 pl., 2 fold. maps.
33 1/2 cm.

11579   Browne, Peter Arrell, 1782-1860.
A lecture on the Oregon territory. I. The title of
the United States to its sovereignty. II. Its capa-
bilities and value to our country. III. And the
necessity of an immediate settlement of it from the
states. By Peter A. Browne... Philadelphia, United
States book and job printing office, 1843.
20 p.   20 1/2 cm.

11580   Browne, Peter Arrell, 1782-1860.
Lecture upon the naturalization law of the United
States, by Peter A. Browne... Philadelphia, J.
Richards, printer, 1845.
24 p.   22 cm.

11581   Browne, Sir Thomas, 1605-1682.
The works of the learned Sr Thomas Brown, Kt.,
Doctor of Physick, late of Norwich. Containing I.
Enquiries into vulgar and common errors. II. Religio
medici: With annotations and observations upon it.
III. Hydriotaphia; or, Vrn-Burial: Together with
The Garden of Cyrus. IV. Certain miscellany tracts.
With alphabetical tables. London, Printed for Tho.
Basset, Ric. Chiswell, Tho. Sawbridge, Charles
Mearn, and Charles Brome, 1686.
4 pt. in 1 v.   front. (port.) illus.   31 1/2 cm.
First collected edition; each part has special
t.-p. and separate paging; [pt.] II ("Religio medici")
has imprint date 1685.

11582   Browne, W[illiam] H[enry James]
Ten coloured views taken during the Arctic expedition
of Her Majesty's ships "Enterprise" and "Investigator",
under the command of Captain Sir James C. Ross...
Drawn by W. H. Browne... With a summary of the...
expeditions in search of Captain Sir John Franklin...
London, Ackermann and co., 1850.
8 p.   10 col. pl. on 7 l.   38 x 28 cm.
English and French in parallel columns.

11583   Brownell, Charles De Wolf, 1822-
The Indian races of North and South America: comprising an account of the principal aboriginal races;
a description of their national customs, mythology,

68

and religious ceremonies: the history of their
most powerful tribes, and of their most celebrated
chiefs and warriors; their intercourse and wars with
the European settlers; and a great variety of anecdote
and description, illustrative of personal and national
character. By Charles De Wolf Brownell... New York,
H. E. & S. S. Scranton, 1853.
　　1 p.l., 720 (i.e. 640) p.　　24 col. pl., 15 port.
(part col.)　　23 cm.

11584　[Brownell, Henry Howard] 1820-1872.
　　　　Lyrics of a day: or, Newspaper-poetry. By a
volunteer in the U. S. Service. New York, Carleton,
1864.
　　ix, [11]-160 p.　　18 cm.

11585　Browning, Meshach, b. 1781.
　　　　Forty-four years of the life of a hunter; being
reminiscences of Meshach Browning, a Maryland hunter.
Roughly written down by himself. Revised and illustrated by E. Stabler. Philadelphia, J. B. Lippincott & co., 1864.
　　xvii, 13-400 p.　　illus., plates.　　19 cm.

11586　Brückner, G
　　　　Amerikas wichtigste charakteristik nach land und
leuten. Von G. Brückner. Mit zahlreichen holz-
schnitten und 3 stahlstichen. Volks-ausg. St. Louis,
Mo., C. Witter [Darmstadt, Druck von C. W. Leske,
1858]
　　2 p.l., 200, [1] p.　　front., illus., plates
(1 double)　　22 1/2 cm.
　　Also published under title: Amerikas geographie
und naturgeschichte.

11587　[Brutus, Lucius Junius] pseud.
　　　　An examination of the President's reply to the
New Haven remonstrance; with an appendix, containing
the President's inaugural speech, the remonstrance
and reply; together with a list of removals from
office, and new appointments, made since the fourth
of March, 1801. New York, Printed and sold by George
F. Hopkins, at Washington's head, 1801.
　　69 p.　　22 cm.
　　Relates to President Jefferson's course in removing
Federalists from office to make way for the appointment of Republicans.

Authorship attributed to William Cranch (Cushing,
Initials and pseudonyms, 1885, p. 42) and to William
Coleman (Sabin, Bibl. amer., v. 4, p. 229)

11588 Bruyas, Jacques, 1635-1712.
       Radices verborum iroquaeorum. Auctore r. p.
Jacobo Bruyas... Neo-Eboraci, typis, J. M. Shea,
1863.
       3 p.l., [3]-123 p.   28 cm.   (Half-title:
Shea's library of American linguistics. X)
       Half-title, added t.-p. and preface in English.
Added t.-p. reads: Radical words of the Mohawk
language, with their derivatives. By Rev. James
Bruyas... New York, Cramoisy press, 1862.
       "The present volume... was written evidently in
the latter part of the seventeenth century, and most
probably on the banks of the Mohawk... The grammatical sketch is rather a series of notes. The main
work... comprises the primitive words of the language
... with derivatives from each word... Except in
strict alphabetical arrangement, it is a very full
Mohawk dictionary, written in Latin, but with the
meaning of the words in French." - Pref.

11589 Bruzen de La Martinière, Antoine Augustin, 1662-1746.
       Introduction à l'histoire de l'Asie, de l'Afrique,
et de l'Amérique. Pour servir de suite à l'Introduction à l'histoire du baron de Pufendorff. Par
Mr. Bruzen la Martinière... Amsterdam, Z. Chatelain,
1735.
       2 v.   fronts., 2 fold. maps.   19 cm.

11590 Bryan, Thomas Barbour, 1828-1906.
       Stephen A. Douglas on the cause and effect of
the rebellion. Letter from Thomas B. Bryan, esq.
[Chicago? 1863]
       2, [1] p.   22 1/2 cm.

11591 Bryant, William Cullen, 1794-1878.
       A discourse on the life, character and genius of
Washington Irving, delivered before the New York
historical society... 3d of April, 1860. By William
Cullen Bryant. New York, G. P. Putnam, 1860.
       46 p.   19 1/2 cm.

11592 Bryant, William Cullen, 1794-1878.
       ... A forest hymn, by William Cullen Bryant. With

illustrations by Iohn A. Hows. New York, W. A.
Townsend & co. [^c1860]
   3 p.l., 4-32 numb. l.   illus.   23 1/2 cm.

11593 Buchanan, Archibald.
     An oration, composed and delivered at the request
of the Republican society of Baltimore, on the
Fourth of July, one thousand seven hundred and
ninety-four. By Archibald Buchanan. Baltimore,
Printed by Clayland, Dobbin, and co., Market-street,
corner of Centre-market, 1795.
    2 p.l., 2-40 p.   23 1/2 cm.   [Duane pamphlets,
v. 78, no. 8]

11594 Buchanan, James, British consul at New York.
     Sketches of the history, manners, and customs of
the North American Indians with a plan for their
melioration. By James Buchanan... New York,
W. Borradaile, 1824.
    2 v.   19 cm.

11595 Buchanan, Joseph Rodes, 1814-1899.
     Free collegiate education. A public lecture deli-
vered by Prof. J. R. Buchanan, on Monday evening,
Jan. 26, 1852, before the Mechanics' institute of
Cincinnati. Together with a statement of the
measures adopted by the trustees and faculty of
the E. M. institute for the establishment of a free
medical college, to be connected with a public
hospital, and which may serve as the nucleus of a
free national university. Cincinnati, W. M.
Naudain, printer, 1852.
    16 p.   22 cm.

11596 [Buchanan, William B   ]
     Baltimore; or, Long, long time ago. By W. B. B.
... Baltimore, Murphy & co., printers, 1853.
    24 p.   22 cm.   [Maryland historical society.
Publications. v. 3, no. 7]
    Poems.
    Contents. - Baltimore: or, Long, long time ago. -
The old church bell. - The city spring. - The old
town-clock.

11597 [Buck, Edward, of Boston]
     The drift of the war... [Boston, A. Williams &
co., 1861]

20 p.   24 1/2 cm.
Brief articles originally published in the Boston
transcript, May-November, 1861.

11598   Bucke, Charles, 1781-1846.
On the beauties, harmonies, and sublimities of
nature; with notes, commentaries, and illustrations;
and occasional remarks on the laws, customs, habits,
and manners, of various nations...   By Charles
Bucke...   A new ed., greatly enl.   London, T. Tegg
and son, 1837.
3 v.   22 cm.
Originally published anonymously, in 1813, under
title: The philosophy of nature.

11599   Buckingham, James Silk, 1786-1855.
America, historical, statistic, and descriptive...
London and Paris, Fisher, son, & co. [1841]
3 v.   front. (port.), fold. map.   23 1/2 cm.

11600   Buckingham, James Silk, 1786-1855.
Autobiography of James Silk Buckingham; including
his voyages, travels, adventures, speculations,
successes and failures, faithfully and frankly
narrated; interspersed with characteristic sketches
of public men with whom he has had intercourse,
during a period of more than fifty years...
London, Longman, Brown, Green, and Longmans, 1855.
2 v.   front. (port.)   19 1/2 cm.

11601   Buckingham, James Silk, 1786-1855.
Canada, Nova Scotia, New Brunswick, and the other
British provinces in North America; with a plan of
national colonization.   By James S. Buckingham.
London, Fisher, son, & co. [1843]
8 p.l., 540 p.   front., double plates, fold.
map.   22 1/2 cm.

11602   Buckingham, James Silk, 1786-1855.
The eastern and western states of America...
London and Paris, Fisher, son & co. [1842]
3 v.   illus.   23 1/2 cm.

11603   Buckingham, James Silk, 1786-1855.
History and progress of the temperance reformation,
in Great Britain and other countries of the globe;
with statistical and documentary evidence of its

beneficial results; and a plea for a Maine law,
to enforce the suppression of all traffic in in-
toxicating drinks. By James Silk Buckingham.
London, Partridge, Oakey, & co., 1854.
  1 p.l., 427-584, 6 p.   diagrs. on fold. pl.
21 1/2 cm.

11604 Buckingham, Joseph H   1806-1880.
       An address delivered before the Massachusetts
       charitable mechanic association, on the occasion of
       their fifteenth triennial festival, October 1, 1851.
       By Joseph H. Buckingham... Boston, Press of T. R.
       Marvin, 1851.
         23, [1] p.   24 cm.

11605 Buckingham, Joseph Tinker, 1779-1861, comp.
       Miscellanies selected from the public journals.
       Boston, Joseph T. Buckingham, 1822-24.
         2 v.   18 cm.

11606 Buckingham, Joseph Tinker, 1779-1861.
       Personal memoirs and recollections of editorial
       life. By Joseph T. Buckingham... Boston, Ticknor,
       Reed, and Fields, 1852.
         2 v.   front. (port.)   17 cm.

11607 Buckingham, Joseph Tinker, 1779-1861, defendant.
       Trial: Commonwealth vs. J. T. Buckingham, on an
       indictment for a libel, before the Municipal court
       of the city of Boston, December term, 1822...
       Boston, Published at the office of the New England
       galaxy [c1822]
         iv, [5]-60 p.   22 1/2 cm.
       Trial for a libel on John N. Maffitt.

11608 Buckminster, Joseph, 1751-1812.
       A discourse, delivered in the South, and in the
       North church in Portsmouth, December 14, 1800: the
       anniversary of the death of George Washington, late
       president of the United States, and commander in
       chief of their armies. By Joseph Buckminster, A. M.
       ... Portsmouth, New Hampshire, Printed at the
       United States' oracle-office by Charles Peirce,
       1800.
         21 p.   21 1/2 cm.
       Half-title: Anniversary sermon on the death of
       Gen. Washington.

11609 [Buckminster, Lydia Nelson (Hastings)] b. 1818.
The Hastings memorial. A genealogical account
of the descendants of Thomas Hastings of Watertown,
Mass. from 1634 to 1864. With an appendix and
index. Boston, S. G. Drake, 1866.
1 p.l., 183 p.   24 cm.

11610 Buffalo. Common council.
Report of the select committee of the Common council,
on the subject of the harbour and business of the
city of Buffalo. Made to the Common council June 1,
1841. Buffalo, Steele's press, 1841.
16 p.   22 cm.
Signed by R. Sears and others.

11611 [Bunce, Oliver Bell] 1828-1890.
The romance of the revolution: being a history
of the personal adventures, romantic incidents, and
exploits incidental to the war of independence...
New York, H. Dayton, 1858.
xxx, [31]-444 p.   front., plates.   19 cm.

11612 Burgoyne, John, 1722-1792.
A supplement to The state of the expedition from
Canada, containing General Burgoyne's orders,
respecting the principal movements, and operations
of the army to the raising of the siege of Ticon-
deroga. London, Printed for J. Robson [etc.]
1780.
1 p.l., 26 p. incl. plan.   26 1/2 x 21 1/2 cm.

11613 Burk, John Daly, d. 1808.
The history of Virginia, from its first settlement
to the present day. By John Burk... Petersburg,
Virginia, Printed for the author, by Dickson &
Pescud, 1804-16.
4 v.   fold. tables.   22 1/2 cm.
Vol. 4 has title: The history of Virginia; com-
menced by John Burk, and continued by Skelton Jones
and Louis Hue Girardin... Petersburg, Virginia -
Printed by M. W. Dunnavant, for the proprietors,
1816.
The history as published extends to 1781 (the
surrender of Cornwallis) though much of the manuscript remains unpublished. cf. Pref. of v. 4.

11614   Burke, AEdanus, 1743?-1802?
        An address to the freemen of the state of South
        Carolina. Containing political observations on the
        following subjects, viz. I. On the citizens making
        a temporary submission to the British arms after the
        reduction of Charlestown in 1780. II. On Governor
        Rutledge's proclamation of the 27th of September,
        1781. III. On the mode of conducting the election,
        for the Assembly at Jacksonborough. IV. On the
        Exclusion act, which cuts off the citizens from the
        rights of election. V. On the Confiscation act.
        VI. On the Amercement act. VII. The conclusion,
        with remarks to prove the necessity of an amnesty,
        or act of oblivion. By Cassius [pseud.] Supposed
        to be written by AEdanus Burke... Philadelphia,
        Printed and sold by Robert Bell, in Third-street,
        price one third of a dollar, 1783.
            32 p.   21 1/2 cm.
        [Duane pamphlets, v. 86, no. 4]

11615   [Burke, Edmund] 1729?-1797.
        An account of the European settlements in America.
        In six parts. I. A short history of the discovery
        of that part of the world. II. The manners and
        customs of the original inhabitants. III. Of the
        Spanish settlements. IV. Of the Portuguese. V. Of
        the French, Dutch, and Danish. VI. Of the English
        ... London, R. and J. Dodsley, 1765.
            2 v.   fronts. (fold. maps)   20 cm.
        Fourth edition.
        Probably the joint work of Edmund and William
        Burke, but usually attributed to the former, who
        called himself merely the reviser of his kinsman's
        work. cf. Dict. nat. biog.; Sabin, Bibl. amer.

11616   Burke, Edmund, 1729?-1797.
        A letter from the Rt. Honourable Edmund Burke to
        His Grace, the Duke of Portland, on the conduct of
        the minority in Parliament, containing fifty-four
        articles of impeachment against the Rt. Hon. C. J.
        Fox, from the original copy in the possession of
        the noble duke. London printed. Philadelphia,
        reprinted for J. Humphreys, 1797.
            56 p.   23 cm.

11617   Burke, Edmund, 1729?-1797.
        Speech of Edmund Burke, esq. on American taxation,

April 19, 1774. The 2d ed. London, Printed for
J. Dodsley, 1775.
iv, 5-96 p.   21 1/2 cm.

11618   Burke, Edmund, 1809-1882.
The protective system considered in connection with
the present tariff, in a series of twelve essays,
originally published in the Washington union over
the signature of "Bundelcund." Written by the Hon.
Edmund Burke. Washington, Printed by J. and G. S.
Gideon, 1846.
40 p.   23 1/2 cm.

11619   Burkitt, Lemuel.
A concise history of the Kehukee Baptist association, from its original rise to the present
time... By Elders Lemuel Burkitt and Jesse Read...
Halifax [N. C.] Printed by A. Hodge, 1803.
4 p.l., [v]-xxvi, [27]-319 p.   16 1/2 cm.

11620   Burmann, Johannes, 1646-1764.
Plantarum americanarum fasciculus primus, con-
tinens plantas, quas olim Carolus Plumierius bota-
nicorum princeps detexit, eruitque, atque in insulis
Antillis ipse depinxit. Has primum in lucem edidit,
concinnis descriptionibus, & observationibus,
Aeneisque tabulis illustravit Johannes Burmannus...
Amsterdam, sumtibus auctoris, atque apud viduam &
fillium S. Schouten; Leiden, apud Gerard. Potvliet
& Theodor. Haak, 1755 [-60]
6 l., 262 p., 4 l., cclxii tables.

11621   Burnaby, Andrew, 1734?-1812.
Travels through the middle settlements in North
America, in the years 1759 and 1760. With observa-
tions upon the state of the colonies. By the Rev.
Andrew Burnaby... London, T. Payne, 1775.
viii, 106 p., 1 l. incl. tables.   27 x 22 cm.
The author's travels extended from Virginia to
New England.
"Diary of the weather," January-December, 1760,
transmitted from Williamsburg, Virginia, by Francis
Fauquier: p. 95-106.

11622   Burnap, George Washington, 1802-1859.
Origin and causes of democracy in America: a
discourse by George W. Burnap. Delivered in

Baltimore, before the Maryland historical society,
on its eighth anniversary celebration; December 20,
1853. [Baltimore, J. D. Toy, printer, 1854]
29 p.   22 cm.   [Maryland historical society.
Publications. vol. III, no. 6]

11623 Burney, James, 1750-1821.
A chronological history of north-eastern voyages
of discovery; and of the early eastern navigations
of the Russians. By Captain James Burney, F. R. S.
London, Payne and Foss [etc.] 1819.
viii, 310 p.   fold. maps.   21 1/2 cm.

11624 Burney, James, 1750-1821.
A memoir on the voyage of D'Entrecasteaux, in
scarch of La Pérouse. By James Burney... London,
Printed by L. Hansard & sons, 1820.
21 p.   22 cm.

11625 Burns, James R
Battle of Williamsburgh, with reminiscences of
the campaign, hospital experiences, debates, etc.
By James R. Burns. New York, The author, 1865.
vi, [7]-119 p.   14 1/2 cm.

11626 Burr, Aaron, 1716-1757.
A discourse delivered at Newark, in New Jersey,
January 1, 1755. Being a day set apart for solemn
fasting and prayer, on account of the late encroach-
ments of the French, and their designs against the
British colonies in America. By Aaron Burr...
New York, Printed and sold by H. Gaine, 1755.
2 p.l., iii-iv, 5-41 p.   20 x 15 1/2 cm.

11627 Burr, Aaron, 1756-1836, defendant.
Message from the President of the United States,
transmitting a copy of the proceedings and of the
evidence exhibited on the arraignment of Aaron Burr,
and others, before the Circuit court of the United
States, held in Virginia, in the year 1807...
City of Washington, A. & G. Way, printers; 1807.
2 p.l., 332, 222 p.   22 1/2 cm.
November 23, 1807. Read and referred to the Committee appointed on so much of the message of the
President of the 27th ultimo, as relates to enter-
prizes against the public peace, and to the means of
preventing the same; and punishing the authors.

"Evidence furnished by the district attorney":
222 p. at end.

11628   Burr, Aaron, 1756-1836, defendant.
Reports of the trials of Colonel Aaron Burr, (late
vice president of the United States) for treason,
and for a misdemeanor, in preparing the means of a
military expedition against Mexico, a territory of
the King of Spain, with whom the United States were
at peace.   In the Circuit court of the United States,
held at the city of Richmond, in the district of Virginia, in the summer term of the year 1807.   To which
is added, an appendix, containing the arguments and
evidence in support and defence of the motion after-
wards made by the counsel for the United States, to
commit A. Burr, H. Blannerhassett [!] and I. Smith
to be sent for trial to the state of Kentucky, for
treason or misdemeanor, alleged to be committed there.
Taken in short hand by David Robertson...   Philadelphia, Published by Hopkins and Earle, Fry and Kam-
merer, printers, 1808.
2 v.   23 cm.

11629   Burr, Fearing.
The field and garden vegetables of America: containing full descriptions of nearly eleven hundred
species and varieties; with directions for propagation,
culture, and use. By Fearing Burr, jr. ...   Boston,
Crosby and Nichols, 1863.
xv, 674 p.   illus.   22 cm.

11630   Burr, Samuel Jones.
The life and times of William Henry Harrison,
by S. J. Burr...   New York, L. W. Ransom; Philadelphia, R. W. Pomeroy, 1840.
viii, [9]-304 p.   front. (port.)   15 1/2 cm.

11631   Burrill, George Rawson, 1770-1818.
An oration, delivered in the Benevolent Congregational meeting-house, on the Fourth of July, A. D.
1797, in commemoration of American independence.
By George R. Burrill... Published by request.
Providence, Printed by Carter and Wilkinson, and
sold at their book-store, 1797.
2 p.l., [3]-18 p.   21 cm.

11632   Burritt, Elihu, 1810-1879.
         Thoughts and things at home and abroad. By Elihu
         Burritt... With a memoir, by Mary Howitt. Boston,
         Phillips, Sampson, and company; New York, J. C.
         Derby, 1854.
         vi, [v]-xxvi, [9]-364 p.   front. (port.)
         20 cm.

11633   Burroughs, Charles, 1787-1868.
         An oration on the moral grandeur of George Washing-
         ton, delivered on the centennial anniversary of his
         birth day, February 22, 1832, at the request of the
         citizens of Portsmouth, N. H. By Charles Burroughs...
         Portsmouth, N. March & co., 1832.
         59, [1] p.   25 1/2 cm.

11634   Burroughs, Stephen, 1765-1840.
         Memoirs of Stephen Burroughs. To which are added,
         notes, and an appendix... Albany, Published by
         B. D. Packard, no. 51 State-street. R. Packard,
         printer, 1811.
         2 v. in 1.   17 1/2 cm.

11635   Burton, John, 1696-1771.
         The duty and reward of propagating principles of
         religion and virtue exemplified in the history of
         Abraham. A sermon preach'd before the Trustees for
         establishing the colony of Georgia in America. And
         before the Associates of the late Rev. Dr. Thomas
         Bray for converting the negroes in the British plant-
         ations, and for other good purposes. At their anni-
         versary-meeting in the parish church of St. Mary-le-
         Bow. On Thursday March 15, 1732. By John Burton...
         Pub. at the desire of the trustees and associates.
         To which is annexed, the general account exhibited
         by the trustees to the right honourable the lord high
         chancellor, and the lord chief justice of His Majesty's
         Court of common-pleas, pursuant to the directions of
         their charter. London, Printed by J. March, 1733.
         50 p.   22 x 17 cm.

11636   Burton, Sir Richard Francis, 1821-1890.
         Explorations of the highlands of the Brazil; with
         a full account of the gold and diamond mines. Also,
         canoeing down 1500 miles of the great river São
         Francisco, from Sabará to the sea. By Captain
         Richard F. Burton, F. R. G. S., etc. London,

Tinsley brothers, 1869.
2 v.   front., illus., map.   22 cm.

11637   Burton, Warren, 1800-1866.
The district school as it was. New York, Arno
Press, 1969.
xii, 171 p.   illus.   23 cm.   (American educa-
tion: its men, ideas, and institutions)
Reprint of the 1928 ed.
Contents. - The district school as it was. - A
supplication to the people of the United States. -
Pages from old spellers.

11638   Burwell, William MacCreary, 1809-1888.
Address delivered before the Society of alumni
of the University of Virginia, at their annual
meeting, June 29, 1847. By William M. Burwell, esq.
Richmond, Printed by Shepherd and Colin, 1847.
27, 7 p.   23 cm.

11639   Busey, Samuel Clagett, 1828-1901.
Immigration, its evils and consequences. By
Samuel C. Busey... New York, De Witt & Davenport
[1856]
162 p.   18 1/2 cm.

11640   Bushnell, Horace, 1802-1876.
Reverses needed. A discourse delivered on the
Sunday after the disaster of Bull Run, in the North
church, Hartford. By Horace Bushnell. Hartford,
L. E. Hunt, 1861.
27 p.   21 1/2 cm.

11641   Bushnell, Horace, 1802-1876.
Speech for Connecticut. Being an historical
estimate of the state, delivered before the Legislature and other invited guests, at the festival of
the normal school in New Britain, June 4, 1851.
By Horace Bushnell. Printed by order of the Legislature. Hartford, Boswell and Faxon, 1851.
43 p.   24 cm.

11642   Bushnell, Horace, 1802-1876.
Women's suffrage; the reform against nature. By
Horace Bushnell. New York, C. Scribner and company,
1869.
184 p.   19 cm.

11643 Bussierre, Marie Théodore Renouard, vicomte de, 1802–
1865.
L'Empire Mexicain; histoire des Toltèques, des
Chichimèques, des Aztèques et de la conquête
espagnole, par le vicomte M. Th. de Bussierre.
Paris, H. Plon, 1863.
2 p.l., 427 p.   22 1/2 cm.

11644 Busteed, Richard, 1822–1898.
An oration, delivered at Huntington, L. I., New
York, by Richard Busteed, esq., on Friday, July 4th,
1862. New York, C. S. Westcott & co., printers,
1862.
21 p.   22 cm.

11645 Busteed, Richard, 1822–1898.
Speech of Richard Busteed, delivered at Faneuil
hall, Boston, October 31st, 1862. On the issues of
the war, and the duty of sustaining the government.
New York, C. S. Westcott & co., printers, 1862.
cover-title, 24 p.   21 1/2 cm.

11646 Butler, Benjamin Franklin, 1795–1858.
Outline of the constitutional history of New York,
an anniversary discourse, delivered at the request
of the New York historical society, in the city of
New York, November 19, 1847. By Benjamin Franklin
Butler... New York, Bartlett & Welford, 1848.
1 p.l., [11]–75 p.   23 cm.

11647 Butler, Benjamin Franklin, 1818–1893.
Speech of Maj.-Gen. Benj. F. Butler, upon the campaign before Richmond, 1864. Delivered at Lowell,
Mass., January 29, 1865. With an appendix: The two
attacks on Fort Fisher; speech on the treatment of
the negro, delivered at Boston, Mass., February 4,
1865; speech of Hon. Geo. S. Boutwell, in reply to
charges of Hon. James Brooks... against Gen. Benj. F.
Butler, delivered in the House of representatives,
January 24, 1865. Boston, Wright & Potter, printers,
1865.
88 p.   23 cm.

11640 Butler, Clement Moore, 1810–1890.
A sermon giving a historical account of St. John's
church, Georgetown, D. C., delivered October 17,
1843; and an address on the occasion of the funeral

of Abel P. Upshur & others, who lost their lives by
the calamity on board the Princeton, Feb. 28, 1844,
and also a farewell sermon delivered April 7, 1844,
on his resignation of the rectorship of St. John's
church. By Rev. C. M. Butler... Washington, J. and
G. S. Gideon, printers, 1844.
40 p.   23 1/2 cm.

11649   Butler, George Bernand, 1809-1886.
... The conscription act: a series of articles
communicated to the Journal of commerce. By George
B. Butler... [New York, 1863]
22 p., 1 l.   22 1/2 cm. (Loyal publication
society. [Pamphlets] no. 40)

11650   Butler, Henry E
God's way of leading the blind. A discourse commemorative of the death of Abraham Lincoln, delivered
by Rev. Henry E. Butler, in the Congregational church,
Keeseville, N. Y., April 23, 1865. Burlington [Vt.]
Free press printing office, 1865.
23 p.   22 1/2 cm.

11651   Butler, John, bp. of Hereford, 1717-1802.
A sermon preached before the incorporated Society
for the propagation of the gospel in foreign parts;
at their anniversary meeting in the parish church
of St. Mary-le-Bow, on Friday, February 20, 1784.
By the Right Reverent John, lord bishop of Oxford.
London, Printed by T. Harrison and S. Brooke, 1784.
21 p.   21 1/2 x 17 cm.
[Theological pamphlets, v. 153, no. 7]

11652   Butterfield, Carlos.
United States and Mexican mail steamship line,
and statistics of Mexico. By Carlos Butterfield...
New York, J. A. H. Hasbrouck & co., printers, 1859.
vi, [7]-109 p., 1 l., v, [7]-152 p.   2 fold.
maps.   23 cm.

11653   Butterfield, Consul Willshire, 1824-1899.
History of Seneca county [Ohio] containing a
detailed narrative of the principal events that have
occurred since its first settlement down to the
present time; a history of the Indians that formerly
resided within its limits; geographical descriptions,
early customs, biographical sketches, &c. &c. With

an introduction, containing a brief history of the
state, from the discovery of the Mississippi river
down to the year 1817, to the whole of which is
added an appendix, containing tabular views, &c.
By Consul W. Butterfield. Sandusky [O.] D. Campbell & sons, 1848.
251, [1] p.   20 cm.

11654 Byam, George.
Wanderings in some of the western republics of
America. With remarks upon the cutting of the great
ship canal through Central America. By George Byam
... London, J. W. Parker, 1850.
xii, 264 p. incl. front., plates.   map.
19 1/2 cm.

11655 Byam, George.
Wild life in the interior of Central America. By
George Byam... London, J. W. Parker, 1849.
viii, 253, [1] p.   front.   17 cm.

11656 Byrd, William, 1674-1744.
History of the dividing line, and other tracts.
From the papers of William Byrd, of Westover, in
Virginia, esquire. Richmond, Va., 1866.
2 v.   illus., map.   21 1/2 cm.   (Half-title:
Historical documents from the Old Dominion, no.
II-III)
Edited by T. H. Wynne.

C

11657 Camp, Phineas, 1788-1868.
Poems of the Mohawk valley, and on scenes in
Palestine, together with an essay on the origin of
poetry, with miscellaneous poems and sketches, by
Phineas Camp. Utica, N. Y., Curtiss & White,
printers, 1859.
vi p., 1 l., [9]-204 p.   18 1/2 cm.

11658 Campbell, Charles, 1807-1876, ed.
Some materials to serve for a brief memoir of John
Daly Burk, author of a History of Virginia. With
a sketch of the life and character of his only
child, Judge John Junius Burk. Ed. by Charles

Campbell. Albany, N. Y., J. Munsell, 1868.
vi, [7]-123 p. 25 cm.

11659 Cardozo, Jacob Newton.
A plan of financial relief, addressed to the legislature of Georgia, and Confederate States Congress,
as originally published in the Atlanta southern confederacy, by J. N. Cardozo. Atlanta, Ga., J. H.
Seals & co.'s power press, 1863.
37 p. 21 cm.

11660 Care, Henry, 1646-1688.
English liberties, or The free-born subject's
inheritance... Comp. first by Henry Care, and continued, with large additions, by William Nelson, of
the Middle-Temple, esq. The 6th ed., cor. and improved. Providence, R. I., Printed and sold by
J. Carter, 1774.
viii, 350 p. 18 cm.

11661 Carey, Mathew, 1760-1839.
Miscellaneous trifles in prose. By Mathew Carey.
Philadelphia, Printed for the author, by Lang and
Ustick, 1796.
176 p. 22 1/2 cm.
Reprinted in part from the Columbian magazine,
American museum, Pennsylvania evening herald, and
Philadelphia gazette.
Contents. - Shipwreck. - Columbian observer, no. I.
No. II. Modern improvement. No. IV. Hist. of Mrs.
Winthrop. - Funding bill. - Life of General Greene.
- Thoughts on the policy of encouraging migration. -
Theatricus: No. I. Mr. Chalmers. No. II. Mrs. Whit-
lock. No. III. Mr. Harwood. No. IV. Mrs. Marshall.
- Advantages of over-trading. - Observations on the
badness of the times.

11662 Cariboo, the newly discovered gold fields of British
Columbia, fully described by a returned digger...
2d ed. London, Darton & Hodge, 1862.
iv, 76 p. 16 cm.

11663 Carlier, Auguste, 1803-1890.
Marriage in the United States, by Auguste Carlier
... Translated from the French by B. Joy Jeffries
... Boston, De Vries, Ibarra & co.; New York,

Leypoldt and Holt, 1867.
xv, 179 p.   18 cm.

11664 Carlile, Thomas, 1792-1824.
An address, delivered before Essex lodge, on the
evening of 28th December, A. L. 5819. By the Rev.
Thomas Carlile... Salem, Printed by W. Palfray,
jr., 1819.
13 p.   22 cm.

11665 Carlyle, Thomas, 1795-1881.
Shooting Niagara: and after? By Thomas Carlyle...
London, Chapman and Hall, 1867.
1 p.l., 55 p.   18 1/2 cm.
Reprinted from Macmillan's magazine for August,
1867. With some additions and corrections.

11666 Carnesworthe, pseud.
Atlantic City. Its early and modern history.
By Carnesworthe. Philadelphia, W. C. Harris & co.,
1868.
96 p.   19 cm.

11667 Carpenter, George W   1802-1860.
A brief description of Phil-Ellena, the country
seat of George W. Carpenter, at Germantown, Philadelphia County, Penn. Situated on the Germantown
Main street, about seven and a half miles from the
city... Philadelphia, Printed by Barrington and
Haswell, 1844.
36 p.   front. (plan) pl.   20 1/2 cm.

11668 Carpenter, Hugh S[mith]
Eulogy on the late William Henry Harrison, presi-
dent of the United States; delivered before the
Eucleian society of the University of the city of
New York, May 28, 1841. By Hugh S. Carpenter.
New York, Hopkins & Jennings, printers, 1841.
16 p.   23 cm.

11669 Carpenter, Matthew Hale, 1824-1881.
The powers of Congress, the constitutionality of
its acts on reconstruction, alarming tendency of
the Seymour Democracy. Speech of Hon. Matt. H. Carpenter, at Chicago, Ill., Aug. 12, 1868... Washington, D. C., Union Republican congressional committee,

1868.
8 p.   23 1/2 cm.

11670   Carpenter, Philip Pearsall, 1819-1877.
Report on the present state of our knowledge with
regard to the Mollusca of the west coast of North
America. By Philip P. Carpenter... London, Printed
by Taylor and Francis, 1857.
1 p.l., 4, 159-368 p.   plates.   22 cm.
From the Report of the British association for
the advancement of science for 1856.
----- Supplementary report... By Philip P. Carpenter... London, Printed by Taylor and Francis,
1864.
1 p.l., 517-686 p.   21 1/2 cm.
From the Report of the British association for
the advancement of science for 1863.

11671   Carpenter, Stephen Cullen, d. ca. 1820.
Select American speeches, forensic and parlia-
mentary, with prefatory remarks: being a sequel to
Dr. Chapman's 'Select speeches.' By S. C. Carpenter
... Philadelphia, Published by J. W. Campbell and
E. Weems, William Fry, printer, 1815.
2 v.   22 1/2 cm.
The speeches here included were delivered during
the period from 1787 to 1814.

11672   Carpenter, William Henry, 1813-1899.
The history of Massachusetts, from its earliest
settlement to the present time. By W. H. Carpenter.
Philadelphia, Lippincott, Grambo & co., 1853.
3 p.l., [5]-330 p.   front. (port.)   17 1/2 cm.
(Half-title: Lippincott's cabinet histories of the
states)

11673   Carpenter, William Henry, 1813-1899.
The history of Vermont, from its earliest settlement to the present time. By W. H. Carpenter, and
T. S. Arthur. Philadelphia, Lippincott, Grambo &
co., 1853.
1 p.l., 260 p.   front.   17 cm.   (Added
t.-p.: Lippincott's cabinet histories)

11674   Carr, John.
Early times in middle Tennessee. By John Carr...
Nashville, Tenn., Pub. for E. Carr, by E. Stevenson

& F. A. Owen, 1857.
vi, 7-248 p.   15 1/2 cm.

11675 Carr, Spencer, 1811-1880.
A brief sketch of La Crosse, Wisc'n, showing the
location of the place, its surrounding scenery,
commercial advantages, early history, and the social,
moral, literary, and religious character of the
inhabitants; and various other interesting items.
By Rev. Spencer Carr... La Crosse, W. C. Rogers,
printer, 1854.
28 p.   20 cm.

11676 [Carrington, John W   ]
The passage of the isthmus; or, Practical hints
to persons about to cross the isthmus of Panama...
By one who has recently crossed. New York, Jennings
& Harrison, 1849.
14 p.   map.   23 1/2 cm.

11677 Carroll, Anna Ella, 1815-1894.
The great American battle; or, The contest between
Christianity and political Romanism. By Anna Ella
Carroll... New York and Auburn, Miller, Orton &
Mulligan, 1856.
xii, 13-365 p.   front., ports.   19 1/2 cm.

11678 Carroll, Anna Ella, 1815-1894.
A review of Pierce's administration; showing its
only popular measures to have originated with the
executive of Millard Fillmore. By Anna Ella Carroll
... Boston, J. French & company; New York, Miller,
Orton & Mulligan, 1856.
iv, [5]-137 p.   18 1/2 cm.

11679 Carroll, Anna Ella, 1815-1894.
The star of the West; or, National men and national
measures. By Anna Ella Carroll... Boston, J. French
and company; New York, Miller, Orton & Mulligan,
1856.
3 p.l., [3]-366 p.   10 port. (incl. front.)
20 cm.
Contents. - The union of the states. - The Pacific
railroad. - Romanism opposed to our liberties. -
Central America. - Review of administrations. -
Biographical sketch of Erastus Brooks; Edwin O.
Perrin; Gardner B. Locke; Alfred B. Ely; Sidney

87

Kopman; Thos. H. Clay; Nathan Ranney.

11680   Carroll, Charles, 1737-1832.
Journal of Charles Carroll of Carrollton, during
his visit to Canada in 1776, as one of the commissioners from Congress; with a memoir and notes by
Brantz Mayer... Published by the Maryland historical
society. Baltimore, J. Murphy, 1845.
84 p.   22 1/2 cm.

11681   Carver, Jonathan, 1710-1780.
... Travels in Wisconsin. From the 3d London ed.
New York, Printed by Harper & bros., 1838.
xxxii, [33]-376 p.   front. (port.) plates,
2 fold. maps.   23 cm.
First edition, London, 1778, published under
title: Travels through the interior parts of North
America, in the years 1766, 1767, and 1768. The
third edition, London, 1781, was edited by John
Coakley Lettsom.

11682   Carver, Jonathan, 1710-1780.
A treatise on the culture of the tobacco plant;
with the manner in which it is usually cured.
Adapted to northern climates, and designed for the
use of the landholders of Great Britain. To which
are prefixed, two plates of the plant and its flowers.
By Jonathan Carver... London, The author, sold by
J. Johnson, 1779.
4 p.l., 54 p.   2 col. pl. (incl. front.)
21 1/2 cm.

11683   Carver, Robin.
History of Boston. By Robin Carver. Boston, Lilly,
Wait, Colman, and Holden, 1834.
viii, [9]-169 p. incl. illus., plates.   front.
15 x 13 cm.

11684   Cary, Thomas Greaves, 1791-1859.
Gold from California, and its effect on prices.
A lecture. Delivered at North Chelsea, Massachusetts.
March 25th, 1856. With some reminiscences of the
place. By Thomas G. Cary. The principal part
having been already published in Hunt's merchants'
magazine, for May, 1856. New York, Printed by
G. W. Wood, 1856.
20 p.   22 cm.

11685 Cary, Thomas Greaves, 1791-1859.
       Letter to a lady in France, on the supposed
       failure of a national bank, the supposed delinquency
       of the national government, the debts of the several
       states, and repudiation; with answers to enquiries
       concerning the books of Capt. Marryat and Mr. Dickens.
       By Thomas G. Cary. 3d ed. Boston, B. H. Greene,
       1844.
          60 p.   23 1/2 cm.
          Cover-title: Letter... in answer to enquiries
       concerning the late imputations of dishonor upon
       the United States.

11686 [Cary, Thomas Greaves] 1791-1859.
       Profits on manufactures at Lowell. A letter from
       the treasurer of a corporation to John S. Pendleton,
       esq., Virginia. Boston, C. C. Little & J. Brown,
       1845.
          23 p.   23 1/2 cm.

11687 Case, Charles, b. 1817.
       The President's special message. Speech of Hon.
       Charles Case, of Indiana. Delivered in the U. S.
       House of representatives, March 11, 1858. [Washing-
       ton, D. C., Buell & Blanchard, printers, 1858]
          16 p.   24 cm.

11688 Case, Wheeler, d. 1793.
       Revolutionary memorials, embracing poems by the
       Rev. Wheeler Case, published in 1778, and an appendix,
       containing General Burgoyne's proclamation (in bur-
       lesque) dated June 23, 1777 - A late authentic
       account of the death of Miss Jane M'Crea - The
       American hero, a Sapphic ode, by Nat. Niles, A. M.,
       etc. Ed. by the Rev. Stephen Dodd... New York,
       M. W. Dodd, 1852.
          iv, [5]-69 p.   18 1/2 cm.
          Includes reprint of original t.-p. (with author's
       name inserted): Poems, occasioned by several cir-
       cumstances and occurrences in the present grand
       contest of America for liberty. By the Rev. Wheeler
       Case, of Dutchess-County, N. Y. New Haven, Printed
       by Theo. and Samuel Green, 1778.
          "General Burgoyne's proclamation" is from the
       Providence gazette of Aug. 16th, 1777. The account
       of the death of Jane M'Crea consists of a letter from
       Asa Fitch (published in the Proceedings of the

Historical society of New Jersey, v. 5, p. 164)
and some extracts from Charles Neilson's account of
Burgoyne's campaign.

11689 The case and claim of the American loyalists impartially
stated and considered. [London] Printed by order
of their agents [1783]
1 p.l., 38 p. 22 cm.
Sabin (Bibl. amer.) mentions copies with the same
collation, and imprint London: G. Wilkie, 1783.

11690 The case of Great Britain and America, addressed to
the king, and both houses of Parliament... London,
Printed; Philadelphia, Re-printed by William and
Thomas Bradford, at the London Coffee-House, 1769.
1 p.l., 16 p. 21 cm.
Authorship attributed to Gervase Parker Bushe
(Bodleian lib., Catalogue, additions, 1835-1847;
Brit. mus., Catalogue, suppl.; Cushing, Anonyms;
Halkett and Laing, Dict.) and to George B. Butler
(Sabin, Bibl. amer.; Boston ath. lib., Catalogue)

11691 The case of the planters of tobacco in Virginia, as
represented by themselves; signed by the president
of the council, and speaker of the House of burgesses. To which is added, A vindication of the
said representation. London, Printed for J. Roberts,
1733.
64 p. 19 1/2 cm.
The case of the planters of tobacco in Virginia,
&c. [signed in the name and behalf of the council,
Robert Carter, president; John Holloway, speaker
of the House of burgesses, Williamsburg, June 28,
1732]: p. 3-15. A vindication of the representation
of the case of the planters of tobacco in Virginia;
made by the General assembly of that colony:
p. 17-64.

11692 Casey, Joseph, 1814-1879.
Speech of Mr. Casey, of Pennsylvania, on the President's message, communicating the constitution of
California. Delivered in the House of representatives of the United States, March 18, 1850. [Washing-
ton, Gideon & co., printers, 1850]
7 p. 24 cm.

11693 Castelnau, Francis, comte de, 1812-1880.
Essai sur le système silurien de l'Amérique septentrionale. Par F. de Castelnau... avec vingt-sept
planches. Paris, P. Bertrand [etc., etc.] 1843.
xv, 56 p.   27 pl. (incl. map)   35 1/2 cm.
"Extrait des Comptes rendus des séances de
l'Académie des sciences, séance du 6 mars 1843."

11694 Caswall, Henry, 1810-1870.
The American church and the American union, by
Henry Caswall... London, Saunders, Otley, and co.,
1861.
x, 311, [1] p.   20 cm.

11695 Caswall, Henry, 1810-1870.
The city of the Mormons; or, Three days at
Nauvoo, in 1843. By the Rev. Henry Caswall... 2d
ed., rev. and enl. ... London, Printed for J. G. F.
& J. Rivington, 1843.
2 p.l., 87, [1] p.   front.   16 cm.

11696 Caswell, Alexis, 1799-1877.
... Meteorological observations made at Providence,
R. I. extending over a period of twenty-eight years
and a half, from December 1831 to May 1860. By
Alexis Caswell... [Washington, Smithsonian institution, 1860]
iv p., 2 l., 179 p.   32 1/2 cm.   (Smithsonian
contributions to knowledge. [vol. XII, art. 4])
Smithsonian institution publication 103.

11697 A catalogue of all the books, printed in the United
States, with the prices, and places where published,
annexed. Published by the booksellers in Boston...
Printed at Boston, for the booksellers, 1804.
79 p.   18 cm.
Original edition.
Reprinted by A. Growoll in his Book-trade bibliography in the United States in the XIXth century,
1808, from the copy belonging to Charles A. Montgomery of Brooklyn. In his introductory note,
Mr. Growoll says "Only two other copies... are known
to be in existence... one... in the library of the
Massachusetts historical society... the other...
the property of Mr. James G. Burnwell."

11698   Catcott, Alexander.
        A treatise on the deluge. Containing I. Remarks on
        the Lord Bishop of Clogher's account of that event.
        II. A full explanation of the Scripture history of it.
        III. A collection of all the principal heathen ac-
        counts. IV. Natural proofs of the deluge, deduced
        from a great variety of circumstances, on and in the
        terraqueous globe. And, under the foregoing general
        articles, the following particulars will be occasion-
        ally discussed and proved, viz. The time when, and
        the manner how America was first peopled. - The Mosaic
        account of the deluge written by inspiration. - The
        certainty of an abyss of water within the earth. -
        The reality of an inner globe or central nucleus. -
        The cause of the subterranean vapour, and of earth-
        quakes. - The origin of springs, lakes, &c. - The
        formation of mountains, hills, dales, vallies, &c. -
        The means by which the bed of the ocean was formed. -
        The cause of caverns or natural grottos; with a des-
        cription of the most remarkable, especially those in
        England. - Also an explication of several lesser
        phaenomena in nature. Illustrated with two copper
        plates; one, representing the state of the earth
        during the height of the flood; the other, the state
        of the earth as it is at present. By Alexander Cat-
        cott... The 2d ed. considerably enl. London,
        Printed for the author, by E. Allen, 1768.
            viii, [8], 423 p.   II pl.   21 1/2 cm.

11699 A caveat against unreasonable and unscriptural separa-
        tions. In a letter, sent from a minister to some
        of his brethren. Boston, Printed and sold opposite
        to the prison in Queen street, 1748.
            30 p.   16 cm.

11700 Caverly, Abiel Moore, 1817-1879.
        An historical sketch of Troy [N. H.] and her
        inhabitants, from the first settlement of the town,
        in 1764, to 1855. By A. M. Caverly... Keene [N. H.]
        Printed at the N. H. sentinel office, 1859.
            ix p., 1 l., [13]-299 p.   front., ports.
        19 1/2 cm.
        Includes genealogical sketches.

11701 Caverly, Robert Boodey, 1806-1887.
        The Merrimac and its incidents. An epic poem by
        Robert B. Caverly. Boston, Innes & Niles, printers,

1866.
3 p.l., 5-80 numb. l.   front., plates.   19 cm.

11702 Caylus, Ernest.
Politique extérieure des États-Unis. Doctrine
Monroe par Ernest Caylus... Paris, E. Dentu, 1865.
31 p.   25 cm.

11703 Cecil, E., pseud.?
Life of Lafayette. Written for children. By
E. Cecil. With six illustrations. Boston, Crosby,
Nichols and company, 1860.
4 p.l., 218 p.   col. front., 4 col. pl.
17 1/2 cm.

11704 Century association, New York.
Proceedings of the Century association in honor
of the memory of Brig.-Gen. James S. Wadsworth and
Colonel Peter A. Porter; with the eulogies read by
William J. Hoppin and Frederic S. Cozzens. December
3, 1864. New York, D. Van Nostrand, 1865.
88 p.   24 cm.

11705 [Cerisier, Antoine Marie] d. 1828.
Le destin de l'Amerique; ou, Dialogues pittoresques
dans lesquels on developpe la cause des evenemens
actuels, la politique et les interests des puissances
de l'Europe relativement a cette guerre, et les
suites qu'elle devroit avoir pour le bonheur de
l'humanité, traduit fidelement de l'anglois...
London, Printed for J. Bew [1780?]
124 p.   22 1/2 cm.
Published anonymously. Not translated from the
English and, apparently, not printed in London.
cf. Sabin, Bibl. amer., v. 3, p. 459; van Doot-
ninck, Vermomde en naamlooze schrijvers, 1883-85,
decl II, p. 418.

11706 Cesnola, Luigi Palma di, 1832-1904.
Ten months in Libby prison. By Louis Palma di
Cesnola... [Philadelphia? 1865]
7 p.   23 cm.
Reprinted from Bulletin of the United States sani-
tary commission, March, 1865.

11707 Chabert de Cogolin, Joseph Bernard, marquis de,
1724-1805.

Voyage fait par ordre du roi en 1750 et 1751,
dans l'Amérique Septentrionale, pour rectifier les
cartes des côtes de l'Acadie, de l'isle Royale & de
l'isle de Terre-Neuve; et pour en fixer les princi-
paux points par des observations astronomiques.
Par m. de Chabert... Paris, Imprimerie royale, 1753.
1 p.l., viii, 288, [10] p.   illus., fold. pl.,
6 fold. maps, fold. tab.   26 x 20 1/2 cm.
[Académie des sciences, Paris. Suite des Mémoires.
Paris, 1720-   v. 12]

11708 Chaix, Paul Georges Gabriel, 1808-1901.
Histoire de l'Amérique Méridionale au seizième
siècle, comprenant les découvertes et conquètes des
Espagnols et des Portugais dans cette partie du
monde; par Paul Chaix... Première partie: Pérou,
avec cinq cartes géographiques... Genève, Paris,
J. Cherbuliez [etc., etc.] 1853.
2 v.   5 fold. maps.   17 1/2 cm.

11709 [Chalmers, George] 1742-1825.
The life of Thomas Pain, the author of Rights of
men. With a defence of his writings. By Francis
Oldys, A. M. of the University of Pennsylvania
[pseud.]   London, Printed for J. Stockdale, 1791.
2 p.l., 128 p.   21 cm.
A hostile account. The words, "With a defence of
his writings" were clearly used as a means of attract-
ing Paine's supporters. The pseudonym was wholly
fictitious, as Chalmers had no such degree and no
connection with the University of Pennsylvania; it
was evidently devised to compete with Paine's honor-
ary degree from the same institution, as well as to
lend dignity to the publication by making it appear
the work of a clergyman. cf. Conway's Life of Paine,
1892, v. 1, p. xiv-xvi, 337-338.

11710 Chambers, William, 1800-1883.
Things as they are in America. Philadelphia,
Lippincott, Grambo & co., 1854.
vi, 364 p.   20 1/2 cm.

11711 [Chambon,   ] fl. 1775.
Le guide de commerce de l'Amérique, principalement
par le port de Marseille... Ouvrage utile aux négo-
cians qui font ce commerce & aux personnes curieuses
de connoître l'histoire de nos colonies. Le tout

orné de cartes & de figures en tailledouce. Par m.
Ch... de Marseille... Avignon, J. Mossy, 1777.
  2 v.   XII pl., maps (part fold.)   25 1/2 cm.
  Published also under titles "Le commerce de
l'Amérique par Marseille" and "Traité général du
commerce de l'Amérique."

11712 Champagny, Jean Baptiste Nompère de, duc de Cadore,
1756-1834.
  Letter from M. Champagny, the French minister for
exterior relations to General Armstrong, the minister
of the United States, at Paris. Accompanying a
message from the president of the United States, received on the 30th March, 1808. April 2, 1808.
Printed by order of the House of representatives.
City of Washington, A. & G. Way, printers, 1808.
  4 p.   21 cm.

11713 [Champion, Richard] 1743-1791.
  Considerations on the present situation of Great
Britain and the United States of North America,
with a view to their future commercial connexions.
Containing remarks upon the pamphlet published by
Lord Sheffield, entitled "Observations on the com-
merce of the American states;" and also on the Act
of Navigation... 2d ed., with great additions...
By Richard Champion... London, J. Stockdale, 1784.
  xxxiv, 274, 36 p.   21 cm.

11714 Champlain, Samuel de, 1567-1635.
  Narrative of a voyage to the West Indies and
Mexico in the years 1599-1602... by Samuel Champlain. Tr. from the original and unpublished manuscript, with a biographical notice and notes by
Alice Wilmere. Ed. by Norton Shaw. London,
Printed for the Hakluyt society, 1859.
  3 p.l., vi, xcix, 48 p.   fold. front. (col.
facsim.) plates (part fold.) fold. maps (part col.)
22 cm.   (Half-title: Works issued by the Hakluyt
society [no. XXIII])
  Caption title: Brief narrative of the most remarkable things that Samuel Champlain of Brouage,
observed in the Western Indies.

11715 Champlain, [Samuel] de, 1567-1635.
  Voyages du sieur de Champlain, ou Journal ès
découvertes de la Nouvelle France... Paris, Imprimé

aux frais du gouvernement pour procurer du travail
aux ouvriers typographes, Août 1830.
2 v.   20 1/2 cm.
Reprint of Les voyages de la Nouvelle France occi-
dentale, 1632, without the map or supplementary
matter.

11716   Chandler, Adoniram.
Address, delivered at the close of the nineteenth
annual fair of the American institute, of the city
of New York, at Castle Garden, October 23, 1846. By
Adoniram Chandler. New York, Van Norden & Amerman,
printers, 1846.
18 p.   23 1/2 cm.
Relates to the tariff.

11717   Chandler, Charles Frederick, 1836-1925.
Report on water for locomotives and boiler in-
crustations: made to the president and directors of
the New York central railroad. By Charles F. Chandler... New York, Printed by J. F. Trow & co., 1865.
35 p.   23 cm.

11718   Chandler, James, 1706-1789.
An answer to Mr. Tucker's letter to Mr. Chandler.
Relative, more especially, to a marginal note or
two in his Sermon preached at Newbury-Port, June 25,
1767, preparatory to their settling of a minister.
By James Chandler, author of said sermon. Boston,
Printed by Edes & Gill, for Bulkeley Emerson, of
Newbury-Port, 1767.
36 p.   20 1/2 cm.

11719   Chandler, Peleg Whitman, 1816-1889.
American criminal trials. By Peleg W. Chandler...
Boston, Charles C. Little and James Brown; London,
A. Maxwell, 1841-44.
2 v.   front. (port., v. 2)   20 cm.
Added t.-p. (v. 1) illustrated with portrait of
Wm. Stoughton.
Vol. 2 has imprint: Boston: Timothy H. Carter and
company. London: A. Maxwell.
Contents. - v. 1. Anne Hutchinson. The Quakers.
Salem witchcraft. Thomas Maule. John Peter Zenger.
New York Negro plot. Leisler's rebellion. Colonel
Bayard's treason. The crew of the Pitt packet.
The Boston massacre. Appendix. - v. 2. Bathsheba

Spooner and others. Colonel Henley. Major André.
Joshua H. Smith. The Rhode Island judges. John
Hauer and others. Appendix: Trial of Mrs. Spooner
and others. Major André. Notes.

11720 Chandler, Peleg Whitman, 1816-1889.
The morals of freedom. An oration delivered before
the authorities of the city of Boston, July 4, 1844.
By Peleg W. Chandler. Boston, J. H. Eastburn, city
printer, 1844.
54 p.   23 1/2 cm.

11721 [Chandler, Thomas Bradbury] 1726-1790.
The American querist: or, Some questions proposed
relative to the present disputes between Great Britain,
and her American colonies. By a North American...
[New York] Printed [by James Rivington] in the year
1774.
2 p.l., 31 p.   21 cm.
Also attributed to Myles Cooper. For evidence of
authorship, cf. Vance, C. H. Myles Cooper. (Columbia
university quarterly, Sept. 1930, vol. XXII, no. 3,
p. 275-276)

11722 [Chandler, Thomas Bradbury] 1726-1790.
What think ye of the Congress now? Or, An enquiry,
how far the Americans are bound to abide by, and
execute the decisions of, the late Congress? ...
New York, Printed by James Rivington, 1775.
48, 4 p.   20 cm.
Also attributed to Myles Cooper.
"A plan of a proposed union, between Great-Britain
and the colonies of New-Hampshire, Massachusetts-Bay,
Rhode-Island, New-York, New-Jersey, Pennsylvania,
Maryland, Delaware counties, Virginia, North Caro-
lina, South Carolina, and Georgia. Which was pro-
duced by one of the delegates from Pennsylvania, in
Congress, as mentioned in the preceding work" (by
Joseph Galloway): 4 p. at end.

11723 Channing, Edward Tyrrel, 1790-1856.
Lectures read to the seniors in Harvard college.
By Edward T. Channing... Boston, Ticknor and Fields,
1856.
xx, 298 p.   18 cm.
"Biographical notice," by Richard H. Dana, jr.:
p. vii-xx.

11724 Channing, Henry, 1760?-1840.
       God admonishing his people of their duty, as
       parents and masters. A sermon, preached at New-
       London, December 20th, 1786, occasioned by the
       execution of Hannah Ocuish, a mulatto girl, aged
       12 years and 9 months, for the murder of Eunice
       Bolles, aged 6 years and 6 months. By Henry Chan-
       ning, M. A. ... New-London, Printed by T. Green,
       1786.
          31 p.   20 1/2 cm.
       Hannah Ocuish was the daughter of a Pequot Indian
       woman.

11725 Channing, Walter, 1786-1876.
       Memoir of the late Enoch Hale, M. D., M. M. S. S.,
       A. A. S. By Walter Channing, M. D. Boston, D.
       Clapp, printer, 1848.
          12 p.   24 cm.

11726 Channing, William F[rancis] 1820-
       The American fire-alarm telegraph: a lecture
       delivered before the Smithsonian institutuion,
       March, 1855. By William F. Channing... Boston,
       Redding & company, 1855.
          19 p.   23 cm.
       "Reprinted from the Annual report of the Smith-
       sonian institution." 1854. p. 147-155.

11727 Channing, William Henry, 1810-1884.
       The civil war in America; or, The slaveholders'
       conspiracy. An address, by William Henry Channing.
       Liverpool, W. Vaughan; London, G. Vickers [etc.,
       1861]
          iv, [5]-100 p.   18 1/2 cm.

11728 Chapin, Alonzo Bowen, 1808-1858.
       Glastenbury for two hundred years: a centennial
       discourse, May 18th, A. D. 1853. With an appendix,
       containing historical and statistical papers of
       interest. By Rev. Alonzo B. Chapin... Hartford,
       Press of Case, Tiffany and company, 1853.
          252 p.   front. (map)   23 cm.
          Genealogical accounts of families: p. 159-200.
          Glastenbury centennial celebration, May 18, 1853:
       p. 219-251.

11729   Chapin, Edwin Hubbell, 1814-1880.
         The American idea, and what grows out of it.
         An oration, delivered in the New York crystal palace,
         July 4, 1854. By E. H. Chapin. Published by request.
         Boston, A. Tompkins, 1854.
            18 p.   21 cm.
            "The... oration was originally printed in the
         New-York tribune."

11730   Chapin, Orange, b. 1790.
         The Chapin genealogy, containing a very large pro-
         portion of the descendants of Dea. Samuel Chapin,
         who settled in Springfield, Mass. in 1642. Collected
         and comp. by Orange Chapin. To which is added a
         "Centennial discourse"... by E. B. Clark... Also,
         an address... by George Bliss. Northampton [Mass.]
         Printed by Metcalf & co., 1862.
            viii, 368 p.   23 1/2 cm.

11731   Chapin, Stephen, 1778-1845.
         The duty of living for the good of posterity.
         A sermon, delivered at North Yarmouth, December 22,
         1820, in commemoration of the close of the second
         century from the landing of the fore-fathers of
         New England. By Stephen Chapin... Portland [Me.]
         Printed by T. Todd & co., 1821.
            48 p.   22 cm.

11732   The Chapin gathering. Proceedings of the meeting of
         the Chapin family, in Springfield, Mass., September
         17, 1862. Springfield, Printed by S. Bowles and
         co., 1862.
            97 p.   21 1/2 cm.

11733   Chapman, Henry Samuel, 1803-1881.
         Thoughts on the money and exchanges of lower Canada.
         By Henry S. Chapman... Montreal, Printed at the
         Montreal gazette office, 1832.
            3 p.l., [5]-64 p. incl. tables.   22 1/2 cm.

11734   Chapman, Isaac A
         A sketch of the history of Wyoming. By the late
         Isaac A. Chapman, esq. To which is added, an appen-
         dix, containing a statistical account of the valley,
         and adjacent country. By a gentleman of Wilkesbarre.
         Wilkesbarre, Penn., S. D. Lewis, 1830.
            209 p.   18 x 10 1/2 cm.

11735   Chapman, John Gadsby, 1808-1889.
        The picture of the baptism of Pocahontas. Painted
        by order of Congress, for the rotundo of the Capitol,
        by J. G. Chapman... Washington, P. Force, 1840.
        22 p.   pl.   25 cm.

11736   Chapman, Mrs. Maria (Weston) 1806-1885.
        Right and wrong in Massachusetts. By Maria Weston
        Chapman... Boston, Dow & Jackson's anti-slavery
        press, 1839.
        177 p.   17 1/2 cm.
        Relates to dissensions in the Massachusetts anti-
        slavery society, 1837-1839.

11737   [Chapman, Mrs. Maria (Weston] 1806-1885, comp.
        Songs of the free, and hymns of Christian freedom...
        Boston, I, Knapp, 1836.
        viii, [9]-227 p.   17 1/2 cm.

11738   Chapman, S[ilas]
        Hand book of Wisconsin. 2d ed., enlarged & im-
        proved. By S. Chapman. Milwaukee, S. Chapman,
        1855.
        117 p.   13 1/2 cm.

11739   Chappelsmith, John.
        ... Account of a tornado near New Harmony, Ind.,
        April 30, 1852, with a map of the track, &c. By
        John Chappelsmith... [Washington, Smithsonian
        institution, 1855]
        11, [1] p.   front. (fold. map) pl., diagrs.
        32 1/2 cm. (Smithsonian contributions to knowledge
        (vol. VII, art. 2])
        Smithsonian institution publication 59.

11740   A chapter of American history. Five years' progress
        of the slave power; a series of papers first published
        in the Boston "Commonwealth," in July, August and
        September, 1851... Boston, B. B. Mussey and com-
        pany, 1852.
        84 p.   23 1/2 cm.

11741   Characters. Containing an impartial review of the
        public conduct and abilities of the most eminent
        personnages in the Parliament of Great Britain:
        considered as statesmen, senators, and public
        speakers. Rev. and cor. by the author, since the

original publication in the Gazetteer. London,
Printed for J. Bew, 1777.
    xv, [1], 152 p.   21 cm.

11742 [Chardon, Daniel Marc Antoine] 1730-1795?
        Essai sur la colonie de Sainte-Lucie. Par un
    ancien intendant de cette isle. Suivi de trois
    mémoires intéressans, deux concernant les Jésuites,
    & le troisieme le general d'Oxat. Neuchatel, Impr.
    de la Société typographique, 1779.
        1 p.l., ii, 154 p.   18 1/2 cm.
        Published anonymously.
        The two "Mémoires concernant les Jésuites" are by
    Louis Nicolas Prétrel.

11743 Charleston, S. C. Apprentices' library society.
        Constitution of the Apprentices' library society
    of Charleston, S. C. Adopted at an adjourned meeting,
    held Wednesday, March 10th, 1841. Charleston, S. C.,
    B. B. Hussey, printer, 1841.
        16 p.   22 1/2 cm.

11744 Charleston, S. C. City council.
        Census of the city of Charleston, South Carolina,
    for the year 1848, exhibiting the condition and
    prospects of the city, illustrated by many statis-
    tical details, prepared under the authority of the
    City council. By J. L. Dawson, M. D., and H. W.
    De Saussure, M. D. Charleston, S. C., J. B. Nixon,
    printer, 1849.
        viii, 262 p.   23 1/2 cm.

11745 Charleston, S. C. City council. Committee on ways
    and means.
        The disabilities of Charleston for complete and
    equal taxation, and the influence of state taxation
    on her prosperity; also, an examination of the measure
    of Mr. James G. Holmes, for the liquidation of the
    debt of the city, with the ordinance adopting the same;
    being reports of the Committee on ways and means,
    made to the City council of Charleston, April, 1857.
    Pub. by order of Council. Charleston, Walker, Evans
    & co., stationers and printers, 1857.
        59, [1] p. incl. tables. fold. tab.   24cm.
        Robert N. Gourdin, first signer.

11746   Charleston, S. C.   Unitarian church.
        The old and the new: or, Discourses and proceed-
ings at the dedication of the re-modelled Unitarian
church in Charleston, S. C., on Sunday, April 2,
1854. Preceded by the farewell discourse delivered
in the old church, on Sunday, April 4, 1852. [With
engravings of the former and present edifices]
Charleston, S. G. Courtenay, 1854.
        3 p.l., [3]-148 p.   plates.   22 1/2 cm.
        Contents. - Farewell to the old church. By Samuel
Gilman. - Dedication of the new church. - Discourse
delivered at the dedication. By Samuel Gilman. -
Prayer of dedication. By Rev. G. W. Burnap. - Inauguration of the new church. By Rev. Charles M.
Taggart. - Salutation of the churches. By Rev.
John Pierpont, jr. - The work of Christ. By Rev.
John H. Heywood. - Unitarian Christianity expounded
and defended. By G. W. Burnap. Concluding address
to the congregation. By Rev. C. J. Bowen.

11747   Charlton, Edwin Azro, 1828-1896.
        New Hampshire as it is... Comp. ... by Edwin A.
Charlton. Claremont, N. H., Tracy and Sanford, 1855.
        592 p.   front., plates, ports.   22 1/2 cm.
        Contents. - pt. I. A historical sketch... to the
adoption of the Federal Constitution in 1788. -
pt. II. A gazetteer... - pt. III. A general view...
containing a description of its soil, productions,
climate... biographical sketches of distinguished
men... together with the constitution of the state.

11748   The Charters of the British colonies in America.
        London, Printed for J. Almon [1774?]
        1 p.l., 142 p.   21 1/2 cm.
        Contents. - Massachusetts Bay. - Connecticut. -
Rhode Island. - First charter granted to Massachu-
setts Bay. - Virginia. - Pennsylvania. - Maryland.
- Georgia.

11749   Charton, Édouard Thomas, 1807-1890, ed.
        Voyageurs anciens et modernes, ou Choix des
relations de voyages les plus intéressantes et les
plus instructives depuis le cinquième siècle avant
Jésus-Christ jusqu'au dix-neuvième siècles, avec
biographies, notes et indications iconographiques,
par m. Édouard Charton... Paris, Aux bureau du
Magasin pittoresque, 1857-63.

4 v.   illus. (incl. ports., maps, plans, diagrs.)
25 1/2 cm.
Vols. 1-3: 1861-63; v. 4: 1857.
Bibliographies accompany each article.
Vols. 1-3, title edition: first published 1854-55.

11750   Chase C   Thurston, b. 1819.
A manual on school-houses and cottages for the
people of the South. Prepared by C. Thurston Chase
... Washington, Govt. print. off., 1868.
83 p.   illus., plans, diagrs.   23 cm.

11751   Chase, Ezra B
Teachings of patriots and statesmen; or, The
"founders of the republic" on slavery. By Ezra B.
Chase... Philadelphia, J. W. Bradley, 1860.
495 p. incl. front. (port.)   19 1/2 cm.

11752   Chase, Francis.
Gathered sketches from the early history of New
Hampshire and Vermont; containing vivid and interesting account of a great variety of the adventures of
our forefathers, and of other incidents of olden
time. Original and selected. Ed. by Francis Chase,
M. A. Claremont, N. H., Tracy, Kenney & co., 1856.
215 p.   front., plates.   18 1/2 cm.

11753   Chase, George Wingate, 1826-1867.
The history of Haverhill, Massachusetts, from its
first settlement, in 1640, to the year 1860, by
George Wingate Chase... Haverhill, Pub. by the
author, 1861.
xvi, [17]-663, [1], xx p.   front., plates,
ports., maps, facsim.   23 1/2 cm.

11754   Chase, Henry.
The North and the South: a statistical view of
the condition of the free and slave states. By
Henry Chase... and Charles W. [!] Sanborn... Comp.
from official documents. Boston, J. P. Jewett and
company; New York, Sheldon, Blakeman, and company
[etc., etc.] 1856.
vi, [7]-134 p.   19 cm.

11755   Chase, Horace, 1788-1875, ed.
The New Hampshire probate directory: containing
all the statute laws relating to courts of probate

and proceedings therein: with a complete collection
of probate forms, adapted to the revised statutes
and acts since passed, including June session, 1854.
With notes, directions, tables, &c., &c. 2d ed.
By Horace Chase. Concord, G. P. Lyon, 1854.
   2 p.l., [iv]-v, [9]-342 p.   19 1/2 cm.

11756 Chase, Pliny Earle, 1820-1886.
       Catalogue of tokens, circulating during the rebel-
       lion of 1861. By Pliny E. Chase. [Philadelphia,
       1863?]
          19 p.   24 cm.
       Reprint from the Proceedings of the American philo-
       sophical society, Philadelphia, vol. IX, p. 242-258.

11757 Chase, Samuel, 1741-1811, defendant.
       The answer and pleas of Samuel Chase, one of the
       associate justices of the Supreme Court of the United
       States, to the articles of impeachment, exhibited
       against him in the said court, by the House of re-
       presentatives of the United States, in support of
       their impeachment against him, for high crimes and
       misdemeanors, supposed to have been by him committed.
       Printed by order of the Senate. Washington, Printed
       by William Duane & son, 1805.
          84, 4 p.   21 1/2 cm.
       Caption title: In the Senate of the United States,
       sitting as a high court of impeachment, on the fourth
       day of February, A. D. 1805. The United States vs.
       Samuel Chase.
       Judge Chase was impeached for alleged misdemeanors
       in the political trials of Fries and Callender. cf.
       Sabin, Dict. of books relating to America.

11758 Chase, Warren, 1813-1891.
       The American crisis; or, Trial and triumph of
       Democracy. By Warren Chase... Boston, B. Marsh,
       1862.
          82 p.   18 1/2 cm.

11759 Chasles, Philarète, 1798-1873.
       Anglo-American literature and manners: from the
       French of Philarète Chasles... New York, C. Scrib-
       ner, 1852.
          1 p.l., [v]-xii, 312 p.   18 1/2 cm.
       Translation somewhat abridged, by Donald MacLeod.

11760　Chasles, Philarète, 1798-1873.
　　　　Beautés de l'histoire du Canada; ou, Époques re-
　　　marquables, traits intéressans, moeurs, usages,
　　　coutumes des habitans du Canada, tant indigènes que
　　　colons, depuis sa découverte jusqu'à ce jour. Par
　　　D. Dainville. Paris, Bossange frères, 1821.
　　　　2 p.l., iv, 511 p.　　plates.　　17 1/2 cm.

11761　Chaudron, Mrs. Adelaide de Vendel.
　　　　Chaudron's spelling book, carefully prepared for
　　　family and school use, by A. de V. Chaudron. Mobile,
　　　S. H. Goetzel, 1865.
　　　　48 p. incl. front., illus.　　18 cm.

11762　Chaumonot, Pierre Joseph Marie, 1611-1693.
　　　　La vie du R. P. Pierre Joseph Marie Chaumonot,
　　　De la Compagnie de Jesus, Missionnaire dans la
　　　Nouvelle France. Ecrite par lui-même par ordre de
　　　son Supérieur, l'an 1688. Nouvelle York, Isle de
　　　Manate, A la Presse Cramoisy de Jean-Marie Shea,
　　　1858.
　　　　108 p.　　20 x 16 cm.　　[Shea's Cramoisy
　　　press series. no. 6]
　　　　This autobiography is supplemented by the
　　　anonymous "Suite de la Vie du R. P. Pierre
　　　Joseph Marie Chaumonot", also published,
　　　1858, by J. G. Shea (Cramoisy press series,
　　　no. 7)

11763　Chauncy, Charles, 1705-1787.
　　　　A discourse on "the good news from a far country."
　　　Deliver'd July 24th [1766] A day of thanks-giving
　　　to almighty God... on occasion of the repeal of the
　　　Stamp-act... By Charles Chauncy... Boston, Printed
　　　by Kneeland and Adams, for T. Leverett, 1766.
　　　　32 p.　　20 cm.
　　　　Reprinted in John W. Thornton's Pulpit of the
　　　American revolution, Boston, 1860.

11764　[Chauncy, Charles] 1705-1787, supposed author.
　　　　A letter from a gentleman in Boston, to Mr. George
　　　Wishart, one of the ministers of Edinburgh, concerning
　　　the state of religion in New England. Edinburgh,
　　　1742.
　　　　24 p.　　20 1/2 cm.
　　　　Ascribed to Charles Chauncy. cf. Ford, P. L.
　　　Bibliotheca Chaunciana, p. 3; Sibley, J. L.　Biog.

sketches of graduates of Harvard, v. 6, p. 462.
A discussion of the effects of George Whitefield's
preaching in New England.

11765   Chautard, Léon.
Escapes from Cayenne. By Leonard Chautard...   Salem,
[Mass.]   Printed at the Observer officer, 1857.
63 p.   23 cm.

11766   Chazotte, Peter Stephen, ca. 1770-ca. 1849.
Facts and observations on the culture of vines,
olives, capers, almonds, &c. in the Southern states,
and of coffee, cocoa, and cochineal in east Florida,
by Peter Stephen Chazotte...   Philadelphia, J. Maxwell, 1821.
24 p.   21 1/2 cm.

11767   Chazotte, Peter Stephen, ca. 1770-ca. 1849.
Historical sketches of the revolutions, and the
foreign and civil wars in the island of St. Domingo,
with a narrative of the entire massacre of the white
population of the island: by Peter S. Chazotte,
esq., an eye witness. New York, W. Applegate, 1840.
71 p.   21 cm.

11768   Cheetham, James, 1772-1810.
An antidote to John Wood's poison. By Warren
[pseud.] New York, Printed by Southwick and Crooker,
354 Water-street, for Denniston and Cheetham, 1802.
63 p.   21 1/2 cm.

11769   Cheetham, James, 1772-1810.
A dissertation concerning political equality, and
the corporation of New York. By James Cheetham.
New York, Printed by D. Denniston, 1800.
vii, 9-50 p.   22 1/2 cm.

11770   Cheetham, James, 1772-1810.
Nine letters on the subject of Aaron Burr's
political defection, with an appendix. By James
Cheetham. New York, Printed by Denniston & Cheetham,
1803.
139 p.   22 cm.

11771   Cheetham, James, 1772-1810.
Peace or war? or, Thoughts on our affairs with
England. By James Cheetham. New York, M. Ward,

1807.
44 p.   23 cm.

11772   Cheever, George Barrell, 1807–1890.
The elements of national greatness. An address
before the New England society of the city of New
York, December 22, 1842. By Rev. George B. Cheever
... New York, J. S. Taylor & co., 1843.
40 p.   22 cm.

11773   Cher, Henry W. B., pseud.
Gnaw-wood; or, New England life in a village.
By Henry W. B. Cher [pseud.] 2d ed. New York, The
National news company, 1868.
cover-title, [3]-22 p.   22 cm.
A parody of Henry Ward Beecher's "Norwood". cf.
Sabin, Bibl. amer.

11774   Cherokee nation.
Address of the "Committee and Council of the
Cherokee nation, in general council convened," to the
people of the United States. [n.p., 1830]
11 p.   16 1/2 cm.
Signed by Lewis Ross, president and 37 others.
"To the reader" (p. 10-11) signed: An American
citizen; dated: Chester County (Pa.) September 24,
1830.

11775   Cherokee nation.
Reply of the delegates of the Cherokee nation to
the pamphlet of the commissioner of Indian affairs.
Washington, 1866.
16 p.   21 1/2 cm.
Regarding the attitude of the Cherokees during
the Civil war.

11776   Cherokee nation. Constitution.
The constitution and laws of the Cherokee nation:
passed at Tah-le-quah, Cherokee nation, 1839.
Washington, Printed by Gales and Seaton, 1840.
36 p.   19 cm.

11777   Cherokee primer. Park Hill, Mission press, J. Candy,
printer, 1840.
24 p.   illus.   13 cm.
Caption and text in Cherokee characters.

11778   Cherry Valley, N. Y.
        The centennial celebration at Cherry Valley,
Otsego co., N. Y., July 4th, 1840. The addresses
of William W. Campbell, esq. and Gov. W. H. Seward,
with letters, toasts, &c. &c. New York, Taylor &
Clement, 1840.
        59 p.   17 1/2 cm.

11779   Chervin, Nicolas, 1783-1843.
        De l'opinion des médecins américains sur la
contagion ou la non-contagion de la fièvre jaune,
ou, Réponse aux allégations de MM. les docteurs
Hosack et Townsend de New York, publiées, l'an
dernier, dans la Revue médicale, la Gazette de France
et le New York Enquirer; par N. Chervin... Paris,
Londres, J. B. Baillière, 1829.
        192 p.   22 cm.

11780   Chesapeake and Ohio canal company.
        Report of the probable revenue of the Chesapeake
and Ohio canal, made to the Baltimore convention,
December, 1834. [Baltimore? 1834]
        16 p.   18 1/2 cm.

11781   Chipman, Nathaniel, 1752-1843.
        Sketches of the principles of government; by
Nathaniel Chipman... Rutland [Vt.] From the press
of J. Lyons, printed for the author, 1793.
        xii, [13]-292 p.   16 1/2 cm.

11782   Christie, Robert, 1788-1856.
        A brief review of the political state of Lower
Canada, since the conquest of the colony, to the
present day. To which are added, memoirs of the
administrations of the colonial government of Lower
Canada, by Sir Gordon Drummond, and Sir John Coape
Sherbrooke, by Robert Christie. New York, W. A.
Mercein, 1818.
        92 p.   22 cm.

11783   Christy, David, b. 1802.
        Ethiopia: her gloom and glory, as illustrated
in the history of the slave trade and slavery, the
rise of the republic of Liberia, and the progress
of African missions. By David Christy... With an
introduction. By W. P. Strickland... Cincinnati,
Rickey, Mallory & Webb, 1857.

iv, 5-255 p.   20 cm.
Originally published as a collection, Columbus,
1853, without collective title but known as Lectures
on African colonization, and kindred subjects.

11784 Christy, David, b. 1802.
Pulpit politics; or, Ecclesiastical legislation
on slavery, in its disturbing influences on the
American union. By Prof. David Christy... 5th ed.
Cincinnati, Farran & McLean, 1863.
xvi, 17-624 p.   21 1/2 cm.

11785 Chronander, Gustav.
... Utilitates, qvae ex commerciis & coloniis in
calidioribus mundi partibus patriae adfluerent...
sub umbone Dn. Petri Kalm... publico examini modeste
submittit Gustavus Chronander... die XXIII. Dec.
MDCCLVII... Aboae, Jacob Merckell [1757]
12 p.   22 cm.

11786 Chronological account of remarkable occurrences from
the commencement of the French revolution to the
31st of December, 1815. Extracted from the Belfast
News letter, commencing January, 1816. Corrected
and enlarged. Belfast, Printed by A. Mackay, 1816.
xi, 324 p.   front. (fold. map)   18 cm.

11787 Church, Benjamin, 1639-1718.
The history of King Philip's war, by Benjamin
Church; with an introduction and notes by Henry
Martyn Dexter. Boston, J. K. Wiggin, 1865.
4 p.l., vii-l p., 1 l., [3], 205, [1] p.
front. (fold. map)   21 1/2 x 17 1/2 cm.   (Half-
title: Library of New England history. No. 2)
Prepared by Thomas Church from the papers of his
father, Benjamin Church. Includes facsim. of
t.-p. of original ed.: Entertaining passages
relating to Philip's war... By T. C. Boston,
Printed by B. Green, 1716.

11788 [Church, Benjamin] 1734-1776.
Elegy on the death of the Reverent Jonathan Mayhew,
D. D., who departed this life July 9th, anno Domini,
1766. aetatis suae 46. Boston, Printed and sold by
Edes and Gill, in Queen street [1766]
15 p.   24 1/2 cm.

11789 [Church, Benjamin] 1734-1776.
　　　Liberty and property vindicated, and the st--pm-n
　　burnt. A discourse occasionally made on burning
　　the effige [!] of the st--pm-n. In New London, in
　　the colony of Connecticut. By a friend to the liberty
　　of his country. Boston, Re-printed and sold at the
　　new printing-office in Milk-street, 1766.
　　　15 p.　　19 cm.
　　A burlesque sermon on the Stamp act. The "epistle
　　dedicatory" is signed: Elizaphan of Parnach.
　　The "stampman" was Jared Ingersoll.

11790 Church, Benjamin, 1734-1776.
　　　An oration; delivered March 5th, 1773, at the
　　request of the inhabitants of the town of Boston;
　　to commemorate the bloody tragedy of the fifth of
　　March, 1770... 3d ed., cor. by the author. Boston,
　　Printed by Edes & Gill, 1773.
　　　18 p.　　20 1/2 x 17 1/2 cm.

11791 Church, George Earl, 1835-1910.
　　　Mexico. Its revolutions: are they evidences of
　　retrogression or of progress? A historical and
　　political review, by George E. Church. Revised
　　from the New York herald of May 25th, 1866. New
　　York, Baker & Godwin, printers, 1866.
　　　84 p.　　23 cm.

11792 Church, John Hubbard, 1772-1840.
　　　A sermon, preached at Concord, before His Excel-
　　lency the Governor, the honorable Council, the
　　honorable Senate, and House of representatives, of
　　the state of New Hampshire, June 3, 1813. Being the
　　anniversary election. By John Hubbard Church,
　　pastor of the church in Pelham. Concord, Printed
　　by George Hough, for the General court, 1813.
　　　2 p.l., [3]-41 p.　　21 1/2 cm.
　　[Theological pamphlets, v. 36, no. 10]

11793 Church, R　　　S　　　H
　　　The two rebellions! A few words to His Excellency,
　　the Hon. C. F. Adams, etc., etc. touching his here-
　　ditary relations to rebellion, from one who like
　　himself is the grandson of an American rebel. By
　　R. S. H. Church... London, W. Ridgway, 1865.
　　　16 p.　　21 cm.

11794 Churchill, Charles.
Memorials of missionary life, in Nova Scotia...
London [etc.] J. Mason [etc.] 1845.
vi, [1], 206 p., 1 l.   15 cm.

11795 Cist, Charles, 1792-1868.
Sketches and statistics of Cincinnati in 1859.
[n.p., 1859]
367 p.   illus.   21 cm.

11796 Civil prudence, recommended to the thirteen United
Colonies of North America. A discourse, showing
that it is in the power of civil prudence to prevent
or cure state distempers, and to make an industrious,
wealthy and flourishing people: - also, to preserve
the balance of trade, with a replenishing indraught
of money in any country, and how it may be done;
holding forth the immense benefits to be obtained
by a good regulation of trade, and the state-ruining
consequences of the contrary... Norwich, Conn.,
Printed and sold by Judah P. Spooner, 1776.
vi, [7]-55 p.   19 cm.

11797 Civis, pseud.
Remarks on the bankrupt law; to which are added,
the proposed amendments of Hopkinson and Webster.
By Civis. New York, Published by Haly and Thomas,
142 Broadway, C. S. Van Winkle, printer, 1819.
71 p.   21 cm.

11798 Claggett, William, 1790-1870.
An address, delivered before the Portsmouth anti-
slavery society, on the fourth of July, A. D. 1839,
being the 63d anniversary of the independence of
the United States of America, by Hon. William Claggett
... Portsmouth, N. H., Printed by C. W. Brewster,
1839.
20 p.   24 cm.

11799 The claim for interest on the advances of Massachusetts
in the war of 1812-15. [n. p., 187-?]
3 p.   22 1/2 cm.

11800 [Clap, Thomas] 1703-1767.
The answer of the friend in the West, to a letter
from a gentleman in the East, entitled, The present
state of the colony of Connecticut considered...

New-Haven, Printed by J. Parker, 1755.
18 p.   20 1/2 cm.

11801   Clap, Thomas, 1703-1767.
A brief history and vindication of the doctrines
received and established in the churches of New
England, with a specimen of the new scheme of religion beginning to prevail. By Thomas Clap, A. M.
president of Yale-college, in New Haven... New
Haven, Printed and sold by James Parker, at the
Post-office, 1755.
44 p.   20 cm.
First edition. Reprinted in 1757. Occasioned
"Some remarks on Mr. president Clap's History and
vindication of the doctrines, &c. of the New England
churches... New Haven, J. Parker, 1757" an anonymous work of Thomas Darling.

11802   Clap, Thomas, 1703-1767.
The religious constitution of colleges, especially
of Yale-college in New Haven, in the colony of
Connecticut. By Thomas Clap... New London,
Printed by T. Green, 1754.
1 p.l., 20 p.   18 1/2 cm.

11803   Clapp, Asahel.
A synopsis; or, systematic catalogue of the medicinal plants of the United States. By A. Clap...
Philadelphia, T. K. and P. G. Collins, printers,
1852.
222 p., 1 l.   23 1/2 cm.
Presented to the American medical association,
at its session of May, 1852.
Published in the Transactions of the association,
v. 5, 1852.
"List of principal botanical works cited": p. 10-15.

11804   Clapp, Charles B   comp.
Bank guide. A list of banks in the New England
states and New Jersey, which have surrendered their
charters, giving the date of surrender, expiration
of time of liability to redeem, &c., &c. Comp. and
pub. by Charles B. Clapp... Augusta [Me.] Printed
at the office of the Kennebec journal, 1865.
34 p., 1 l.   16 1/2 cm.

11805 Clark, Aaron.
An oration. A project for the civilization of the
Indians of North America. Delivered before the
P. B. Ph. society, Schenectady, July 22, 1816, in
pursuance of their appointment. By Aaron Clark...
Albany, Printed by Packard & Van Benthuysen, 1819.
24 p.   24 cm.

11806 Clark, Benjamin Franklin, 1808-1879.
The province of law in distinction from that of
truth. A sermon delivered before the executive
and legislative departments of the government of
Massachusetts, at the annual election, Wednesday,
Jan. 6, 1869. By B. F. Clark.   Boston, Wright &
Potter, state printers, 1869.
55 p.   21 1/2 cm.
No. 3 in a volume lettered: Massachusetts election
sermons, 1867-84.
Printed by order of the Massachusetts Senate.

11807 Clark, Charles, d. 1881.
A few more words upon Canada.   By Charles Clark...
London, Longman, Orme, Brown, Green, and Longmans,
1838.
30 p.   21 1/2 om.

11808 Clark, Charles, d. 1881.
"Principles that ought naturally to govern the
conduct of neutrals and belligerents"; a paper read
before the Juridical society, 1 February 1864.   By
Charles Clark...   London, Butterworths, 1864.
42 p.   20 cm.

11809 Clark, Charles, d. 1881.
A summary of colonial law, the practice of the
Court of appeals from the plantations, and of the
laws and their administration in all the colonies;
with charters of justice, orders in Council, &c. ...
By Charles Clark...   London, S. Sweet [etc., etc.]
1834.
2 p.l., viii, 746 p.   22 cm.

11810 Clark, Daniel Atkinson, 1779-1840.
Independence-sermon, delivered July 4, 1814, at
Hanover, N. Jersey.   By Daniel A. Clark.   Newark,
Printed by John Tuttle & co., 1814.
24 p.   22 cm.

11811   Clark, Hamlet, 1823-1867.
            Letters home from Spain, Algeria, and Brazil,
        during past entomological rambles. By the Rev.
        Hamlet Clark... London, J. Van Voorst, 1867.
            iv, 178 p.   front., col. pl.   16 1/2 cm.

11812   Clark, Henry, 1829-1899.
            An historical address, delivered at Hubbardton,
        Vt., on the eighty-second anniversary of the battle
        of Hubbardton, July 7, 1859. By Henry Clark. With
        an appendix containing an account of the celebration
        ... Rutland, Press of G. A. Tuttle & co., 1859.
            cover-title, 16 p.   23 cm.

11813   Clark, Hiram C
            History of Chenango county, containing the divisions
        of the county and sketches of the towns; Indian
        tribes and titles... By Hiram C. Clark. Norwich,
        N. Y., Thompson & Pratt, 1850.
            119, [1] p.   front., illus., plates, ports.
        23 cm.

11814   Clark, Horace Francis, 1815-1873.
            Speech of Hon. H. F. Clark, of New York, upon the
        subject of the admission of Kansas as a state under
        the Lecompton constitution. Delivered in the House
        of representatives, March 24, 1858. [Washington,
        1858]
            16 p.   24 cm.

11815   Clark, Sir James, bart., 1788-1870.
            ... The sanative influence of climate; with an
        account of the best places of resort for invalids
        in England, the south of Europe, &c. By Sir James
        Clark... From the 3d London ed. Philadelphia,
        A. Waldie, 1841.
            ix, [11]-196 p. incl. tables.   21 1/2 cm.
        (Dunglison's American medical library)
            Previously issued under title: The influence of
        climate in the prevention and cure of chronic
        diseases.

11816   Clark, Joel W
            Miniature of Dansville village: humbly inscribed
        to the first settlers, and their immediate descend-
        ants. By J. W. Clark. Dansville, N. Y., J. W.

Clark, 1844.
5 p., 1 1., [7]-72 p.   21 cm.

11817   Clark, Jonas, 1730-1805.
The fate of blood-thirsty oppressors, and God's
tender care of his distressed people. A sermon,
preached at Lexington, April 19, 1776. To commemorate the murder, bloodshed, and commencement of hostilities, between Great Britain and America, in that
town, by a brigade of troops of George III, under the
command of Lieutenant-Colonel Smith, on the nineteenth
of April, 1775. To which is added a brief narrative
of the principal transactions of that day. By Jonas
Clark... Boston, Printed by Powars & Willis, 1776.
31, 8 p.   23 cm.

11818   Clark, Jonathan.
Life of General Washington, late president of the
United States; together with his Farewell address,
and a short account of the American revolutionary
war. By Jona. Clark... Albany, Printed by Packard
& Van Benthuysen, 1813.
vi, [7]-143, [1] p. incl. front. (port.)
14 1/2 cm.

11819   Clark, Joseph, 1751-1813.
A sermon on the death of the Hon. William Paterson
... one of the associate justices of the Supreme
Court of the United States... Preached in the Presbyterian church, in New Brunswick (New Jersey) on
the twenty-first day of September. By the Reverend
Joseph Clark... New Brunswick, Printed by A. Blau-
velt, 1806.
24 p.   21 1/2 cm.

11820   Clark, Joseph G
Lights and shadows of sailor life, as exemplified
in fifteen years' experience, including the more
thrilling events of the U. S. exploring expedition,
and reminiscences of an eventful life on the "Mountain
wave". By Joseph G. Clark. Boston, B. B. Mussey &
co., 1848.
xii, [13]-324 p.   front., plates.   19 1/2 cm.

11821   Clark, Joseph Sylvester, 1800-1861.
A historical sketch of the Congregational churches
in Massachusetts, from 1620 to 1858. With an appendix.

By Joseph S. Clark... Boston, Congregational board
of publication, 1858.
   xii, 344 p.   20 1/2 cm.

11822   Clark, Joshua Victor Hopkins, 1803-1869.
   Lights and lines of Indian character, and scenes
of pioneer life. By J. V. H. Clark... Syracuse,
E. H. Babcock and co.; New York, J. C. Derby [etc.,
etc.] 1854.
   vi, [7]-375 p.   front. (port.)   19 1/2 cm.
   "Some few of these pieces have previously appeared
in the New York 'Commercial advertiser,' and other
papers. Some of them may be found in the 'History
of Onondaga.'" - Pref.

11823   Clark, Lincoln, 1800-1886.
   Eulogy upon the life, character and death of Gen.
Andrew Jackson, delivered on the 19th of July, 1845,
by Lincoln Clark: before the societies and citizens
of Tuscaloosa; and pub. at their request. Tuscaloosa, Printed by M. D. J. Slade, 1845.
   40 p.   21 cm.

11824   Clark, Mary, 1792?-1841.
   Biographical sketches of the fathers of New England,
intended to acquaint youth with the lives, characters
and sufferings of those who founded our civil and
religious institutions. By Mary Clark. Concord
[N. H.] Marsh, Capen and Lyon, 1836.
   v, [7]-180 p.   14 1/2 cm.
   Contents. - John Robinson. - John Carver. - Edward
Winslow. - William Brewster. - William Bradford. -
Robert Cushman. - Myles Standish. - John Winthrop. -
Roger Williams. - Appendix.

11825   Clark, Peter, 1694-1768.
   Religion to be minded, under the greatest perils
of life. A sermon on Psal. CXIX. 109. containing a
word in season to soldiers. Preach'd on April 6,
1755. Being the Lord's-day, before muster of a
number of soldiers in the North-parish in Danvers,
who had enlisted in the publick service of the
king and country, in the intended expedition... By
Peter Clark... Boston, Printed and sold by S. Kneeland in Queen-street, 1755.
   2 p.l., 29 p.   19 1/2 cm.

11826 Clark, Peter H
        The black brigade of Cincinnati; being a report of
        its labors and a muster-roll of its members; together
        with various orders, speeches, etc., relating to it.
        By Peter H. Clark. Cincinnati, Printed by J. B.
        Boyd, 1864.
        30 p.   22 1/2 cm.

11827 Clark, Rufus Wheelwright, 1813-1886.
        A discourse on the life and character of Howard
        Townsend, M. D., late professor of materia medica
        and physiology in the Albany medical college;
        preached in the North Dutch church, Albany, Sunday
        morning, Jan. 20th, 1867. By Rufus W. Clark, D. D.
        Albany, S. R. Gray, 1867.
        18 p.   23 1/2 cm.

11828 Clark, Rufus Wheelwright, 1813-1886.
        Fifty arguments in favor of sustaining and enfor-
        cing the Massachusetts anti-liquor law. By Rev.
        Rufus W. Clark.   Boston, J. P. Jewett & co., Cleve-
        land, O., Jewett, Proctor, & Worthington, 1853.
        47 p.   19 1/2 cm.

11829 Clark, Rufus Wheelwright, 1813-1886.
        The heroes of Albany. A memorial of the patriot-
        martyrs of the city and county of Albany, who sacri-
        ficed their lives during the late war in defense of
        our nation 1861-1865, with a view of what was done
        in the county to sustain the United States government;
        and also brief histories of the Albany regiments.
        By Rufus W. Clark, D. D. Albany, S. R. Gray, 1866.
        viii p., 1 l., [11]-870 p.   col. front., illus.,
        plates, ports.   24 cm.

11830 Clark, Rufus Wheelwright, 1813-1886.
        The unity of the American nationality. A discourse
        delivered in the North Ref. Prot. Dutch church of
        Albany, November 26th, 1863, the day of the national
        Thanksgiving. By Rufus W. Clark... Albany, Steam
        press of C. Van Benthuysen, 1863.
        42 p.   23 cm.

11831 Clark, Thomas, 1787-1860.
        Sketches of the naval history of the United States;
        from the commencement of the revolutionary war, to
        the present time... likewise an appendix, wherein

the chief part of the important documents concerning
the Navy are collected. By Thomas Clark... Philadelphia, M. Carey, 1813.
   1 p.l., xiv, [13]-177 p., 1 l., cxxxix p.   front.
19 1/2 cm.
   Afterward issued under the title: Naval history
of the United States.

11832   Clark, Thomas March, bp., 1812-1903.
         Oration delivered before the municipal authorities
      and citizens of Providence, on the eighty-fourth
      anniversary of American independence, July 4, 1860.
      By Thomas M. Clark, D. D.   Providence, Knowles,
      Anthony & co., city printers, 1860.
         32 p.   21 cm.
      Printed by order of the City council.

11833   [Clark, William Adolphus] 1825-1906.
         Our modern Athens; or, Who is first? A poem.
      By Anicetus [pseud.]   Boston, Redding & co., 1860.
      x p., 1 l., [13]-70 p.   19 1/2 cm.
         Revised version appeared in 1872 under title:
      Hard knocks; or, Who is first?

11834   Clarke, A   B   of Westfield, Mass.
         Travels in Mexico and California: comprising a
      journal of a tour from Brazos Santiago, through
      central Mexico, by way of Monterey, Chihuahua, the
      country of the Apaches, and the river Gila, to the
      mining districts of California. By A. B. Clarke.
      Boston, Wright & Hasty, printers, 1852.
         138 p.   19 1/2 x 11 1/2 cm.

11835   Clarke, Abraham Lynsen, 1768?-1810.
         A discourse, occasioned by the death of General
      George Washington, at Mount-Vernon, Dec. 14, 1799.
      Delivered before the right worshipful master and
      brethren of Mount-Vernon lodge, and the congregation
      of St. John's church, in Providence, on Saturday
      the 22d of February, A. L. 5800. By Abraham L.
      Clarke... Providence, Printed by John Carter, 1800.
         26 p.   24 cm.

11836   Clarke, Edward, 1810-1891.
         A sermon delivered at Middlefield, Mass., March 26,
      1845, at the funeral of Deacon David Mack, by Rev.
      Edward Clarke... With an appendix... Amherst,

J. S. & C. Adams, printers, 1845.
   16 p.   23 cm.
   Appendix A: Ancestry of D. Mack.

11837 Clarke, Sir Edward George, 1841-
       A treatise upon the law of extradition. With the
       conventions upon the subject existing between England
       & foreign nations, and the cases decided thereon.
       By Edward Clarke... London, Stevens and Haynes,
       1867.
       x p., 1 l., 183 p.   19 1/2 cm.

11838 Clarke, Frank Wigglesworth, 1847-
       Views around Ithaca: being a description of the
       waterfalls and ravines of this remarkable locality,
       by F. W. Clarke... Ithaca, N. Y., Andrus, McChain
       & co. [c1869]
       155 p.   photos.   18 1/2 cm.

11839 Clarke, John, lieutenant of marines.
       An impartial and authentic narrative of the battle
       fought on the 17th of June, 1775, between His Britan-
       nic Majesty's troops and the American provincial army,
       on Bunker's Hill, near Charles Town, in New England.
       With a true and faithful account of the officers who
       were killed and wounded in that memorable battle.
       To which are added, some particular remarks and
       anecdotes which have not yet transpired. The whole
       being collected and written on the spot. By John
       Clarke, first lieutenant of marines. London, Printed
       for the author; and sold by J. Millan, Whitehall;
       J. Bew, in Pater-noster Row; and - Sewell, in Corn-
       hill, 1775.
       1 p.l., 32 p.   20 1/2 cm.
       "A list of officers killed and wounded on Saturday
       the 17th of June, 1775" and "Regiments in the field
       of battle...": p. 9-14. "Officers dead of their
       wounds": p. 32.

11840 Clarke, John, of Philadelphia.
       A treatise on the mulberry tree and silkworm. And
       on the production and manufacture of silk... By
       John Clarke... Philadelphia, Thomas, Cowperthwait
       & co., 1839.
       363 p.   illus.   19 1/2 cm.

11841   Clarke, John, 1755-1798.
A sermon delivered at the church of Brattle-
street, January 2, 1784, at the interment of the
Rev. Samuel Cooper, D. D. who expired, December 29,
1783. By John Clarke... Boston, Printed by John
Gill, 1784.
35 p.   20 cm.
"The... character of Doctor Cooper, drawn by
another hand... taken from the Continental journal,
of January 22, 1874": p. [30]-35.

11842   Clarke, John Hopkins, 1789-1870.
Speech of Mr. Clarke, of Rhode Island, on the
California claims. Delivered in the Senate of the
United States, April 25, 1848. Washington, Printed
by J. T. Towers, 1848.
15 p.   22 1/2 cm.

11843   Clarke, Matthew St. Clair.
Legislative and documentary history of the Bank
of the United States: including the original Bank
of North America. Comp. by M. St. Clair Clarke &
D. A. Hall. Washington, Printed by Gales and Seaton,
1832.
vi, [9]-832, [799]-808 p.   23 cm.

11844   Clarke, Matthew St. Clair.
Report made to the Hon. John Forsyth, secretary
of state of the United States, on the subject of the
Documentary history of the United States, now publishing under an act of Congress, by M. St. Clair Clarke,
and Peter Force. Washington, 1834.
cover-title, 39 p.   25 1/2 cm.

11845   Clarke, Pitt, 1763-1835.
Memorial of Rev. Pitt Clarke, pastor of the First
Congregational church in Norton, Mass.; and of Mary
Jones Clarke (his wife)   Printed for private dis-
tribution. Cambridge, Press of J. Wilson and son,
1866.
94 p., 1 l.   23 1/2 x 18 cm.
Preface signed: Edward H. Clarke.
"Confession of faith [by Rev. Clarke]": p. [27]-38.
"Poems by Mrs. Mary Jones Clarke, with an intro-
ductory sketch": p. [39]-94.

11846   Clarke, Samuel, 1599-1682.
A mirrour or looking-glasse both for saints, and
sinners, held forth in some thousands of examples;
wherein is presented, as Gods wounderful mercies to
the one, so his severe judgments against the other.
Collected out of the most classique authors, both
ancient, and modern, with some late examples observed
by my self, and others. Whereunto are added a Geographical description of all the countries in the
known world: as also the wonders of God in nature;
and the rare, stupendious, and costly works made by
the art, and industry of man. As the most famous
cities, temples, structures, statues, cabinets of
rarities, &c. which have been, or are now in the
world. By Sa. Clark... The 3d ed. very much enlarged... London, Printed by T. R. and E. M. for
Tho. Newberry, 1657.
9 p.l., 702, [10] p., 2 l., 225, [8] p.   29 cm.

11847   Clarke, Samuel Clarke, b. 1806.
Records of some of the descendants of William
Curtis, Roxbury, 1632. Comp. from the ms. of Miss
Catherine P. Curtis, and other sources. By Samuel
C. Clarke. Boston, Printed by D. Clapp & son, 1869.
29 p.   24 1/2 cm.

11848   Clarke, Samuel Fulton, 1818-1861.
A centennial discourse delivered September 9, 1850,
before the First church and society in Athol, at the
celebration of the one hundredth anniversary of the
organization of said church. With an appendix. By
Samuel F. Clarke, minister of the First church in
Athol... Boston, W. Crosby & H. P. Nichols, 1851.
95 p.   23 cm.
[Waterman pamphlets, v. 123, no. 7]

11849   Clarke, Thomas Curtis, 1827-1901.
An account of the iron railway bridge across the
Mississippi River at Quincy, Illinois. By Thomas
Curtis Clarke, C. E., engineer-in-chief. Illustrated
by twenty-one lithographic plates. New York, D. Van
Nostrand, 1869.
70 p., 1 l.   21 fold. pl. (incl. front.)
28 1/2 x 21 1/2 cm.

11850   Clarke, Walter, 1812-1871.
Half century discourse. The first church in

Buffalo. Delivered on the evening of Feb. 3d, 1862.
By Walter Clarke, D. D. Buffalo, T. Butler, 1862.
   vii p., 1 l., [11]-92 p.   23 cm.
"Poem: read at the semi-centennial celebration.
Monday evening, Feb. 3, 1862." By Rev. A. T. Chester:
p. [83]-92.

11851   Clarkson, Thomas, 1760-1846.
   An essay on the comparative efficiency of regulation or abolition, as applied to the slave trade;
shewing that the latter only can remove the evils
to be found in that commerce. London, Printed by J.
Phillips, 1789.
   xi, 82 p.   20 cm.

11852   Clarkson, Thomas, 1760-1846.
   An essay on the slavery and commerce of the human
species, particularly the African, translated from
a Latin dissertation, which was honoured with the
first prize in the University of Cambridge, for the
year 1785, with additions... London, printed;
Philadelphia, re-printed by Crukshank, 1786.
   xix, [21]-155 p.   20 cm.

11853   Clarkson, Thomas, 1760-1846.
   A letter to the clergy of various denominations,
and to the slave-holding planters, in the southern
parts of the United States of America. By Thomas
Clarkson. London, Printed by Johnston and Barrett,
1841.
   64 p.   21 cm.

11854   Clarkson, Thomas, 1760-1846.
   Memoirs of the private and public life of William
Penn. By Thomas Clarkson... Philadelphia, Bradford
and Inskeep [etc.] 1814.
   2 v.   fronts. (port.)   18 cm.

11855   [Clarkson, Thomas] 1760-1846.
   The true state of the case, respecting the insurrection at St. Domingo. Ipswich, J. Bush, 1792.
   8 p.   20 1/2 cm.

11856   Clarkson, Thomas Streatfeild.
   A biographical history of Clermont, or Livingston
manor, before and during the war for independence,
with a sketch of the first steam navigation of

Fulton and Livingston. By Thomas Streatfeild Clarkson... Clermont, N. Y., 1869.
vii p., 1 l., [2], [11]-319 p.   5 phot. (incl.
front.)   23 1/2 cm.

11857   Clary, Dexter.
History of the churches and ministers connected
with the Presbyterian and Congregational convention
of Wisconsin, and of the operations of the American
home missionary society in the state for the past
ten years; with an appendix. By Rev. Dexter Clary.
Beloit, Printed by B. E. Hale, 1861.
128 p.   19 cm.

11858   Clary, Timothy Farrar, 1817-1912.
Honorable old age. A discourse occasioned by the
centennial anniversary of Hon. Timothy Farrar, LL. D.,
delivered at Hollis, N. H., July 11, 1847. By
Timothy Farrar Clary... Andover, Printed by W. H.
Wardwell, 1847.
28 p.   21 1/2 cm.

11859   [Clason, Isaac Starr] 1789?-1834.
Horace in New York. Part 1 ... New York, J. M.
Campbell, 1826.
2 p.l., [7]-8 p., 1 l., [9]-47 p.   19 1/2 cm.
No more published.

11860   The Clifford family; or, A tale of the Old Dominion,
by one of her daughters... New York, Harper &
brothers, 1852.
1 p.l., [5]-430 p.   19 1/2 cm.

11861   Cline, A   J
Secession unmasked, or An appeal from the madness
of disunion to the sobriety of the Constitution and
common sense. By A. J. Cline... Washington, Printed
by H. Polkinhorn, 1861.
cover-title, [3]-16 p.   22 1/2 cm.

11862   Clinton, De Witt, engineer.
Correspondence on the importance & practicability
of a rail road, from New York to New Orleans, in
which is embraced a report on the subject, by De
Witt Clinton... New York, Vanderpool and Cole,
printers, 1830.
2 p.l., 23 p.   21 1/2 cm.

The "correspondence" consists of a letter from
A. Dey and six others (2d prelim. leaf) and the
report of Mr. Clinton in answer (p. [1]-23)

11863 Cobbett, William, 1763-1835.
       A treatise on Cobbett's corn, containing instruct-
ions for propagating and cultivating the plant, and
for harvesting and preserving the crop; and also an
account of the several uses to which the produce is
applied, with minute directions relative to each
mode of application. By William Cobbett... London,
W. Cobbett, 1828.
       iv, [290] p.   III pl.   19 1/2 cm.

11864 Coffin, Charles Carleton, 1823-1896.
       Following the flag. From August, 1861, to November,
1862, with the Army of the Potomac. By "Carleton".
Boston, Ticknor and Fields, 1865.
       vi, [2], 336 p. incl. plans.   pl.   17 1/2 cm.

11865 Coit, Thomas Winthrop, 1803-1885.
       Puritanism: or, A churchman's defense against its
aspersions, by an appeal to its own history... By
Thomas W. Coit... New York, D. Appleton & co.;
Philadelphia, G. S. Appleton, 1845.
       xii, [13]-527, [1] p.   19 1/2 cm.

11866 Coke, Thomas, 1747-1814.
       ... A journal of the Rev. Dr. Coke's third tour
through the West Indies: in two letters, to the
Rev. J. Wesley. London, Printed by G. Paramore,
North-green, Worship street; and sold by G. Whitfield, at the Chapel, City road; and at the Methodist
preaching-houses in town and country, 1791.
       12 p.   17 cm.

11867 Colvocoresses, George Musalas, 1816-1872.
       Four years in a government exploring expedition;
to the island of Madeira, Cape Verd islands, Brazil
... &c., &c. ... By Lieut. Geo. M. Colvocoresses...
New York, Cornish, Lamport & co., 1852.
       371 p. incl. plates.   front., plates.
18 1/2 cm.
       "Compiled from a journal... which the author kept
in obedience to a 'General order' from the Navy
department." - Pref.

11868 Comitatus, Zedekiah, pseud.
            Reconstruction on "my policy"; or, Its author at
        the confessional. By Zedekiah Comitatus, M. P. E. C.
        [pseud.] Skaggaddahunk [New York?] Scantlewood,
        Timberlake & co., printers to the "North River
        society," 1866.
            29 p.   23 cm.

11869 The companion: being a selection of the beauties of
        the most celebrated authors, in the English language.
        In prose and verse... Providence, Printed by
        Nathaniel and Benjamin Heaton, for Joseph J. Todd,
        at the sign of the Bible and anchor, 1799.
            viii, [9]-280 p.   14 1/2 cm.

11870 [Cone, Edward Winfield] 1814-1871.
            Some account of the life of Spencer Houghton Cone,
        a Baptist preacher in America. New York, Livermore
        & Rudd, 1856.
            iv, [2], [7]-484 p.   front. (port.) illus.
        18 1/2 cm.
            By Edward W. Cone and Spencer Wallace Cone.

11871 Confederate States of America. Congress. Senate.
        Committee on finance.
            ... Report of the Committee on finance on the bill
        (H. R. 18) to lay taxes for the common defence and
        carry on the government of the Confederate States.
        [Richmond, 1863]
            14 p.   24 cm.
            [Senate report, no. 9] April 6, 1863.

11872 Confederate States of America. Constitution.
            Provisional and permanent constitutions, together
        with the Acts and resolutions of the first session
        of the Provisional congress, of the Confederate
        States, 1861. Montgomery, Ala., Shorter & Reid,
        printers and binders, 1861.
            160 p.   22 1/2 cm.

11873 Confederate States of America. Post-Office Department.
            Report of the Postmaster General, Post-Office
        Department, Richmond, May 2, 1864. [Richmond?
        1864]
            16 p.   23 cm.

11874 Confederate States of America. President.
      President's message... [Richmond? 1864]
      5 p.   23 1/2 cm.
      Signed: Jefferson Davis; dated: May 2, 1864.

11875 Confederate States of America. War dept.
      General orders from Adjutant and Inspector-
      General's office, Confederate States army, from
      January, 1862, to December, 1863, (both inclusive)
      In two series. Prpared from files of head-quarters,
      Department of S. C., Ga., and Fla. With full indexes.
      Columbia, Presses of Evans and Cogswell, 1864.
        2 v. in 1.   18 cm.
      Includes also (v. 2, p. 243-276) certain of the
      General orders issued from January to March, 1864.

11876 A Continuation of the state of New-England; being a
      farther account of the Indian warr, and of the
      engagement betwixt the joynt forces of the United
      English colonies and the Indians, on the 19th. of
      December 1675. With the true number of the slain
      and wounded, and the transactions of the English army
      since the said fight. With all other passages that
      have there hapned from the 10th. of November, 1675
      to the 8th. of February, 1678. Together with an
      account of the intended rebellion of the negroes
      in the Barbadoes... London, Printed by T. M. for
      D. Newman, 1676.
        20 p.   30 cm.
      A continuation, apparently by the same writer, of
      The present state of New England, with respect to
      the Indian war, London, 1675. Includes two letters
      from Boston, the first dated February 9, 1675, the
      second dated February 8, 1678, and signed, N. S.
      The letter from Barbados is dated November 30, 1675,
      and signed, G. W.

11877 Convention of banks of the city of Charleston, 1841.
      Minutes of the Convention of banks, of the city of
      Charleston, held on the 3d and 6th of Feb. 1841,
      to consider the act of the legislature, passed at
      the last session; with the opinions of the solicitors
      of each bank. Charleston, S. C., Printed by A. E.
      Miller, 1841.
        27 p.   22 1/2 cm.

11878 Cooper, Thomas, 1759-1839.
  Consolidation. An account of parties in the
United States, from the Convention of 1787, to the
present period. 2d ed. By Thomas Cooper...
Columbia, S. C., Printed at the "Times and gazette"
office, 1830.
  37 p. 22 cm. [With South Carolina. General
assembly. The debate in the... legislature, in
December, 1830, on the reports... in favor of convention...]

11879 Cooper, Thomas, 1759-1839, supposed author.
  Strictures addressed to James Madison on the
celebrated report of William H. Crawford, recom-
mending the intermarriage of Americans with the
Indian tribes. Ascribed to Judge Cooper, and
originally published by John Binns, in the Democratic press. Philadelphia, Printed by J. Harding,
1824.
  iv, [5]-22 p. 24 cm.
Letters signed Americanus, and dated Washington
city, April 10-30, 1816. The last letter, addressed
to the secretary at war, is signed Tabitha Spinster,
and fictitiously dated Maidenhead, New Jersey,
May 1, 1816.
"... Attributed to Cooper... in my opinion
without justification." - D. Malone. The public
life of Thomas Cooper, London, 1926, p. 406.

11880 Cooper union for the advancement of science and art,
New York.
  Charter, trust deed, and by-laws of the Cooper
union for the advancement of science and art:
with the letter of Peter Cooper, accompanying the
trust deed. New York, W. C. Bryant & co.,
printers [1859]
  61 p. 24 cm.

11881 Cradlebaugh, John.
  Utah and the Mormons. Speech of Hon. John Cradlebaugh, of Nevada, on the admission of Utah as a state.
Delivered in the House of representatives, February
7, 1863. [Washington? 1863]
  67 p. 23 cm.

11882 Cugnet, Francois Joseph, 1720-1789, comp.
  Extraits des edits, declarations, ordonnances et

reglemens, de Sa Majesté très chretienne. Des
reglemens et jugemens des gouverneurs generaux et
intendans concernans la justice; et des reglemens
et ordonnances de police rendues par les intendans,
faisans partie de la legislature en force en la
colonie du Canada, aujourd'hui province de Québec.
Tirés des regîtres du Conseil superieur et de ceux
d'Intendance. Par Francois Joseph Cugnet...
Quebec, G. Brown, 1775.
1 p.l., 106 p.   18 1/2 x 15 1/2 cm.

11883   Cugnet, Francois Joseph, 1720-1789.
Traité de la loi des fiefs. Qui a toujours été
suivie en Canada depuis son établissement, tirée
de celle contenuë en la Coûtume de la prevôté et
vicomté de Paris, à laquelle les fiefs et seigneuries
de cette province sont assujettis, en vertu de leurs
titres primitifs de concession, et des edits, reglemens, ordonances et declarations de Sa Majesté très
chrétienne, rendus en consequence; et des diferens
jugemens d'intendans rendus à cet égard, en vertu
de la loi des fiefs, et des dits edits, reglemens,
ordonances et declarations... par Francois Joseph
Cugnet... Québec, G. Brown, 1775.
2 p.l., ix-xiv, 71 p.   20 1/2 cm.

11884   Cugnet, François Joseph, 1720-1789.
Traité de la police. Qui a toujours été suivie
en Canada, aujourd'hui province de Québec, depuis
son etablissement jusqu'à la conquête, tiré des
diférens réglemens, jugemens et ordonnances d'intendans, à qui par leurs commissions, cette partie
du gouvernement était totalement atribuée, à l'ex-
clusion de tous autres juges, qui n'en pouvaient
connaitre qu'en qualité de leurs subdélégués.
Traité qui pourrait être de quelqu' utilité aux
grand voyers, et aux juges de police en cette province. Par François Joseph Cugnet... Quebec, Chez
G. Brown, 1775.
2 p.l., iii, 5-25, [1] p.   19 cm.

11885   Cugoano, Ottobah.
Thoughts and sentiments on the evil and wicked
traffic of the slavery and commerce of the human
species, humbly submitted to the inhabitants of
Great Britain, by Ottobah Cugoano, a native of

Africa... London, Printed in the year 1787.
2 p.l., iv, 148 p.   22 1/2 cm.

11886 Cullen, Cassius C
The American melodies, in three parts, and
Miscellaneous poems, by Cassius C. Cullen. Trenton,
N. J., Murphy & Bechtel, printers, 1864.
96 p.   17 1/2 cm.

11887 Cullen, Edward.
Isthmus of Darien ship canal; with a full history
of the Scotch colony of Darien, several maps, views
of the country, and original documents. By Dr.
Cullen... 2d ed., much enlarged. London, E. Wilson,
1853.
xii, 204 p.   front., maps (part fold.)   23 cm.

11888 Cullom, William, 1810-1896.
Speech of Hon. Wm. Cullom, of Tennessee, on the
Nebraska and Kansas bill, in the House of represent-
atives, April 11, 1854. Washington, Printed at the
Congressional globe office, 1854.
13 p.   22 1/2 cm.

11889 Cullum, George Washington, 1809-1892.
Register of the officers and graduates of the
U. S. military academy, at West Point, N. Y., from
March 16, 1802, to January 1, 1850. Comp. by
Captain George W. Cullum... From the official
records of the War department, and other reliable
sources. New York, J. F. Trow, printer, 1850.
3 p.l., [33]-303 p.   19 cm.

11890 Cumback, William, 1829-
Politics of the country. Speech of Hon. Will.
Cumback, of Indiana. In the House of representatives,
December 17, 1856. Washington, Buell & Blanchard,
printers, 1857.
7 p.   23 cm.

11891 Cumings, Henry, 1739-1823.
An eulogy on the late patriot Washington, addressed
to the people of Billcrica, Jan. 10, 1800; when they
honoured him with funeral solemnities. By Henry
Cumings. Amherst, Printed by Samuel Preston, Feb.,
1800.
16 p.   22 1/2 cm.

11892   Cumings, Henry, 1739-1823.
        An half-century discourse, addressed to the people
of Billerica, Feb. 21, 1813. By their reverend
pastor, Henry Cumings, S. T. D. Published at the
unanimous request of the town. Cambridge, Mass.,
Printed by Hilliard and Metcalf, 1813.
        31 p.   21 1/2 cm.

11893   Cumings, Henry, 1739-1823.
        A sermon preached before His Honor Thomas Cushing...
the honorable the Council, and the two branches of
the General court of the commonwealth of Massachusetts, May 28, 1783. Being the anniversary of general
election. By Henry Cumings...   Boston, Printed by
T. & J. Fleet, 1783.
        55 p.   23 1/2 cm.

11894   Cumings, Henry, 1739-1823.
        A sermon preached in Billerica, on the 23d of
November, 1775. Being the day appointed by civil
authority, for a public thanksgiving throughout the
province of Massachusetts-bay. By Henry Cumings,
A. M., pastor of the church there. Massachusetts-
bay: Worcester, Printed by I. Thomas near the Court-
house [1775?]
        29 p.   24 cm.

11895   Cumings, Samuel.
        The western pilot, containing charts of the Ohio
river, and of the Mississippi from the mouth of the
Missouri to the gulf of Mexico, accompanied with
directions for navigating the same, and a gazetteer,
or description of the town on their banks, tributary
streams, &c. Also, a variety of matter interesting
to travellers and all concerned in the navigation of
those rivers. By Samuel Cumings. Cincinnati, N. & G.
Guilford, 1829.
        3 p.l., [5]-104 p.   4 pl., port., 44 maps.
22 cm.
        A revised and altered edition of the author's
"Western navigator", 1822.
        "Cumings's editions of the 'Navigator' and 'Pilot'
... were amplifications of [The navigator] of [Zadoc]
Cramer, without acknowledgment of the main source of
their material." - Sabin, Bibl. amer., v. 5, p. 126.

11896　Cumming, Alexander, 1726-1763.
　　　　　Animadversions on the Reverend Mr. Croswell's
　　　　late letter &c. Designed to remove prejudices it
　　　　tends to excite against the truth: and to shew that
　　　　the principal doctrines contained and contended for
　　　　therein, are not only not according to truth, but
　　　　opposite thereto. By A. Cumming... Boston,
　　　　Printed and sold by S. Kneeland, in Queen-street,
　　　　1763.
　　　　　2 p.l., 40 p.　　19 1/2 cm.

11897　[Cumming, Hiram]
　　　　　Secret history of the perfidies, intrigues, and
　　　　corruptions of the Tyler dynasty, with the mysteries
　　　　of Washington city, connected with that vile adminis-
　　　　tration, in a series of letters to the ex-acting
　　　　President, by one most familiar with the subject...
　　　　Washington and New York, The author, 1845.
　　　　　64 p.　　23 cm.

11898　Cumming, Hooper, 1788-1825.
　　　　　An oration, commemorative of Washington. Delivered
　　　　Feb. 22, 1821. By Hooper Cumming, A. M., pastor of
　　　　the Third Presbyterian church in the city of Albany.
　　　　Albany, D. Steele, 1821.
　　　　　26 p.　　21 1/2 cm.

11899　Cummings, Ebenezer Edson, 1800-1886.
　　　　　Annals of the Baptist churches in New Hampshire.
　　　　A sermon, preached before the New Hampshire Baptist
　　　　state convention, at its tenth annual meeting, held
　　　　at Deerfield, October 20, 1835. By Ebenezer E.
　　　　Cummings... Concord, N. H., Marsh, Capen & Lyon,
　　　　1836.
　　　　　52 p.　　22 cm.

11900　Cummings, Preston, 1800-1875.
　　　　　A dictionary of Congregational usages and prin-
　　　　ciples, according to ancient and modern authors;
　　　　to which are added brief notices of some of the
　　　　principal writers, assemblies, and treatises referred
　　　　to in the compilation. By Preston Cummings...
　　　　Boston, S. K. Whipple and co., 1852.
　　　　　xii, [13]-419 p.　　19 cm.

11901　Cummings, Thomas Seir, 1804-1894.
　　　　　Historic annals of the National academy of design,

New York drawing association, etc., with occasional
dottings by the way-side, from 1825 to the present
time. By Thos. S. Cummings... Philadelphia, G. W.
Childs, 1865.
iv, [5]-364 p.   23 1/2 cm.

11902 Cummins, George David, bp., 1822-1876.
Life of Mrs. Virginia Hale Hoffman, late of the
Protestant Episcopal mission to western Africa.
By the Rev. George D. Cummins... Philadelphia,
Lindsay & Blakiston, 1859.
xv, 17-256 p.   front. (port.)   18 1/2 cm.

11903 Cummins, George David, bp., 1822-1876.
The pestilence - God's messenger and teacher.
Discourse in behalf of the sufferers of Norfolk
and Portsmouth, Va., delivered in Trinity church,
Washington, September 9, 1855, by Rev. George D.
Cummins... Washington, G. S. Gideon, printer,
1855.
13 p.   22 1/2 cm.

11904 [Cunningham, J   ] supposed author.
An essay on trade and commerce: containing observations on taxes, as they are supposed to affect
the price of labour in our manufactories: with
some interesting reflections on the importance of
our trade to America... By the author of Considerations on taxes, &c. London, S. Hooper, 1770.
xiv, 302 p.   21 cm.
By J. Cunningham? - Brit. mus. Catalogue.

11905 Cunningham, Letitia.
The case of the Whigs who loaned their money on
the public faith fairly stated. Including a
memento for Congress to review their engagements,
and to establish the honour and honesty of the
United States of America. By Letitia Cunningham.
Philadelphia, Printed by Francis Bailey, in Market-
street, 1783.
51 p.   16 cm.

11906 Cunningham, William, 1767-1823.
An eulogy delivered at Lunenburg, on Saturday
the 22d of February, 1800. The day recommended by
Congress to commemorate the unequalled virtues and
preeminent services of Gen. George Washington:

first president of the United States of America,
and commander in chief of the American forces during
the revolutionary war. By William Cunningham, jun.
... Worcester, Printed by Isaiah Thomas, jun.,
March, 1800.
16 p.   23 1/2 cm.

11907   Currey, Richard Owen.
A sketch of the geology of Tennessee: embracing a
description of its minerals and ores, their variety
and quality, modes of assaying and value; with a
description of its soils and productiveness, and
palaeontology. By Richard O. Currey... Knoxville,
Tenn., Printed by Kinsloe & Rice, 1857.
x, 128 p.   front. (fold. map)   22 cm.

11908   Currie, William, 1754-1828.
An historical account of the climates and diseases
of the United States of America; and of the remedies
and methods of treatment... By William Currie...
Philadelphia, Printed by T. Dobson, 1792.
2 p.l., 4, 409, v p.   20 1/2 cm.

11909   Currie, William, 1754-1828.
Memoirs of the yellow fever, which prevailed in
Philadelphia, and other parts of the United States
of America, in the summer and autumn of the present
year, 1798... To which is added, a collection of
facts respecting the origin of the fever. By
William Currie... Philadelphia, Printed by J.
Bioren, for T. Dobson, 1798.
1 p.l., 145 p.   22 1/2 cm.

11910   Currie, William, 1754-1828.
A treatise on the synochus icteroides, or yellow
fever; as it lately appeared in the city of Philadelphia. Exhibiting a concise view of its rise,
progress and symptoms, together with the method of
treatment found most successful; also remarks on
the nature of its contagion, and directions for
preventing the introduction of the same malady, in
future. By William Currie... Philadelphia, Printed
by Thomas Dobson, no. 41, South second-street, 1794.
iv, [vi]-viii, 85 p.   21 cm.

11911   A cursory glimpse of the state of the nation, on the
twenty-second of February, 1814, being the eighty-

first anniversary of the birth of Washington; or,
A physico-politico-theologico, lucubration upon the
wonderful properties of nitrous oxide, or the newly
discovered exhilarating gas, in its effects upon
the human mind, and body; as they were exhibited, by
actual experiment, on the evening of the twenty-third
instant. Philadelphia, Published by Moses Thomas
(J. Maxwell, printer) 1814.
    23 p.   21 cm.

11912 Cursory remarks on men and measures in Georgia. [n.p.]
    Printed in the year 1784.
      1 p.l., 30 p.   22 1/2 cm.
    Signed: A citizen.

11913 [Curtis, Benjamin Robbins] 1809-1874.
    Address to the people of Massachusetts. [Boston,
    1851?]
      16 p.   23 cm.
    On the coalition of 1851 between the Democratic
    and Free-soil parties in Massachusetts.
    Signed by William Aspinwall and 166 other Whig
    members of the General court of Massachusetts.

11914 Curtis, Benjamin Robbins, 1809-1874.
    Executive power. By B. R. Curtis. Boston, Little,
    Brown and company, 1862.
      viii, [9]-29 p.   18 1/2 cm.

11915 Curtis, George Ticknor, 1812-1894.
    ... Address of Hon. George Ticknor Curtis, at
    Philadelphia, Sept. 30, 1864. [New York, 1864]
      16 p.   22 cm.   (Campaign document. no. 10)

11916 Curtis, George Ticknor, 1812-1894.
    The just supremacy of Congress over the territories.
    By George Ticknor Curtis... Boston, A. Williams
    and company, 1859.
      44 p.   23 1/2 cm.
    "Written as an answer to the article by the Hon.
    Stephen A. Douglas, which originally appeared in
    Harper's magazine, entitled 'The dividing line
    between federal and local authority; popular
    sovereignty in the territories.'" - Introd. note.

11917 [Curtis, George Ticknor] 1812-1894.
    The merits of Thomas W. Dorr and George Bancroft,

as they are politically connected. By a citizen of
Massachusetts. Boston, Printed by J. H. Eastburn
[1844]
   36 p.   23 cm.
   [Waterman pamphlets, v. 160, no. 21]

11918 [Curtis, George Ticknor] 1812-1894.
     Observations on the Rev. Dr. Gannett's sermon,
entitled "Relation of the North to slavery".
Republished from the editorial columns of the Boston
courier, of June 28th and 30th, and July 6th, 1854.
Boston, Redding and company, 1854.
   29 p.   21 1/2 cm.

11919 Curtis, George Ticknor, 1812-1894.
     The strength of the Constitution. A discourse
delivered at the Lowell institute, in Boston, 7
Feburary, 1850, as the conclusion of a course of
twelve lectures on the history of the Constitution
of the United States. By George Ticknor Curtis.
Boston, Ticknor, Reed, and Fields, 1850.
   39 p.   22 1/2 cm.

11920 Curtis, George William, 1824-1892.
     The duty of the American scholar to politics and
the times. An oration, delivered on Tuesday,
August 5, 1856, before the literary societies of
Wesleyan university, Middletown, Conn. By George
William Curtis. New York, Dix, Edwards & co.,
1856.
   46 p.   24 cm.

11921 Curtis, Josiah, 1816-1883.
     Brief remarks on the hygiene of Massachusetts,
but more particularly of the cities of Boston and
Lowell: being a report to the American medical
association; submitted, as member for Massachusetts
of the Committee on public hygiene, at their annual
meeting in Boston, May, 1849. By Josiah Curtis...
Philadelphia, T. K. and P. G. Collins, printers,
1849.
   70 p., 1 l. incl. tables.   24 cm.
   From the Transactions of the American medical
association, vol. II.

11922 Curtis, Lucius Quintius, 1812-1901.
     Civil government an ordinance of God: a sermon,

delivered in the 1st Congregational church, Colchester, April 21st, 1861, by L. Curtis. Hartford, O. F. Jackson, printer, 1861.
   15 p.   19 1/2 cm.

11923 Curwen, Samuel, 1715-1802.
   Journal and letters of the late Samuel Curwen, judge of Admiralty, etc., an American refugee in England, from 1775 to 1784, comprising remarks on the prominent men and measures of that period. To which are added, biographical notices of many American loyalists, and other eminent persons. By George Atkinson Ward... New York, C. S. Francis and co.: Boston, J. H. Francis, 1842.
   xii, [9]-578, [2] p.   front. (port.) pl. 23 cm.

11924 Cushing, Caleb, 1800-1879.
   A eulogy on La Fayette, pronounced at the request of the young men of Dover, September 6, 1834. By Caleb Cushing. Dover, N. H., G. Wadleigh, 1834.
   27 p.   22 cm.

11925 Cushman, Robert Woodward, 1800-1868.
   Plymouth's Rock: "the rock whence we were hewn." A discourse delivered in Plymouth at the Cushman festival, August 15th, 1855, on the CCXXXVth anniversary of the embarkation of the Pilgrims for America. By Robert W. Cushman... Boston, J. M. Hewes, printer, 1855.
   31 p.   23 1/2 cm.

11926 Cutler, Joseph, 1815-1885
   The insolvent laws of Massachusetts. With notes. By Joseph Cutler... Boston, B. B. Mussey, 1846.
   xii, 108 p.   24 cm.

11927 Cutler, Manasseh, 1742-1823.
   A sermon, delivered at Hamilton, on the day of the national fast, April 25, 1799; appointed by the President of the United States of America. By Manasseh Cutler... Pub. at the request of the hearers. Salem, Printed by Joshua Cushing, 1799.
   32 p.   21 cm.

11928 Cutler, Rufus King.
   Address of Hon. R. King Cutler, United States

senator of Louisiana. Proceedings in Congress.
The Louisiana delegation. United States officers
in Louisiana. The President, cabinet and Congress.
The Louisiana constitution. Compensation and negro
suffrage. Governor Wells. General Hurlbut. The
conservative Union and liberty party. Advice to
Louisianians. August, 1865. New Orleans, Printed
at Rea's steam job printing office, 1865.
cover-title, 22 p.   22 1/2 cm.

11929 Cutter, Charles William.
An oration pronounced before the Whigs of Portsmouth, on the fourth of July, A. D. 1834. By Charles
W. Cutter. Portsmouth, N. H., J. F. Shores, 1834.
32 p.   22 1/2 cm.

11930 Cutter, William, 1801-1867.
The life of Israel Putnam, major-general in the
army of the American revolution. Comp. from the
best authorities. By William Cutter. New York,
C. F. Cooledge & brother, 1847.
2 p.l., [iii]-xx, [21]-383 p.   front. (port.)
plates, maps.   19 1/2 cm.

11931 Cutting, Francis Brockholst, 1805-1870.
"Hards" and "softs." Reply of Mr. Cutting, of
New York, in the House of representatives, Jan. 17,
1854, to a question put to him by Mr. Smith, of
Alabama, in Committee of the whole. [Washington,
Printed at the Congressional globe office, 1854]
7 p.   23 cm.

11932 Cuyler, Cornelius C   1783-1850.
Believers, sojourners on earth, and expectants
of heaven; a sermon occasioned by the death of
Robert Ralston, esq., who died in Philadelphia
on the 11th August, 1836, in the 75th year of his
age. Preached in Second Presbyterian church,
Philadelphia, August 21, 1836, by Cornelius C.
Cuyler... Philadelphia, W. S. Martien, 1836.
36 p., 1 l., [2] p.   23 cm.

11933 The Cynick. By Growler Gruff, esquire [pseud.]
Aided by a confederacy of lettered dogs... v. 1;
Sept. 21-Dec. 12, 1811. Philadelphia, 1812.
1 p.l., iv, 210 p.   15 cm.   weekly.
"The principal purpose of the little paper was to

censure... the theatrical managers of the city for abolishing the old theatre boxes." - Smyth, Philadelphia magazines, p. 241.

D

11934 Dabadie, F
A travers l'Amérique du Sud. Paris, F. Sartorius, 1858.
2 p.l., 386 p., 1 l.   16 cm.

11935 [Daggett, John] 1805-1885.
Remarks and documents concerning the location of the Boston and Providence rail-road through the burying ground in East Attleborough. To which are added, the statutes for the protection of the sepulchres of the dead, with remarks on some of the powers and rights of corporations in this state. By a freeman of Massachusetts. Boston, Printed by Light & Horton, 1834.
28 p.   24 cm.

11936 Daggett, John, 1805-1885.
Sketch of the history of Attleborough, from its settlement to the present time. By John Daggett. Dedham [Mass.] H. Mann, printer, 1834.
136 p.   22 1/2 cm.

11937 Dagnall, John Malone, 1818-1917.
Daisy Swain, the flower of Shenandoah. A tale of the rebellion. By John M. Dagnall... Brooklyn, N. Y., 1865.
vi, [7]-167 p. incl. front., illus., pl.
16 1/2 cm.
In verse.

11938 Dake, Orsamus Charles.
Nebraska legends and poems, by Orsamus Charles Dake. New York, Pott & Amery, 1871.
165 p.   19 1/2 cm.

11939 Dall, Caroline [Wells] (Healey) "Mrs. C. H. A. Dall," 1822-1912.
The college, the market, and the court; or, Woman's relation to education, labor, and law. By Caroline H. Dall... Boston, Lee and Shepard,

1867.
xxxv, 498 p., 1 l.   19 1/2 cm.

11940   Dall, Caroline [Wells] (H[ealey]) "Mrs. C. H. A.
Dall," 1822-1912.
Woman's rights under the law; in three lectures,
delivered in Boston, January, 1861, by Caroline H.
Dall... Boston, Walker, Wise and company, 1861.
xix, 164 p., 1 l.   18 cm.

11941   Dall, William Healey, 1845-1927.
Alaska and its resources, by William H. Dall...
Boston, Lee and Shepard, 1870.
xii, 627, [1] p.   front., illus., plates,
fold. map.   21 cm.
Bibliography: p. 595-609.

11942   Dallas, George Mifflin, 1792-1864.
Mr. Dallas' letter on the Mexican treaty; reprinted from the Public ledger of June 15, 1849.
Philadelphia, United States book and job printing
establishment, 1849.
29 p.   21 1/2 cm.

11943   Dallas, Robert Charles, 1754-1824.
The history of the Maroons, from their origin to
the establishment of their chief tribe at Sierra
Leone; including the expedition to Cuba, for the
purpose of procuring Spanish chasseurs; and the
state of the island of Jamaica for the last ten
years: with a succinct history of the island
previous to that period... By R. C. Dallas, esq.
London, T. N. Longman and O. Rees, 1803.
2 v.   fronts., 2 fold. maps.   22 1/2 cm.

11944   Dalliba, James.
A narrative of the battle of Brownstown, which
was fought on the 9th of August, 1812, during the
campaign of the north western army under the command
of Brigadier General Hull. By James Dalliba...
New York [D. Longworth] 1816.
vi, [7]-37 p.   23 1/2 cm.

11945   Dalrymple, Alexander, 1737-1808, ed.
A collection of voyages chiefly in the southern
Atlantick ocean. Published from the original m.s.s. [!]
by Alexander Dalrymple. London, Printed for the

author, 1775.
   3 p.l., 19, 88, 22, [2], 83, 16, 16 p.   [1], 13,
3 fold. maps.   27 1/2 cm.
   Contents. - La Roche. - Halley, two voyages. -
Bouvet. - Leon. - Journals of winds and weather at
Falkland's islands.

11946   Dalrymple, [Alexander] 1737-1808.
   A letter from Mr. Dalrymple to Dr. Hawkesworth,
occasioned by some groundless and illiberal imputations in his account of the late voyages to the
south. London, J. Nourse [etc.] 1773.
   2 p.l., 35 p. fold. map.   28 x 21 cm.   [With
Cluny, Alexander. The American traveller. London,
1769]

11947   [Dalrymple, Sir John, bart.] 1726-1810.
   The address of the people of Great Britain to the
inhabitants of America. London, Printed for T.
Cadell, 1775.
   2 p.l., 60 p.   22 cm.
   "This address is said, and believed, to have been
written by Sir J. D. and printed at the public
expence, to be distributed in America." - Monthly
review, June 1775, v. 52, p. 540.

11948   Dalton, William, of Crackenthorpe, Westmoreland.
   Travels in the United States of America, and part
of Upper Canada. By Wm. Dalton... Appleby [Eng.]
Printed for the author, by R. Bateman, 1821.
   vii (i.e. viii), 256 p.   19 1/2 cm.

11949   Daly, Augustin, 1838-1899.
   A legend of "Norwood"; or, Village life in New
England. An original dramatic comedy of American
life, in four acts. Founded on a novel by Rev.
Henry Ward Beecher. By Augustin Daly... New York,
Printed for the author, 1867.
   79 (i.e. 41) p.   26 1/2 cm.

11950   Daly, Charles Patrick, 1816-1899.
   Are the southern privateersmen pirates? Letter to
the Hon. Ira Harris, United States senator. By
Charles P. Daly... New York, J. B. Kirker, 1862.
   13 p.   22 cm.

11951   Dan to Beersheba; or, Northern and southern friends.
        London, Chapman and Hall, 1864.
            iv, 336 p.   19 1/2 cm.

11952   Dana, James, 1735-1812.
            A century discourse, delivered at the anniversary
        meeting of the freemen of the town of Wallingford
        [Conn.]   April 9, 1770...   New Haven, T. & S. Green
        [1770?]
            51 p.   16 cm.

11953   Dana, James, 1735-1812.
            The character and reward of the good and faithful
        servant.   A sermon occasioned by the much lamented
        death of Charles Whittelsey, esq.; who departed
        this life July 2d, 1764, in the 41st year of his age.
        Preached the Lord's-day after his funeral, by James
        Dana...   Boston, Printed by Richard & Samuel Draper,
        in Newbury-street, 1764.
            30 p.   19 1/2 cm.

11954   Dana, James Dwight, 1813-1895.
            Manual of geology, treating of the principles of
        the science, with special reference to American
        geological history, for the use of colleges, aca-
        demies, and schools of science.   By James D. Dana...
        Illustrated by a chart of the world, and over one
        thousand figures, mostly from American sources.
        Philadelphia, T. Bliss & co.; London, Trübner & co.,
        1863.
            xvi, 798 p. incl. front., illus.   fold. map.
        22 cm.

11955   Dana, James Dwight, 1813-1895.
            Manual of mineralogy, including observations on
        mines, rocks, reduction of ores, and the applications
        of the science to the arts.   With 260 illustrations.
        Designed for the use of schools and colleges.   By
        James D. Dana...   2d ed.   New Haven, Durrie & Peck;
        Philadelphia, H. C. Peck, 1849.
            xii, [13]-432 p.   illus., diagrs.   19 cm.

11956   Dana, James Freeman, 1793-1827.
            Outlines of the mineralogy and geology of Boston
        and its vicinity, with a geological map.   By J.
        Freeman Dana, M. D. and Samuel L. Dana, M. D. ...
        Boston, Published by Cummings and Hilliard,

no. 1 Cornhill, University press... Hilliard
and Metcalf, 1818.
108 p.   front. (fold. map)   26 cm.

11957   Deane, Samuel, 1733-1814.
The New-England farmer; or, Georgical dictionary:
containing a compendious account of the ways and
methods in which the most important art of husbandry,
in all its various branches, is, or may be, practised
to the greatest advantage in this country. By
Samuel Deane, A. M. Fellow of the American academy
of arts and sciences... Printed at Worcester,
Massachusetts, By Isaiah Thomas, sold at his book-
store in Worcester, and by him and company in Boston,
1790.
viii, 335 p.   1 illus. (diagr.)   21 cm.

11958   Deane, Samuel, 1733-1814.
An oration, delivered in Portland, July 4th, 1793,
in commemoration of the independence of the United
States of America. By Samuel Deane, D. D. Portland, Printed by Thomas B. Wait, 1793.
14 p.   20 x 15 1/2 cm.

11959   Deane, Silas, 1737-1789.
An address to the free and independent citizens
of the United States of North-America. By Silas
Deane, esquire. Hartford, Printed by Hudson &
Goodwin, 1784.
30 p.   18 cm.
Relates to his conduct while commissioner of the
United States in France. Dated: London, August 10,
1783. Appendix dated: London, October 12, 1783.
Also published the same year in more extended form,
with appended documents, under title: An address
to the United States of North America.

11960   Deane, Silas, 1737-1789.
Paris papers; or, Mr. Silas Deane's late inter-
cepted letters to his brothers, and other intimate
friends, in America. To which are annexed for comparison, the Congressional declaration of independency in July 1776, and that now inculating among
the revolted provinces, with the never-to-be-for-
gotten orders of the rebel general in August 1776,
for preventing a pacification. New-York, Re-printed
by James Rivington [1782]

xii, 141, xxxi p.   14 1/2 cm.
The Declaration of Independence and the "Counter-
declaration published at New-York in 1781" are
printed on opposite pages numbered in duplicate
1-11.
Reprinted from Rivington's "Royal gazette"
Oct. 24-Dec. 12, 1781. cf. Collections of the N. Y.
hist. soc. Pub. fund. v. 22, p. 501.

11961 Deane, William Reed, 1809-1871.
A biographical sketch of Elkanah Watson, founder
of agricultural societies in America, and the pro-
jector of canal communication in New York state,
with a brief genealogy of the Watson family, early
settled in Plymouth colony. By Wm. R. Deane...
Albany [N. Y.] J. Munsell, 1864.
15 p.   front. (port.) illus.   24 1/2 cm.
Reprinted from the N. E. hist. and gen. reg.:
Biographical sketch, v. 17, p. 97; Genealogy,
v. 18, p. 363.

11962 Deane, William Reed, 1809-1871.
Brief memoirs of John and Walter Deane, two of
the first settlers of Taunton, Mass., and of the
early generations of their descendants... By
William Reed Deane, assisted by others. Boston,
Printed by Coolidge & Wiley, 1849.
16 p.   front. (port.) illus. (incl. facsims.,
coat of arms)   24 cm.

11963 [De Beck, William L   ]
Murder will out. The first step in crime leads
to the gallows. The horrors of the Queen city...
By an old citizen. Cincinnati, 1867.
128 p.   21 cm.

11964 De Bonelli, L   Hugh.
Travels in Bolivia; with a tour across the Pampas
to Buenos Ayres, &c. By L. Hugh De Bonelli...
London, Hurst and Blackett, 1854.
2 v.   19 1/2 cm.

11965 Decatur, Mrs. Susan (Wheeler)
Documents relative to the claim of Mrs. Decatur,
with her earnest request that the gentlemen of
Congress will take the trouble to read them. George-

town, D. C., J. C. Dunn, printer, 1826.
62 p.   21 1/2 cm.

11966 Decius, pseud.
       Letters of Decius, in answer to the criticism
       upon the Political account of Trinidad; and upon
       the defence of the crimes of Governor Picton, in
       the Anti-Jacobin review, under the title of the
       "Pictonian prosecution". London, Printed and sold
       by J. Morton, 1808.
       1 p.l., 85 p.   21 cm.

11967 A Declaration of independence published by the Congress
       at Philadelphia in 1776. With a counter-declaration
       published at New-York in 1781. [New York? 1781?]
       1 p.l., 24 (i.e. 34) p.   16 cm.
       Pages 2-11 are numbered in duplicate; text begins
       on verso of t.-p., the counter-declaration and the
       Declaration on opposite pages. The counter-declara-
       tion is a criticism of the acts of Congress, and a
       renunciation of "all allegiance... to the Congress,
       or to any government under them." At end, "We
       mutually pledge to each other, and to the crown and
       empire of Great Britain, our lives, our fortunes,
       and our sacred honour..." Unsigned.
       Pages 13-24 contain a letter dated Philadelphia,
       August 20, 1781, addressed to Mr. Rivington, and
       signed: A friend to America and to peace.

11968 A defence of the resolutions and address of the
       American Congress, in reply to Taxation no tyranny.
       By the author of Regulus. To which are added,
       General remarks on the leading principles of that
       work, as published in the London evening post of
       the 2d and 4th of May; and A short chain of deduct-
       ions from one clear position of common sense and
       experience. London, Printed for J. Williams [1775]
       2 p.l., [3]-96 p.   21 1/2 cm.
       "General remarks on the leading principles of
       Taxation no tyranny" (p. 74-92) signed Regulus.

11969 A defence of the Rockingham party, in their late
       coalition with the Right Honourable Frederic, Lord
       North. London, J. Stockdale, 1783.
       1 p.l., 53 p.   21 cm.

11970   Dehay, Timothée, 1794-1851.
        Les colonies et la métropole, le sucre exotique
        et le sucre indigène, trésor, marine, commerce,
        agriculture, émancipation commerciale de nos colo-
        nies, et abolition de l'esclavage. Par Timothée
        Dehay... Paris, Hortet et Ozanne, 1839.
        xv, 340 p.   19 1/2 cm.

11971   Dehon, Theodore, bp., 1776-1817.
        A discourse, delivered in Newport, Rhode-Island;
        before the congregation of Trinity church, the
        Masonic society, and the Newport guards; the Sunday
        following the intelligence of the death of General
        George Washington. By Theodore Dehon... Newport,
        Printed by Henry Barber, 1880.
        17, [1] p., 1 l.   20 1/2 x 16 1/2 cm.

11972   Dehon, Theodore, bp., 1776-1817.
        A discourse, delivered in Trinity church, in
        Newport, on Thursday, 27th November, 1805, an
        appointed day of public thanksgiving and praise.
        By Theodore Dehon, A. M., rector of Trinity church.
        Published by particular desire. Newport, (Rhode
        Island) Printed at the office of the Newport
        Mercury, 1806.
        14 p.   19 x 14 1/2 cm.

11973   De Kay, James Ellsworth, 1792-1851.
        Anniversary address on the progress of the
        natural sciences in the United States: delivered
        before the Lyceum of natural history of New York,
        Feb. 1826. By James E. De Kay. New York, G. & C.
        Carvill, 1826.
        78 p.   21 cm.

11974   [Delacroix, Jacques Vincent] 1743-1832.
        Memoires d'un Américain, avec une description
        de la Prusse et de l'isle de Saint Domingue. Par
        l'auteur des Lettres d'Affi à Zurac, & de celles
        d'un philosophe sensible... Lausanne et se trouve
        à Paris, chez la v. Regnard & Demonville, 1771.
        2 v.   17 cm.

11975   Delafield, Edward, 1794-1875.
        Biographical sketch of J. Kearny Rodgers... by
        Edward Delafield, M. D. Read before the New York
        academy of medicine on Wednesday, October 6th, 1852,

and published under its authority. New York,
G. A. C. Van Beuren, printer, 1852.
28 p.   23 1/2 cm.

11976 Delafield, John, 1812-1865 or 6.
A brief topograhpical [!] description of the
county of Washington, in the state of Ohio, by J.
Delafield, junr. ... New York, Printed by J. M.
Elliott, 1834.
39 p.   fold. front.   22 1/2 cm.

11977 De Lancey, William Heathcote, bp., 1797-1865.
A sermon preached at the centennial celebration
of the opening of St. Peter's church, Philadelphia,
September 4th, 1861, by William Heathcote De
Lancey... Published by request of the vestry.
Philadelphia, King & Baird, printers, 1862.
3 p.l., [3]-78 p.   22 1/2 cm.

11978 [Delaplaine, Joseph] 1777-1824.
The author turned critic; or, The reviewer re-
viewed; being a reply to a feeble and unfounded
attack on Delaplaine's repository, in the Analectic
magazine and Naval chronicle, for the month of
September 1816. [Philadelphia, 1816]
34 p.   22 cm.

11979 Dell, William, d. 1664.
T[he] doctrin[e] of baptisms, reduced from its
ancient and modern corruptions; and restored to its
primitive soundness [a]nd [int]egrity: [accord]in[g
to] the word of [tru]th; the sub[stance] o[f fa]ith,
and the nature of Christ's kingdom. [B]y William
Dell... The 5th ed. L[o]ndon printed; [Philad]el-
phia, Reprinted, by B. Franklin, and D. Hall, 1759.
iv, 5-43 p.   19 cm.

11980 Dell, William, d. 1664.
The trial of spirits, both in teachers and hearers.
Wherein is held forth the clear discovery, and
certain downfal, of the carnal and anti-Christian
clergy of these nations. Testified from the Word
of God, to the University congregations in Cambridge.
By William Dell, minister of the gospel, and master
of Gonvil and Caius college, in Cambridge. London,
First printed in the year 1666. Philadelphia,

Re-printed by B. Franklin, and D. Hall, 1760.
55 p.   19 1/2 cm.

11981   Del Mar, Alexander, 1836–
... The great paper bubble; or, The coming financial
explosion. By Alex. Delmar... A campaign document
for 1864. New York, Office of the "Metropolitan
record," 1864.
cover-title, 94 p., 1 l.   pl.   18 1/2 cm.

11982   Demarest, James, 1832–
Thanksgiving sermon. A sermon preached in the
Second Reformed Dutch church, Hackensack, N. J.,
on Thanksgiving morning, Nov. 28, 1861. By Rev.
James Demarest, jr. ... Hackensack, Printed at
the office of the Bergen County patriot, 1861.
16 p.   22 1/2 cm.

11983   Demersay, Alfred, d. 1891.
... Étude économique sur le maté ou thé du Para-
guay, par le docteur Alfred Demersay... Paris,
Ve Bouchard-Huzard, 1867.
2 p.l., 45 p., 1 l.   front., pl.   24 1/2 cm.
At head of title: Société impériale et centrale
d'agriculture de France.
Extrait des Mémoirs de la Société d'agriculture,
année 1865.

11984   Demersay, Alfred, d. 1891.
Une mission géographique dans les archives
d'Espagne et de Portugal 1862-1863; fragments lus
à la Société de géographie dans sa séance générale
du 15 avril 1864 par M. Alfred Demersay... Paris,
L. Hachette et cie, 1864.
45 p.   25 cm.
"Extrait du Bulletin de la Société de géographie
(juin 1864)"

11985   Démeunier, Jean Nicolas, 1741-1814.
Supplément ou suite aux rémarques de Mr. Démeunier,
sur la constitution et les états de Nouvelle-Yorck
et Virginie, qui ne se trouvent point dans les trois
volumes de l'Amérique indépendante. Gand, P. F. de
Goesin, 1791.
1 p.l., 120 p.   22 1/2 cm.

11986 [Dewey, Dellon Marcus]
       ... History of the strange sounds or rappings,
       heard in Rochester and western New-York, and usually
       called the mysterious noises! Which are supposed
       by many to be communications from the spirit world,
       together with all the explanation that can as yet be
       given of the matter. Rochester, D. M. Dewey, 1850.
       1 p.l., ii, [13]-79 p. incl. plan.   20 cm.

11987 A dissertation upon the constitutional freedom of
       the press in the United States of America. By an
       impartial citizen... Boston, Printed by David
       Carlisle, for Joseph Nancrede, no. 49, Marlborough
       street, 1801.
       54 p.   23 cm.

11988 Dix, Dorothea Lynde, 1802-1887.
       Remarks on prisons and prison discipline in the
       United States. By D. L. Dix... Boston, Printed
       by Munroe & Francis, 1845.
       104 p.   21 cm.

11989 Dodge, William Castle, 1827-1914.
       Breech-loaders versus muzzle-loaders: or, How to
       strengthen our army and crush the rebellion, with
       a saving of life and treasure. By by [!] W. C.
       Dodge... Washington, D. C., W. C. Dodge, 1865.
       31, 2 p.   22 cm.
       On cover: 3d ed.
       "Most of the contents of this pamphlet were ori-
       ginally published in the form of a memorial to the
       Secretary of war." - p. [3]

11990 Downing, Andrew Jackson, 1815-1852.
       A treatise on the theory and practice of landscape
       gardening, adapted to North America; with a view to
       the improvement of country residences. Comprising
       historical notices and general principles of the
       art, directions for laying out grounds and arranging
       plantations, the description and cultivation of
       hardy trees, decorative accompaniments to the house
       and grounds, the formation of pieces of artificial
       water, flower gardens, etc. with remarks on rural
       architecture... By A. J. Downing. New York & London,
       Wiley and Putnam; Boston, C. C. Little & co., 1841.
       2 p.l., viii, [9]-451 p.   front., illus.
       24 1/2 cm.

11991   Drake, Samuel Gardner, 1798-1875.
        A particular history of the five years French and
Indian war in New England and parts adjacent, from
its declaration by the King of France, March 15,
1744, to the treaty with the eastern Indians, Oct.
16, 1749, sometimes called Governor Shirley's war.
With a memoir of Major-General Shirley, accompanied
by his portrait and other engravings. By Samuel
G. Drake. Albany, J. Munsell, 1870.
        312 p.   front. (port.) illus.   21 1/2 x 18 cm.

11992   [Duché, Jacob] 1737-1798.
        Caspipina's letters; containing observations on
a variety of subjects, literary, moral, and religious. Written by a gentleman who resided some time
in Philadelphia. To which is added, the life and
character of Wm. Penn, esq.; original proprietor
of Pennsylvania... Bath, Reprinted by R. Cruttwell,
and sold by E. and C. Dilly and J. Phillips,
London, 1777.
        2 v. in 1.   16 cm.
        The life of Penn is by Edmund Rack. cf. Sabin,
Bibl. amer.; etc., etc.
        Published in 1774 under title: Observations on a
variety of subjects, literary, moral and religious.
        Letter in French inserted.

11993   Duganne, Augustine Joseph Hickey, 1823-1884.
        The fighting Quakers; a true story of the war for
our union. By A. J. H. Duganne. With letters from
the brothers to their mother: and a funeral sermon
by Rev. O. B. Frothingham. By authority of the
Bureau of Military record. New York, J. P. Robens,
1866.
        1 p.l., 116 p.   front.   19 cm.
        Later edition, 1869, published under title: The
Quaker soldiers.

                            E

11994   Eastburn, Robert, 1710-1778.
        ... The dangers and sufferings of Robert Eastburn,
and his deliverance from Indian captivity... with
introduction and notes by John R. Spears. Cleveland, Burrows brothers, 1904.
        76 p.   facsim.   20 1/2 cm.

11995 Eastman, Francis Smith, 1803–1846 or 7.
        A history of the state of New York, from the first
        discovery of the country to the present time: with
        a geographical account of the country, and a view
        of its original inhabitants. By F. S. Eastman.
        A new ed. New York, A. K. White, 1833.
        3 p.l., [5]–455, [1] p.   front., plates, ports.
        19 cm.

11996 Eastman, Mrs. Mary (Henderson) b. 1818.
        Chicóra and other regions of the conquerors and
        the conquered. Philadelphia, Lippincott, Grambo
        and co., 1854.
        iv p., 2 l., [9]–126 p.   XXI pl. (incl. front.)
        28 cm.
        A collection of engravings from drawings by
        Captain Seth Eastman, accompanied by descriptive
        text, illustrative of the history and customs of
        various tribes of North American Indians.

11997 Easton, Pa. Library company.
        Catalogue of the books belonging to the Easton
        library company; containing, also, the articles of
        association, and the rules and regulations of the
        library... Phillipsburg, Cooley & Wise, printers,
        1855.
        98 p., 1 l.   21 cm.

11998 Eaton, B   A
        The minstrel, and other poems. By B. A. Eaton.
        Boston, Russell, Odiorne, and company, 1833.
        54 p.   15 cm.

11999 Eaton, Edward Byrom.
        "The crisis." The crisis – its solution – the
        causes – their removal. A lecture delivered at
        Oxford, England, by the permission of the Rev. the
        vice chancellor, and the worshipful tho [!] mayor,
        on March 14th, 1863. By Philodemos (friend of the
        people) Edward Byrom Eaton... London, Heardley
        & co., 1863.
        x, [11]–32 p.   21 1/2 cm.
        Originally published in the San Francisco herald,
        California, U. S., October, 1861.

12000 Eaton, Francis Brown, 1825–1904.
        History of Candia: once known as Charmingfare;

with notices of some of the early families. By
F. B. Eaton. Manchester, N. H., J. O. Adams,
printer, 1852.
151, [1] p. front., plates, fold. map.
21 1/2 cm.

12001 Eaton, Horace, 1810-1883.
The early history of Palmyra: a Thanksgiving
sermon, delivered at Palmyra, N. Y., November 26,
1857, by Horace Eaton... Published by request of
the descendants of the first settlers. Rochester,
Press of A. Strong & co., 1858.
26 p. 22 1/2 cm.

12002 Eaton, John Henry, 1790-1856.
Candid appeal to the American public: in reply
to Messrs. Ingham, Branch, and Berrien, on the
dissolution of the late cabinet. By John H. Eaton.
City of Washington, Printed at the Globe office,
1831.
55 p. 22 cm.

12003 Edge, Frederick Milnes.
The Alabama and Kearsarge. An account of the
naval engagement in the British channel, on Sunday,
June 19th, 1864, from information furnished to the
writer by the wounded and paroled prisoners of the
... Alabama, and the officers of the... Kearsarge,
and citizens of Cherbourg. By Frederick Milnes
Edge. London, W. Ridgway, 1864.
48 p. 20 cm.
Also published under title: An Englishman's view
of the battle between the Alabama and the Kearsarge.

12004 Edwards, Jonathan, 1745-1801.
Observations on the language of the Muhhekaneew
Indians; in which the extent of that language in
North-America is shewn; its genius is grammatically
traced; some of its peculiarities, and some instances
of analogy between that and the Hebrew are pointed
out. Communicated to the Connecticut society of
arts and sciences, and pub. at the request of the
Society. By Jonathan Edwards... New-Haven, Printed
by J. Meigs, 1787; London, Reprinted by W. Justins,
1788.
iv, [5]-15, [1] p. 22 1/2 cm. (In Occom,
Samson, 1723?-1792. A sermon at the execution of

Moses Paul. London, 1788. [pt. 2])

12005 Elder, William, 1806-1885.
Biography of Elisha Kent Kane. By William Elder.
Philadelphia, Childs & Peterson; London, Trübner
& co., 1858.
1 p.l., 416 p. front. (port.) plates.
22 1/2 cm.

12006 Eliot, John, 1604-1690.
A late and further manifestation of the progress
of the gospel amongst the Indians in New-England.
Declaring their constant love and zeal to the
truth: with a readiness to give accompt of their
faith and hope; as of their desires in church
communion to be partakers of the ordinances of
Christ. Being a narrative of the examinations of
the Indians, about their knowledge in religion, by
the elders of the churches. Related by Mr. John
Eliot. Pub. by the corporation, established by
act of Parliament, for propagating the gospel there
... London, Printed by M. S., 1655.
4 p.l., 23 p. 17 1/2 x 13 1/2 cm.
The eighth of a series of 11 pamphlets, commonly
known as the "Eliot tracts", published in London
from 1643 to 1671 in the interests of missionary
work among the Indians of New-England.
"The examination of the Indians at Roxbury, the
13th day of the 4th month, 1654 [reported by William
Walton]": p. 11-20.

12007 Eliot, John, 1754-1813.
A biographical dictionary, containing a brief
account of the first settlers, and other eminent
characters among the magistrates, ministers,
literary and worthy men, in New England. By John
Eliot, D. D. corresponding secretary of the Massachusetts historical society... Published by
Cushing and Appleton, Salem, and Edward Oliver,
no. 70, State street, Boston, 1809. E. Oliver,
printer.
viii, 511, [1] p. 22 cm.

12008 Eliot, Jonathan, 1784-1846.
The funding system of the United States and of
Great Britain, with some tabular facts of other
nations touching the same subject. Prepared under

152

a resolution of the House of representatives of the
United States, by Jonathan Elliot... Washington,
Blair and Rives, printers, 1845.
xxiv, 1299 p.   23 cm.   (On p. [I]: 28th Cong.,
1st sess. House. Doc. no. 15)

12009 Eliot, Samuel, 1821-1898.
The functions of a city. An oration before the
city authorities of Boston, on the Fourth of July,
1868. By Samuel Eliot, LL. D. Boston, A. Mudge &
son, city printers, 1868.
31 p.   23 cm.

12010 Eliot, Thomas Dawes, 1808-1870.
Address of Thomas D. Eliot, of the 1st congressional
district of Massachusetts, to his constituents.
[Washington, H. Polkinhorn, printer, 1861]
8 p.   24 1/2 cm.

12011 [Eliot, William Havard] 1796-1831.
A description of Tremont house, with architectural
illustrations... Boston, Gray and Bowen, 1830.
2 p.l., 36 p.   XXXI pl. (1 col.) incl. front.
33 1/2 cm.

12012 Elizaga, Lorenzo.
Ensayos políticos. Coleccion de artículos
escritos y publicados en diversos periódicos,
durante la usurpacion de Maximiliano, por Lorenzo
Elizaga. Mexico, Tip. de J. Abadiano, 1867.
v, 464 p.   front. (mounted port.)   22 1/2 cm.

12013 Elkins, Hervey.
Fifteen years in the senior order of Shakers:
a narration of facts, concerning that singular
people. By Hervey Elkins... Hanover [N. H.]
Dartmouth press, 1853.
136 p.   23 cm.
"Lines by Charlotte Cushman, suggested by a visit
to the Shaker settlement, near Albany, N. Y.":
p. [5]-6; "Answer to lines by Charlotte Cushman
[by a Shaker girl]": p. [7]-8.

12014 Ellet, Charles, 1810-1862.
The Army of the Potomac, and its mismanagement;
respectfully addressed to Congress. By Charles

Ellet, jr. ... New York, Ross & Tousey, 1862.
16 p.   23 1/2 cm.

12015 Ellet, Charles, 1810-1862.
... Contributions to the physical geography of
the United States. Part I. Of the physical geography of the Mississippi valley, with suggestions
for the improvement of the navigation of the Ohio
and other rivers. By Charles Ellet, jr. ...
[Washington, Smithsonian institution, 1850]
64 p.   diagrs. (1 fold.)   31 1/2 cm.
(Smithsonian contributions to knowledge, vol. II,
art. 4)
No more published.
Smithsonian institution publication 13.

12016 Ellet, Charles, 1810-1862.
An essay on the laws of trade, in reference to
the works of internal improvement in the United
States. By Charles Ellet, jr. ... Richmond,
P. D. Bernard, 1839.
viii, [9]-284 p.   fold. pl.   20 1/2 cm.

12017 Ellet, Charles, 1810-1862.
Military incapacity, and what it costs the
country. By Charles Ellet, jr. ... New York, Ross
& Tousey; Philadelphia, J. R. Callender, 1862.
15 p.   22 cm.
A criticism of General McClellan.

12018 Ellet, Charles, 1810-1862.
The Mississippi and Ohio rivers: containing
plans for the protection of the delta from inunda-
tion; and investigations of the practicability and
cost of improving the navigation of the Ohio and
other rivers by means of reservoirs, with an appendix, on the bars at the mouths of the Mississippi.
By Charles Ellet, jr. ... Philadelphia, Lippincott,
Grambo, and co., 1853.
viii, [17]-367 p.   12 pl. (2 fold.) tables.
25 cm.   (Half-title: Inundations of the delta of
the Mississippi)

12019 [Ellet, Charles] 1810-1862.
The Wheeling bridge. [Philadelphia, 1852]
6 p.   25 1/2 cm.

12020   Ellet, Mrs. Elizabeth Fries (Lummis) 1818-1877.
        The court circles of the republic; or, The beauties
        and celebrities of the nation; illustrating life
        and society under eighteen presidents; describing
        the social features of the successive administrations
        from Washington to Grant... By Mrs. E. F. Ellet...
        with sketches by Mrs. R. E. Mack. Hartford, Conn.,
        Hartford publishing co.; New York, J. D. Denison
        [etc., etc.] 1869.
        2 p.l., [iii]-xiv, [15]-586 p. incl. ports.
        front.   22 1/2 cm.

12021   Ellet, Mrs. Elizabeth Fries (Lummis) 1818-1877.
        Pioneer women of the West. By Mrs. Ellet...
        New York, C. Scribner, 1852.
        xi, [13]-434 p.   front.   18 1/2 cm.

12022   Ellet, Mrs. Elizabeth Fries (Lummis) 1818-1877.
        The queens of American society. By Mrs. Ellet...
        New York, C. Scribner & company, 1867.
        1 p.l., ii, [3]-464 p.   front., ports.
        20 1/2 cm.

12023   Ellet, Mrs. Elizabeth Fries (Lummis) 1818-1877.
        The women of the American revolution. By Elizabeth
        F. Ellet... 2d ed. New York, Baker and Scribner,
        1848-50.
        3 v.   fronts. (v. 1-2) ports.   19 cm.
        Vol. 3: 1st edition.

12024   Ellicott, Andrew, 1754-1820.
        The journal of Andrew Ellicott, late commissioner
        on behalf of the United States during part of the
        year 1796, the years 1797, 1798, 1799, and part of
        the year 1800: for determining the boundary between
        the United States and possessions of His Catholic
        Majesty in America, containing occasional remarks
        on the situation, soil, rivers, natural productions,
        and diseases of the different countries on the Ohio,
        Mississippi, and gulf of Mexico, with six maps com-
        prehending the Ohio, the Mississippi from the mouth
        of the Ohio to the gulf of Mexico, the whole of West
        Florida, and a part of East Florida. To which is
        added an appendix, containing all the astronomical
        observations made use of for determining the boundary
        ... likewise a great number of thermometrical ob-
        servations... Philadelphia, Printed by William Fry,

155

1814.
   vii, 299, 151 p.   illus. (diagr.) 8 fold. pl.,
6 fold. maps.   28 x 22 cm.

12025 Ellington, George, pseud.
    The women of New York; or, The under-world of
the great city. Illustrating the life of women of
fashion, women of pleasure, actresses and ballet
girls... etc. By George Ellington... New York,
The New York book company, 1869.
    650 p. incl. front.   plates.   22 1/2 cm.

12026 Elliot, Jonathan, 1784-1846, comp.
    The American diplomatic code embracing a collection
of treaties and conventions between the United
States and foreign powers: from 1778 to 1834.
With an abstract of important judicial decisions,
on points connected with our foreign relations.
Also, A concise diplomatic manual, containing a
summary of the law of nations, from the works of
Wicquefort, Martens, Kent, Vattel, Ward, Story,
&c. &c. ... by Jonathan Elliot... Washington,
Printed by J. Elliot, jun., 1834.
    2 v.   23 1/2 cm.

12027 Elliot, Jonathan, 1784-1846, comp.
    Diplomatic code of the United States of America:
embracing a collection of treaties and conventions
between the United States and foreign powers, from
the year 1778 to 1827. With an index to the principal
cases decided in the courts of the United States,
upon points connected with their foreign relations;
and various official acts, papers, and useful information, for public ministers and consuls. To which
is annexed, extracts from treaties and conventions,
at present subsisting between Great Britain, France,
Spain, &c. chiefly intended to elucidate the policy
pursued towards America, about the period of the
late general pacification in Europe. By Jonathan
Elliot. Washington, Printed by J. Elliot, junior,
1827.
    3 p.l., [xxi]-xxv, [27]-668 p.   24 1/2 cm.

12028 Elliot, Jonathan, 1784-1846.
    Historical sketches of the ten miles square forming
the District of Columbia; with a picture of Washington,
describing objects of general interest or curiosity

at the metropolis of the Union: also, a description
of the river Potomac - its fish and wild fowl; the
proposed route and plan of the Chesapeake and Ohio
canal, from Georgetown to Pittsburgh; and an account
of Mount Vernon. Together with public documents
and statistical facts, touching the affairs of the
District. By Jonathan Elliot. Washington, Printed
by J. Elliot, jr., 1830.
    554 p.   front.   14 1/2 cm.

12029 Elliot, Samuel, 1777-1845.
    A humble tribute to my country: or, Practical
essays, political, legal, moral, and miscellaneous,
including a brief account of the life, sufferings,
and memorable visit of General Lafayette... By
Samuel Elliot. Boston, Otis, Broaders and company,
1842.
    viii, [9]-240, v p.   15 1/2 cm.

12030 Elliot, Samuel Hayes, 1809-1869.
    The attractions of New Haven, Connecticut; a guide
to the city... By S. H. Elliot... New York, N.
Tibbals & co., 1869.
    2 p.l., 141 p.   double front., plates, fold. map.
15 1/2 cm.

12031 [Elliot, Sir Thomas Frederick] 1808-1880.
    The Canadian controversy; its origin, nature, and
merits... London, Printed for Longman, Orme, Brown,
Green & Longmans, 1838.
    2 p.l., 84 p.   23 1/2 cm.
    Published anonymously.

12032 Elliot, William.
    The patentee's manual: containing a list of
patents granted by the United States for the encouragement of arts & sciences, alphabetically arranged,
from 1790 to 1830. [To be continued by supplements]
Also, the laws of Congress for granting patents;
with a digest of all the decisions which have taken
place in the courts of the United States respecting
patents. Washington, Printed by S. A. Elliot, 1830.
    xviii, 3-118, [137]-153 p.   22 1/2 cm.

12033 Elliot, William.
    The Washington guide... By William Elliot.
Washington city, F. Taylor, 1837.

1 p.l., [v]-xii, 310 p.   front., fold. map,
plans.   15 1/2 cm.
List of Officers of Congress (1 leaf inserted
between p. 56 and 57)

12034   Elliott, Benjamin, 1786-1836.
An oration, delivered in St. Philip's church,
before the inhabitants of Charleston, South Carolina;
on Friday, the fourth of July, 1817.   In commemoration of American independence; by appointment of
the '76 association, and published at the request
of that society.   By Benjamin Elliot, esq. ...
Charleston, Printed by W. P. Young, 1817.
23 p.   22 cm.   [Seventy-six association,
Charleston, S. C.   Orations and addresses.   1817]

12035   Elliott, Charles, 1792-1869.
History of the great secession from the Methodist
Episcopal church in the year 1845, eventuating in
the organization of the new church, entitled the
"Methodist Episcopal church, South."   By Rev.
Charles Elliott, D. D.   Cincinnati, Pub. by Sworm-
stedt & Poe, for the Methodist Episcopal church,
1855.
xxix p., 1 l., 1144 col.   24 1/2 cm.

12036   Elliott, Charles, 1792-1869.
The life of the Rev. Robert R. Roberts, one of
the bishops of the Methodist Episcopal church.   By
Rev. Charles Elliott, D. D.   New York, Published
by G. Lane & C. B. Tippett, for the Methodist
Episcopal church, 1844.
407, [1] p. incl. 1 illus., plates, facsims.
front. (port.)   18 1/2 cm.

12037   Elliott, Charles Wyllys, 1817-1883.
Mysteries; or, Glimpses of the supernatural, containing accounts of the Salem witchcraft, the Cock-
lane ghost, the Rochester rappings, the Stratford
mysteries, oracles, astrology, dreams, demons,
ghosts, spectres, &c. &c.   By Charles Wyllys
Elliott.   New York, Harper & brothers, 1852.
vi, [7]-273 p.   19 cm.

12038   Elliott, Franklin Reuben, 1817-1878.
Elliott's fruit book; or, The American fruit-
grower's guide in orchard and garden.   Being a compend

158

of the history, modes of propagation, culture,
&c., of fruit trees and shrubs, with descriptions
of nearly all the varieties of fruits cultivated
in this country; notes of their adaptation to localities and soils, and also a complete list of fruits
worthy of cultivation. By F. R. Elliott. New York,
C. M. Saxton, 1854.
ix, [11]-503, [2] p.   illus.   20 cm.
Subsequently issued under title: The western fruit
book...
"Abbreviations and books quoted": p. [11]-14.

12039 Elliott, Jesse Duncan, 1782-1845.
Speech of Com. Jesse Duncan Elliott, U. S. N.
delivered in Hagerstown, Md. on 14th November, 1843.
Published by the Committee of arrangement of Washington county, Maryland. Philadelphia, G. B. Zieber &
co., 1844.
2 p.l., 55, 82 p.   illus., fold. plan, fold.
diagrs.   23 cm.

12040 Elliott, John, 1768-1824.
The gracious presence of God, the highest felicity
and security of any people. A sermon, preached
before His Excellency the governor, and the honorable
legislature of the state of Connecticut, convened
at Hartford, on the anniversary election, May 10th,
1810. By John Elliott, A. M., pastor of a church
in Guilford. Hartford, Printed by Hudson and Goodwin, 1810.
52 p.   23 cm.

12041 Elliott, Stephen, 1771-1830.
A sketch of the botany of South Carolina and
Georgia... By Stephen Elliott. Charleston, S. C.,
J. R. Schenck, 1821-24.
2 v.   XII pl.   22 1/2 cm.

12042 Elliott, Stephen, bp., 1806-1866.
God's presence with our army at Manassas. A
sermon, preached in Christ church, Savannah, on
Sunday, July 28th, being the day recommended by the
Congress of the Confederate States, to be observed
as a day of thanksgiving, in commemoration of the
victory at Manassas Junction, on Sunday the 21st
of July, 1861. By the Rt. Rev. Stephen Elliott...

Savannah, W. T. Williams, 1861.
iv, 22 p., 1 1.   22 cm.

12043   Elliott, Stephen, bp., 1806-1866.
A high civilization the moral duty of Georgians.
A discourse delivered before the Georgia historical
society, on the occasion of its fifth anniversary,
on Monday, 12th February, 1844. By the Rt. Rev.
Stephen Elliott, jr. Savannah, The Society, 1844.
21 p.   24 1/2 cm.

12044   Elliott, Stephen, bp., 1806-1866.
"New wine not to be put into old bottles." A
sermon preached in Christ church, Savannah, on
Friday, February 28th, 1862, being the day of
humiliation, fasting, and prayer, appointed by the
President of the Confederate States. By the Rt.
Rev. Stephen Elliott... Savannah, Press of J. M.
Cooper & co., 1862.
18 p.   23 cm.

12045   Elliott, Stephen, bp., 1806-1866.
A reply to a resolution of the Georgia historical
society, read before the Society at its anniversary
meeting, February 12th, 1866, by Rt. Rev. Stephen
Elliott, president of the Society. Published at the
request of the Society. Savannah, Ga., Purse and
son, printers, 1866.
13 p.   21 cm.

12046   Elliott, Stephen, bp., 1806-1866.
Sermons by the Right Reverend Stephen Elliott...
with a memoir by Thomas M. Hanckel, esq. New York,
Pott and Amery, 1867.
xxxv, 594 p.   front. (mounted port.)   23 cm.

12047   Elliott, Stephen, bp., 1806-1866.
The silver trumpets of the sanctuary. A sermon
preached to the Pulaski Guards in Christ church,
Savannah, on the second Sunday after Trinity.
Being the Sunday before their departure to join the
army in Virginia, by the Rt. Rev. Stephen Elliott,
D. D. ... Published by request. Savannah, Press
of John M. Cooper & company, 1861.
12 p.   20 1/2 cm.

12048 Elliott, William, 1788-1863.
       Carolina sports by land and water; including
incidents of devil-fishing, wild-cat, deer and bear
hunting, etc., by the Hon. Wm. Elliott... New York,
Derby & Jackson, 1859.
       v p., 2 l., 11-292 p. incl. front.   5 pl.
18 1/2 cm.
       "Several of the sketches... have already been
published under the signatures of 'Piscator' and
'Venator'." - Pref.

12049 Elliott society of natural history, Charleston, S. C.
       Proceedings of the Elliott society of natural
history of Charleston, South Carolina. v. 1-2;
Nov. 1853-Nov. 1890. Charleston, Russell & Jones
[etc., etc.] 1859-[91]
       2 v. in 1.   illus., plates.   23 1/2 cm.
       In November 1867 the name of the society was
changed to Elliott society of science and art (cf.
Proceed., v. 2, p. 54) and this name is used in
the caption of v. 2.
       No more published.
       With this is bound: Instance of incomplete longi-
tudinal fission in Actinia cavernosa Bosc. By John
M'Grady. Read before the Elliott society of natural
history of Charleston, S. C., February 15th, 1859
(4 p.)

12050 Ellis, Ferdinand, 1780-1858.
       Civil government an ordinance of God. A sermon,
delivered at Concord, before His Excellency the
Governor, the honorable Council, and both branches
of the legislature of the state of New Hampshire,
June 8, 1826. By Ferdinand Ellis, A. M., pastor of
the Baptist church in Exeter. Concord, Printed by
Jacob B. Moore, for the state, 1826.
       26 p.   23 cm.
Printed by order of the New Hampshire General court.

12051 Ellis, G   A
       New Britain. A narrative of a journey, by Mr.
Ellis, to a country so called by its inhabitants,
discovered in the vast plain of the Missouri, in
North America, and inhabited by a people of British
origin... London, W. Simpkin and R. Marshall, 1820.
       vii, [1], 336 p.   22 cm.

"A work of fiction, descriptive of an Utopian
state of society." - O. Rich, Bibliotheca americana
nova, London, 1846.

12052 Ellis, George Edward, 1814-1894.
        I. The aims and purposes of the founders of Massa-
chusetts. II. Their treatment of intruders and
dissentients. Two lectures of a course by members
of the Massachusetts historical society, delivered
before the Lowell institute on Jan. 8 and Jan. 12,
1869. By George E. Ellis. Boston, Press of J.
Wilson and son, 1869.
        100 p.   24 1/2 cm.

12053 Ellis, George Edward, 1814-1894.
        A half-century of the Unitarian controversy, with
particular reference to its origin, its course, and
its prominent subjects among the Congregationalists
of Massachusetts. With an appendix. By George E.
Ellis. Boston, Crosby, Nichols, and company, 1857.
        xxiv, 511 p.   22 1/2 cm.

12054 Ellis, George Edward, 1814-1894.
        Memoir of Luther V. Bell, M. D., LL. D. Prepared
by vote of the Massachusetts historical society.
By George E. Ellis... Boston, Printed by J. Wilson
and son, 1863.
        75 p.   front. (port.)   26 1/2 cm.
        "Reprinted from the 'Proceedings'."

12055 Ellis, George Edward, 1814-1894.
        An oration delivered at Charlestown, Massachusetts,
on the 17th of June, 1841, in commemoration of the
battle of Bunker-Hill. By George E. Ellis. Boston,
W. Crosby & co., 1841.
        72 p.   map.   22 cm.

12056 Ellis, George Edward, 1814-1894.
        "The preservation of the States united:" a discourse
delivered in Harvard church, Charlestown, on Thanksgiving day, Nov. 29, 1860. By George E. Ellis.
Charlestown [Mass.] A. E. Cutter, 1860.
        29 p.   23 cm.

12057 Ellis, George W
        A poem on the awful catastrophe on board the U. S.
steam frigate Princeton. By George W. Ellis, M. D.

Together with a full description of the terrible
calamity, the proceedings at Washington, and the
funeral obsequies. Boston, Printed by A. J.
Wright, 1844.
72 p.   1 illus.   15 1/2 cm.

12058   Ellis, Henry, 1721-1806.
A voyage to Hudson's Bay, by the Dobbs galley
and California, in the years 1746 and 1747, for
discovering a North west passage; with an accurate
survey of the coast, and a short natural history of
the country. Together with a fair view of the facts
and arguments from which the future finding of such
a passage is rendered probable. By Henry Ellis...
To which is prefixed, an historical account of the
attempts hitherto made for the finding that way to
the East-Indies... London, Printed for H. Whit-
ridge, 1748.
xxxvii, 336 p.   front. (fold. map) plates (part
fold.)   23 cm.

12059   Ellis, John B
The sights and secrets of the national capital:
a work descriptive of Washington city in all its
various phases, by Dr. John B. Ellis. New York,
United States publishing company, 1869.
xix, [21]-512 p.   front., plates (part double)
23 cm.

12060   Ellis, Rufus, 1819-1885.
The last sermon preached in First church, Chauncy
street, May 10, 1868; being the Lord's day previous
to the removal of the congregation to the chapel of
their fifth house of worship, on the corner of
Berkeley and Marlborough streets. By Rufus Ellis,
pastor... with an appendix... Boston, Press of J.
Wilson and son, 1868.
32 p.   front., pl.   22 1/2 cm.

12061   Elton, Romeo, 1790-1870.
Life of Roger Williams, the earliest legislator
and true champion for a full and absolute liberty
of conscience. By Romeo Elton... London, A. Cock-
shaw [c1852]
viii, 173, [1] p.   16 1/2 cm.

163

12062   Engels, L
          Nordamerika - Ohio. Reise nach Nordamerika.
        Beobachtungen und erfahrungen in Ohio 1848 und 1849.
        Für meine deutschen brüder, von L. Engels...
        Elberfeld, J. Bädeker, 1850.
          3 p.l., [3]-108 p.   18 cm.

12063   English, Henry, 1803-1855.
          A general guide to the companies formed for
        working foreign mines, with their prospectuses,
        amount of capital, number of shares, names of
        directors, &c., and an appendix, showing their pro-
        gress since their formation... with a table of the
        extent of their fluctuations in price, up to the
        present period. By Henry English... London, Boosey
        & sons, 1825.
          2 p.l., 106, [2] p.   22 cm.
          A second pt. was published in 1826, with title:
        A compendium of useful information relating to the
        companies formed for working British mines... A
        third pt. was published in 1827, with title: A
        complete view of the joint stock companies formed
        during the years 1824 and 1825... cf. Brit. mus.
        catalogue.
          "Both of these parts are included in this edition."

12064   English, William Hayden, 1822-1896.
          Speech of Hon. W. H. English, of Indiana, on the
        Smithsonian institution, in the House of represent-
        atives, February 27, 1855. [Washington, Printed at
        the Congressional globe office, 1855]
          7 p.   23 1/2 cm.

12065   The English practice: a statement, showing some of
        the evils and absurdities of the practice of the
        English common law, as adopted in several of the
        United States, and particularly in the state of
        New York... By a lover of improvement. New York,
        Printed by J. Seymour, 1822.
          71 p.   21 cm.

12066   An enquiry into the chymical character and properties
        of that species of coal, lately discovered at Rhode
        Island: together with observations on the useful
        application of it to the arts and manufactures of
        the eastern states. Boston, Printed by Snelling and

Simons, Devonshire street, 1808.
　　21 p.　　18 cm.

12067　An entertaining account of all the countries of the
　　　　known world: describing the different religions,
　　　　habits, tempers, customs, traffick, and manufactures,
　　　　of their inhabitants... London, Printed for R.
　　　　Goadby, and sold by W. Owen, 1752.
　　　　　266, [8] p.　　plates (part fold.)　　20 cm.
　　　　　Contents. - The discovery of the West Indies
　　　　[called the New world] by Christopher Columbus. -
　　　　An account of the island Formosa, by George Candi-
　　　　dius. - The travels of His Excellency E. Ysbrants
　　　　Ides. - The voyage of Ferdinand Maglianes, or
　　　　Magellan, from the South seas to the East Indies. -
　　　　The journal of Sir Thomas Roe, ambassador from His
　　　　Majesty King James the First of England, to Ichan
　　　　Guire, the mighty emperor of India. - Index.

12068　Epaminondas, pseud.
　　　　　Epaminondas: originally published in numbers,
　　　　in the New-York gazette... New-York, Printed for
　　　　John Lang, by G. F. Hopkins, 1801.
　　　　　17 p.　　20 cm.
　　　　　Signed: Epaminondas; addressed: To the Federal
　　　　members of the House of representatives of the
　　　　United States. Urges Federalist support of Burr
　　　　for president.
　　　　　Sometimes attributed to Augustus Brevoort Woodward,
　　　　who used the pseudonym Epaminondas on occasion.
　　　　Internal evidence against his authorship is convincing.

12069　An epistle from a young lady to an ensign in the Guards,
　　　　upon his being ordered to America... London, Printed
　　　　for J. Sewell, in Cornhill; Whieldon and Waller, and
　　　　R. Faulder, 1779.
　　　　　17 p.　　27 cm.
　　　　　In verse.

12070　An epistle from Edward, an American prisoner in England,
　　　　to Harriet, in America... London, Printed for
　　　　Fielding and Walker, and sold by Mr. Breadewer
　　　　and Mr. Maurice, 1779.
　　　　　1 p.l., 9 p.　　26 1/2 x 21 1/2 cm.
　　　　　In verse.

12071 Epitaphs and elegies... New York, Printed by S.
Wood & sons, 1816.
iv, [5]-72 p.   illus.   14 1/2 cm.

12072 Erasmus, Desiderius, d. 1536.
The plea of reason, religion and humanity, against
war. By Erasmus... New York, Collins & co., 1813.
viii, [9]-48 p.   20 1/2 cm.
"Extracted from a work, written by Erasmus, entitled Antipolemus, or The plea of reason, religion
and humanity, against war; translated and published
in London 1794." - Advertisement.

12073 Ermatinger, Edward, 1797-1876.
The Hudson's Bay territories; a series of letters
on this important question. By Edward Ermatinger.
Toronto, Maclear, Thomas & co., printers, 1858.
32 p.   24 1/2 cm.

12074 Ermatinger, Edward, 1797-1876.
Life of Colonel Talbot, and the Talbot settlement,
its rise and progress, with sketches of the public
characters, and career of some of the most conspicuous men in Upper Canada... By Edward Ermatinger.
St. Thomas [Ont.] Printed at A. McLachlin's Home
journal office, 1859.
iv, [2], 230 p.   17 1/2 cm.

12075 Erni, Henry.
Coal oil and petroleum: their origin, history,
geology, and chemistry... By Henry Erni... Philadelphia, H. C. Baird, 1865.
viii, [13]-196 p.   illus.   19 1/2 cm.
"The main portions of the present treatise...
were written for and published by the Sunday morning
chronicle [Washington, D. C.]" - Pref.

12076 An essay for discharging the debts of the nation,
by equivalents: in a letter to the Right Hon.
Charles, earl of Sunderland. And the South-Sea
scheme consider'd; in a letter to the Right Hon.
Robert Walpole, esq; ... London, Printed for
J. Noon [etc.] 1720.
1 p.l., vii, [2], 50 p., 1 l., iv, [57]-98 p.
20 cm.

12077　Essay on political society... Whitehall: Printed by
　　　　W. Young, Philadelphia, 1800.
　　　　　　3 p.l., [9]-234 p.　　23 cm.
　　　　　　Contents. - Of general politics. - Of the polity
　　　　of the American states. - Of forms of government.

12078　An essay on sugar, proving it the most pleasant, salu-
　　　　brious, and useful vegetable to mankind; especially
　　　　as refin'd and brought to its present perfection in
　　　　England.　With remarks on a method lately published
　　　　of procuring a fermentation in the West-Indies.
　　　　London, Printed for E. Comyns, 1752.
　　　　　　3 p.l., 33 p.　　19 1/2 cm.

12079　An essay on the trade of the northern colonies of
　　　　Great Britain in North America.　Printed at Phila-
　　　　delphia.　London, Reprinted for T. Becket & P. A.
　　　　De Hondt, 1764.
　　　　　　2 p.l., 38 p.　　21 cm.

12080　Essay on the warehousing system and government credits
　　　　of the United States.　Philadelphia, Printed by
　　　　order of the Philadelphia Chamber of commerce, W.
　　　　Brown, printer, 1828.
　　　　　　57 p.　　21 1/2 cm.
　　　　　　"The following essays originally appeared in the
　　　　editorial columns of the Aurora and Pennsylvania
　　　　gazette, and are now republished in a connected
　　　　form." - p. [5]

12081　Essex institute, Salem, Mass.
　　　　　　Act of incorporation, constitution and by-laws
　　　　of the Essex institute, incorporated February, 1848.
　　　　With a catalogue of the officers and members.
　　　　Salem, W. Ives and G. W. Pease, printers, 1855.
　　　　　　24 p.　　24 cm.

12082　Estancelin, L[ouis] 1777-1858.
　　　　　　Recherches sur les voyages and découvertes des
　　　　navigateurs normands en Afrique, dans les Indes
　　　　Orientales et en Amérique... Par L. Estancelin...
　　　　Paris, Delaunay [etc.] 1832.
　　　　　　2 p.l., xii, 361, [1] p., 1 l.　　21 1/2 cm.

12083　Estaugh, John, 1676-1742.
　　　　　　A call to the unfaithful professors of truth.
　　　　Written by John Estaugh in his life-time; and now

published for general service. To which is added
divers epistles of the same author. Philadelphia,
Printed by B. Franklin, 1744.
xviii, [19]-119 p.   14 cm.

12084 Este, David Kirkpatrick, 1785-1875.
Discourse on the life and public services of the
late Jacob Burnet, delivered at Smith and Nixon's
hall, by D. K. Este, on the evening of the 21st of
June, 1853. Cincinnati, Press of the Cincinnati
gazette co., 1853.
25 p.   23 cm.

12085 Estee, Charles Frederick, comp.
The excise tax law. Approved July 1, 1862; and
all the amendments, together with the instructions
and blank forms, decisions, and regulations of the
commissioner... and a minute analytical index.
Also, the January statement of the commissioner of
internal revenue to the secretary of the Treasury.
Comp. by Charles F. Estee... New York, Fitch, Estee
& co., 1863.
vi, [7]-355 p. incl. tables, forms.   24 cm.

12086 European delineation of American character, as contained in a letter from a foreign traveller in New
York, to his friend in London... New York, Printed
for the booksellers, J. Gray & co., printers, 1820.
16 p.   21 1/2 cm.
"From No. 2 of the Literary and scientific repository [pp. 516-529]" - t.-p.
Originally published under title: Letter from a
foreigner in New York. 1820.

12087 The European traveller in America. Contained in three
letters to his friend in London... Hartford, Printed
by Hudson & Goodwin, 1785.
40 p.   20 1/2 cm.   ·
"In a copy I sold in 1859, several of these letters
had the autograph signature of Jo. Young; but in
Mr. Brown's catalogue they are ascribed to the Rev.
Mr. Brockway of Lebanon, Connecticut." - Sabin,
Bibl. amer.

12088 Eustace, John Skey, 1760-1805.
Official and private correspondence of Major-
General J. S. Eustace, citizen of the state of New

168

York; aide-de-camp to General Lee and General
Sullivan; colonel and adjutant-general in the service
of Georgia, during the American war: and maréchal-
de-camp in the armies of the Republic of France.
Part I... Paris, Printed by Adlard and son, 1796.
   1 p.l., vi, 151 p.   21 cm.
   No more published?
   Includes letters written and received by Eustace.
   Contents. - Dedication and preface. - Project of
a tobacco contract. - Project to emancipate the provinces of Caracas and Cumana. - Notes on the project
for emancipating Caracas and Cumana. - Private
letters respecting my visit to the court of Spain. -
Letter from a paternal friend [Edward Church] -
Certificate of my services in the armies of the
United States. - Documents of service in France in
the general-staff of the army.

12089 Evans, Caleb, 1737-1791.
   Political sophistry detected, or Brief remarks
on the Rev. Mr. Fletcher's late tract, entitled
"American patriotism". In a letter to a friend.
By Caleb Evans... Bristol [Eng.] Printed and sold
by W. Pine, 1776.
   36 p.   19 1/2 cm.

12090 Evans, Estwick, 1787-1866.
   Essay on state rights. (The first of a series)
The object of which is to define and illustrate the
spirit of our institutions and of liberty, and to
renovate our political elements. By Estwick Evans,
of the North. Washington City, Printed by W. Greer,
1844.
   40 p.   24 cm.
   No more published?

12091 Evans, Estwick, 1787-1866.
   Mr. Evans for the presidency. [Washington, 1864]
   4 p.   24 cm.

12092 Evans, Francis A
   The emigrant's directory and guide to obtain lands
and effect a settlement in the Canadas. By Francis
A. Evans... Dublin, W. Curry, jr. and co. [etc.,
etc.] 1833.
   vi, iv, [2], 180 p.   20 cm.

12093　Evans, Frederick William, 1808-1893.
　　　　　Autobiography of a Shaker, and Revelation of the
　　　　Apocalypse. With an appendix... Mt. Lebanon,
　　　　N. Y., F. W. Evans, 1869.
　　　　　162 p.　　21 cm.

12094　Evans, Frederick William, 1808-1893.
　　　　　Shakers. Compendium of the origin, history,
　　　　principles, rules and regulations, government, and
　　　　doctrines of the United society of believers in
　　　　Christ's second appearing. With biographies of
　　　　Ann Lee, William Lee, Jas. Whittaker, J. Hocknell,
　　　　J. Meacham, and Lucy Wright. By F. W. Evans...
　　　　New York, D. Appleton and company, 1859.
　　　　　x, [11]-189 p.　　18 cm.

12095　[Evans, Sir George De Lacy] 1787-1870.
　　　　　Facts relating to the capture of Washington, in
　　　　reply to some statements contained in the memoirs
　　　　of Admiral Sir George Cockburn, G. C. B. By the
　　　　officer serving as quartermaster general with the
　　　　forces engaged. London, H. Colburn, 1829.
　　　　　1 p.l., 20 p.　　23 cm.

12096　Evans, Israel, 1747-1807.
　　　　　A discourse, delivered at Easton, on the 17th of
　　　　October, 1779, to the officers and soldiers of the
　　　　western army, after their return from an expedition
　　　　against the Five nations of hostile Indians. By the
　　　　Rev. Israel Evans, A. M., and chaplain to General
　　　　Poor's brigade. Now published at the particular
　　　　request of the generals and field officers of the
　　　　army; and to be distributed among the soldiers. -
　　　　Gratis. Philadelphia, Printed by Thomas Bradford,
　　　　at the Coffee-house, 1779.
　　　　　40 p.　　20 cm.
　　　　　[Hazard pamphlets, v. 51, no. 3]

12097　Evans, Israel, 1747-1807.
　　　　　A discourse delivered near York in Virginia, on
　　　　the memorable occasion of the surrender of the
　　　　British army to the allied forces of America and
　　　　France, before the brigade of New York troops and
　　　　the division of American light-infantry, under the
　　　　command of the Marquis de la Fayette. By Israel
　　　　Evans, A. M., chaplain to the troops of New Hampshire

... Philadelphia, Printed by Francis Bailey, 1782.
45, [1] p.   18 1/2 cm.

12098 Evans, Lemuel Dale, 1810-1877.
Speech of Hon. Lemuel D. Evans, of Texas, on the
foreign policy of the United States, delivered in
the House of representatives of the United States
on the 24th of July, 1856. Washington, D. C.,
American organ, print., 1856.
32 p.   22 1/2 cm.

12099 Evans, Nathaniel, 1742-1767.
Poems on several occasions, with some other com-
positions. By Nathaniel Evans, A. M., late missionary (appointed by the Society for propagating the
gospel) for Gloucester county, in New Jersey; and
chaplain to the Lord Viscount Kilmorey, of the kingdom of Ireland. Philadelphia, Printed by John
Dunlap, in Market-street, 1772.
xxviii, 160, 24 p., 1 l.   21 cm.
The preface, signed William Smith, contains brief
biographical sketch of the author.

12100 Evans, Oliver, 1755-1819.
The young mill-wright & miller's guide. In five
parts - embellished with twenty-five plates... By
Oliver Evans, of Philadelphia. Philadelphia, The
author, 1795.
4 p.l., 160, ii, [3]-178, x, [11]-90, 10, [12] p.
26 pl. (2 fold.) tables.   21 cm.
Part 5 by Thomas Ellicott.

12101 Evans, Thomas Wiltberger, 1823-1897.
Lettres d'un oncle à son neveu sur le gouvernement
des États-Unis. Pouvoir législatif. Pouvoir exécu-
tive. Pouvoir judicaire des états. Constitution
des États-Unis. Par le Dr. Thomas W. Evans. Paris,
E. Dentu, 1866.
3 p.l., [3]-73 p.   25 cm.

12102 Evans, William Jones, M. R. C. S.
A clinical treatise on the endemic fevers of the
West Indies, intended as a guide for the young
practitioner in those countries. By W. J. Evans...
London, J. Churchill, 1837.
viii, 309 p.   22 1/2 cm.

171

12103   Evans, William Julian.
            The sugar-planter's manual. Being a treatise
        on the art of obtaining sugar from the sugar cane.
        By W. J. Evans, M. D.   Philadelphia, Lea and Blan-
        chard, 1848.
            2 p.l., [5]-264 p.   illus., 2 fold. pl., diagrs.
        20 1/2 cm.

12104   [Evarts, Jeremiah] 1781-1831.
            Essays on the present crisis in the condition of
        the American Indians; first published in the National
        intelligencer, under the signature of William Penn
        [pseud.]   Boston, Perkins & Marvin, 1829.
            112 p.   23 cm.

12105   [Everett, Alexander Hill] 1790-1847.
            America: or, A general survey of the political
        situation of the several powers of the western con-
        tinent, with conjectures on their future prospects...
        By a citizen of the United States...   Philadelphia,
        H. C. Carey and I. Lea, 1827.
            2 p.l., [9]-364 p.   22 cm.

12106   [Everett, Alexander Hill] 1790-1847.
            The conduct of the administration...   Boston,
        Stimpson & Clapp, 1832.
            86 p.   24 cm.
            Reprinted from the Boston daily advertiser and
        patriot.

12107   Everett, Alexander Hill, 1790-1847.
            A defence of the character and principles of
        Mr. Jefferson; being an address delivered at Wey-
        mouth, Mass., at the request of the anti-Masonic
        and Democratic citizens of that place, on the 4th
        of July, 1836. By Alexander H. Everett. Boston,
        Beals and Greene, 1836.
            iv, [5]-76 p.   22 1/2 cm.

12108   [Everett, Alexander Hill] 1790-1847.
            Europe: or, A general survey of the present
        situation of the principal powers; with conjectures
        on their future prospects. By a citizen of the
        United States. Boston, O. Everett [etc.] 1822.
            3 p.l., [5]-451 p.   22 1/2 cm.

12109　[Everett, Alexander Hill] 1792-1847.
　　　　　Remarks on the governor's speech. By an American.
　　　　Boston, Printed at the Patriot office, 1814.
　　　　　xii, [13]-76 p.　24 cm.

12110　Everett, Edward, 1794-1865.
　　　　　An address delivered at Bloody Brook, in South
　　　　Deerfield, September 30, 1835, in commemoration of
　　　　the fall of the "Flower of Essex," at that spot,
　　　　in King Philip's war, September 18, (o. s.) 1675.
　　　　By Edward Everett... Boston, Russell, Shattuck, &
　　　　Williams, 1835.
　　　　　44 p.　24 1/2 cm.

12111　Everett, Edward, 1794-1865.
　　　　　The claims of citizens of the United States of
　　　　America on the governments of Naples, Holland, and
　　　　France. By Edward Everett. Cambridge, Printed by
　　　　Hilliard and Metcalf, 1826.
　　　　　152 p.　21 1/2 cm.
　　　　Reissue, with modifications, of two articles
　　　　published in the North American review for October
　　　　1825 and October 1826.　cf. Note.

12112　Everett, Edward, 1794-1865.
　　　　　The discovery and colonization of America, and
　　　　immigration to the United States. A lecture deli-
　　　　vered before the New York historical society, in
　　　　Metropolitan hall, on the 1st of June, 1853.　By
　　　　Edward Everett. Boston, Little, Brown, and company,
　　　　1853.
　　　　　32 p.　22 1/2 cm.

12113　Everett, Edward, 1794-1865.
　　　　　Eulogy on Lafayette, delivered in Faneuil hall,
　　　　at the request of the young men of Boston, September
　　　　6, 1834.　By Edward Everett. Boston, N. Hale; and
　　　　Allen & Ticknor, 1834.
　　　　　104 p.　23 cm.

12114　Everett, Edward, 1794-1865.
　　　　　Eulogy on Thomas Dowse, of Cambridgeport, pro-
　　　　nounced before the Massachusetts historical society,
　　　　9th December, 1858.　By Edward Everett. With the
　　　　introductory address by Robert C. Winthrop, president
　　　　of the society; and an appendix. Boston, Printed by

J. Wilson and son, 1859.
　　82 p.　　front., pl., port.　　24 cm.

12115　Everett, Edward, 1794-1865.
　　　... The Monroe doctrine. Paper by Edward
　　Everett. Letter of John Quincy Adams. Extract
　　from speech of Geo. Canning... New York, W. C.
　　Bryant & co., printers, 1863.
　　　cover-title, 17 p.　　21 1/2 cm.　　(Loyal public-
　　ation society. [Pamphlets] no. 34)

12116　Everett, Edward, 1794-1865.
　　　The Mount Vernon papers. By Edward Everett.
　　New York [etc.] D. Appleton and company, 1860.
　　　xxi, 490 p., 1 l.　　19 1/2 cm.
　　　These papers were written at the request of Robert
　　Bonner, editor.
　　　Papers contributed to the New York ledger. The
　　author received for the series ten thousand dollars,
　　to aid the Mount Vernon ladies association in the
　　purchase of the home of George Washington.

12117　Everett, Edward, 1794-1865.
　　　An oration delivered on the battlefield of
　　Gettysburg (November 19, 1863) at the consecration
　　of the cemetery... By Edward Everett. To which
　　is added interesting reports of the dedicatory
　　ceremonies; descriptions of the battlefield; inci-
　　dents and details of the battles, &c. New York,
　　Baker & Godwin, printers, 1863.
　　　48 p.　　illus. (plan)　　23 1/2 cm.

12118　Everett, Edward, 1794-1865.
　　　An oration pronounced at Cambridge, before the
　　society of Phi beta kappa. August 26, 1824...
　　By Edward Everett. Boston, O. Everett, 1824.
　　　67 p.　　21 1/2 cm.
　　　No. 4 in a volume of pamphlets with binder's
　　title: Orations and eulogies. [1821-29]

12119　Everett, Edward Franklin, 1840-1899.
　　　Genealogy of the Everett family. By Edward F.
　　Everett... Reprinted from the New England histo-
　　rical and genealogical register, for July, 1860.
　　Boston, H. W. Dutton & son, printers, 1860.
　　　7 p.　　23 cm.

12120 Everett, Horace, 1780-1851.
       Speech of Mr. H. Everett, of Vermont, on the case
       of Alexander McLeod. Delivered in the House of
       representatives of the United States, September 3,
       1841. Washington, Printed at the National intelli-
       gencer office, 1841.
       24 p.   22 1/2 cm.

12121 Evershaw, Mary.
       Five years in Pennsylvania. By Mary Evershaw.
       London, W. Strange, 1840.
       1 p.l., 227 p.   18 1/2 cm.

12122 Ewbank, Thomas, 1792-1870.
       Inorganic forces ordained to supersede human
       slavery. By Thomas Ewbank... [Originally read
       before the American ethnological society] New York,
       W. Everdell & sons, 1860.
       32 p.   22 cm.

12123 Ewell, James, 1773-1832.
       The medical companion, or family physician:
       treating of the diseases of the United States, with
       their symptoms, causes, cure, and means of prevent-
       ion... By James Ewell... 10th ed., rev., enl.,
       and very considerably improved... Philadelphia,
       Pub. by Crissy & Markley, for J. A. Geer, 1848.
       xxvi, [27]-692 p. incl. tab.   front. (port.)
       pl.   23 1/2 cm.
       First published 1807 under title: The planter's
       and mariner's medical companion.

12124 Ewer, John, bp. of Bangor, d. 1774.
       A sermon preached before the incorporated Society
       for the propagation of the gospel in foreign parts;
       at their anniversary meeting in the parish church
       of St. Mary-le-Bow, on Friday, February 20, 1767.
       By the Right Reverend father in God, John lord
       bishop of Landaff. London printed; New-York, Re-
       printed and sold by James Parker, in Beaver-street,
       1768.
       18 p.   19 cm.
       [Hazard pamphlets, v. 14, no. 1]

12125 Ewing, Thomas, 1789-1871.
       Letter of the Hon. Thomas Ewing to his excellency
       Benj. Stanton, lieut. governor of Ohio, in answer to

his charges against our generals who fought the
battle of Shiloh, on the 6th of April, 1862.
Columbus, R. Nevins, printer, 1862.
    cover-title, 24 p.   23 cm.
Letter dated October 4, 1862.

12126   An examination into the conduct of the present adminis-
        tration, from the year 1774 to the year 1778. And a
        plan of accommodation with America. By a member of
        Parliament. London, J. Almon, 1778.
            1 p.l., 69 p.   19 1/2 cm.

12127   An examination into the principles, conduct, and
        designs of the Earl of Shelburne, taken from a late
        speech... London, Printed for J. Stockdale, 1783.
            1 p.l., 61 p.   21 cm.
            Published the same year under title: An examination
        into the principles, conduct and designs of the
        Minister.

12128   An examination into the prospective effects of the
        national banks upon the public welfare. New York,
        Hall, Clayton, & Medole, printers, 1863.
            cover-title, 23 p.   23 1/2 cm.

12129   An examination of a pamphlet, entitled, His Catholic
        Majesty's manifesto, &c., with reasons for not
        paying the 95000 l. London, T. Gardner, 1739.
            1 p.l., ii, 59 p.   18 1/2 cm.

12130   [Examination of the controversy between Georgia and
        the Creeks] First published in the New-York review,
        August, 1825. [New York, 1825?]
            173-195 p.   23 cm.
            A review of several United States and state docu-
        ments relating to the removal of the Creeks from
        Georgia.

12131   An examination of the opinion contained in the Report
        of the Onondaga commissioners, of the seventeenth of
        February, 1800, to His Excellency the governor; and
        by him transmitted to the honourable the Legislature:
        with a view to its refutation. By a western citizen
        ... Albany, Printed for the author [1800?]
            24 p.   19 1/2 cm.

176

12132　An examination of the rights of the colonies, upon
　　　　principles of law.　By a gentleman at the bar...
　　　　London, R. Dymott and J. Almon, 1766.
　　　　　42 p.　　21 cm.

12133　An exhibit of the losses sustained at the office of
　　　　discount and deposit, Baltimore, under the adminis-
　　　　tration of James A. Buchanan, president, and James
　　　　W. McCulloh, cashier; comp. by the president and
　　　　directors of the office at Baltimore, in pursuance
　　　　of an order from the president and directors of the
　　　　Bank of the United States:　to which is appended a
　　　　Report of the conspiracy cases tried at Harford
　　　　county in Maryland.　Baltimore, Printed by T. Murphy,
　　　　1823.
　　　　　28, xix, 280, 116, [2] p.　　3 fold. tab.　　23 cm.
　　　　　Report of the conspiracy cases occupies all after
　　　　p. 28, and has separate t.-p.:　A report of the
　　　　conspiracy cases, lately decided at Belle Air...
　　　　comp. and digested under the direction... of Robert
　　　　Goodloe Harper...　Baltimore, Printed by T. Murphy,
　　　　1823.
　　　　　James A. Buchanan, James W. M'Culloh and George
　　　　Williams are named as traversers.

12134　Exposé des droits des colonies britanniques, pour
　　　　justifier le projet de leur indépendance.　Amsterdam,
　　　　M. M. Rey, 1776.
　　　　　2 p.l., 36, 43 p.　　21 cm.

12135　An Exposé of facts, concerning recent transactions,
　　　　relating to the corps of cadets of the United States'
　　　　Military academy, at West-Point, New-York.　Newburgh,
　　　　N. Y., Printed by Uriah C. Lewis, 1819.
　　　　　vii, 68, 24, [3]-9 p.　　23 1/2 cm.
　　　　　By a committee, consisting of W. M. C. Fairfax,
　　　　T. Ragland, C. R. Vining, N. H. Loring and C. R.
　　　　Holmes, who were elected by the cadets to represent
　　　　to the superintendent of the Military academy the
　　　　treatment which they had received from Captain Bliss.
　　　　　Includes Defence before a general court-martial,
　　　　held at West-Point, in the state of New-York, in the
　　　　month of May, eighteen hundred and nineteen.　By
　　　　Cadet Thomas Ragland.　Newburgh, N. Y., Printed by
　　　　Uriah C. Lewis, 1819 (24 p.) and Memorial to Congress
　　　　[by N. H. Loring and others] ([3]-9 p.)　In this
　　　　edition a list of Errata is added on p. 68.

12136   Fanning, David, 1756?-1825.
        The narrative of Colonel David Fanning (a Tory
in the Revolutionary war with Great Britain):
giving an account of his adventures in North Carolina from 1775 to 1783, as written by himself.
With an introduction and explanatory notes. New
York, Reprinted for Joseph Sabin, 1865.
        xxvi, 86 p.   24 cm.   (Half-title: Sabin's
reprints, 2d ser., no. 1)
        Edited by T. N. Wynne.
        Includes t.-p. of original edition, Richmond,
Va., 1861. The original is no. 1 of Historical
documents relating to the Old North state.

12137   Fanning, Edmund, 1769-1841.
        Voyages to the South seas, Indian and Pacific
oceans, China Sea, North-west coast, Feejee Islands,
South Shetlands, &c. ... with an account of the
new discoveries made in the southern hemisphere,
between the years 1830-1837... By Edmund Fanning.
3d ed. New York, W. H. Vermilye, 1838.
        xii, [13]-324 p.   front.   19 cm.

12138   Farmer, John, 1789-1838.
        A gazetteer of the state of New-Hampshire. By
John Farmer and Jacob B. Moore. Embellished with
an accurate map of the state, and several other
engravings: by Abel Bowen. Concord, J. B. Moore,
1823.
        iv, [5]-276 p.   front. (fold. map) illus.,
plates.   18 cm.

12139   Featherstonhaugh, George William, 1780-1866.
        Excursion through the slave states, from Washington
on the Potomac, to the frontier of Mexico; with
sketches of popular manners and geological notices.
By G. W. Featherstonhaugh... New York, Harper &
brothers, 1844.
        x, [11]-168 p.   23 cm.

12140   The Federalist.
        The Federalist, on the new Constitution, written
in the year 1788, by Alexander Hamilton, James

Madison and John Jay, with an appendix, containing
the original Articles of confederation; the letter
of General Washington, as president of the Convention, to the president of Congress; the Constitution
of the United States, and the amendments to the Constitution. A new ed., with a table of contents, and
... index. The numbers written by Mr. Madison
corrected by himself. Washington, Thompson &
Homans, 1831.
vii, [3]-420 p.   18 1/2 cm.

12141   Fernández de Castro, Manuel, 1825-1895.
Ferro-carril central de la isla de Cuba. Articulos
insertos en el Diario de la marina, para demostrar
su conveniencia y la posibilidad de construirlo en
5 ó 6 años, sin grandes sacrificios por parte del
estado ni de los contribuyentes, por D. Manuel
Fernandez de Castro... Habana, Impr. del Tiempo,
1862.
106 p.   22 cm.

12142   Ferris, Jacob.
The states and territories of the great west;
including Ohio, Indiana, Illinois, Missouri, Michigan,
Wisconsin, Iowa, Minnestoa [!], Kansas, and Nebraska;
their geography, history, advantages, resources, and
prospects; comprising their local history, institutions, and laws. Giving a table of distances and
the most direct routes and modes of conveyance;
also, pointing out the best districts for agricultural, commercial, lumbering, and mining operations.
With a map and numerous illustrations... New York
and Auburn, Miller, Orton, and Mulligan; Buffalo,
E. F. Beadle, 1856.
xii, 13-352 p.   illus., fold. map.   20 cm.

12143   [Fessenden, Thomas Green] 1771-1837.
Democracy unveiled; or, Tyranny stripped of the
garb of patriotism. By Christopher Caustic [pseud.]
... Boston, Printed by David Carlisle, For the
author, 1805.
viii, 220 p.   20 1/2 cm.
Poem, with the author's foot-notes.

12144   Fisher, Ellwood.
Lecture on the North and the South, delivered in
College Hall, before the Young Men's Mercantile

Library Association of Cincinnati, by Ellwood
Fisher, January 16, 1849. Cincinnati, Chronicle
book and job rooms, 1849.
64 p.   22 1/2 cm.

12145   Flórez Estrada, Alvaro, 1766?-1854?
An impartial examination of the dispute between
Spain and her American colonies. By Alvaro Florez
Estrada. Tr. from the original, by W. Burdon.
London, Printed by C. Squire, for Sherwood, Neely
and Jones, 1812.
viii, 199 p.   22 1/2 cm.
Spanish original, London, 1812, published under
title: Exámen imparcial de las disensiones de la
América con la España...

12146   Flournoy, John Jacobus.
An essay on the eminent services and illustrious
character of Henry Clay... By John James Flournoy.
Athens, Ga., Printed at the Whig office, 1840.
46 p.   22 cm.

12147   Foote, Andrew Hull, 1806-1863.
Africa and the American flag. By Commander
Andrew H. Foote... New York [etc.] D. Appleton &
co., 1854.
390 p. incl. col. front.   col. plates, map.
19 1/2 cm.

12148   Ford, Thomas.
A history of Illinois, from its commencement as
a state in 1818 to 1847. Containing a full account
of the Black Hawk War, the rise, progress, and fall
of Mormonism, the Alton and Lovejoy riots, and other
important and interesting events... Chicago, S. C.
Griggs; New York, Ivison & Phinney, 1854.
xvii, 18-447 p.   21 cm.

12149   Forry, Samuel, 1811-1844.
The climate of the United States and its endemic
influences. Based chiefly on the records of the
Medical department and Adjutant general's office,
United States army. By Samuel Forry... New York,
J. & H. G. Langley; Philadelphia, Barrington &
Haswell [etc., etc.] 1842.
xii, [13]-378, [2] p., 1 l.   front. (map) diagr.
23 1/2 cm.

12150 Forster, Johann Reinhold, 1729-1798, comp.
        A catalogue of the animals of North America.
        Containing, an enumeration of the known quadrupeds,
        birds, reptiles, fish, insects, crustaceous and
        testaceous animals... to which are added short
        directions for collecting, preserving, and trans-
        porting, all kinds of natural history curiosities.
        By John Reinhold Forster... London, Sold by B.
        White, 1771.
        43 p.   front.   22 cm.

12151 Foster, John Wells, 1815-1873.
        The Mississippi valley: its physical geography,
        including sketches of the topography, botany,
        climate, geology, and mineral resources; and of
        the progress of development in population and
        material wealth. By J. W. Foster... Illustrated
        by maps and sections... Chicago, S. C. Griggs and
        company [etc., etc.] 1869.
        xvi, 443 p.   maps.   24 cm.

12152 Fothergill, John, 1676-1744.
        An account of the life and travels, in the work
        of the ministry, of John Fothergill. To which are
        added, divers epistles to friends in Great-Britain
        and America, on various occasions. London, printed;
        Philadelphia, reprinted and sold by James Chattin,
        in Church-alley, 1754.
        iv, 280 p.   16 1/2 cm.

12153 Fowler, William Chauncey, 1793-1881.
        Local law in Massachusetts and Connecticut, his-
        torically considered. By William Chauncey Fowler,
        LL. D. Prepared from the New England historical
        and genealogical register, with additions. Albany,
        J. Munsell, 1872.
        104 p.   22 1/2 cm.

12154 [Fox, Charles Barnard] 1833-1895.
        Record of the service of the Fifty-fifth regiment
        of Massachusetts volunteer infantry. Printed for
        the regimental association. Cambridge, Press of
        J. Wilson and son, 1868.
        2 p.l., 144 p.   25 cm.
        The diary kept by Col. Fox, revised by a committee,
        and published with very little change from the
        original draft. cf. Pref.

12155 Fox, Ebenezer, 1763-1843.
     The revolutionary adventures of Ebenezer Fox...
Boston, Munroe & Francis, 1838.
     vi, [7]-238 p.   front. (port.)   15 1/2 cm.

12156 [Foxcroft, Thomas] 1697-1769.
     The ruling & ordaining power of congregational
bishops, or presbyters, defended. Being remarks on
some part of Mr. P. Barclay's Persuasive, lately
distributed in New-England. By an impartial hand.
In a letter to a friend. Boston, Printed for
Samuel Gerrish and sold at his shop near the Brick
meeting-house in Cornhill, 1724.
     1 p.l., 45 p.   17 1/2 cm.   [With Checkley,
John. A modest proof of the order and government
... in the church. Boston, 1723]
     "Design'd as an appendix to [E. Wigglesworth's]
Sober remarks." - Edward Wigglesworth. Sober remarks on a book... entituled, A modest proof.
2d ed. Publisher's preface.

12157 Francis, Convers, 1795-1863.
     A discourse delivered at Plymouth, Mass. Dec. 22,
1832, in commemoration of the landing of the fathers.
By Convers Francis... Pub. by request of the committee of the First parish. Plymouth, Printed by A.
Danforth, 1832.
     56 p.   22 cm.

12158 Francis, John Wakefield, 1789-1861.
     New York during the last half century: a discourse
in commemoration of the fifty-third anniversary of
the New-York historical society, and of the dedication
of their new edifice (November 17, 1857) By John W.
Francis... New York, J. F. Trow, printer, 1857.
     3 p.l., [5]-232 p.   24 1/2 cm.

12159 Francis, John Wakefield, 1789-1861.
     Old New York; or, Reminiscences of the past
sixty years. Being an enlarged and revised edition
of the anniversary discourse delivered before the
New York historical society (November 17, 1857)
by John W. Francis... New York, C. Roe, 1858.
     384 p.   19 cm.

12160 Francis, John Wakefield, 1789-1861.
     Reminiscences of Samuel Latham Mitchill, M. D.,

LL. D. By John W. Francis, M. D., etc. Enlarged
from Valentine's city manual. New York, J. F.
Trow, printer, 1859.
31, [1] p.   22 1/2 cm.

12161   Francklin, Thomas, 1721-1784.
A sermon preached before the honourable Trustees
for establishing the colony of Georgia in America,
and the Associates of the late Rev. Dr. Bray, at
their anniversary meeting, March 16, 1749-50, in
the parish church of St. Margaret, Westminster.
By Thomas Francklin... Pub. at the desire of the
trustees and associates. London, Printed for R.
Francklin, 1750.
20 p.   27 1/2 x 22 cm.

12162   [Franklin, Benjamin] 1706-1790.
An account of the new invented Pennsylvanian
fire-places: wherein their construction and manner
of operation is particularly explained; their advantages above every other method of warming rooms
demonstrated; and all objections that have been
raised against the use of them, answered and ob-
viated. With directions for putting them up, and
for using them to the best advantage. And a copper-
plate, in which the several parts of the machine
are exactly laid down, from a scale of equal parts.
Philadelphia, Printed and sold by B. Franklin, 1744.
1 p.l., 37, [1] p.   2 diagr. (1 fold.)   22 cm.

12163   Franklin and Marshall college, Lancaster, Pa.
Dedication of Franklin and Marshall college.
Lancaster, Pa., May 16th, 1856. Introductory by E. V.
Gerhart... Address by Emlen Franklin, esq. Chambers-
burgh, Pa., Printed by M. Kieffer & co., 1856.
24 p.   23 cm.

12164   Fransioli, Joseph, 1817-1890.
... Patriotism, a Christian virtue. A sermon
preached by the Rev. Joseph Fransioli, at St. Peter's
(Catholic) church, Brooklyn, July 26th, 1863. [New
York, 1863]
8 p.   22 1/2 cm.   (Loyal publication society.
[Pamphlets] no. 24)

12165   Fraser, Eliza Anne.
Narrative of the capture, sufferings, and miraculous

183

escape of Mrs. Eliza Fraser, wife of the late
Captain Samuel Fraser, commander of the ship
Sterling Castle, which was wrecked on 25th May,
in latitude 34, and longitude 155, 12 east, on
Eliza reef, on her passage from New South Wales to
Liverpool... thrown on an unknown island, inhabited
by savages... and... for several weeks held in bondage... New York, C. S. Webb, 1837.
24 p. incl. front.   23 cm.

12166   Free-masonry, in reply to Anti-masonry, in the American
quarterly review, for March, 1830. Boston, J. Marsh
& co., 1830.
40 p.   18 1/2 cm.
Reply to a review of Henry Brown's Narrative of
the anti-masonic excitement.

12167   Freedman, John Joseph, 1835-1921.
Is the act, entitled "An act for enrolling and
calling out the national forces, and for other purposes," commonly called the Conscription act, passed
March 3, 1863, constitutional or not? By John J.
Freedman... New York, G. S. Diossy, 1863.
62 p.   23 cm.

12168   [Freeman, James] 1759-1835.
The character of Rev. John Eliot, D. D., pastor
of the New-North church, Boston... Boston, Published
by Thomas Wells, 3 Hanover-street, Watson & Bangs,
Printers, 1813.
23 p.   22 1/2 cm.

12169   Freeman, Samuel.
The emigrant's hand book, and guide to Wisconsin,
comprising information respecting agricultural and
manufacturing employment, wages, climate, population
&c; sketch of Milwaukee, the queen city of the lakes;
its rise and progress; business and population; list
of public offices, with a full and accurate table of
statistical information of that and other ports on
lake Michigan; also, table of routes from New York,
Boston, &c. ... By Samuel Freeman. Milwaukee,
Sentinel and gazette power press print., 1851.
148 p.   22 1/2 cm.

12170   Frémont, Jessie (Benton) 1824-1902.
The story of the guard: a chronicle of the war.

By Jessie Benton Frémont... Boston, Ticknor and
Fields, 1863.
xiii, [15]-227, [2] p.   18 1/2 cm.

12171 [French, Benjamin Franklin] 1799-1877.
Biographia americana; or, A historical and critical
account of the lives, actions, and writings of the
most distinguished persons in North America; from the
first settlement to the present time... By a gentleman of Philadelphia. New York, D. Mallory, 1825.
1 p.l., vii, 356 p.   front. (port.)   22 1/2 cm.

12172 French, George.
The history of Col. Parke's administration, whilst
he was captain-general and chief governor of the
Leeward Islands; with an account of the rebellion
in Antegoa:wherein he, with several others, were
murther'd on the 7th of December, 1710. By Mr.
George French... London, Printed, and sold by the
booksellers of London and Westminster, 1717.
6 p.l., 427 p.   19 cm.

12173 Frost, John, 1800-1859.
The book of the colonies; comprising a history of
the colonies composing the United States, from the
discovery in the tenth century until the commencement of the revolutionary war. Comp. from the best
authorities by John Frost... New York, D. Appleton
& co.; Philadelphia, G. S. Appleton, 1846.
viii, 9-280 p.   front., illus. (incl. ports.)
19 cm.

12174 Frost, John, 1800-1859.
The book of the navy; comprising a general history
of the American marine; and particular accounts of
all the most celebrated naval battles, from the
Declaration of independence to the present time.
Comp. from the best authorities, by John Frost...
With an appendix... engravings from original drawings,
by William Croome... New York, D. Appleton & co.;
Philadelphia, G. S. Appleton, 1843.
viii, 9-344 p. incl. illus., plates.   fronts.,
ports.   19 1/2 cm.
"Naval and patriotic songs": p. 301-328.

12175 Frost, John, 1800-1859.
Historical collections of all nations; comprising

notices of the most remarkable events and distinguished characters in the history of the world;
with anecdotes of heroes, statesmen, patriots and
sovereigns, who have signalized their names in
ancient and modern history: with special notices
of the heroes of the West. By John Frost... Hartford, Tiffany & co., 1852.
1008 p. incl. illus., pl., port.   25 cm.

12176   Frost, John, 1800-1859.
History of the United States; for the use of
common schools. By John Frost... Philadelphia,
E. C. Biddle, 1837.
324 p. incl. front., illus.   15 1/2 x 10 cm.
Abridged from the author's History of the United
States; for the use of schools and academies.

12177   Frost, John, 1800-1859, ed.
Indian battles, captivities, and adventures.
From the earliest period to the present time. Ed.
by John Frost... New York, J. C. Derby; Boston,
Phillips, Sampson & co. [etc., etc.] 1856.
3 p.l., 5-408 p.   front., plates.   19 cm.

12178   Frost, John, 1800-1859.
The Mexican war and its warriors; comprising a
complete history of all the operations of the
American armies in Mexico; with biographical
sketches and anecdotes of the most distinguished
officers in the regular army and volunteer force.
By J. Frost... New Haven and Philadelphia, H.
Mansfield, 1850.
6, [vii]-viii, 9-332, 11, [1] p. incl. col.
front., illus., plates, ports., map.   pl.
20 cm.

12179   Frothingham, Nathaniel Langdon, 1793-1870.
Christian patriotism. A sermon, on occasion of
the death of John Adams, preached in Chauncy-place,
Boston, July 9th, 1826. By N. L. Frothingham...
Boston, Printed by Munroe and Francis, 1826.
20 p.   23 cm.

12180   Fry, Benjamin St. James, 1824-1892.
The life of Robert R. Roberts, one of the bishops
of the Methodist Episcopal church. By Benjamin
St. James Fry. New-York, Carlton & Phillips,

1856.
126 p.   15 1/2 cm.

12181 Fuller, Timothy, 1778-1835.
An oration, delivered at Faneuil hall, Boston,
July 11, 1831, at the request of the Suffolk anti-
masonic committee, by Timothy Fuller. Boston,
Printed at the office of the Boston press for the
Publishing committee, 1831.
11 p.   23 1/2 cm.

12182 Fulton, James Alexander.
Peach culture. By James Alexander Fulton... New
York, O. Judd and company [c1870]
190 p.   illus.   19 1/2 cm.

G

12183 Gale, Benjamin, 1715-1790.
Doct. Gale's letter to J. W., esquire, containing,
a narrative of the principal matters, of a public
and interesting nature, which were subjects of the
debates and resolves of the General assembly of the
colony of Connecticut, during their sessions in
May, 1769... Hartford, Printed and sold by Green
& Watson, near the Great-bridge, 1769.
34 p.   17 cm.
Much space given to a consideration of the Susquehanna company's memorial on lands on the Susquehanna
river.
With this is bound: Remarks on Dr. Gale's letter
to J. W., esq. [By Eliphalet Dyer] [Hartford] 1769;
the author's Observations, on a pamphlet, entitled
Remarks on Dr. Gale's letter to J. W., esq., signed
E. D. of which the Hon. Eliphalet Dyer is the
reputed author... Hartford [1769]

12184 Gale, George, 1816-1868.
Upper Mississippi: or, Historical sketches of the
mound-builders, the Indian tribes, and the progress
of civilization in the North-west; from A. D. 1600
to the present time. By George Gale. Chicago,
Clarke and company; New York, Oakley and Mason,
1867.
vii p., 1 l., [11]-460 p. incl. illus., plates,

ports., maps.   front., pl., port.   19 1/2 cm.
P. 419-420 missing in all copies examined.

12185   Galland, Isaac, 1790-1858.
        Galland's Iowa emigrant: containing a map, and
        general descriptions of Iowa Territory. Chillicothe
        [O.] W. C. Jones, 1840.
        32 p.   fold. map.   22 1/2 cm.

12186   Gallatin, Albert, 1761-1849.
        A memoir on the north-eastern boundary, in connexion
        with Mr. Jay's map, by the Hon. Albert Gallatin...
        together with a speech on the same subject by the
        Hon. Daniel Webster... delivered at a special
        meeting of the New-York historical society, April
        15th, 1843. Illustrated by a copy of the "Jay
        map." New York, Printed for the Society, 1843.
        1 p.l., iii, [5]-74 p.   front. (fold. map)
        22 1/2 cm.

12187   Gallatin, Albert, 1761-1849.
        A sketch of the finances of the United States.
        By Albert Gallatin. New York, Printed by William
        A. Davis, No. 438 Pearl street, 1796.
        2 p.l., [9]-205 (i.e. 203), [1] p. incl. tables.
        4 fold. tab.   23 1/2 cm.

12188   Gallatin, Albert, 1761-1849.
        Views of the public debt, receipts & expenditures
        of the United States. New York, Printed by M. L.
        & W. A. Davis, 1800.
        61 p.   tables.   23 cm.

12189   [Galloway, Joseph] 1731-1803.
        An account of the conduct of the war in the middle
        colonies. Extracted from a late author. 2d ed.
        London, Printed in the year 1780.
        iv, [5]-28 (i.e. 56) p.   16 1/2 cm.
        Published anonymously.
        A reprint, with some changes, of Galloway's Letters
        to a nobleman, on the conduct of the war in the
        middle colonies (1st ed. pub. London, 1779)

12190   [Galloway, Joseph] 1731-1803.
        Observations on the fifth article of the treaty
        with America: and on the necessity of appointing a
        judicial enquiry into the merits and losses of the

American loyalists. Printed by order of their
agents. [London] 1783.
vi, [7]-19 p.   20 cm.
"Chiefly by Joseph Galloway." - Halkett and
Laing, Dict. of the anon... lit. of Gt. Brit.,
1885, v. 3, col. 1778.

12191 [Galt, John M   ]
Political essays. [n.p., 1852?]
38 p.   21 1/2 cm.
Contents. - pt. I-II. The annexation of Texas.
[Dated Apr. 10 and Apr. 26, 1844, and signed G.] -
[pt. III] The future of democracy [signed: A voice
from Virginia. Williamsburg, Va., Nov., 1852]

12192 Gamel', Iosif Khristianovich, 1788-1861.
England and Russia; comprising the voyages of
John Tradescant, the elder, Sir Hugh Willoughby,
Richard Chancellor, Nelson, and others, to the
White Sea, etc., by Dr. J. Hamel. Translated by
John Studdy Leigh, F. R. G. S. London, R. Bentley,
1854.
xi, 422 p.   22 1/2 cm.
Published in 1843 under title: Tradescant der
Aeltere 1618 in Russland.

12193 Gammell, William, 1812-1889.
Life of Roger Williams, the founder of the state
of Rhode Island. By William Gammell... Boston,
Gould and Lincoln, 1854.
4, [v]-ix p., 1 l., [5]-221 p.   front. (port.)
facsim.   18 1/2 cm.

12194 Gannett, Ezra Stiles, 1801-1871.
Peace - not war. A sermon preached in the Federal
street meeting-house, December 14, 1845. By Ezra S.
Gannett... Boston, J. Dowe, 1845.
24 p.   23 1/2 cm.

12195 Garcilaso de la Vega, el Inca, 1539-1616.
Histoire de la conquête de la Floride: ou Relation
de ce qui s'est passé dans la découverte de ce païs
par Ferdinand de Soto; composée en espagnol par
l'Inca Garcillasso de la Vega, & traduit en françois
par sr. Pierre Richelet. Nouv. ed. ... cor. & augm.,
avec tres belles cartes & figures en taille douce...

Leide, P. van der Aa, 1731.
2 v.   front. (fold. map)   fold. plates.
17 1/2 cm.

12196   [Gardiner, Walter Clarke]
A letter to the corporation of Trinity-church,
New-York; accompanied with copies of sundry papers
and documents, relative to the Episcopal church at
Hudson; by the late rector of that church... [New
York? 1802?]
2 p.l., [3]-33 p.   25 cm.

12197   [Gardner, John]
A brief consideration of the important services,
and distinguished virtues and talents, which recommend
Mr. Adams for the presidency of the United States.
Boston, Printed by Manning & Loring, and to be sold
by J. Nancrede, 1796.
31 p.   16 1/2 cm.
Originally published in the Columbian centinel,
Boston, over the signature of Aurelius.

12198   Garnett, James Mercer, 1770-1843.
Constitutional charts; or, Comparative views of
the legislative, executive and judiciary departments,
in the constitutions of all the states in the Union,
including that of the United States. With an appendix. By James M. Garnett. Richmond, T. W. White,
1829.
6, [49]-64 p.   6 fold. charts.   27 1/2 x
22 1/2 cm.

12199   Gasparin, Agénor Étienne, comte de, 1810-1871.
America before Europe. Principles and interests.
By Count Agénor de Gasparin. Tr. from advance
sheets, by Mary L. Booth. London, S. Low, son, &
co., 1862.
xi, 419 p.   19 cm.

12200   [Gay, John] 1685-1732.
The Mohocks. A tragi-comical farce. As it was
acted near the Watch-house in Covent-Garden. By
Her Majesty's servants... London, B. Lintott, 1712.
4 p.l., 21, [1] p.   19 cm.

12201   Gazelle, a true tale of the great rebellion; and
other poems. Boston, Lee & Shepard; New York, The

American news co., 1866.
194 p.   17 1/2 cm.

12202 Geldard, James.
Hand-book on cotton manufacture; or, A guide to
machine-building, spinning and weaving, with practical examples, all needful calculations, and many
useful and important tables... By James Geldard...
New York, J. Wiley & son, 1867.
vi, [7]-298 p. incl. tables.   front., 10 pl.
20 1/2 cm.

12203 Genesee consociation.
A reply of the Genesee consociation, to the letter
of the Rev. Joseph Emerson... addressed to them on
the subject of their resolution relative to masonic
ministers, and masonic candidates for the ministry.
Rochester, N. Y., Printed by E. Scrantom, 1829.
43 p.   22 1/2 cm.

12204 [Genet, Edmond Charles] 1763-1834.
A letter to the electors of president and vice-
president of the United States. By a citizen of
New York. Accompanied with an extract of the secret
debates of the Federal convention, held in Philadelphia, in the year 1787, taken by Chief Justice
Yates. New-York, Printed by Henry C. Southwick,
no. 2, Wall-street, 1800.
22 p.   21 cm.

12205 Geneva. American residents.
Celebration of the ninetieth anniversary of
American independance [!] in Geneva (Suisse)
July 4th, 1866. Pub. under the direction of the
committee of arrangements. [Geneva, 1866]
41 p.   22 1/2 cm.

12206 Genin, Sylvester, 1822-1850.
Selections from the works of the late Sylvester
Genin, esq., in poetry, prose, and historical
design. With a biographical sketch. New York,
Maigne & Hall, printers, 1855.
252 p.   front. (port.) 15 pl. (incl. ports.)
23 cm.
The plates are reproductions of the author's
paintings.

191

12207   Gentz, Friedrich von, 1764-1832.
        The origin and principles of the American revo-
        lution, compared with the origin and principles of
        the French revolution. Translated from the German
        of Gentz; by an American gentleman. Copy-right
        secured. Philadelphia, Published by Asbury Dickins,
        opposite Christ-church, H. Maxwell, printer, Columbia-
        house, 1800.
        73 p.   21 cm.
        Translated by John Quincy Adams.

12208   A genuine account of earthquakes, especially that at
        Oxford, in the year 1695 [i.e. 1683]; and of another
        terrible one at Port-Royal, in Jamaica, in the year
        1692. Giving an account of the nature and cause
        of them, their dire effects and destructive faculties
        ... published for the information and instruction
        of the publick in general, and collected from the
        best authors, and personal witnesses to the several
        fatal occurrences... London, Printed for H. Slater,
        1750.
        viii, 24 p.   20 1/2 cm.

12209   A genuine account of the late secret expedition to
        Martinico and Guardaloupe, under Commodore Moore
        and General Hopson, written at Guardaloupe, by a
        sea-officer who went out with Commodore Hughes...
        [London] Printed for R. Griffiths, 1759.
        23 p.   21 cm.
        "A reprint of newspaper articles." - Sabin, Bibl.
        Amer.

12210   Georgetown, D. C. Ordinances, etc.
        Ordinances of the corporation of Georgetown.
        With an appendix, containing the law for laying out
        the town, the original and supplementary charters,
        the act of cession, and such other laws of Maryland
        as relate immediately to the town; and sundry acts
        of Congress relating to the town and district
        generally. Georgetown, D. C., Printed by J. C.
        Dunn, 1821.
        2 p.l., [3]-126, 64, xiv p., 1 l.   23 1/2 cm.

12211   Georgia. Constitution.
        The constitution of the state of Georgia. Savannah,
        Ga., Printed by William Lancaster, 1777.
        2 p.l., 11 p.   22 cm.

12212　Georgia.　Convention, 1861.
　　　　　　Journal of the public and secret proceedings of
　　　　the Convention of the people of Georgia, held in
　　　　Milledgeville and Savannah in 1861.　Together with
　　　　the ordinances adopted.　Pub. by order of the con-
　　　　vention.　(From state archives)
　　　　　　(In The Confederate records of the state of Georgia.
　　　　Atlanta, Ga., 1909.　26 cm.　v. 1, p. 212-773)
　　　　　　George W. Crawford, president.
　　　　　　Running title:　Journal of seccession convention.
　　　　　　Includes communications from commissioners and
　　　　officers of other states relative to secession,
　　　　the constitution of the Confederate States of Ame-
　　　　rica, etc.

12213　Georgia.　Governor, 1857-1865 (Joseph E. Brown)
　　　　　　Message of His Excellency Joseph E. Brown to the
　　　　extra session of the legislature, convened March 10th,
　　　　1864...　Milledgeville, Ga., Boughton, Nisbet, Barnes
　　　　& Moore, state printer, 1864.
　　　　　　48 p.　　22 1/2 cm.

12214　Georgia historical society.
　　　　　　... Collections.　v. 1-　　　Savannah, Ga., The
　　　　Georgia historical society, 1840-
　　　　　　v.　fronts., illus., plates (part fold.)
　　　　fold. maps, plans (part fold.)　fold. tables.
　　　　24-25 cm.

12215　Georgia historical society.
　　　　　　Constitution, by-laws and list of members of the
　　　　Georgia historical society.　Savannah, Steam press
　　　　of J. M. Cooper & co., 1859.
　　　　　　15 p.　　22 cm.

12216　Germantown academy, Germantown, Pa.
　　　　　　A history of the Germantown academy...　[Phila-
　　　　delphia, Press of S. H. Burbank & co.] 1910-35.
　　　　　　2 v.　　fronts., illus., plates, ports., facsims.
　　　　(1 double)　　26 1/2 cm.
　　　　　　[Vol. 1] published 1910 upon the one hundred and
　　　　fiftieth anniversary of the school's founding relates
　　　　the history of the school to 1877; v. 2, by Horace M.
　　　　Lippincott, published 1935 upon the one hundred and
　　　　seventy-fifth anniversary of the school's founding,
　　　　covers the period 1876 to 1936.

12217   Gerstäcker, Friedrich, 1816-1872.
      Western lands and western waters... With illus-
trations and designs by eminent artists. London,
S. O. Beeton, 1864.
     xii, 388 p.   illus.   23 cm.

12218   Gesner, Abraham, 1797-1864.
      The industrial resources of Nova Scotia. Com-
prehending the physical geography, topography, geology, agriculture, fisheries, mines, forests...
commerce, emigration... natural history and resources, of the province. By Abraham Gesner...
Halifax, N. S. [A. & W. MacKinlay] 1849.
     2 p.l., iv, iii, 341 (i.e. 337), 15 p., 1 l.,
4 p.   fold. front., pl., fold. map.   22 cm.

12219   Gesner, Abraham, 1797-1864.
      New Brunswick; with notes for emigrants. Compre-
hending the early history, an account of the Indians,
settlement... By Abraham Gesner... London, Sim-
monds & Ward, 1847.
     1 p.l., [v]-xv, [1], 388 p.   5 pl.   22 cm.

12220   Gesner, Abraham, 1797-1864.
      A practical treatise on coal, petroleum, and
other distilled oils, by Abraham Gesner... 2d ed.,
rev. and enl. By George Weltden Gesner... New York,
Baillière brothers; London, H. Baillière [etc., etc.]
1865.
     vi, [7]-181 p.   front., illus.   23 1/2 cm.

12221   Gesner, Abraham, 1797-1864.
      Remarks on the geology and mineralogy of Nova
Scotia. By Abraham Gesner... Halifax, Nova Scotia,
Printed by Gossi and Coade, 1836.
     xi, 272 p.   fold. front., 2 pl. (1 fold.)
fold. map.   21 cm.

12222   Gessner, Ludwig, 1828-1890.
      ... Le droit des neutres sur mer. Berlin, Stilke
et van Muyden [etc., etc.] 1865.
     xiv, 437, [1] p.   23 cm.   (Bibliothèque diplo-
matique)

12223   Gholson, Thomas Saunders, 1809-1868.
      Speech of Hon. Thos. S. Gholson, of Virginia, on
the policy of employing negro troops, and the duty

of all classes to aid in the prosecution of the war.
Delivered in the House of representatives of the
Congress of the Confederate States, on the 1st of
February, 1865. Richmond, G. P. Evans & co.,
printers, 1865.
20 p.   24 cm.

12224 Gholson, William Yates, 1807-1870.
Address of Hon. W. Y. Gholson, on the subject of
the payment of the bonds of the United States in
coin, delivered to the Grant club at Avondale, on
Friday, October 2, 1868... Cincinnati, R. Clarke
& co., printers, 1868.
32 p.   23 1/2 cm.
Republished from the Cincinnati commercial of
Saturday, October 3, 1868.

12225 [Gibbes, George M   ]
A letter to the American peace society from a
member of the Committee of peace in Paris. Paris,
Printed by E. Brière, 1842.
31 p.   21 1/2 cm.
"Proposal for the establishment of a daily journal
in the French language, at Paris... for the purposes
... of promoting peace, and international philan-
thropy."

12226 Gibbes, Robert Wilson, 1809-1866.
Cuba for invalids. By R. W. Gibbes... New York,
W. A. Townsend and company, 1860.
xii, 214 p.   19 1/2 cm.

12227 Gibbons, Israel, d. 1866.
Crescent-shine; or, Gleams of light on all sorts
of subjects from the columns of the "New Orleans
crescent"... By Israel Gibbons... New Orleans,
J. O. Nixon, 1866.
vi, [7]-194 p.   22 1/2 cm.

12228 Gibbons, James.
Miscellaneous and patriotic poems. By James
Gibbons... Philadelphia, Printed for private circulation, 1870.
64 p.   17 1/2 cm.
Some of poems published originally in his Irish
patriotic songs.

195

12229   Gibbons, James Sloan, 1810-1892.
      The public debt of the United States. Its orga-
nization; its liquidation; administration of the
Treasury; the financial system. By J. S. Gibbons
... New York, C. Scribner & co. [etc., etc.] 1867.
xii, 276 p.   20 1/2 cm.

12230   Gibbs, Frederick Waymouth, 1821-
      The Foreign enlistment act. By Frederick Waymouth
Gibbs, C. B. London, W. Ridgway, 1863.
1 p.l., 74 p.   20 1/2 cm.

12231   Gibbs, Frederick Waymouth, 1821-
      Recognition: a chapter from the history of the
North American & South American states, by Frederick
Waymouth Gibbs, C. B. London, W. Ridgway [etc.,
etc.] 1863.
1 p.l., 46 p.   20 1/2 cm.

12232   Gibbs, George, 1815-1873.
      Alphabetical vocabularies of the Clallam and
Lummi. By George Gibbs. New York, Cramoisy press,
1863.
vii, [9]-40 p.   28 1/2 cm.   (Half-title:
Shea's library of American linguistics. XI)
"Vocabulary of the Lummi": p. [21]-40.

12233   Gibbs, George, 1815-1873.
      A dictionary of the Chinook jargon, or, Trade
language of Oregon. By George Gibbs. New York,
Cramoisy press, 1863.
xiv, [2], 43, [1] p.   36 x 28 cm.   (Half-title:
Shea's library of American linguistics. XII)
"Bibliography of the Chinook jargon": p. [xiii]-
xiv.
      Published also, Washington, 1863 (Smithsonian
institution publication 161) and reissued in Smithsonian miscellaneous collections, vol. 7, 1867.

12234   [Gibbs, George] 1815-1873.
      The judicial chronicle, being a list of the judges
of the courts of common law and Chancery in England
and America, and of the contemporary reports, from
the earliest period of the reports to the present
time. Cambridge, J. Munroe & company, 1834.
iv p., 2 l., 55 p.   22 1/2 cm.

12235 Gibbs, William, b. 1785.
        Family notices collected by William Gibbs, of
        Lexington, Mass. [Lexington, Mass., 1845]
        8 p.   21 1/2 cm.
        Descendants of Robert Gibbs of Boston.

12236 Gibbs, William H
        Address delivered before the Literary association,
        Blandford, Mass., Sept. 21, 1850, upon the history
        of that town. By William H. Gibbs... Springfield,
        G. W. Wilson, printer, 1850.
        76 p.   fold. geneal. tab.   18 1/2 cm.

12237 Gibstone, Henry.
        L'esclavage aux États-Unis; Dean le quarteron,
        par Henry Gibstone. [Paris] E. Dentu, 1863.
        3 p.l., 340 p.   18 cm.

12238 Giddings, Joshua Reed, 1795-1864.
        The exiles of Florida; or, The crimes committed
        by our government against the maroons, who fled from
        South Carolina, and other slave states, seeking pro-
        tection under Spanish laws. By Joshua R. Giddings
        ... 9th thousand. Columbus, O., Follett, Foster
        and company, 1858.
        viii, 338 p.   front., ports.   20 1/2 cm.

12239 Giddins, Edward.
        An inquiry into the causes of the rise and fall of
        the Lakes, embracing an account of the floods and
        ebbs of Lake Ontario as determined by a long series
        of actual observations, and an examination of the
        various opinions in regard to the late unprecedented
        flood throughout the chain of Great Lakes. To which
        is annexed a letter to Dr. H. H. Sherwood on his
        theory of magnetism. By Edward Giddins. Lockport,
        N. Y., Printed at the Courier office, 1838.
        31 p.   19 cm.

12240 Gihon, John H
        Geary and Kansas. Governor Geary's administration
        in Kansas. With a complete history of the territory.
        Until June 1857. Embracing a full account of its
        discovery, geography, soil, rivers, climate, products;
        its organization as a territory... All fully authen-
        ticated. By John H. Gihon... Philadelphia, J. H. C.
        Whiting, 1857.

xii, [13]-348 p.   19 cm.
Also published under title: Gihon's history of
Kansas.

12241 Giles, Charles, 1783-1867.
Pioneer: a narrative of the nativity, experience,
travels, and ministerial labors of Rev. Charles
Giles... With incidents, observations, and reflections. New York, G. Lane & P. P. Sandford, 1844.
333 p.   front. (port.)   18 1/2 cm.

12242 Giles, Joel.
Practical liberty. An oration delivered before
the city authorities of Boston in the Tremont
temple, July 4, 1848. By Joel Giles. Boston,
Eastburn's press, 1848.
24 p.   24 cm.

12243 Giles, William Branch, 1762-1830.
Address of the Honorable William B. Giles, to
the people of Virginia. [n.p., 1813]
123 p.   20 cm.

12244 Giles, William Branch, 1762-1830.
The speeches of Mr. Giles and Mr. Bayard, in the
House of representatives of the United States,
February, 1802. On the bill received from the
Senate, entitled, "An act to repeal certain acts
respecting the organization of the courts of the
United States." Boston, Printed by Munroe & Francis,
Half-court square, opposite the south-east corner
of the Mercury-office. Sold by them, and at the
several book-stores, 1802.
56 p.   21 cm.

12245 Giles, William F[ell] 1807-1879.
The annual address, delivered before the Maryland
historical society, on the evening of December 17th,
1866, by Hon. William F. Giles. Baltimore, Printed
by J. Murphy & co., 1867.
29 p.   23 1/2 cm.

12246 Gill, Theodore Nicholas, 1837-1914.
Catalogue of the fishes of the eastern coast of
North America, from Greenland to Georgia. By
Theodore Gill... [Philadelphia, Academy of natural
sciences, 1861]

63 p.   23 cm.
Presented to the academy and ordered to be printed,
Jan. 1, 1861.

12247   Gill, Theodore Nicholas, 1837-1914.
Synopsis of the fresh water fishes of the western
portion of the island of Trinidad, W. I., by Theodore
Gill... Reprinted from the Annals of the Lyceum of
natural history, New York, vol. VI. New York, H.
Baillière [etc., etc.] 1858.
70 p.   29 cm.

12248   Gilleland, J   C
History of the late war, between the United States
and Great Britain; containing an accurate account
of the most important engagements by sea and land.
Interspersed with interesting geographical sketches
of those parts of the country where the principal
battles were fought.   2d ed.   By J. C. Gilleland.
Baltimore, Printed and published by Schaeffer &
Maund, 1817.
190 p.   15 cm.
"Appendix.   Treaty of peace":   p. [173]-190.

12249   Gillespie, Alexander.
Gleanings and remarks: collected during many
months of residence at Buenos Ayres, and within the
upper country; with a prefatory account of the expedition from England, until the surrender of the
colony of the Cape of Good Hope, under the joint
command of Sir D. Baird... and Sir Home Popham...
By Major Alexander Gillespie... Illustrated with
a map of South-America, and a chart of Rio de la
Plata, with pilotage directions. Leeds, Printed by
B. Dewhirst for the author, 1818.
1 p.l., ii, 242 (i.e. 342) p.   front. (map)
chart.   22 cm.

12250   Gillespy, Edward, comp.
The Columbian naval songster; being a collection
of original songs, odes, etc. composed in honour of
the five great naval victories, obtained by Hull,
Jones, Decatur, Bainbridge and Lawrence, over the
British ships Guerriere, Frolic, Macedonian, Java
and Peacock. Comp. and arranged by Edward Gillespy.
New York, Printed and published by Edward Gillespy,

no. 24 William-street, nearly opposite the Post
office, 1813.
94, [2] p.   19 cm.

12251   Gillet, Eliphalet, 1768-1848.
A discourse, delivered at Hallowell, April 25th,
1799. Being the day appointed by the chief magistrate of the United States, for a national fast.
By Eliphalet Gillet... Hallowell, printed; New-
York, reprinted for, and sold by Cornelius Davis,
no. 94, Water-street, 1799.
22 p., 1 l.   21 1/2 cm.

12252   Gillet, Eliphalet, 1768-1848.
An oration, delivered January 8, 1800, before the
citizens of Hallowell, and its vicinity, in commemoration of the much lamented death of General
George Washington. By Eliphalet Gillet... Hallowell (District of Maine) Printed by Peter Edes,
1800.
19 p.   19 1/2 x 16 cm.

12253   Gillet, Ransom Hooker, 1800-1876.
Democracy in the United States. What it has done,
what it is doing, and what it will do. By Ransom H.
Gillet... New York, D. Appleton and company, 1868.
xiv, 414 p.   front., port.   20 1/2 cm.

12254   Gillet, Ransom Hooker, 1800-1876.
The federal government; its officers and their
duties. By Ransom H. Gillet... New York, Chicago,
Woolworth, Ainsworth & company, 1871.
x, [13]-444 p.   20 cm.

12255   [Gillette, Charles]
A few historic records of the church in the diocese
of Texas, during the rebellion. Together with a
correspondence between the Right Rev. Alexander
Gregg... and the Rev. Charles Gillette... New York,
J. A. Gray & Green, printers, 1865.
131 p.   23 cm.

12256   Gilliam, Albert M   d. 1859.
Travels over the table lands and cordilleras of
Mexico. During the years 1843 and 44; including a
description of California... and the biographies of
Iturbide and Santa Anna. By Albert M. Gilliam...

Philadelphia, J. W. Moore [etc., etc.] 1846.
xv, [17]-455 p.   front., plates, ports., fold.
maps.   22 cm.

12257 [Gillmore, Parker]
       Gun, rod, and saddle. Personal experiences. By
       Ubique [pseud.] New York, W. A. Townsend & Adams,
       1869.
       275 p.   front.   18 cm.
       Articles originally published in "Land and water".
       cf. Pref.

12258 Gillmore, Robert H
       The thrilling narrative of Edgell, Pearson, Gatwood
       and Savage, who were rescued, after having been
       buried alive seven hundred feet under ground, for
       fourteen days and thirteen hours without food. In
       the Blue Rock coal mines. By Robert H. Gillmore.
       Zanesville, O., Gillmore & Bennett, printers, 1856.
       48 p.   illus.   17 1/2 cm.

12259 Gilman, Arthur, 1837-1909.
       A genealogical and biographical record of that
       branch of the family of Gilman, descended from the
       Honorable Counsellor John Gilman, of Exeter, N. H.
       With which is incorporated some account of his
       ancestors and the English branch of the Gilman
       family. Comp. by Arthur Gilman. Albany, Printed
       for the use of the family, by J. Munsell, 1863.
       51 p.   25 1/2 cm.

12260 Gilman, Daniel Coit, 1831-1908.
       A historical discourse delivered in Norwich,
       Connecticut, September 7, 1859, at the bi-centennial
       celebration of the settlement of the town. By
       Daniel Coit Gilman... 2d ed., with additional notes.
       Boston, G. C. Rand and Avery, city printers, 1859.
       128 p.   23 cm.

12261 Gilman, Daniel Coit, 1831-1908.
       Our national schools of science. By Daniel C.
       Gilman... Boston, Ticknor and Fields, 1867.
       28 p.   21 cm.
       Reprinted from the North American review for
       October, 1867.
       Bibliography: p. [3]

12262 [Gilman, Samuel] 1791-1858.
Monody on the victims and sufferers by the late
conflagration in the city of Richmond, Virginia.
Boston, Published by Charles Williams. T. B. Wait
and co., printers, 1812.
24 p.   24 cm.

12263 [Gilmer, George Rockingham] 1790-1859.
Sketches of some of the first settlers of upper
Georgia, of the Cherokees, and the author. New
York, D. Appleton and company, 1855.
587 p.   front. (port.) illus.   23 1/2 cm.

12264 Gilmer, John H
Letter addressed to Hon. Wm. C. Rives, by John H.
Gilmer, on the existing status of the revolution,
&c. [Richmond? 1864]
16 p.   23 1/2 cm.
Caption title. Dated Richmond, November 1, 1864.
An arraignment of the Confederate executive for
refusing to discharge from service the 1st Maryland
artillery, at the expiration of its 3 year term of
service.

12265 Gilmer, John H
War of races. By whom it is sought to be brought
about. Considered in two letters, with copious
extracts from the recent work of Hilton [!] R.
Helper, by John H. Gilmer. Richmond, 1867.
16 p.   21 1/2 cm.

12266 Gilmore, Joseph Henry, 1834-
"Hath God forgotten to be gracious." A thanksgiving sermon preached before the united religious
societies of Fisherville, N. H., Nov. 26, 1863, by
J. H. Gilmore... Concord, P. B. Cogswell, printer,
1864.
14 p.   23 cm.

12267 Gilmore, Patrick Sarsfield, 1829-1892.
History of the National peace jubilee and great
musical festival, held in the city of Boston, June,
1869, to commemorate the restoration of peace
throughout the land. By P. S. Gilmore. Illustrated
with steel engravings. Published by the author, and
for sale by Lee and Shepard, Boston; Lee, Shepard,
and Dillingham, New York, 1871.

x, 758 p.   front. (port.) illus. (music)
4 pl.   24 cm.

12268 Gilpin, Henry Dilworth, 1801-1860.
The character of Franklin. Address delivered
before the Franklin institute of Pennsylvania, on
the evening of the fourth of December, 1856. By
Henry D. Gilpin. Philadelphia, King & Baird,
printers, 1857.
50 p.   23 cm.

12269 Gilpin, Henry Dilworth, 1801-1860.
An eulogy on Silas Wright, delivered before the
Young men's Democratic association of the city and
county of Philadelphia, on the 12th of November,
1847, by Henry D. Gilpin. Philadelphia, United
States book and job printing office, 1847.
30 p.   22 cm.

12270 Gilpin, Henry Dilworth, 1801-1860.
A speech delivered at the Democratic celebration
by the citizens of the second congressional district
of Pennsylvania, of the fifty-eighth anniversary of
the Declaration of independence, July 4th, 1834.
By Henry D. Gilpin. [Philadelphia, Mifflin & Parry,
1834]
27 p.   22 cm.

12271 Gilpin, Joshua.
A memoir on the rise, progress, and present state
of the Chesapeake and Delaware canal, accompanied
with original documents and maps. By Joshua Gilpin
... Wilmington, Printed by R. Porter, 1821.
1 p.l., 50, 72 p.   maps (part fold.)   23 cm.

12272 Gilpin, Thomas, 1776-1853.
An essay on organic remains, as connected with
an ancient tropical region of the earth. By Thomas
Gilpin... Philadelphia, E. H. Butler, 1843.
39, [1] p.   24 cm.

12273 [Gilpin, Thomas] 1776-1853.
On the representation of minorities of electors
to act with the majority, in elected assemblies.
Philadelphia, J. C. Clark, printer, 1844.
2 p.l., [3]-15 p.   24 cm.

12274   Giordan, [Jean] François.
        Description et colonisation de l'isthme de Tehuan-
        tepec, précédées d'une notice historique par F¹ˢ
        Giordan... Paris, Le Doyen [etc.] 1838.
        2 p.l., 144, [4] p.   fold. map, fold. tab.
        23 1/2 cm.

12275   Girard, Stephen, 1750-1831.
        The will of the late Stephen Girard, esq., procured
        from the office for the probate of wills, with a
        short biography of his life... Philadelphia,
        Thomas L. Bonsal, 1832.
        35 p.   21 1/2 cm.

12276   Girard college, Philadelphia.
        A description of the Girard college for orphans,
        contained in a final report of the Building committee
        to the Select and Common councils of Philadelphia,
        a report to the Building committee, by Thomas U.
        Walter, architect. Together with the address deli-
        vered on laying the corner stone, July 4, 1833, by
        Nicholas Biddle. And the address delivered on the
        occasion of placing the crowning stone, August 29,
        1846, by Joseph R. Chandler. And an account of the
        final transfer of the buildings and grounds to the
        Board of directors. To which is appended the will
        of Stephen Girard. Philadelphia, 1848.
        64 p.   pl.   22 1/2 cm.

12277   Girdlestone, Thomas, 1758-1822.
        Facts tending to prove that General Lee was never
        absent from this country, for any length of time,
        during the years 1767, 1768, 1769, 1770, 1771, 1772,
        and that he was the author of Junius. By Thomas
        Girdlestone... London, Printed for P. Martin, 1813.
        vii, 138 p.   front. (port.) 2 facsim. (1 fold.)
        22 cm.

12278   Gisborne, Lionel, 1823-1861.
        The isthmus of Darien in 1852. Journal of the
        expedition of inquiry for the junction of the
        Atlantic and Pacific oceans. By Lionel Gisborne.
        With four maps. London, Saunders and Stanford,
        1853.
        1 p.l., [v]-vi, 238 p.   3 fold. maps.
        19 1/2 cm.

Also printed, for private circulation, London, 1853, under title: Journal of a trip to Darien.

12279 Gladden, Washington, 1836-1918.
From the Hub to the Hudson: with sketches of nature, history and industry in north-western Massachusetts. By Washington Gladden. Boston, New England news co., 1869.
iv, [5]-149 p.   plates.   17 cm.

12280 Gladstone, Thomas H
The Englishman in Kansas; or, Squatter life and border warfare. By T. H. Gladstone... With an introduction, by Fred. Law Olmsted... New York, Miller & company, 1857.
iv, 328 p.   19 cm.

12281 Gladstone, Thomas H
Kansas; or, Squatter life and border warfare in the far West. By Thomas H. Gladstone... with additions and corrections... London, New York, G. Routledge & co., 1857.
viii, 295 p.   front., pl., fold. map.   17 cm.
"Reprinted, by permission, from 'The Times.'"

12282 Glascott, Cradock, 1743?-1831.
The best method of putting an end to the American war. Being the substance of a sermon preached on the 13th of December, 1776; the day of the general fast, at Tottenham-Court chapel... by the Rev. Cradock Glascott... With an address from Henry Peckwell... to his fellow subjects on that solemn occasion. London, Printed by J. W. Pasham, 1776.
31 p.   21 cm.
[Hazard pamphlets, v. 89, no. 10]

12283 Glazier, Lewis.
History of Gardner, Massachusetts, from its earliest settlement to 1860. By Lewis Glazier. Worcester, Printed by C. Hamilton, 1860.
vii, [1], [9]-163 p.   19 1/2 cm.

12284 Gleason, Benjamin, 1777-1847.
An oration on the anniversary of American inde-pendence. Pronounced before the senior class of Rhode-Island college, in college chapel, on the evening of the 5th of July, 1802. At their parti-

cular request. By Benjamin Gleason... Boston,
Munroe & Francis, printers, 1802.
16 p.   21 cm.
[Miscellaneous pamphlets, v. 245, no. 15]

12285   Glezen, Levi, 1774?-1842.
An oration delivered at Lenox, on the twenty-
second of February, 1800. By Levi Glezen...
Stockbridge [Mass.] Printed at the office of
H. Jones & co. by H. Willard, 1800.
20 p.   21 cm.
"Published at the polite request of a select
committee."

12286   Gloria Britannorum; or, The British worthies. A poem.
Being an essay on the characters of the most illustrious persons in camp or cabinet, since the
glorious revolution to this present time. More
particularly, of the present ministry, under our
most renowned sovereign lord King George. To which
is added, an ode on His Majesty's coronation, and
an elegy on the death of the late glorious Duke of
Marlborough. By a lover of the present happy constitution... Boston, Printed by J. Franklin for
N. Buttolph, 1723.
1 p.l., 30 p.   16 cm.
Incidentally refers to Harvard college (p. 1-2)

12287   Glover, Richard, 1712-1785.
The evidence delivered on the petition presented
by the West-India planters and merchants to the
Hon. House of commons, as it was introduc'd at the
bar, and summ'd up by Mr. Glover. [London, 1775]
1 p.l., 95 p.   18 1/2 cm.
On the question of commercial relations between
the British West Indies and the thirteen colonies.
The two witnesses examined were George Walker and
John Ellis.

12288   Glover, Samuel Taylor, 1813-1884.
Slavery in the United States - emancipation in
Missouri. Speech of Samuel T. Glover, at the ratification meeting in St. Louis, held at the Court
house, July 22, 1863. St. Louis, Daily union
steam printing house, 1863.
cover-title, 18 p.   22 cm.

12289 The go-between; or, Two edged sword. Being an impartial address to the citizens of the United
States, as regards their true and general interest,
welfare and security. By a gentleman from South
Carolina... New York, Printed for the author,
1807.
37 p.   21 1/2 cm.
Signed: Hornet.

12290 Gobright, Lawrence Augustus, 1816-1879.
Recollection of men and things at Washington,
during the third of a century. By L. A. Gobright.
Philadelphia, Claxton, Remsen & Haffelfinger;
Washington, W. H. & O. H. Morrison, 1869.
xi, 13-420 p.   19 cm.

12291 Godard-Lange,
La congrégation; ou, Une mission chez les Iroquois;
poème ascéti-épique, en 9 chants, avec des notes
critiques, historiques, anecdotiques et édifiantes,
tirées, pour la plupart, des ouvrages des benoits
pères jesuites... Par Godard-Lange... Paris,
Chez l'auteur, 1846.
xvi, 397 p., 1 l.   front.   23 cm.
"A satire without a word regarding the Iroquois
or any other savages, except those of Paris." -
T. W. Fields (cf. Sabin)

12292 Goddard, Frederick Bartlett, 1834-
Where to emigrate and why, describes the climate -
soil - productions - minerals and general resources
... in nearly all sections of the United States;
and contains a description of the Pacific railroad
... rates of wages... etc. ... By Frederick B.
Goddard... New York, F. B. Goddard, 1869.
1 p.l., xvi, [9]-591 p.   2 pl., maps (part fold.)
23 cm.

12293 Goddard, William, 1740-1817.
The partnership: or, The history of the rise and
progress of the Pennsylvania chronicle, &c. Wherein
the conduct of Joseph Galloway, esq., speaker of the
honourable House of representatives of the province
of Pennsylvania, Mr. Thomas Wharton, sen., and their
man Benjamin Towne, my late partners, with my own,
is properly delineated, and their calumnies against
me fully refuted. By William Goddard... No. I[-II]

Philadelphia, Printed by William Goddard, in Arch-
street, between Front and Second streets, 1770.
1 p.l., 72 p., 1 l.   20 cm.

12294   Godwin, Morgan, fl. 1685.
The negro's ʕ Indians advocate, suing for their
admission into the church: or A persuasive to the
instructing and baptizing of the negro's and Indians
in our plantations. Shewing, that as the compliance
therewith can prejudice no man's just interest: so
the wilful neglecting and opposing of it, is no less
than a manifest apostacy from the Christian faith.
To which is added, a brief account of religion in
Virginia. By Morgan Godwyn... London, Printed for
the author, by J. D., 1680.
7 p.l., 174 p.   18 cm.
"The state of religion in Virginia, as it was
some time before the late rebellion, represented in
a letter to Sir W. B. then governour thereof":
p. 167-174.
----- A supplement to The negro's ʕ Indian's advocate:
or, some further considerations and proposals for
the effectual and speedy carrying on of the negro's
Christianity in our plantations (notwithstanding the
late pretended impossibilities) without any prejudice
to their owners. By M. G. a presbyter of the
church of England... London, Printed by J. D., 1681.
12 p.   20 1/2 x 15 1/2 cm.

12295   Goedel, C
Sklaverei und emancipation der schwarzen rasse
in den Vereinigten Staaten von Nordamerika.
Geschichtliche abhandlugen, von C. Goedel. Hrsg.
vom Züricher comité zur unterstützung der befreiten
farbigen. Zürich, Schabelitz (C. Schmidt) 1866.
2 p.l., 150 p., 1 l.   21 1/2 cm.

12296   Golder, John, comp.
Life of the Honourable William Tilghman, late
chief justice of the state of Pennsylvania. Comp.
from the eulogies of two distinguished members of
the Philadelphia bar, who delivered them in commemoration of his virtues. By John Golder, esq.
Philadelphia, The author, 1829.
148 p.   port.   21 cm.
Appendix (p. [71]-148): An eulogium in commemoration of Doctor Caspar Wistar, late president of

the American philosophical society... by the Hon.
William Tilghman... 1818; An address delivered
before the Philadelphia society for promoting agriculture. By the Hon. William Tilghman... 1820.

12297 Goldsborough, Charles Washington, 1779-1843.
The United States' naval chronicle... By Charles
W. Goldsborough. vol. 1. Washington, J. Wilson,
1824.
395, xii p.   22 cm.

12298 Goldsmith, Lewis, 1763?-1846.
An exposition of the conduct of France towards
America: illustrated by cases decided in the
council of prizes in Paris. By Lewis Goldsmith...
London, Printed for J. M. Richardson, 1810.
iv, 133 p.   20 1/2 cm.

12299 Gómez de Avellaneda y Arteaga, Gertrudis, 1814-1873.
Guatimozin, último emperador de Méjico. Novela
histórica por la Señorita Gómez de Avellaneda.
Méjico, Impr. de J. R. Navarro, 1853.
178 p., 1 l.   27 1/2 cm.

12300 [Goodenow, John Milton] 1782-1838.
Historical sketches of the principles and maxims
of American jurisprudence, in contrast with the
doctrines of the English common law on the subject
of crimes and punishments... Steubenville, Printed
by James Wilson, 1819.
vii, [1], 426 (i.e. 418), vi p.   24 cm.

12301 Goodhue, Josiah Fletcher, 1791-1863.
History of the town of Shoreham, Vermont, from
the date of its charter, October 8th, 1761, to the
present time, by Rev. Josiah F. Goodhue. Pub. by
the town. Middlebury, A. H. Copeland, 1861.
vi, [2], 198 p.   front., plates, port.
23 1/2 cm.
Written by request of the Middlebury historical
society.

12302 Goodrich, Chauncey Enoch, 1801-1864.
A sermon, on the death of Amariah Brigham, M. D.,
superintendent of the New-York state lunatic asylum,
who died September 8, 1849. Delivered at the asylum,
October 8, 1849, and again in the First Presbyterian

church, Utica, November 11, 1849. By the Rev.
Chauncey E. Goodrich... With an appendix. New
York, J. F. Trow, printer, 1850.
   35 p.   24 cm.

12303 Goodrich, Elizur, 1734-1797.
       The principles of civil union and happiness con-
       sidered and recommended. A sermon, preached before
       His Excellency Samuel Huntington, esq., L. L. D.,
       governor and commander in chief, and the honorable
       the General assembly of the state of Connecticut.
       Convened at Hartford, on the day of the anniversary
       election, May 10th, 1787. By Elizur Goodrich, D. D.,
       pastor of the Church of Christ in Durham. Hartford,
       Printed by Hudson and Goodwin, 1787.
          58 p.   20 cm.
       Printed by order of the Connecticut General
       assembly.

12304 [Goodricke, Henry]
       Observations on Dr. Price's Theory and principles
       of civil liberty and government, preceded by a
       letter to a friend, on the pretensions of the
       American colonies, in respect of right and equity
       ... York [Eng.] Printed by A. Ward, 1776.
          4 p.l., 147 p.   21 cm.

12305 [No entry - number inadvertently omitted]

12306 Goodwin, Henry Martyn, 1820-1893.
       The Pilgrim fathers. A glance at their history,
       character and principles, in two memorial discourses,
       delivered in the First Congregational church,
       Rockford, May 22, 1870, by Rev. H. M. Goodwin...
       Rockford, Ill., Bird, Conick, & Flint, printers,
       1870.
          36 p.   23 cm.

12307 Goodwin, Hermon Camp, 1813-1891.
       Pioneer history; or, Cortland county and the
       border wars of New York. From the earliest period
       to the present time. By H. C. Goodwin... New York,
       A. B. Burdick, 1859.
          viii, [9]-456 p.   front., ports.   19 cm.

12308 Goodwin, Thomas, 1600-1680.
       An apologeticall narration, hvmbly submitted to

the honourable houses of Parliament. By Tho.
Goodwin, Philip Nye, Sidrach Simpson, Jer. Bur-
roughes, William Bridge. London, Printed for R.
Dawlman, 1643.
2 p.l., 31 p.   18 1/2 x 14 1/2 cm.

12309   Gookin, Daniel, 1612?-1687.
Historical collections of the Indians in New
England. Of their several nations, numbers, customs,
manners, religion and government, before the English
planted there. Also a true and faithful account of
the present state and condition of the praying
Indians (or those who have visibly received the
gospel in New England) declaring the number of that
people, the situation and place of their towns and
churches, and their manner of worshipping God...
Together with a brief mention of the instruments and
means, that God hath been pleased to use for their
civilizing and conversion, briefly declaring the
prudent and faithful endeavours of the Right honourable the Corporation at London, for promoting that
affairs. Also suggesting some expedients for their
further civilizing and propagating the Christian
faith among them. By Daniel Gookin... Now first
printed from the original manuscript... Boston, At
the Apollo press, by Belknap and Hall, 1792.
89 p.   20 cm.
Published by the Massachusetts historical society.
"A short account of Daniel Gookin": p. 88-89.

12310   Gordon, James Bentley, 1750-1819.
An historical and geographical memoir of the North-
American continent; its nations and tribes: by the
Rev. James Bentley Gordon. With a summary account
of his life, writings, and opinions. Dublin,
Printed by J. Jones, 1820.
civ, x p., 1 l., 305 p. incl. front. (port.)
27 x 21 1/2 cm.
Edited by Thomas Jones, of Nutgrove school, Rath-
farnham.

12311   Gordon, John, d. 1845, defendant.
A full report of the trial of John Gordon and
William Gordon, charged with the murder of Amasa
Sprague; before the Supreme court of Rhode-Island,
March term, 1844: with all the incidental questions
raised in the trial carefully preserved - the

testimony of the witnesses nearly verbatim - and
the arguments of council and a correct plat of all
the localities described in the testimony, prepared
expressly for this report. Reported by Edward C.
Larned and William Knowles. Providence, Printed at
the office of the Daily transcript, 1844.
45, [2] p.   fold. map.   26 1/2 cm.

12312   Gordon, Thomas Francis, 1787-1860.
A gazetteer of the state of New Jersey. Comprehending a general view of its physical and moral
condition, together with a topographical and statistical account of its counties, towns, villages,
canals, rail roads &c., accompanied by a map. By
Thomas F. Gordon. Trenton, D. Fenton, 1834.
iv, 266 p.   front. (fold. map)   23 cm.
[With his History of New Jersey. Trenton, 1834]

12313   Gordon, Thomas Francis, 1787-1860.
The history of New Jersey, from its discovery by
Europeans, to the adoption of the federal Constitution. By Thomas F. Gordon. Trenton, D. Fenton,
1834.
xii, 339 p.   23 cm.

12314   Gordon, William, 1728-1807.
The separation of the Jewish tribes, after the
death of Solomon, accounted for, and applied to the
present day, in a sermon preached before the General
court, on Friday, July the 4th, 1777. Being the
anniversary of the Declaration of independency.
By William Gordon. Pastor of the Third church in
Roxbury. Boston, Printed by J. Gill, printer to
the General assembly, 1777.
37 p.   22 x 13 cm.

12315   Gordon, William Robert, 1811-1897.
The peril of our ship of state: a sermon on the
day of fasting and prayer, January 4th, 1861...
The folly of our speculations: a New-Year's sermon,
January 6, 1861... Strictures on a recent sermon
by Rev. H. J. Van Dyke. By Rev. W. R. Gordon, D. D.,
pastor of the Reformed Dutch church of Schraalenbergh,
N. J. New York, J. A. Gray, printer, 1861.
38 p.   22 1/2 cm.

12316   Gordon, William Robert, 1811-1897.
        Reliance on God, our hope of victory. A sermon
preached on the day of fasting and prayer, September
26th, 1861. By Rev. W. R. Gordon... New York,
J. A. Gray, printer, 1861.
        30 p.   23 cm.

12317   Gordon, William Robert, 1811-1897.
        The sin of reviling, and its work. A funeral
sermon, occasioned by the assassination of President
Lincoln, April 14th, 1865. By W. R. Gordon, D. D.,
pastor of the Ref. Prot. Dutch church of Schraalen-
berg, N. J. Preached on May 7, 1865... New York,
J. A. Gray & Green, printers, 1865.
        24 p.   23 1/2 cm.

12318   [Gore, Christopher] 1758-1827.
        Manlius; with notes and references. [Boston?
1794]
        54 p.   21 cm.
        A defense of Washington's administration, in seven
letters originally published in the Columbian
centinel, Boston, Sept. 3-24, 1794.

12319   Gore, Montague.
        Observations on the disturbances in Canada. By
Montague Gore, esq. London, Saunders and Otley,
1838.
        38 p.   22 cm.

12320   Gorrie, Peter Douglass, 1813-1884.
        The churches and sects of the United States:
containing a brief account of the origin, history,
doctrines, church government, mode of worship,
usages, and statistics of each religious denomination, so far as known. By Rev. P. Douglass Gorrie.
New York, L. Colby, 1850.
        1 p.l., [v]-xii, [13]-240 p.   19 1/2 cm.

12321   Gorrie, Peter Douglass, 1813-1884.
        Episcopal Methodism, as it was, and is; or, An
account of the origin, progress, doctrines, church
polity, usages, institutions, and statistics, of the
Methodist Episcopal church in the United States.
Embracing also a sketch of the rise of Methodism
in Europe, and of its origin and progress in Canada.
By Rev. P. Douglass Gorrie... Auburn [N. Y.]

Derby and Miller, 1852.
xxii, 354 p.   20 cm.

12322   Gorton, Samuel, 1592–1677.
Simplicity's defence against seven-headed policy.
By Samuel Gorton... with notes explanatory of the
text: and appendixes containing original documents
referred to in the work. By William R. Staples...
Providence, Marshall, Brown and company, 1835.
[7]-278 p.   22 cm.   (In Rhode Island historical
society. Collections. Providence, 1835. vol. II)
With reproduction of original t.-p., London,
J. Macock, 1646; also that of the edition printed,
London, J. Macock, 1647.

12323   Goss, Ephraim.
Supervisor's book: containing an abstract of all
laws now in force relating to the powers and duties
of supervisors, of the several towns and counties
of the state of New York, with suitable forms, notes
and references appended thereto. Together with a
copy of the legislative and parliamentary rules, so
far as applicable to boards of supervisors. By
Ephraim Goss... Rochester, D. M. Dewey, 1849.
212 p.   21 cm.

12324   Gosse, Philip Henry, 1810–1888.
The birds of Jamaica. By Philip Henry Gosse;
assisted by Richard Hill, esq., of Spanish-town.
London, J. Van Voorst, 1847.
x, 447, [1] p.   19 1/2 cm.

12325   Gosse, Philip Henry, 1810–1888.
The romance of natural history. By Philip Henry
Gosse... Boston, Gould and Lincoln; New York,
Sheldon and company [etc., etc.] 1861.
xiv p., 1 l., 372 p. incl. front.   pl.   20 cm.

12326   Gouge, William M   1796–1863.
An inquiry into the expediency of dispensing
with bank agency and bank paper in fiscal concerns
of the United States. By William M. Gouge...
Philadelphia, Printed by W. Stavely, 1837.
iv, [5]-56 p.   22 cm.

12327   Gouge, William M   1796–1863.
A short history of paper money and banking in

the United States, including an account of provincial
and continental paper money. To which is prefixed,
An inquiry into the principles of the system... By
William M. Gouge. Philadelphia, Printed by T. W.
Ustick, 1833.
   xii, 140, 240 p.   17 1/2 cm.

12328 Gould, Augustus Addison, 1805-1866.
   Otia conchologica: descriptions of shells and
mollusks, from 1839 to 1862. By Augustus A. Gould,
M. D. Boston, Gould and Lincoln, 1862.
   2 p.l., 256 p.   22 1/2 cm.
   "Short papers... have been published in several
periodicals. Extra copies of the sheets relating to
the shells of the exploring expeditions under Cap-
tains Wilkes and Rodgers were secured as they were
originally printed." - Pref.

12329 [Gould, Augustus Addison] 1805-1866.
   Report on the Invertebrata of Massachusetts, comprising the Mollusca, Crustacea, Annelida, and
Radiata. Pub. agreeably to an order of the legislature, by the commissioners on the Zoological and
botanical survey of the state. Cambridge, Folsom,
Wells, and Thurston, printers, 1841.
   xiii, 373 p.   15 pl.   24 1/2 cm.

12330 Gould, Benjamin Apthorp, 1824-1896.
   ... Boston harbor: a series of communications to
the Boston daily advertiser, by Benjamin A. Gould,
republished by order of the City council of Boston.
Boston, J. E. Farwell & company, printers to the
city, 1863.
   64 (i.e. 65) p.   24 cm.   (City document, no.
108)

12331 Gould, Benjamin Apthorp, 1824-1896.
   Reply to the "Statement of the trustees" of the
Dudley observatory, by Benj. Apthorp Gould, jr.
Albany, Printed by C. Van Benthuysen, 1859.
   v p., 1 l., 366 p.   23 cm.

12332 [Gould, Benjamin Apthorp] 1824-1896.
   Specimens of the garbling of letters by the
majority of the trustees of the Dudley observatory.
Albany, Van Benthuysen, printer, 1858.
   19 p.   23 cm.

215

12333   Gould, Hannah Flagg, 1789-1865.
      Poems, by Miss H. F. Gould. Boston, Hilliard,
Gray, Little and Wilkins, 1832.
      viii, 174 p.   pl.   15 1/2 cm.
      Issued in 1836 with additions as "vol. I" of a
2 vol. edition. Vol. III appeared in 1841. cf.
Sabin, Bibl. amer.

12334   Gould, Jay, 1836-1892.
      History of Delaware county, and border wars of
New York. Containing a sketch of the early settle-
ments in the county, and a history of the late anti-
rent difficulties in Delaware, with other historical
and miscellaneous matter, never before published.
By Jay Gould. Roxbury [N. Y.] Keeny & Gould, 1856.
      xvi, 426 p.   front. (port.)   20 cm.
      Life and adventures of Timothy Murphy: p. 305-343;
Adventures of a Yankee woman, by Maud Sutherland,
Jr.: p. 344-356.

12335   Gould, John W   1814-1838.
      John W. Gould's private journal of a voyage from
New-York to Rio de Janeiro; together with a brief
sketch of his life, and his occasional writings.
Ed. by his brothers. Printed for private circulation
only. New York, 1839.
      2 p.l., [3]-207 p.   fold. map.   24 cm.

12336   Gould, Nathaniel D[uren] 1781-1864.
      Church music in America, comprising its history
and its peculiarities at different periods, with
cursory remarks on its legitimate use and its abuse;
with notices of the schools, composers, teachers,
and societies. By Nathaniel D. Gould... Boston,
A. N. Johnson, 1853.
      xii, [13]-240 p.   19 cm.
      "List of collections of sacred music, for schools
and churches, in the United States, since... 1810":
p. [231]-233.

12337   Gourlay, Robert Fleming, 1778-1863.
      General introduction to Statistical account of
Upper Canada, compiled with a view to a grand system
of emigration, in connexion with a reform of the
poor laws. By Robert Gourlay... London, Simpkin
and Marshall [etc.] 1822.
      xii, div, 47 p.   front. (fold. map)   21 1/2 cm.

The "Statistical account of Upper Canada" appeared the same year in 2 vols.

12338 Gourlay, Robert Fleming, 1778-1863.
Plans for beautifying New York, and for enlarging and improving the city of Boston. Being, studies to illustrate the science of city building. By Robert Fleming Gourlay... Boston, Crocker & Brewster [etc.] 1844.
2 p.l., [3]-38, 381-384 p.   illus., fold. plan. 23 1/2 cm.

12339 Gourlie, John Hamilton.
An address, delivered before the Mercantile library association at its eighteenth annual meeting, January 8, 1839. (Embodying a history of the association) By John H. Gourlie. New York, Printed by J. Van Norden, 1839.
20 p.   23 cm.

12340 Grace, Henry, b. 1730?
The history of the life and sufferings of Henry Grace, of Basingstoke in the county of Southampton, being a narrative of the hardships he underwent during several years captivity among the savages in North America, and of the cruelties they practise to their unhappy prisoners. In which is introduced an account of the several customs and manners of the different nations of Indians; as well as a compendious description of the soil, produce and various animals of those parts. Written by himself. Reading [Eng.] Printed for the author, 1764.
56 p.   18 1/2 cm.

12341 Graham, John Andrew, 1764-1841.
A descriptive sketch of the present state of Vermont. One of the United States of America. By J. A. Graham... London, Printed and sold for the author, by H. Fry, 1797.
vii, 186 p., 1 l. incl. front. (port.) illus. 22 cm.

12342 Graham, John Andrew, 1764-1841.
Speeches, delivered at the City-hall of the city of New-York; in the courts of Oyer and terminer, Common pleas, and General sessions of the peace. By John A. Graham... 2d ed., with additions.

New-York, Printed and published by George Forman,
and sold by him, at no. 178 Greenwich-street.
Also by Gould, Banks & Gould, sign of Lord Coke,
corner of Wall and Broad-st. and M. & W. Ward,
City-hotel, Broad-way, and William Gould & co.
State-street, Albany, 1812.
viii, [9]-140 p.   front. (port.)   21 1/2 cm.

12343   Graham, William, 1798-1854.
The contrast; or, The Bible and abolitionism:
an exegetical argument, by Rev. William Graham...
Cincinnati, Printed at the Daily Cincinnati atlas
office, 1844.
48 p.   21 cm.

12344   Grahame, James, 1790-1842.
Who is to blame? or, Cursory review of "American
apology for American accession to negro slavery".
By James Grahame, esq. ... London, Smith, Elder &
co., 1842.
112 p.   23 cm.

12345   A grammatical sketch of the Heve language, tr. from
an unpublished Spanish manuscript. By Buckingham
Smith. New York, Cramoisy press, 1861.
26 p.   26 cm.   (Half-title: [Shea's] library
of American linguistics. III)
"The title of the work, in manuscript, from which
the grammatical notices have been elaborated, is
Arte y vocabulario de la lingua [!] dohema heve, ó
eudeva." - Foot-note.

12346   Grandpierre, Jean Henri, 1799-1874.
A Parisian pastor's glance at America. By Rev.
J. H. Grandpierre... Boston, Gould and Lincoln,
1854.
5, [iii]-v p., 1 l., [11]-132 p.   18 1/2 cm.
Appendix, found in original and in Dutch translation, omitted in this translation.

12347   Grandpierre, Jean Henri, 1799-1874.
Quelques mois de séjour aux États-Unis d'Amérique,
par J.-H. Grandpierre... Paris, Grassart, 1854.
207 p., 1 l.   18 cm.

12348   [Granger, Gideon] 1767-1822.
An address to the people of New England. By

Algernon Sidney [pseud.] December 15th, 1808.
Washington city, Printed by Dinmore and Cooper,
1808.
    38 p., 1 l.   23 cm.

12349 [Granger, Gideon] 1767-1822.
    A vindication of the measures of the present admi-
    nistration. By Algernon Sidney [pseud.] ...
    Washington, Printed by Samuel H. Smith, 1803.
        20 p.   22 1/2 cm.
    "Taken from the National intelligencer."

12350 Grant, Charles, viscount de Vaux.
    Proposals for a subscription to form colonies in
    Canada, of French emigrant loyalists, and ecclesias-
    tics, now in England. By Charles Grant, viscount
    de Vaux. [n. p., 1793?]
        8 p.   21 1/2 cm.

12351 Grant, Joseph W
    The flying regiment. Journal of the campaign of
    the 12th regt. Rhode Island volunteers. By Capt.
    J. W. Grant. Providence, S. S. Rider & bro., 1865.
        152 p.   15 1/2 cm.
    Also published, 1863, anonymously, under title:
    "My first campaign."

12352 Graves, William, 1724?-1801.
    Two letters respecting the conduct of Rear Admiral
    Graves on the coast of the United States, July to
    November, 1781. By William Graves... Morrisania,
    N. Y., 1865.
        2 p.l., 39 p.   30 cm.
    Edited by H. B. Dawson.

12353 Gravier, Jacques, 1651-1708.
    Relation de ce qvi s'est passé dans la Mission de
    l'Immaculée Conception, au Pays des Ilinois,
    depuis le Mois de Mars 1693, jusqu'en Fevrier 1694.
    Par le R. Père Jacques Gravier, de la Compagnie de
    Jésus. A Manate, De la Presse Cramoisy de Jean-Marie
    Shea, 1857.
        65, [1] p.   19 cm.   [Shea's Cramoisy press
    series. no. 1]

12354 Gray, Alonzo, 1808-1860.
    Elements of geology. By Alonzo Gray... and

219

C. B. Adams... New York, Harper & brothers, 1853.
xv, 354 p. illus. 20 cm.

12355 Gray, Asa, 1810-1888.
Genera florae Americae boreali-orientalis illus-
trata. The genera of the plants of the United States
illustrated by figures and analyses from nature, by
Isaac Sprague... Superintended, and with descriptions,
&c., by Asa Gray... Boston, J. Munroe and company;
New York and London, J. Wiley, 1848-49.
2 v. 186 pl. 24 cm.

12356 Gray, Edward, 1764-1810.
An oration, delivered July 5, 1790. At the request
of the inhabitants of the town of Boston, in celebration of the anniversary of American independence.
By Edward Gray... Boston, Printed and sold by
Samuel Hall, 1790.
16 p. 20 1/2 cm.

12357 [Gray, Francis Calley] 1790-1856.
Letter to Governor Lincoln, in relation to Harvard
university. Boston, W. L. Lewis, printer, 1831.
48 p. 23 cm.

12358 Gray, Francis Calley, 1790-1856.
Oration delivered before the Legislature of Massachusetts, at their request, on the hundredth anniversary of the birth of George Washington. By Francis
C. Gray. Boston, Dutton and Wentworth, printers to
the state, 1832.
80 p. 24 cm.
"Celebration of the centennial anniversary of the
birth day of George Washington, by the Legislature of
Massachusetts. February 22, 1832": p. [78]-80.

12359 Gray, Frederick Turell, 1804-1855.
Extract from a sermon delivered at the Bulfinch-
street church, Boston, Jan. 9, 1853, the Sunday
following the interment of the late Amos Lawrence.
By Rev. F. T. Gray. Boston, J. Wilson & son, 1853.
16 p. 16 1/2 cm.

12360 Gray, Horatio, 1828-1903.
Memoirs of Rev. Benjamin C. Cutler, D. D., late
rector of St. Ann's church, Brooklyn, N. Y. By Rev.
Horatio Gray... New York, A. D. F. Randolph, 1865.

3 p.l., v-vii, 439 p.   front. (port.) pl.
20 1/2 cm.

12361   Gray, Robert, 1761-1822.
A sermon delivered at Hopkinton, before the hon.
General court of the state of New Hampshire, at the
annual election, holden on the first Wednesday in
June, 1798. By Robert Gray, A. B., pastor of the
church in Dover. Dover, Printed by Samuel Bragg,
jun., for the General court [1798]
29 p.   21 1/2 cm.

12362   Gray, Thomas.
California politics. Letter of Thos. Gray, of
San Francisco, California, to the secretary of the
Treasury. [Washington, 1861]
15 p.   22 cm.
Dated Washington city, April 2, 1861. An applica-
tion for the position of collector of the port of
San Francisco, preceded by a review of his political
affiliations and work.

12363   Gray, Thomas, 1772-1847.
Half century sermon, delivered on Sunday morning,
April 24, 1842, at Jamaica Plain. By Thomas Gray...
Boston, Printed by I. R. Butts, 1842.
6 p., 1 l., [5]-44 p.   23 cm.

12364   Gray, Thomas, 1772-1847.
A sermon on the death of His Excellency, William
Eustis, late governor of the commonwealth of Massa-
chusetts, preached in the First church in Roxbury,
February 13, 1825... By Thomas Gray... Boston,
Office of the Christian register, F. Y. Carlile,
printer, 1825.
26 p.   23 1/2 cm.

12365   Gray, William Cunningham, 1830-1901.
Life of Abraham Lincoln. For the young man and the
Sabbath school. By Wm. C. Gray... Cincinnati,
Western tract and book society, 1867.
vi, 7-200 p.   front., plates.   17 1/2 cm.

12366   [Gray, William Farley]
Letter to His Excellency Wm. H. Seward, governor
of the state of New York, touching the surrender of
certain fugitives from justice... New York, Printed

221

by W. Osborn, 1841.
   100 p.   23 cm.
   Signed: A Virginian, now a citizen of New York.
   Leaflet prefixed to t.-p.: Note. It was the
intention of the writer to have appended the whole
letter of Governor Seward to the executive of Virginia... Upon reflection... he has not deemed it
necessary or advisable.

12367   Graydon, Alexander, 1752-1818.
   Memoirs of his own time. With reminiscences of
the men and events of the revolution. By Alexander
Graydon. Ed. by John Stockton Littell... Philadelphia, Lindsay & Blakiston, 1846.
   xxiv, [13]-504 p.   23 cm.
   First edition, Harrisburg, 1811, appeared under
title: Memoirs of a life, chiefly passed in Pennsylvania...

12368   Gt. Brit. Sovereigns, etc., 1649-1658 (Oliver Cromwell)
   A manifesto of the Lord protector of the commonwealth of England, Scotland, Ireland, &c., published
by consent and advice of his Council. Wherein is
shewn the reasonableness of the cause of this republic against the depredations of the Spaniards.
Written in Latin by John Milton, and first printed
in 1655, now translated into English... To which
is added, Britannia, a poem; by Mr. Thomson, first
published in 1727. London, A. Millar, 1738.
   40 p.   20 1/2 cm.
   First published in London, 1655 in two editions,
English and Latin, the English edition with title
"A declaration of His Highnes, by advice of his
Council; setting forth, on behalf of this commonwealth, the justice of their cause against Spain";
the Latin edition, "Scriptum Dom. protectoris...
ex consensu atque sententia Concilii sui editum:
in quo hujus reipublicae causa contra Hispanos justa
esse demonstratus".
   "This very interesting tract details a great number
of instances of cruelty and oppression towards
English mariners and others at Hispaniola, Providence, Tortugas, etc." - Sabin, Bibl. amer., v. 12,
p. 190.

12369   ... The great issue to be decided in November next!
Shall the Constitution and the Union stand or fall,

shall sectionalism triumph? Lincoln and his supporters... [Washington, National Democratic executive
committee, 1860?]
    24 p.   25 cm.   (Breckinridge and Lane campaign
documents, no. 19)

12370   The great surrender to the rebels in arms. The armis-
tice. "Immediate efforts to be made for a cessation
of hostilities." - Peace and disunion platform of the
Chicago copperhead convention. [Washington, Printed
by McGill & Witherow, 1864]
    7, [1] p.   24 cm.   [Republican congressional
committee, 1863-1865. Publications. Campaign of
1864. No. 4]

12371   Great trans-continental tourist's guide... from the
Atlantic to the Pacific Ocean... [1st rev. ed.]
New York, G. A. Crofutt & co., 1870.
    208 p. incl. front., illus.   fold. map.   18 cm.

12372   Grece, Charles Frederick.
    Facts and observations respecting Canada, and the
United States of America: affording a comparative
view of the inducements to emigration presented in
those countries. To which is added an appendix of
practical instructions to emigrant settlers in the
British colonies. By Charles F. Grece... London,
Printed for J. Harding, 1819.
    xv, 172 p.   23 cm.
    Appendix (p. [81]-[164]) consists of various
articles relating to Canadian agriculture, commerce,
etc.

12373   Greeley, Horace, 1811-1872.
    Art and industry as represented in the exhibition
at the Crystal Palace, New York - 1853-4; showing
the progress and state of the various useful and
esthetic pursuits. From the New York Tribune.
Rev. and ed. by Horace Greeley. New York, Redfield,
1853.
    xxv, [13]-386 p.   18 1/2 cm.

12374   Greeley, Horace, 1811-1872.
    Hints toward reforms, in lectures, addresses,
and other writings: by Horace Greeley... New-York,
Harper & brothers, 1850.
    400 p.   19 1/2 cm.

12375 Greely, Allen, 1781-1866.
       A sermon delivered in Bangor, June 23, 1824,
before the Maine missionary society, at their
seventeenth anniversary. By Allen Greely...
Hallowell, Printed by S. K. Gilman, 1824.
       32 p.   24 cm.
       "Report of the Trustees of the Maine missionary
society, at the annual meeting, in Bangor, June 23,
1824": p. [23]-32.

12376 Green, Ashbel, 1762-1848.
       Discourses, delivered in the College of New Jersey;
addressed chiefly to candidates for the first degree
in the arts; with notes and illustrations, including
a historical sketch of the college, from its origin
to the accession of President Witherspoon. By Ashbel
Green... Philadelphia, E. Littell; New York, R. N.
Henry [etc., etc.] 1822.
       xi, 419 p.   23 cm.

12377 Green, Ashbel, 1762-1848.
       Memoirs of the Rev. Joseph Eastburn, stated
preacher in the Mariner's church, Philadelphia...
By Ashbel Green, D. D. Philadelphia, G. W. Mentz,
1828.
       vi, 208 p.   front. (port.)   18 1/2 cm.
       Second appendix (p. [183]-208): A faithful narra-
tive of the many dangers and sufferings... of Robert
Eastburn, during his late captivity among the Indians
... By Robert Eastburn... Philadelphia, Printed by
W. Dunlap, 1758.

12378 [Green, Duff] 1791-1875.
       ... The United States and England. By an American.
London, 1842.
       122 p.   front. (fold. map)   22 cm.
       At head of title: "The Great western magazine.
September, 1842," [v. 2, no. 6]

12379 [Green, Jacob] 1722-1790.
       Observations, on the reconciliation of Great-
Britain, and the colonies, in which are exhibited
arguments for, and against, that measure. By a
friend of American liberty... Philadelphia, Printed
by Robert Bell, in Third-Street, 1776.
       40 p.   20 cm.
       [Colonial pamphlets, v. 16, no. 6]

224

12380 Green, John, 1835-1913.
　　　　City hospitals. By John Green... Boston, Little,
　　Brown, and company, 1861.
　　　　viii, [9]-66 p.　　illus., v pl.　(2 phot., incl.
　　front.; 3 plans)　　24 cm.

12381 Green, John B[remner] d. 1905.
　　　　An address at the funeral of Hon. Henry Wyles Cush-
　　man; delivered in Bernardston, Mass., Nov. 24, 1863.
　　By John B. Green... Boston, Printed by J. Wilson
　　and son, 1864.
　　　　23 p.　　21 1/2 cm.

12382 Green, John Orne, 1841-
　　　　A memorial of John C. Dalton, M. D.; an address
　　delivered before the Middlesex north district medical
　　society, April 27, 1864, by John O. Green... Cam-
　　bridge, University press, 1864.
　　　　35 p.　　24 cm.

12383 [Green, Joseph] 1706-1780.
　　　　Entertainment for a winter's evening: being a
　　full and true account of a very strange and wonderful
　　sight seen in Boston on the twenty-seventh of
　　December at noonday.　The truth of which can be
　　attested by a great number of people, who actually
　　saw the same with their own eyes.　By me, the
　　Hon'ble B. B. esq. ... Boston, Printed and sold
　　by G. Rogers, next to the prison in Queen-street
　　[1750]
　　　　1 p.l., ii, [5]-15 p.　　20 cm.
　　　　[Hazard pamphlets, v. 36, no. 9]
　　　　"A versified satire on a masonic procession, &c.,
　　which caused in its day much ill feeling." - Sabin,
　　Bibl. amer.
　　　　Names of persons alluded to are supplied in manus-
　　cript.

12384 Green, Matthew, 1696-1737.
　　　　The spleen.　An epistle to Mr. C. Jackson.　By
　　Matthew Green... Boston, Printed for S. H. Parker,
　　1804.
　　　　1 p.l., 31 p.　　17 1/2 cm.

12385 Green, Samuel, d. 1822.
　　　　Life of Samuel Green, executed at Boston, April 25,
　　1822, for the murder of Billy Williams, a fellow

225

convict with Green, in the state prison. Written
by himself... Boston, D. Felt, 1822.
   47, [1] p.   front. (port.)   23 cm.

12386   Green, Samuel, 1793-1834.
      A discourse, delivered at Plymouth, Dec. 20, 1828,
on the two hundred and eighth anniversary of the
landing of the Pilgrim fathers. By Samuel Green...
Boston, Pierce & Williams, 1829.
   36 p.   23 1/2 cm.

12387   Green-back, pseud.
      Green-back to his country friends. [New York, 1862]
cover-title, 17 p.   22 1/2 cm.

12388   [Greene, Asa] 1789-1838.
      A glance at New York: embracing the city govern-
ment, theatres, hotels, churches, mobs, monopolies,
learned professions, newspapers, rogues, dandies,
fires and firemen, water and other liquids, &c.,
&c. ... New York, A. Greene, 1837.
   vi, 264 p.   15 cm.

12389   Greene, Benjamin, 1764-1837.
      An oration, pronounced at Lexington, July 4th,
1809, being the anniversary of American independence.
By Benj. Greene, esq. Boston, Printed by Munroe,
Francis & Parker, no. 4 Cornhill, 1809.
   24 p.   22 1/2 cm.

12390   Greene, Charles S
      Thrilling stories of the great rebellion: com-
prising heroic adventures and hair-breadth escapes
of soldiers, scouts, spies, and refugees; daring
exploits of smugglers, guerrillas, desperadoes,
and others; tales of loyal and disloyal women;
stories of the Negro, etc. etc. With incidents of
fun and merriment in camp and field. Together with
an account of the death of President Lincoln; fate
of the assassins; capture of Jefferson Davis, and
end of the war. By Lieutenant-Colonel Charles S.
Greene... Philadelphia, J. E. Potter & co. [c1864]
   494 p.   col. front., col. plates.   19 cm.

12391   Greene, Christopher Rhodes, 1786-1825.
      An oration, delivered in St. Michael's church,
Charleston, South-Carolina; on Tuesday, the Fourth

of July, 1815; in commemoration of American independence; by appointment of the South-Carolina state Society of Cincinnati, and published at the request of that society; and also of the American revolution society. By Christopher R. Greene... Charleston, Printed by W. P. Young, no. 44, Broad-street, 1815.
    3 p.l., [5]-26 p.   20 cm.

12392 Greene, David, 1797?-1866.
    Ministerial fidelity exemplified. A sermon at the funeral of the Rev. Daniel Crosby, late pastor of the Winthrop church, Charlestown, March 3, 1843. By David Greene. Boston, T. R. Marvin, 1843.
    39 p.   24 cm.

12393 Greene, George Washington, 1811-1883.
    A discourse delivered before the Rhode-Island historical society, on the evening of Thursday, February 1, 1849. By George Washington Greene... Providence, Gladding and Proud, 1849.
    22 p., 1 l.   23 1/2 cm.
    "Sketch of the progress of historical science."

12394 Greene, George Washington, 1811-1883.
    Historical view of the American revolution... Boston, Ticknor and Fields, 1865.
    ix p., 1 l., 459 p.   18 1/2 cm.

12395 Greene, George Washington, 1811-1883.
    Nathaniel Greene. An examination of some statements concerning Major-General Greene, in the ninth volume of Bancroft's History of the United States. By George Washington Greene... Boston, Ticknor and Fields, 1866.
    vi, 7-86 p.   23 1/2 cm.

12396 Greene, Jerome B
    The world's progress, and other poems. By J. B. Greene. Worcester, Mass., The author, 1856.
    vi, [7]-112 p.   17 cm.

12397 Greene, Jonathan Harrington, b. 1812.
    Gambling unmasked! or, The personal experience of J. H. Green, the reformed gambler; designed as a warning to the young men of this country. Written by himself... Philadelphia, G. B. Zieber

& co., 1847.
2 p.l., 3-312 p.   front. (port.)   plates.
19 cm.

12398   Greene, Richard Henry, 1839-
The Todd genealogy; or, Register of the descendants
of Adam Todd, of the names of Todd, Whetten, Bre-
voort, Coolidge, Bristed, Sedgwick, Kane, Renwick,
Bull, Huntington, Dean, Astor, Bentzen, Langdon,
Boreel, Wilks, De Nottbeck, Ward, Chanler, Cary,
Tiebout, Bruce, Robbins, Waldo, Woodhull, Odell,
Greene and Foster, with notices and genealogies of
many persons and families connected with the before-
mentioned descendants. By Richard Henry Greene,
A. M. New York, Wilbur & Hastings, 1867.
viii, [9]-143, xvii p.   23 1/2 cm.

12399   Greene, Samuel D   b. 1788.
The broken seal; or, Personal reminiscences of the
Morgan abduction and murder. By Samuel D. Greene.
Boston, The author, 1872.
304 p.   20 cm.
Cover-title: Free masonry developed.

12400   Greene, Samuel Stillman, 1810-1883.
A genealogical sketch of the descendants of Thomas
Green[e] of Malden, Mass. By Samuel S. Greene,
Providence, R. I. Boston, H. W. Dutton & son,
printers, 1858.
1 p.l., 80 p.   24 cm.

12401   Greene, William, 1797-1883.
An oration on the life and character of John Quincy
Adams. Delivered at Cincinnati, 25 March, 1848,
before the bar of Hamilton County, at their request,
by William Greene. Cincinnati [Cincinnati chronicle
print] 1848.
35 p.   21 1/2 cm.

12402   Greene, William Batchelder, 1819-1878.
The sovereignty of the people. By William B.
Greene... Boston, A. Williams and co., 1868.
35 p.   23 1/2 cm.

12403   Greene, William H
Maine liquor law. Report of the case of William
H. Greene vs. Nathan M. Briggs, et al. The

plaintiff's opening argument, and the opinion of
the U. S. Circuit court for the Rhode-Island district. By Joseph S. Pitman... Boston, Little,
Brown & co.; Providence, G. H. Whitney, 1853.
   60 p.   23 1/2 cm.

12404 Greenhow, Rose (O'Neal) 1814-1864.
       My imprisonment and the first year of abolition
       rule at Washington. By Mrs. Greenhow. London,
       R. Bentley, 1863.
          x, 352 p.   front. (port.)   19 1/2 cm.

12405 Greenleaf, Jonathan, 1785-1865.
       A genealogy of the Greenleaf family. By Jonathan
       Greenleaf... New York, Printed by E. O. Jenkins,
       1854.
          iv, 5-116 p.   23 1/2 cm.

12406 Greenleaf, Jonathan, 1785-1865.
       A history of the churches, of all denominations,
       in the city of New York, from the first settlement
       to the year 1846. By Jonathan Greenleaf... New
       York, E. French; Portland, Hyde, Lord & Duren, 1846.
          viii, 379, [1] p.   16 cm.

12407 Greenleaf, Lawrence Nichols, b. 1838.
       King Sham, and other atrocities in verse; including
       a humorous history of the Pike's Peak excitement.
       By Lawrence N. Greenleaf. New York, Hurd and
       Houghton, 1868.
          vi, [7]-139, [1] p.   18 cm.

12408 Greenleaf, Moses, 1777-1834.
       A statistical view of the district of Maine; more
       especially with reference to the value and importance
       of its interior. Addressed to the consideration of
       the legislators of Massachusetts, by Moses Green-
       leaf... Boston, Published by Cummings and Hilliard,
       at the Boston bookstore, no. 1, Cornhill, 1816.
          viii, [9]-154 p.   23 cm.

12409 Greenleaf, Moses, 1777-1834.
       A survey of the state of Maine, in reference to
       its geographical features, statistics and political
       economy; illustrated by maps. By Moses Greenleaf.
       Portland, Shirley and Hyde, 1829.

viii, [9]-468 p., 1 l. incl. tables.   22 cm.
and atlas of 5 fold. maps, 2 fold. diagr.
33 1/2 cm.

12410   Greenleaf, Simon, 1783-1853.
A discourse commemorative of the life and character
of the Hon. Joseph Story, LL. D., an associate
justice of the Supreme court of the United States,
and Dane professor of law in Harvard university;
pronounced on the eighteenth day of September,
A. D. 1845, at the request of the corporation of
the University, and the members of the Law school,
by Simon Greenleaf... Boston, C. C. Little and J.
Brown, 1845.
48 p.   22 1/2 cm.

12411   Greenough, William Whitwell, d. 1899.
The conquering republic. An oration delivered
before the municipal authorities of the city of
Boston, July 4, 1849... by William W. Greenough.
Boston, J. H. Eastburn, city printer, 1849.
39 p.   22 cm.

12412   [Greenough, William Whitwell] d. 1899.
Descendants of Richard Gardner, of Woburn, of the
name of Gardner. Boston, Printed for private circulation [Press of G. C. Rand and Avery] 1858.
14 p.   24 cm.

12413   Greenwood, Andrew, 1776-1816.
An oration, composed at the request of the select-
men, and delivered before the inhabitants of the
town of Bath, on Saturday, 22d February, 1800. By
Andrew Greenwood, esq. Hallowell (District of Maine)
Printed by Peter Edes, 1800.
16 p.   18 1/2 x 15 1/2 cm.

12414   Greenwood, Francis William Pitt, 1797-1843.
Funeral sermon on the late Hon. Christopher Gore,
formerly governor of Massachusetts. Preached at
King's chapel, Boston, March 11, 1827. By F. W. P.
Greenwood... Boston, Wells and Lilly, 1827.
19 p.   21 1/2 cm.

12415   Greenwood, Francis William Pitt, 1797-1843.
A history of King's chapel, in Boston, the first
Episcopal church in New England; comprising notices

230

of the introduction of Episcopacy into the northern
colonies. By F. W. P. Greenwood... Boston, Carter,
Hendee & co. [etc.] 1833.
   xii, 215 p.   front., illus.   17 1/2 cm.

12416   Gregg, Alexander, bp., 1819-1893.
        History of the old Cheraws: containing an account
   of the aborigines of the Pedee, the first white
   settlements, their subsequent progress, civil changes,
   the struggle of the revolution, and growth of the
   country afterward; extending from about A. D. 1730
   to 1810, with notices of families and sketches of
   individuals. By the Right Rev. Alexander Gregg...
   New York, Richardson and company, 1867.
        viii, 546 p., 1 l.   front., illus., maps, plans.
   22 cm.

12417   Gregg, Jarvis, 1808-1836.
        Eulogy on Lafayette, delivered in the chapel of
   Dartmouth college, July 4, 1834. By Jarvis Gregg.
   Hanover, N. H., T. Mann, printer, 1834.
        28 p.   21 cm.

12418   Gregg, William, 1800-1867.
        Essays on domestic industry: or, An inquiry into
   the expediency of establishing cotton manufactures
   in South-Carolina. Originally published in the
   Charleston courier, and now re-published at the
   request of several gentlemen of Charleston. By
   William Gregg. Charleston [S. C.] Burges & James,
   1845.
        v, [7]-63 p.   22 1/2 cm.
        Published in the Courier under the head of
   "Domestic industry", and signed "South Carolina".

12419   Grégoire, Henry, constitutional bp. of Blois, 1750-
        1831.
        Critical observations on the poem of Mr. Joel
   Barlow, The Columbiad. By M. Gregoire... Washington city, Printed by Roger Chew Weightman, 1809.
        15 p.   21 1/2 cm.
        [Miscellaneous pamphlets, v. 799, no. 6]
        Translated from the French.

12420   Grégoire, Henri, constitutional bp. of Blois, 1750-
        1831.
        De la liberté de conscience et de culte à Haïti.

Par m. Grégoire, ancien évêque de Blois. Paris,
Baudouin frères, 1824.
2 p.l., 43 p.   18 1/2 cm.

12421 Grégoire, Henri, constitutional bp. of Blois, 1750-
1831.
De la littérature des Nègres, ou Recherches sur
leurs facultés intellectuelles, leurs qualités
morales et leur littérature; suivies de notices
sur la vie et les ouvrages des Nègres qui se sont
distingués dans les sciences, les lettres et les
arts; par H. Grégoire... Paris, Maradan, 1808.
xvi, 287, [1] p.   20 cm.

12422 Grégoire, Henri, constitutional bp. of Blois, 1750-
1831.
An enquiry concerning the intellectual and moral
faculties, and literature of negroes; followed with
an account of the life and works of fifteen negroes
& mulattoes, distinguished in science, literature
and the arts. By H. Grégoire... Tr. by D. B. Warden
... Brooklyn, Printed by Thomas Kirk, Main-street,
1810.
1 p.l., viii, [9]-253, [2] p.   22 cm.

12423 Gregory, John, civil engineer.
Industrial resources of Wisconsin. By John Gregory
... Milwaukee, Starrs' book and job printing office,
1855.
v, [6]-329 p., 1 l.   16 1/2 cm.

12424 [Grenville, George] 1712-1770.
The speech of a Right Honourable gentleman, on
the motion for expelling Mr. Wilkes, Friday,
February 3, 1769. London, Printed for J. Almon,
1769.
54 p., 1 l.   20 1/2 cm.

12425 Grew, Henry.
A narrative of proceedings in the Bank street
church, Philadelphia, relative to the reception of
an adhering Free mason; with an examination of
masonic oaths, and of the principles of discipline
adopted by said church, by Henry Grew... Philadelphia, 1836.
36 p.   18 cm.

12426 [Grey, Sir Charles Edward] 1785-1865.
　　　　Remarks on the proceedings as to Canada, in the
present session of Parliament: by one of the commissioners. 10th April, 1837. London, J. Ridgway
and sons, 1837.
　　　　67 p.　　23 cm.

12427 [Grey, Isaac]
　　　　A serious address to such of the people called
Quakers, on the continent of North-America, as profess
scruples relative to the present government: exhibiting the ancient real testimony of that people,
concerning obedience to civil authority. Written
before the departure of the British army from Philadelphia, 1778, by a native of Pennsylvania. To which
are added, for the information of all rational en-
quirers, an appendix, consisting of extracts from An
essay concerning obedience to the supreme powers,
and the duty of subjects in all revolutions, published in England soon after the revolution of 1688.
The 2d ed. Philadelphia, Printed by Styner and
Cist, at the north-east corner of Race- and Second-
streets, 1778.
　　　　48 p.　　19 1/2 cm.

12428 Grider, Henry, 1796-1866.
　　　　Speech of Mr. Henry Grider, of Kentucky, on the
sub-treasury bill. Delivered in the House of representatives U. S. April 1st, 1846. Washington,
J. & G. S. Gideon, printers, 1846.
　　　　15 p.　　24 cm.

12429 Gridley, John.
　　　　History of Montpelier: a discourse delivered in
the Brick church, Montpelier, Vermont, on Thanksgiving day, Dec. 8, 1842. By Rev. John Gridley...
Montpelier, E. P. Walton and sons, 1843.
　　　　48 p.　　21 1/2 cm.

12430 Gridley, Philo, 1796-1864.
　　　　An address delivered before the literary societies
of Hamilton college, July 22, 1845, Clinton, N. Y.
By Hon. Philo Gridley. Utica, R. W. Roberts,
printer, 1845.
　　　　29 p.　　23 cm.

12431   Griffin, Augustus, 1767-1866.
        Griffin's journal. First settlers of Southold;
        the names of the heads of those families, being only
        thirteen at the time of their landing; first pro-
        prietors of Orient; biographical sketches, &c. &c.
        &c., by Augustus Griffin. Orient, L. I., A. Griffin,
        1857.
        [3]-312 p.   front. (port.)   19 cm.

12432   Griffin, Frederick.
        Junius discovered. By Frederick Griffin...   Boston,
        Little, Brown and company [etc., etc.] 1854.
        vi, [7]-310 p., 1 l.   17 1/2 cm.
        An attempt to identify Junius with Thomas Pownall.
        "List of Governor Pownall's works": p. [301]-303.

12433   Griffin, John, 1769-1834.
        Memoirs of Capt. James Wilson, containing an
        account of his enterprises and sufferings in India,
        his conversion to Christianity, his missionary
        voyage to the South seas, and his peaceful and
        triumphant death. By John Griffin. 2d American ed.
        With an appendix, exhibiting the glorious results
        of the South sea mission. Portland, J. Adams, jr.,
        1827.
        iv, [9]-220 p.   18 1/2 cm.

12434   Griffith, John, 1713-1776.
        A journal of the life, travels, and labours in
        the work of the ministry, of John Griffith...
        London Printed; Philadelphia, Re-printed by Joseph
        Crukshank in Market-street, between Second and
        Third-streets, 1780.
        1 p.l., iv, 426 p.   20 1/2 cm.
        With this is bound his Some brief remarks upon
        sundry important subjects... principally addressed
        to the people called Quakers. London, 1781.

12435   Griffith, Thomas Waters, 1767-1838.
        Sketches of the early history of Maryland. By
        Thomas W. Griffith. Baltimore, F. G. Schaeffer,
        1821.
        75, [2] p., 1 l.   front. (port.) pl.   20 cm.

12436   [Griffith, William] 1766-1826.
        Eumenes: being a collection of papers, written
        for the purpose of exhibiting some of the more pro-

minent errors and omissions of the constitution of
New-Jersey, as established on the second day of
July, one thousand seven hundred and seventy-six;
and to prove the necessity of calling a convention,
for revision and amendment. Trenton, Printed by
G. Craft, 1799.
vi, [9]-149, [4] p., 1 l.   20 1/2 cm.

12437   Griffith, William, 1766-1826.
Historical notes of the American colonies and revo-
lution, from 1754 to 1775, by William Griffith...
Published by his executors. Burlington, N. J.,
Sold by J. L. Powell, 1843.
ix, [11]-300 p.   23 1/2 cm.

12438   Griffith, William, 1766-1826.
An oration, delivered to the citizens of Burlington,
on the 22d of February, 1800, in commemoration of
Gen. George Washington... By William Griffith, esq.
To which is added, a prayer on the same occasion.
By Charles H. Wharton... Trenton, Printed by G.
Craft, 1800.
25 p.   21 1/2 cm.

12439   Grigsby, Hugh Blair, 1806-1881.
Discourse on the life and character of the Hon.
Littleton Waller Tazewell, delivered in the Free-
mason street Baptist church, before the bar of
Norfolk, Virginia, and the citizens, generally, on
the 29th of June, 1860, by Hugh Blair Grigsby...
Norfolk, J. D. Ghiselin, jr., 1860.
123, [1] p.   23 1/2 cm.

12440   Grigsby, Hugh Blair, 1806-1881.
The Virginia convention of 1776. A discourse
delivered before the Virginia Alpha of the Phi beta
kappa society, in the chapel of William and Mary
college, in the city of Williamsburg, on the after-
noon of July the 3rd, 1855. By Hugh Blair Grigsby.
[Published by a resolution of the Society] Richmond,
J. W. Randolph, 1855.
206 p.   23 cm.

12441   Grigsby, Hugh Blair, 1806-1881.
The Virginia convention of 1829-30. A discourse
delivered before the Virginia historical society,
at their annual meeting, held in... Richmond,

December 15th, 1853. By Hugh B. Grigsby. Pub. by
the society. Richmond, Macfarland & Fergusson,
1854.
104 p.   20 1/2 cm.
Published also in the Virginia historical reporter,
v. 1, 1854, p. 15-116.

12442 [Grim, Charles Frederic]
An essay towards an improved register of deeds.
City and county of New-York. To December 31, 1799,
inclusive. New-York, Gould, Banks, & co., 1832.
371 p.   22 1/2 cm.

12443 Grimké, Frederick, 1791-1863.
Considerations upon the nature and tendency of
free institutions. By Frederick Grimke. Cincinnati,
H. W. Derby & co. [etc., etc.] 1848.
viii, 544 p.   22 cm.

12444 Grimké, Thomas Smith, 1786-1834.
A letter to the Honorable John C. Calhoun, vice-
president of the United States, Robert Y. Hayne,
senator of the United States, George M'Duffie, of
the House of representatives of the United States,
and James Hamilton, jr., governor of the state of
South Carolina. By Thomas S. Grimke. 2d ed.
Charleston, Printed by J. S. Burges, 1832.
15 p.   23 1/2 cm.

12445 Grimké, Thomas Smith, 1786-1834.
An oration, delivered in St. Philip's church,
before the inhabitants of Charleston, on the fourth
of July, 1809, by the appointment of the South Carolina state society of Cincinnati, and published at
the request of that society, and of the American
revolution society. By Thomas S. Grimké... Charleston, Re-printed by W. Riley, 1829.
32 p.   22 cm.   (In his Oration on the absolute
necessity of union. Charleston, 1829)
First published in 1809.

12446 Grimké, Thomas Smith, 1786-1834.
Speech of Thomas Smith Grimké, one of the senators
from St. Philip's and St. Michael's, delivered in
the Senate of South Carolina, in December, 1828,
during the debate on sundry resolutions, of the
Senate and House of representatives, respecting the

tariff... Charleston, Printed by W. Riley, 1829.
129 p.   22 cm.   (In his Oration on the
absolute necessity of union. Charleston, 1829)

12447   Grimshaw, William, 1782-1852.
An exposition of the situation, character, and
interests, of the American republic, absolute and
relative. By William Grimshaw... Philadelphia,
1822.
31 p.   18 cm.

12448   Grimshaw, William, 1782-1852.
The history of South America, from the discovery
of the New world by Columbus, to the conquest of
Peru by Pizarro; interspersed with amusing anecdotes,
and containing a minute description of the manners
and customs... of the Indians. By William Grimshaw... New York, Collins & Hannay, and Collins &
co., 1830.
252 p.   18 cm.

12449   Griscom, John Hoskins, 1809-1874.
A history, chronological and circumstantial, of
the visitations of yellow fever at New York. By
John H. Griscom... New York, Hall, Clayton & co.,
printers, 1858.
cover-title, 36 p.   1 illus.   23 1/2 cm.
"From the American medical monthly, February,
1858."

12450   Griscom, John Hoskins, 1809-1874, comp.
Memoir of John Griscom, LL. D., late professor
of chemistry and natural philosophy; with an account
of the New York high school; Society for the prevention of pauperism; the House of refuge; and other
institutions. Comp. from an autobiography and other
sources, by John H. Griscom, M. D. New York, R.
Carter and brothers, 1859.
427 p.   front. (port.)   24 cm.

12451   Griscom, John Hoskins, 1809-1874.
The sanitary condition of the laboring population
of New York. With suggestions for its improvement.
A discourse (with additions) delivered on the 30th
December, 1844, at the repository of the American
institute. By John H. Griscom... New York, Harper

& brothers, 1845.
2 p.l., 58 p.   22 1/2 cm.

12452 Grisebach, August Heinrich Rudolf, 1814-1879.
Flora of the British West Indian islands. By
A. H. R. Grisebach... London, L. Reeve & co.,
1864.
xvi, 789 p.   23 cm.

12453 Griswold, Alexander Viets, bp., 1766-1843.
A sermon, delivered in Trinity church, Boston,
at the first meeting of the convention of the Eastern
diocese, 19th September, 1810. By Alexander V.
Griswold, rector of St. Michael's church, Bristol
(R. I) bishop elect. Published by desire of the
convention. Boston, Printed by Munroe & Francis,
no. 4 Cornhill, 1811.
19, 15 p.   fold. tab.   21 cm.
"The constitution of the Protestant Episcopal
church in the Eastern diocese of the United States
of America. ... An act to incorporate sundry persons, by the name of the trustees of donations to
the Protestant Episcopal church...": 15 p. at end.

12454 Griswold, Chauncey D
The Isthmus of Panama, and what I saw there. By
C. D. Griswold... New York, Dewitt and Davenport,
1852.
3 p.l., [v]-viii, 9-180 p.   front., maps.
18 1/2 cm.

12455 Griswold, Rufus Wilmot, 1815-1857.
The biographical annual: containing memoirs of
eminent persons, recently deceased. Ed. by Rufus
W. Griswold... New York, Linen and Fennell, 1841.
1 p.l., [ix]-xii, [13]-307 p.   front., ports.
19 cm.

12456 [Griswold, Rufus Wilmot] 1815-1857.
The Cyclopedia of American literature, by Evart
A. Duyckinck and George L. Duyckinck. A review...
New York, Baker & Godwin, printers, 1856.
32 p.   22 cm.
From the New York Herald of February 13, 1856.

12457 Griswold, Rufus Wilmot, 1815-1857.
Statement of the relations of Rufus W. Griswold

with Charlotte Myers (called Charlotte Griswold)
Elizabeth F. Ellet, Ann S. Stephens, Samuel J.
Waring, Hamilton R. Searles, and Charles D. Lewis,
with particular reference to their late unsuccessful
attempt to have set aside the decree granted in
1852 by the Court of common pleas of Philadelphia
County, in the case of Griswold vs. Griswold. Philadelphia, Printed by H. B. Ashmead, 1856.
    32 p.   23 1/2 cm.

12458 The groans of Jamaica, express'd in a letter from a
gentleman residing there, to his friend in London:
containing a clear detection, and most convincing
narrative of some of the crying grievances, and
fraudulent oppressions, which gave the first rise
to the present growing discontents, divisions, and
animosities, among the inhabitants of that island:
as also particular characters of the chief authors
and promoters of these distractions... London,
Printed in the year 1714.
    viii, 48 p.   18 cm.

12459 Groot, Jeldert Jansz.
    Beknopt en getrouw verhaal, van de reys van comman-
deur Jeldert Jansz Groot, uit Texel na en in Groenland
etc. Voorgevallen in ao. 1777 en 1778. Amsterdam,
Gedrukt voor den autheur [etc., etc., 1779]
    16+ p.   21 x 16 cm.

12460 [Grose, Francis] 1731?-1791.
    Advice to the officers of the British army: with
the addition of some hints to the drummer and private soldier... 5th ed. London, Printed by W.
Richardson for G. Kearsley, 1783.
    iv, 134 p.   fold. front.   17 1/2 cm.

12461 [Gross, Charles Heebner] 1838-1902.
    A reply to Horace Binney's pamphlet on the habeas
corpus. Philadelphia, 1862.
    40 p.   22 1/2 cm.

12462 Gross, Samuel David, 1805-1884, ed.
    Lives of eminent American physicians and surgeons
of the nineteenth century. Ed. by Samuel D. Gross...
Philadelphia, Lindsay & Blakiston, 1861.
    xi p., 2 l., [17]-836 p.   front. (port.)
23 cm.

12463   Gross, Samuel David, 1805-1884.
        Memoir of Valentine Mott, M. D., LL. D., professor
    of surgery in the University of the city of New York,
    member of the Institute of France. By S. D. Gross...
    New York, D. Appleton and co.; Philadelphia, Lindsay
    and Blakiston, 1868.
        viii p., 1 l., 96 p.   front. (port.)   24 cm.

12464   Gross, William, 1796-1823, defendant.
        ... The last words and dying confession of Wm.
    Gross, who was executed on the 7th of February,
    1823, for the murder of Kesiah Stow, in the city of
    Philadelphia. Being that which was given by Wm.
    Gross to Mr. Roberts, while under sentence of
    death, containing his full confession and experience
    while in prison... Philadelphia, Printed and pub-
    lished for the purchasers, to be had at 91 S. Front
    St. and at the Printing office, in the court back
    of 110 Walnut St. [1823]
        20 p.   1 illus.   21 cm.

12465   Grosvenor, David Adams, 1802-1866.
        The last hours of the Christian: a discourse,
    occasioned by the death of Mrs. Mary Harris Ely,
    wife of Mr. Heman Ely, jr., delivered on Sabbath
    A. M., March 4th, 1849, by David A. Grosvenor...
    Cleveland, M. C. Younglove & co., 1849.
        13 p.   22 cm.

12466   Grosvenor, Ebenezer, 1739-1788.
        A sermon preached at the ordination of the Rev.
    Mr. Daniel Grosvenor, to the pastoral care of the
    church in Grafton. October 19, 1774. By Ebenezer
    Grosvenor, A. M., pastor of the First church in
    Scituate. Boston, Printed by Thomas and John Fleet,
    1774.
        31 p.   21 1/2 cm.
        Half-title: Mr. Grosvenor's sermon at the ordi-
    nation of his brother.

12467   Grosvenor, Lemuel.
        History of the First Congregational church and
    society of Woodstock, Conn. A Thanksgiving dis-
    course, by L. Grosvenor, November 24th, 1859...
    Worcester, Spy steam printing house, 1860.
        28 p.   22 cm.

12468 Grotius, pseud.
       Pills for the delegates: or, The chairman chastised,
       in a series of letters, addressed to Peyton Randolph,
       esq; on his conduct, as president of the general
       Congress: held at the city of Philadelphia, Septem-
       ber 5, 1774. By Grotius. Originally published in
       the Massachusetts gazette, and now first collected.
       New York, Printed by James Rivington, 1775.
       32 p.   20 cm.

12469 Groton, Mass. First parish church. Ecclesiastical
       council. 1826.
       The rights of the Congregational churches of Massa-
       chusetts. The result of an ecclesiastical council,
       convened at Groton, Massachusetts, July 17, 1826.
       Boston, T. R. Marvin, printer, 1827.
       63 p.   23 cm.
       Written by Rev. Lyman Beecher, a member of the
       council. cf. Beecher, Lyman. Autobiography.
       New York, 1864-65. v. 2, p. 79.

12470 Groton, Mass. Public library.
       Catalogue of the Groton public library, with the
       by-laws and regulations. Groton, G. H. Brown,
       printer, 1855.
       26 p.   21 1/2 cm.

12471 Grout, Henry Martyn.
       Commemorative of Hon. Edward Southworth, who died
       at West Springfield, Mass., December 11, 1869.
       Prepared by Rev. Henry M. Grout, and printed by
       request of the bereaved family... Springfield,
       Mass., S. Bowles and company, printers, 1870.
       38 p.   front. (port.)   23 cm.

12472 Grout, William Wallace, 1836-1902.
       An oration before the Re-union society of Vermont
       officers, in the Representatives' hall, Montpelier,
       Vt., November 4, 1869. By Gen. William W. Grout...
       Rutland, Tuttle & co., printers, 1869.
       29 p.   23 cm.

12473 Groux, Daniel Edward.
       Prospectus of an important work in three volumes,
       to be called Numismatical history of the United
       States... By Professor Daniel E. Groux... Boston,

241

Franklin printing house [1856?]
10, [4], [13]-16 p.   pl.   23 1/2 cm.

12474 Grove, Joseph, d. 1764.
A letter to a right honourable patriot; upon the
glorious success at Quebec. In which is drawn a
parallel between a good and bad general, a scene
exhibited, wherein are introduced, (besides others)
three of the greatest names in Britain; and a particular account of the manner of General Wolfe's
death, with a postscript, which enumerates the
other conquests mentioned in the London address.
By Mr. Grove of Richmond... London, Printed for
J. Burd, 1759.
1 p.l., 58 p.   21 1/2 cm.

12475 Grover, Martin, 1811-1875.
Speech of Mr. Grover of New York, on the Oregon
question. Delivered in the House of representatives,
Monday, January 26, 1846. Washington, Blair &
Rives, Printers, 1846.
8 p.   21 1/2 cm.

12476 The growth of New York... New York, G. W. Wood, 1865.
49 p.   22 1/2 cm.

12477 Grund, Francis Joseph, 1805-1863.
The Americans, in their moral, social, and political
relations. By Francis J. Grund. From the London
edition of Longman... Two volumes in one. Boston,
Marsh, Capen and Lyon, 1837.
1 p.l., [9]-423 p.   19 1/2 cm.

12478 Grund, Francis Joseph, 1805-1863.
Thoughts and reflections on the present position
of Europe, and its probable consequences to the
United States. By Francis J. Grund... Philadelphia,
Childs & Peterson, 1860.
iv, ii, [5]-245 p.   19 1/2 cm.

12479 Grundy, Felix, 1777-1840.
Speech of Mr. Grundy, of Tennessee, on Mr. Foot's
resolution, proposing an inquiry into the expediency
of abolishing the office of surveyor general of
public lands, and for discontinuing further surveys,
&c. Delivered in the Senate of the United States,
February 29, 1830. Washington, Printed by D. Green,

1830.
   16 p.   23 1/2 cm.   [Miscellaneous pamphlets,
v. 955, no. 10]

12480 Guadalajara, Mexico. Catedral. Cabildo.
       Coleccion de ducomentos [!] relativos a la
conducta del cabildo eclesiastico de la diocesi de
Guadalajara y del clero secular y regular de la
misma, en cuanto a reusar el juramento de la segunda
parte del artículo sétimo de la Constitucion del
estado libre de Jalisco. [Guadalajara?] Impr. del
ciudadano Mariano Rodriguez, 1825.
       1 p.l., 136 p.   20 1/2 cm.

12481 Güell y Renté, José, 1819-1884.
       Leyendas americanas, por Don José Güell y Renté...
Madrid, Impr. de las Novedades é ilustracion, 1856.
       283 p.   front. (port.)   18 cm.

12482 Guernsey, Egbert, 1823-1903.
       History of the United States of America, designed
for schools. Extending from the discovery of America
by Columbus to the present time... together with
a notice of American antiquities, and the Indian
tribes... By Egbert Guernsey, A. M.   7th ed.
New York, Cady and Burgess, 1850.
       xii, [13]-456 p.   illus., maps.   18 1/2 cm.

12483 Guest, Richard.
       A compendious history of the cotton-manufacture;
with a disproval of the claim of Sir Richard Ark-
wright to the invention of its ingenious machinery.
By Richard Guest. Manchester, Printed by J. Pratt,
1823.
       2 p.l., [3]-70, 3 p.   12 pl.   28 x 22 cm.

12484 A guide to the city of Chicago; its public buildings,
places of amusement, commercial, benevolent, and
religious institutions; churches, hotels, railroads,
etc., etc. With a map... Chicago, T. E. Zell & co.,
1868.
       197 p.   illus., plates, map.   16 cm.

12485 Guide to the White mountains and lakes of New Hampshire:
with minute & accurate descriptions of the scenery
and objects of interest on the route... Concord,

N. H., Tripp & Morril, 1850.
48 p., 1 l.   15 cm.

12486   Guide-book of the Central railroad of New Jersey, and
its connections through the coal-fields of Pennsylvania. New York, Harper & brothers, 1864.
120 p. incl. front., illus., plates.   fold. map.
19 1/2 cm.

12487   Guignard, Philippe, 1820-
Notice historique sur la vie et les travaux de m.
Fevret de Saint-Mémin, par Ph. Guignard... Dijon,
Impr. Loireau-Feuchot, 1853.
22 p.   21 1/2 cm.
Extrait des Mémoires de l'Académie des sciences,
arts et belles-lettres de Dijon.

12488   Guild, Calvin, 1808-1897.
Genealogy of the descendants of John Guild,
Dedham, Massachusetts. By Calvin Guild... Providence,
Providence press company, printers, 1867.
xii, 120 p.   20 cm.

12489   [Guild, Reuben Aldridge] 1822-1899.
An account of the writings of Roger Williams.
[Providence, 1862]
11 p.   23 1/2 cm.

12490   Guild, Reuben Aldridge, 1822-1899.
History of Brown university, with illustrative
documents. By Reuben Aldridge Guild... Providence,
R. I. [Providence press company, printers] 1867.
xv, 443 p.   front., illus., 3 port.   23 cm.

12491   Guild, Reuben Aldridge, 1822-1899.
The librarian's manual; a treatise on bibliography,
comprising a select and descriptive list of bibliographical works; to which are added, sketches of
public libraries. Illustrated with engravings. By
Reuben A. Guild... New York, C. B. Norton, 1858.
10, 304 p.   illus.   22 x 18 cm.
"Descriptive list of four hundred and ninety-five
separate works... of the first importance for a
library apparatus... and historical sketches of
fourteen of the largest publick libraries in this
country and in Europe." - Pref.

12492   Guild, Reuben Aldridge, 1822-1899.
        Life, times, and correspondence of James Manning,
and the early history of Brown university. By
Reuben Aldridge Guild... Boston, Gould and Lincoln;
New York, Sheldon and company [etc., etc.] 1864.
        xxii, [23]-523 p.   2 pl., 2 port. (incl. front.)
21 cm.

12493   [Guild, Samuel Eliot] 1819-1862.
        The question before us. Boston, Printed by J.
Wilson and son, 1862.
        12 p.   23 cm.
        Discussion of slavery in its relation to the war.

12494   Guild, William.
        A chart and description of the Boston and Worcester
and Western railroads; in which is noted the towns,
villages, station, bridges, viaducts, tunnels,
cuttings, embankments, gradients, &c., the scenery
and its natural history, and other objects passed
by this line of railway. With numerous illustrations.
Constituting a novel and complete companion for
the railway carriage. By William Guild. Boston,
Bradbury & Guild, 1847.
        vi, 7-84 p. incl. front., illus.   19 1/2 cm.

12495   Guild, William.
        ... New York and the White Mountains; with a
complete map, and numerous wood-cut views of the
principal objects of interest upon the line [of
the Harlem and other railroads] By William Guild.
Boston, Bradbury & Guild, 1852.
        80 p.   front. (fold. map) illus.   20 1/2 cm.
(Bradbury and Guild's railroad maps, no. 4)

12496   Guillermin de Montpinay, Gilbert.
        Précis historique des derniers événemens de la
partie de l'est de Saint-Domingue, depuis le 10 août
1808, jusqu'à la capitulation de Santo-Domingo.
Avec des notes historiques, politiques et statis-
tiques sur cette partie; des réflexions sur l'Amérique
septentrionale, et des considérations sur l'Amérique
méridionale, et sur la restauration de Saint-
Domingue... Par M. Gilbert Guillermin... Paris,
Arthus-Bertrand, 1811.
        2 p.l., 20, [2], [21]-494 p.   front. (port.)
fold. pl., fold. plan.   21 1/2 cm.

12497 Guinnard, Auguste, b. 1832?
Three years' slavery among the Patagonians:
an account of his captivity, by A. Guinnard...
From the 3d French ed., by Charles S. Cheltnam...
London, R. Bentley and son, 1871.
x, 375 p.   front. (map)   20 1/2 cm.

12498 Guinnard, Auguste, b. 1832?
Trois ans d'esclavage chez les Patagons; recit
de ma captivité, par A. Guinnard... 2. éd.
Paris, P. Brunet, 1864.
3 p.l., v, 340 p.   front. (port.) fold. map.
18 cm.

12499 Guirey, William.
A funeral sermon, on the death of General George
Washington... Delivered by request, before the
Methodist Episcopal church at Lynn, January 7, 1800.
Being the day set apart by that society to testify
their most affectionate regard for the memory of
their most illustrious fellow citizen. By the Rev.
William Guirey. Salem, Printed by Joshua Cushing,
for the proprietors, 1800.
22 p.   21 cm.

12500 Guiteras, Pedro José, 1814-1890.
Historia de la conquista de la Habana (1762)
Escrita por Pedro J. Guiteras. Filadelfia, Parry
and McMillan, 1856.
188 p.   20 cm.

12501 Guizot, François Pierre Guillaume, 1787-1874.
Essay on the character and influence of Washington
in the revolution of the United States of America,
by M. Guizot. Translated from the French. 2d ed.
New York, J. Miller, 1863.
xi, [13]-160 p.   front.   17 1/2 cm.
"The following essay is a translation of the intro-
duction, by M. Guizot, to a French version of Sparks's
Life of Washington, and of selected portions of
Washington's writings, which... appeared in Paris
[1840]" - Translator's pref., signed: George S.
Hillard.

12502 Guizot, [François Pierre Guillaume] 1787-1874.
Report upon the international exchanges undertaken by M. Alexandre Vattemare and upon the actual

state of letters and especially of historical
investigations in the United States of America:
by M. Guizot. Meeting February 24th, 1855. Tr.
from the French by Maunsell B. Field, A. M.
[Paris, Printed by P. Dupont, 1855]
     55, [1] p.   24 cm.
     Added t.-p. in French; text, French and English
on opposite pages.
     "Extract from the Minutes of the Proceedings of
the Academy of moral and political sciences...
Publication of March 1855, vol. XXXI."

12503   Gunn, Alexander, 1784-1829.
     Memoirs of the Rev. John Henry Livingston... by
the late Rev. Alexander Gunn... New ed. cor. and
condensed, with the addition of some new matter.
New York, Board of publication of the Reformed Protestant Dutch church, 1856.
     x, [11]-405 p.   front. (port.)   18 cm.

12504   Gunnison, John Williams, 1812-1853.
     The Mormons, or, Latter-day saints, in the valley
of the Great salt lake: a history of their rise
and progress, peculiar doctrines, present condition,
and prospects, derived from personal observation,
during a residence among them. By Lieut. J. W.
Gunnison... Philadelphia, Lippincott, Grambo & co.,
1853.
     ix, 13-168 p.   front., illus.   19 1/2 cm.

12505   Gurley, Phineas Densmore, 1816-1868.
     Man's projects and God's results. A sermon:
preached by the Rev. P. D. Gurley... on Thursday,
August 6, 1863, being the day of national thanksgiving, praise and prayer. Washington, D. C.,
W. Ballantyne, 1863.
     20 p.   23 cm.

12506   Gurley, Ralph Randolph, 1797-1872.
     A discourse, delivered on the fourth of July,
1825, in the city of Washington. By Ralph Randolph
Gurley. Washington, Printed by Gales & Seaton,
1825.
     21 p.   20 1/2 cm.

12507   Gurley, Ralph Randolph, 1797-1872.
     Life and eloquence of the Rev. Sylvester Larned,

first pastor of the First Presbyterian church in
New-Orleans. By R. R. Gurley. New York, Wiley &
Putnam, 1844.
   xii, [13]-412 p.   front. (port.)   18 1/2 cm.
"Sermons": p. [123]-412.

12508   Gurley, Ralph Randolph, 1797-1872.
   Life of Jehudi Ashmun, late colonial agent in
Liberia. With an appendix, containing extracts from
his journal and other writings; with a brief sketch
of the life of the Rev. Lott Cary. By Ralph Randolph
Gurley. Washington, Printed by J. C. Dunn, 1835.
   vii, [17]-396 p., 1 l., 160 p.   21 1/2 cm.

12509   Gutiérrez, Blas J   defendant.
   Vindicacion del juez de circuito de Sonora, Sina-
loa & Baja California, lic. Blas J. Gutierrez,
acusado de perturbador del orden publico por el
exmo. sr. d. Pomposo Verdugo, por no haber consen-
tido en la violacion del Estatuto orgánico provisional para la república, oponiéndose, á mocion del
ministerio fiscal, á obedecer por sí y sus subalter-
nos el decreto que sobre contribuciones espidió el
mismo exmo. sr. Verdugo en 28 de junio de este ano,
pretendiendo llevarlo á efecto sin la sancion
suprema. Mejico, Impr. de J. R. Navarro, 1856.
   31 p.   22 cm.

12510   Gutiérrez, Juan M[aría] 1809-1878.
   Apuntes biograficos de escritores, oradores y
hombres de estado de la Republica Arjentina. Por
el Dr. D. Juan M. Gutierrez... Buenos Aires,
Impr. de Mayo, 1860.
   294 p., 1 l.   17 1/2 cm.   (Half-title:
Bibioteca [!] americana, t. VII)

12511   Gutiérrez, Juan María, 1809-1878.
   Poesias de Juan María Gutiérrez. Buenos Aires,
C. Casavalle, 1869.
   x p., 1 l., [3]-339 p.   21 1/2 cm.

12512   Guyer, Isaac D
   History of Chicago; its commercial and manufacturing interests and industry; together with
sketches of manufacturers... with glances at some
of the best hotels; also the principal railroads
which enter Chicago. By I. D. Guyer. Chicago,

Church, Goodman & Cushing, printers, 1862.
200 p. incl. front., illus.   plates.   27 cm.

12513 [Guzmán, Antonio Leocádio] 1801-1884.
Ojeada al proyecto de constitucion que el Liber-
tador ha presentado a la republica Bolivar. Por
A. L. G. Lima, Imprenta republicana administrada
por J. M. Concha, 1826.
2 p.l., [3]-52 p.   17 1/2 cm.   [With Peru.
Constitution. Proyecto de constitucion para la
Republica peruana. Lima, 1826]

12514 Gyles, John, 1678?-1755.
Memoirs of odd adventures, strange deliverances,
etc. in the captivity of John Giles, esq., commander
of the garrison on Saint George river, in the district of Maine. Written by himself. Originally
published at Boston, 1736. Printed for William
Dodge. Cincinnati, Spiller & Gates, printers,
1869.
v, [7]-64 p.   24 cm.

H

12515 Hackelton, Mrs. Maria W
Jamestown of Pemaquid: a poem. By Mrs. Maria W.
Hackelton. Read on the site of Fort Frederic, on
the reception of the committee of the Maine historical society by the citizens of Bristol, August 26,
1869. Published under the direction of the society.
New York, Hurd and Houghton, 1869.
40 p.   19 1/2 cm.
Prefatory notice by Edward Ballard; Historical
sketch signed M. W. H.
Settlement destroyed in 1689.

12516 Hackett, Horatio Balch, 1808-1875.
Christian memorials of the war; or, Scenes and
incidents illustrative of religious faith and
principle, patriotism and bravery of our Army.
With historical notes. By Horatio B. Hackett...
Boston, Gould and Lincoln; New York, Sheldon and
co. [etc., etc.] 1864.
xiv, 256 p.   20 cm.

12517   Hackett, James.
            Narrative of the expedition which sailed from
        England in 1817, to join the South American
        patriots; comprising every particular connected
        with its formation, history, and fate; with obser-
        vations and authentic information elucidating the
        real character of the contest, mode of warfare,
        state of the armies, &c. By James Hackett...
        London, J. Murray, 1818.
            1 p.l., xv, 144 p.   21 1/2 cm.

12518   Hadfield, William, 1806-1887.
            Brazil, the river Plate, and the Falkland islands;
        with the Cape Horn route to Australia. Including
        notices of Lisbon, Madeira, the Canaries and Cape
        Verds. By William Hadfield... Illustrations by
        permission, from the South American sketches of
        Sir W. Gore Ouseley... and, by permission, from the
        drawings of Sir Charles Hotham... London, Longman,
        Brown, Green, and Longmans, 1854.
            1 p.l., vi, 384 p.   front., illus., port., maps.
        22 1/2 cm.

12519   Hadfield, William, 1806-1887.
            Brazil and the river Plate in 1868: by William
        Hadfield, showing the progress of those countries
        since his former visit in 1853. London, Bates,
        Hendy and co., 1869.
            271 p.   front., pl.   22 cm.

12520   Hadley, William Hobart, comp.
            The American citizen's manual of reference; being
        a comprehensive historical, statistical, topographical,
        and political view of the United States of North
        America, and of the several states and territories.
        Carefully comp. from the latest authorities, and
        pub. by W. Hobart Hadley... New York, Printed by
        S. W. Benedict, 1840.
            1 p.l., 102 p.   23 cm.

12521   Hadley, Mass.
            Celebration of the two hundredth anniversary of
        the settlement of Hadley, Massachusetts, at Hadley,
        June 8, 1859; including the address by Rev. Prof.
        F. D. Huntington... poem by Edward C. Porter...
        and the other exercises of the occasion. Northampton,

250

Bridgman & Childs, 1859.
98 p.   24 cm.

12522   Hagadorn, William, jr.
        A comparison of American and British slavery.
        By Wm. Hagadorn, jr.   New York, Printed by E. B.
        Thomas, 1851.
        32 p.   23 cm.

12523   Hagen, Hermann August, 1817-1893.
        ... Synopsis of the Neuroptera of North America.
        With a list of the South American species.   Prepared
        for the Smithsonian institution by Hermann Hagen.
        Washington, Smithsonian institution, 1861.
        xx, 347 p.   23 1/2 cm.   (Smithsonian mis-
        cellaneous collections. [vol. IV, art. I])
        Translated from the Latin manuscript by P. R.
        Uhler.

12524   Hager, Albert David, 1817-1888.
        The marbles of Vermont: an address pronounced
        October 29, 1858, before the Vermont historical
        society, in the presence of the General assembly
        of Vermont, by Albert D. Hager.   Pub. by order of
        the General assembly.   Burlington, Times job office
        print, 1958.
        16 p.   22 cm.   [With White, Pliny H   The life
        & services of Matthew Lyon.   An address pronounced
        October 29, 1858, before the Vermont historical
        society...   Burlington, 1858]

12525   Hagner, Charles Valerius, 1796-1878.
        Early history of the falls of Schuylkill, Mana-
        yunk, Schuylkill and Lehigh navigation companies,
        Fairmount waterworks, etc., by Charles V. Hagner.
        Philadelphia, Claxton, Remsen and Haffelfinger,
        1869.
        viii, [9]-102 p.   front., port.   21 cm.
        Includes biographies.

12526   Hagner, Thomas Holme.
        An address delivered in the Senate chamber of
        Maryland, before "The association of the Theta
        Delta Phi" of St. John's college, 4th July, 1837.
        By Thomas Holme Hagner...   Annapolis, Printed by
        J. Hughes, 1837.

32 p.   23 1/2 cm.
On the colonial history of Maryland.

12527   Hague, William, 1808-1887.
A discourse occasioned by the death of the Hon.
John Quincy Adams, delivered in the Rowe street
Baptist church, February 27, 1848.   By William
Hague...   Boston, W. D. Ticknor & company, 1848.
22 p.   23 1/2 cm.

12528   Hague, William, 1808-1887.
An historical discourse delivered at the celebration of the second centennial anniversary of the
First Baptist church in Providence, November 7,
1839.   By William Hague...   Providence, B. Cranston
and company; Boston, Gould, Kendall and Lincoln,
1839.
192 p.   19 cm.

12529   Haigh, Samuel.
Sketches of Buenos Ayres and Chile.   By Samuel
Haigh.   London, J. Carpenter and son, 1829.
xviii p., 1 l., 316 p.   front. (fold. map)
col. pl.   21 1/2 cm.

12530   Hain, Augustus H   F
A brief essay on the civil service of the United
States, by Augustus H. F. Hain.   Washington, D. C.,
R. Beresford, printer, 1869.
8 p.   22 cm.

12531   Haines, Elijah Middlebrook, 1822-1889, ed.
A compilation of the laws of the state of Illinois,
relating to township organization; to which are
added numerous practical forms.   And notes, by way
of instruction, supported by references to adju-
dicated cases.   Rev., and adapted to the new constitution of 1870.   By Elijah M. Haines...   Chicago,
E. B. Myers and company, 1870.
xii, [13]-392 p.   23 cm.

12532   Haines, Elijah Middlebrook, 1822-1889.
Historical and statistical sketches of Lake
county, state of Illinois.   In two parts.   The
first consisting of general observations; the
second, gives a minute review of each township,
in its order.   By Elijah M. Haines.   Waukegan, Ill.,

E. G. Howe, 1852.
112 p.   front.   15 cm.

12533 Haines, William A
       Catalogue of the terrestrial shells in the collection
       of William A. Haines. New York, Printed by the New
       York printing company, 1868.
       1 p.l., 118 p., 1 l.   23 cm.

12534 Hale, B   E
       Familiar conversations upon the Constitution of the
       United States; designed for the use of common schools.
       By B. E. Hale. West Bradford [Mass.] Hale and com-
       pany; Boston, E. R. Broaders, 1835.
       132 p. incl. front.   15 1/2 cm.

12535 [Hale, Benjamin] 1797-1863.
       Valedictory letter to the trustees of Dartmouth
       college. [Hanover? 1835]
       24 p.   19 cm.

12536 Hale, Mrs. C   L
       Woodland lays, legends and charades. By Mrs. C. L.
       Hale. Philadelphia, Printed for the author by
       Lippincott & co., 1868.
       viii, [9]-282 p.   19 cm.

12537 Hale, Charles, 1831-1882.
       "Our houses are our castles." A review of the
       proceedings of the nunnery committee, of the
       Massachusetts legislature; and especially their
       conduct and that of their associates on occasion
       of the visit to the Catholic school in Roxbury,
       March 26, 1855. Boston, C. Hale, 1855.
       62 p.   24 cm.

12538 Hale, Edward Everett, 1822-1909.
       Memories of a hundred years, by Edward Everett
       Hale... New York, The Macmillan company; London,
       Macmillan & co., ltd., 1902.
       2 v.   fronts., illus., ports., facsims (part
       double)   21 cm.
       Republished from the Outlook.

12539 Hale, Edward Everett, 1822-1909.
       The public duty of a private citizen: a sermon
       preached in the South Congregational church, Boston,

253

Sept. 3, 1865, the Sunday following the death of
Mr. George Livermore. By Edward E. Hale. Cambridge,
Press of J. Wilson and sons, 1865.
14 p.   23 1/2 cm.

12540   Hale, Enoch, 1790-1848.
History and description of an epidemic fever,
commonly called spotted fever, which prevailed at
Gardiner, Maine, in the spring of 1814. By E. Hale,
jr. ... Boston, Printed by Wells and Lilly, 1818.
xvi, 246 p.   24 cm.

12541   [Hale, Salma] 1787-1866.
... History of the United States, from their first
settlement as colonies, to the close of Mr. Tyler's
administration, in 1845. To which are added
Questions, adapted to the use of schools. New ed.
... Cooperstown, N. Y., H. & E. Phinney, 1846.
326, 28 p.   front., maps.   18 cm.

12542   Hales, John Groves.
A survey of Boston and its vicinity; shewing the
distance from the Old state house... to all the
towns and villages not exceeding fifteen miles
therefrom... together with a short topographical
sketch of the country... By John G. Hales...
Boston, Printed by E. Lincoln, 1821.
156 p.   front., fold. map.   18 1/2 cm.

12543   Haley, Thomas.
Trotting record for 1869.   Rev. and cor. Containing a complete and reliable record of all the
trotting events of the past season, compiled and
arranged with great care, and respectfully dedicated
to American turfmen, by Thomas Haley. New York,
Torrey brothers, printers, 1870.
144 p.   19 1/2 cm.

12544   Haliburton, Robert Grant.
Intercolonial trade our only safeguard against
disunion, by R. G. Haliburton... Ottawa, Printed
by G. E. Desbarats, 1868.
42 p.   21 1/2 cm.

12545   [Haliburton, Thomas Chandler] 1796-1865.
The letter-bag of the Great western; or, Life in
a steamer... By the author of "The sayings and

doings of Samuel Slick", &c. &c. Philadelphia,
Lea & Blanchard, 1840.
xvi, 17-189 p.   17 1/2 cm.
With this are bound: Charcoal sketches; or,
Scenes in a metropolis, by Joseph C. Neal... New
ed. Philadelphia, 1845; The Augustan age (1841?)
and Lecture on Jerusalem (1841) both by C. D. Meigs.

12546 [Haliburton, Thomas Chandler] 1796-1865.
Nature and human nature. By the author of "Sam
Slick the clockmaker"... New York, Stringer and
Townsend, 1855.
1 p.l., ix-xi, [13]-336 p.   19 1/2 cm.

12547 Haliburton, Thomas Chandler, 1796-1865.
The old judge; or, Life in a colony. By Judge
Haliburton... New York, Stringer & Townsend, 1849.
239 p.   23 cm.

12548 [Haliburton, Thomas Chandler] 1796-1865.
Rule and misrule of the English in America; by
the author of "Sam Slick the clock-maker"...
New York, Harper & brothers, 1851.
1 p.l., [xi]-xii, [13]-379 p.   20 1/2 cm.
Also issued under title: The English in America.

12549 [Haliburton, William]
Effects of the stage on the manners of a people:
and the propriety of encouraging and establishing
a virtuous theatre. By a Bostonian. Boston,
Printed by Young and Etheridge, Market-Square,
sold by them and the several booksellers, 1792.
75, [1] p.   20 1/2 cm.

12550 Halkett, John, 1768-1852.
Historical notes respecting the Indians of North
America: with remarks on the attempts made to convert
and civilize them... By John Halkett, esq. London,
Printed for A. Constable and co., Edinburgh [etc.]
1825.
vii, [1], 408 p.   22 cm.

12551 Hall, Aaron, 1751-1814.
A sermon, preached at Concord, June 2d, 1803,
before His Excellency the Governor, the honorable
Council, Senate, and House of representatives, of
the state of New Hampshire. By Aaron Hall, A. M.,

minister of Keene. Concord, Printed by George Hough,
for the honorable General court, June, 1803.
   23 p.   21 1/2 cm.
   [Theological pamphlets, v. 36, no. 5]

12552 [Hall, Anna Maria (Fielding) "Mrs. S. C. Hall"]
      1800-1881.
      The buccaneer. A tale... London, R. Bentley,
      1832.
      3 v.   19 1/2 cm.

12553 [Hall, Arethusa] 1802-1891.
      Life and character of the Rev. Sylvester Judd.
      Boston, Crosby, Nichols, and company; New York,
      C. S. Francis and co., 1854.
      x p., 1 l., 531 p.   front. (port.)   20 1/2 cm.

12554 [Hall, Baynard Rush]
      The new purchase; or, Early years in the far west.
      By Robert Carlton, esq. [pseud.]... Illustrated by
      Momberger. Second edition, revised by the author.
      Two volumes in one. New Albany, Ind., Jno. R. Nune-
      macher; New York, D. Appleton and co.; Philadelphia,
      J. B. Lippincott and co. [1855]
      471 p.   illus.   20 cm.

12555 Hall, Benjamin Franklin, 1814-1891.
      The early history of the north western states,
      embracing New York, Ohio, Indiana, Illinois,
      Michigan, Iowa and Wisconsin, with their land laws,
      etc., and an appendix containing the constitutions
      of those states. By B. F. Hall. Buffalo, G. H.
      Derby & co.; Cincinnati, H. W. Derby & co. [etc.,
      etc.] 1849.
      1 p.l., [15]-477 p.   22 cm.

12556 Hall, Benjamin Franklin, 1814-1891.
      The land owner's manual. Containing a summary of
      statute regulations, in New York, Ohio, Indiana,
      Illinois, Michigan, Iowa and Wisconsin, concerning
      land titles, deeds, mortgages, wills of real estate,
      descents, land taxes, tax sales, redemptions,
      limitations, exemptions, interest of money and
      usury, with an appendix, containing the constitu-
      tions of the said states. By Benjamin F. Hall...
      Auburn, N. Y., J. C. Derby & co.; Buffalo, Derby &

Hewson [etc., etc.] 1847.
1 p.l., [15]-477 p.   22 cm.

12557   Hall, Benjamin Franklin, 1814-1891.
        The Republican party and its presidential candi-
        dates... With... sketches... of Fremont and Dayton.
        By Benjamin F. Hall...   New York and Auburn, Miller,
        Orton & Mulligan, 1856.
        xii, [13]-512 p.   front., port.   18 1/2 cm.

12558   Hall, Benjamin Homer, 1830-1893.
        A collection of college words and customs.   By
        B. H. Hall...   Rev. and enl. ed.   Cambridge [Mass.]
        J. Bartlett, 1856.
        vi, 508 p.   20 cm.

12559   Hall, Benjamin Homer, 1830-1893.
        History of eastern Vermont, from its earliest
        settlement to the close of the eighteenth century.
        With a biographical chapter and appendixes.   By
        Benjamin H. Hall.   New York, D. Appleton & co.,
        1858.
        xii p., 1 l., 799 p.   illus. (incl. ports.,
        facsims.)   23 cm.
        That portion of the state east of the Green
        Mountains comprised in old counties of Cumberland
        and Gloucester (now Windham, Windsor, Orange,
        Washington, Caledonia, Essex and Orleans counties)

12560   Hall, Charles Francis, 1821-1871.
        Arctic researches, and life among the Esquimaux;
        being the narrative of an expedition in search of
        Sir John Franklin, in the years 1860, 1861, and
        1862.   By Charles Francis Hall...   New York, Harper
        & brothers, 1865.
        1 p.l., xxviii, [29]-595 p. incl. illus., plates.
        front., fold. map.   23 1/2 cm.

12561   Hall, Charles Henry, 1820-1895.
        A mournful Easter.   A discourse delivered in the
        Church of the Epiphany, Washington, D. C., on
        Easter day, April 19 [i.e. 16] 1865, by the rector,
        Rev. Charles H. Hall, D. D., being the second day
        after the assassination of the President of the
        United States, and a similar attempt upon the
        secretary of state, on the night of Good Friday.

Washington, Gideon & Pearson, printers, 1865.
15 p.   22 1/2 cm.

12562 Hall, Daniel Weston, 1841-
Arctic rovings: or, The adventures of a New Bedford
boy on sea and land. By Daniel Weston Hall. Boston,
A. Tompkins, 1861.
viii, [9]-171 p.   front. (port.)   17 1/2 cm.

12563 Hall, David, 1683-1756.
A mite into the treasury; or, Some serious remarks
on that solemn and indispensable duty of duly
attending assemblies for divine worship, incumbent
upon all persons come to years of understanding
(especially the professors of truth) whilst favoured
with health, strength and liberty; together with
some due animadversions upon the neglect thereof;
as also a word of consolation to such sincere hearted
Friends, as are rendered incapable of personally
attending them, by reason of old age, some bodily
disorder, or confinement, &c. To which is subjoined,
An epistle to Friends of Knaresborough Monthly-
meeting. By David Hall. [Eight lines of Biblical
quotations] London Printed; Philadelphia, Re-printed
by B. Franklin, and D. Hall, 1758.
x, 53 p.   18 cm.

12564 Hall, Edward Brooks, 1800-1866.
A discourse delivered before the Rhode-Island
historical society February 6, 1855. On the life
and times of John Howland, late president of the
society. By Edward B. Hall, D. D. Providence,
G. H. Whitney, 1855.
36 p.   23 cm.

12565 Hall, Edward Brooks, 1800-1866.
Discourses comprising a history of the First
Congregational church in Providence. Delivered
June 19, 1836. After the close of a century from
the formation of the church. By Edward B. Hall,
pastor. Published by request of the society.
Providence, Printed by Knowles, Vose & co., 1836.
62 p.   22 cm.

12566 Hall, Edward Hepple.
... Ho! for the West!! The traveller and emigrants'
hand-book to Canada and the north-west of the

American union: comprising the states of Illinois,
Wisconsin, and Iowa, and the territories of Minnesota, and Kansas; with a description of their
climate, resources, and products; and much other
useful information compiled from the latest authentic
sources, and designed particularly for the use of
travellers, emigrants, and others. To which is
added, a list of railway stations, routes, and distances... By Edward H. Hall... London, Algar &
Street [etc.] 1858.
32 p.   20 1/2 cm.
At head of title: Third edition.

12567 Hall, Edward Hepple.
The summer tourist's pocket guide to American
watering-places. With map and tables of distances.
By E. Hepple Hall... New York, Cathcart & Hall;
London, Sampson, Low, son & Marston, 1869.
4 p.l., xxx, [5]-156 p. incl. tables.   front.
(fold. map)   14 1/2 x 11 1/2 cm.

12568 Hall, Edwin, 1802-1877, comp.
The ancient historical records of Norwalk, Conn.;
with a plan of the ancient settlement, and of the
town in 1847. Comp. by Edwin Hall... Norwalk, J.
Mallory & co.; New York, Baker & Scribner, 1847.
320 p.   front. (fold. map) fold. plates.
19 cm.
"Town records": p. 41-145.
"The genealogical register": p. 181-320.

12569 Hall, Francis, d. 1833.
Colombia: its present state, in respect of
climate, soil, productions, population, government,
commerce, revenue, manufactures, arts, literature,
manners, education, and inducements to emigration.
With itineraries... By Colonel Francis Hall...
Philadelphia, A. Small, 1825.
131 p.   18 1/2 cm.

12570 Hall, Frederick, 1780-1843.
Eulogy: on the late Solomon Metcalf Allen,
professor of languages in Middlebury college. Pronounced according to appoinment [!] of the president
and fellows, March 17, 1818. By Frederick Hall,
A. A. S., professor of math. and nat. philosophy.
Published by request of the corporation. Middlebury,

Vt., Printed by Francis Burnap, 1818.
16 p.   21 cm.

12571   Hall, Frederick, 1780-1843.
Statistical account of the town of Middlebury,
in the state of Vermont. Part first. By Frederick
Hall... Boston, Printed by S. Phelps, 1821.
38 p.   22 cm.
Published also in Massachusetts historical society
Collections, ser. 2, v. 9, p. 123-158.

12572   Hall, Gordon, 1823-1879.
Divine mercy a cause for humiliation. A discourse
preached on the occasion of the state fast, April 13,
1865, by Gordon Hall... Northampton, Mass., Trumbull
& Gere, printers, 1865.
15 p.   22 1/2 cm.

12573   Hall, James, 1793-1868.
Notes on the western states; containing descriptive
sketches of their soil, climate, resources, and
scenery. By James Hall... Philadelphia, H. Hall,
1838.
xxiii, 13-304 p. incl. tables.   18 1/2 cm.
The earlier editions appeared under title: "Statistics of the West."
Western steamboats [including alphabetical lists]:
p. 213-263, 290-304.

12574   Hall, James, 1811-1898.
Key to a chart of the successive geological form-
ations, with an actual section from the Atlantic to
the Pacific ocean. Illustrated by the characteristic
fossils of each formation. By James Hall... Boston,
Gould and Lincoln, 1852.
72 p.   16 1/2 cm.

12575   Hall, John, 1806-1894.
History of the Presbyterian church in Trenton,
N. J., from the first settlement of the town. By
John Hall... New York, A. D. F. Randolph, 1859.
vi p., 1 l., [9]-453 p., vii p.   front., illus.
19 1/2 cm.
"Index to subjects, and to books cited": vii p.
at end.

12576 [Hall, John Taylor]
         Memorial of Lewis and Susan Benedict. [New York?]
         Printed for the family, 1870.
         55 p.   2 port. (incl. front.)   25 1/2 cm.

12577 Hall, John W
         Marine disasters on the western lakes, during the
         navigation of 1869, with the loss of life and property;
         vessels bought and sold; new vessels and their
         tonnage; also, those which have passed out of exist-
         ence; with the names of vessels laid up at various
         lake ports. Carefully comp. by Capt. J. W. Hall...
         Detroit, Mich., W. E. Tunis, 1870.
         120 p.   16 1/2 cm.

12578 Hall, Jonathan Prescott, 1796-1862.
         A discourse delivered before the New England
         society, in the city of New York, December 22, 1847.
         By J. Prescott Hall. New York, G. F. Nesbitt,
         printer, 1848.
         77 p.   22 cm.

12579 Hall, Joseph, 1761-1848.
         An oration, pronounced July 4, 1800, at the request
         of the inhabitants of the town of Boston, in comme-
         moration of the anniversary of American independence.
         By Joseph Hall. Boston, From the printing-office of
         Manning & Loring, Spring-lane [1800]
         24 p.   22 cm.

12580 Hall, Newman, 1816-1902.
         The American war. By Newman Hall, LL. B. A lecture
         to working men, delivered in London, Oct. 20, 1862.
         London, J. Nisbet & co. [etc., 1862]
         31 p.   18 1/2 cm.

12581 Hall, Newman, 1816-1902.
         From Liverpool to St. Louis. By the Rev. Newman
         Hall. London, New York, G. Routledge & sons, 1870.
         xxv, 294 p.   front.   18 cm.
         Reprint of papers contributed to the Broadway
         magazine. Cf. Pref.

12582 Hall, Mrs. Sarah (Ewing) 1761-1830.
         Selections from the writings of Mrs. Sarah Hall,
         author of Conversations on the Bible, with a memoir
         of her life. Philadelphia, H. Hall, 1833.

261

xxxiv p., 1 l., 180 p.   front. (port.)
17 1/2 cm.
    Edited by her son, Harrison Hall. cf. Appendix.
Verse and prose.

12583 Hall, Willard, 1780-1875.
    Defence of the American Sunday school union,
against the charges of its opponents, in an address
delivered at the first anniversary of the New Castle
county Sabbath school union, March 26, 1828. By
the Hon. Willard Hall... Philadelphia, American
Sunday school union, 1831.
    16 p.   21 1/2 cm.

12584 Hall, Rev. William A
    The historic significance of the southern revo-
lution. A lecture delivered by invitation in Peters-
burg, Va., March 14th and April 29th, 1864. And in
Richmond, Va., April 7th and April 21st, 1864. By
Rev. William A. Hall of New Orleans... Petersburg,
Printed by A. F. Crutchfield & co., 1864.
    45 p.   23 cm.

12585 [Halleck, Fitz-Greene] 1790-1867.
    Alnwick castle, with other poems. New York,
G. & C. Carvill, 1827.
    64 p.   22 cm.

12586 Halleck, Fitz-Greene, 1790-1867.
    The poetical works of Fitz-Greene Halleck. New ed.
New York, Redfield, 1852.
    1 p.l., iv, [9]-232 p.   19 cm.

12587 Hallett, Benjamin Franklin, 1797-1862, ed.
    A legislative investigation into masonry; being a
correct history of the examination, under civil oath,
of more than fifty adhering and seceding masons,
before a committee of the General assembly of Rhode-
Island, held at Providence and Newport, between
December 7, 1831, and January 7, 1832. Reported
from minutes taken at the time by B. F. Hallett,
Geo. Turner and others, and carefully compared.
[Boston] Office of the Boston daily advocate, 1832.
    85, [2] p.   27 cm.
    An unofficial report of the testimony, interspersed
with comments and criticisms, apparently prepared by
authority of the Antimasonic party of Rhode Island.

12588 [Halliburton, Sir Brenton] 1773-1860.
Observations on the importance of the North American
colonies to Great Britain. By an old inhabitant of
British America. London, J. Murray, 1831.
2 p.l., [3]-49 p. 22 cm.
First ed. Halifax, 1825. Reprinted in G. W. Hill's
Memoir of Sir Brenton Halliburton. 1864. p. 121-143.

12589 Halliday, Sir Andrew, 1781-1839.
The West Indies: the natural and physical history
of the Windward and Leeward colonies; with some
account of the moral, social, and political condition
of their inhabitants, immediately before and after
the abolition of Negro slavery: by Sir Andrew
Halliday... London, J. W. Parker, 1837.
vii, 408 p. front., fold. maps, fold. tab.
19 cm.

12590 Hallock, Robert T
The child and the man: or, Anniversary suggestions,
by Dr. R. T. Hallock. An oration delivered in New
York, on the Fourth of July, 1856. To which are
added extemporaneous speeches, by S. B. Brittan,
William H. Burleigh, and others, on the same occasion.
New York, Ellinwood and Hills, 1856.
iv, [5]-37 p. 23 cm.

12591 Hallock, William Allen, 1794-1880.
Memoir of Harlan Page; or, The power of prayer and
personal effort for the souls of individuals. By
William A. Hallock... New York, American tract
society [1835]
2 p.l., [3]-230 p. front. (port.) pl. 15 cm.

12592 [Hallock, William H   ]
Life of Gerard Hallock, thirty-three years editor
of the New York journal of commerce. Illustrated
in biography, professional writings, correspondence,
controversies, etc. New York, Oakley, Mason & co.,
1869.
vi, [7]-287 p. front. (port.) 19 cm.

12593 Halsey, Lewis, 1843-1914.
The falls of Taughannock: containing a complete
description of this the highest fall in the state
of New York. With historical and descriptive
sketches. By Lewis Halsey... New York, J. A. Gray &

Green, printers, 1866.
95 p. incl. front., 1 illus.   14 1/2 x 11 cm.

12594   Halsey, William, 1765?-1843.
An oration, delivered the twenty-second of February,
MDCCC. Before the brethren and a select audience, in
the hall of St. John's lodge, no. 2, Newark, New
Jersey. By William Halsey, esq. Newark, Printed by
Jacob Halsey, 1800.
23 p.   24 cm.

12595   Hambden, pseud.
First reflections on reading the President's
message to Congress, of December 7, 1830. By
"Hampden"... Washington, Printed by Gales & Seaton,
1831.
15 p.   22 1/2 cm.
On the tariff.
"Published originally in the National intelligencer."

12596   Hambleton, James Pinkney.
A biographical sketch of Henry A. Wise, with A
history of the political campaign in Virginia in
1855. To which is added a review of the position of
parties in the Union, and a statement of the political
issues: distinguishing them on the eve of the
presidential campaign of 1856. By James P. Hambleton,
M. D. Richmond, Va., J. W. Randolph, 1856.
xxxvi, 509 p.   front. (port.)   23 1/2 cm.

12597   Hamersly, Lewis Randolph, 1847-1910.
The records of living officers of the U. S. Navy
and Marine corps; with a history of naval operations
during the rebellion of 1861-5, and a list of the
ships and officers participating in the great battles,
comp. from official sources by Lewis R. Hamersly...
Philadelphia, J. B. Lippincott & co., 1870.
350 p.   24 cm.

12598   [Hamilton, Alexander] 1757-1804.
An address to the electors of the state of New
York. New York, Re-printed, April, 1801.
23 p.   21 cm.

12559   [Hamilton, Alexander] 1757-1804.
The examination of the President's message, at the

opening of Congress December 7, 1801. Rev. and cor.
by the author... New York, New York Evening post,
1802.
127 p.   22 cm.
Eighteen articles signed: Lucius Crassus.
Originally published in the New York evening post.
President Jefferson's message, Dec. 8, 1801,
appended, p. 120-127.

12600 [Hamilton, Alexander] 1757-1804.
The Farmer refuted: or, A more impartial and
comprehensive view of the dispute between Great
Britain and the colonies, intended as a further
vindication of the Congress: in answer to a letter
from A. W. Farmer, intitled A view of the controversy
between Great Gritain and her colonies: including,
a mode of determining the present disputes finally
and effectually, &c. ... New York, Printed by James
Rivington, 1775.
iv, 78 p.   20 cm.
[Hazard pamphlets, v. 44, no. 13]
Signed: A sincere friend to America.

12601 Hamilton, Alexander, 1757-1804.
Letter from Alexander Hamilton, concerning the
public conduct and character of John Adams, esq.,
president of the United States. Written in the
year 1800. New ed., with a preface. Boston,
Printed by E. G. House, No. 5, Court street, 1809.
56 p.   20 1/2 cm.
[Bailey pamphlets, v. 41, no. 4]

12602 [Hamilton, Alexander] 1757-1804.
A letter from Phocion to the considerate citizens
of New York, on the politics of the day. New York,
Printed by Samuel Loudon; Boston, Re-printed by T.
and J. Fleet, 1784.
19 p.   22 cm.
Urges moderation in the treatment of the American
loyalists.

12603 Hamilton, Alexander, 1757-1804.
Letters of Pacificus and Helvidius on the proclamation of neutrality of 1793, by Alexander Hamilton
(Pacificus,) and James Madison (Helvidius,) to which
is prefixed the proclamation. Washington, J. and

G. S. Gideon, 1845.
102 p.   22 cm.

12604 Hamilton, Alexander, 1757-1804.
Observations on certain documents contained in
no. v & vi of "The history of the United States for
the year 1796," in which the charge of speculation
against Alexander Hamilton, late secretary of the
Treasury, is fully refuted. Written by himself.
Philadelphia, Printed pro bono publico, 1800.
37, lviii p.   22 1/2 cm.

12605 Hamilton, Andrew Jackson, 1815-1875.
Address of A. J. Hamilton, military governor, to
the people of Texas. New Orleans, Printed at the
Era office, 1864.
19 p.   22 1/2 cm.
Hamilton was appointed military governor of Texas
in 1862 by President Lincoln, and provisional
governor in 1865 by President Johnson.

12606 Hamilton, Lord Archibald, d. 1754.
An answer to an anonymous libel, entitled,
Articles exhibited against Lord Archibald Hamilton,
late governour of Jamaica; with sundry depositions
and proofs relating to the same. By Lord Archibald
Hamilton. London, 1718.
92 p.   19 cm.

12607 Hamilton, Lady Augusta.
Marriage rites, customs, and ceremonies, of all
nations of the universe. By Lady Augusta Hamilton.
London, Printed for Chapple and son [etc.] and E.
Barrett, Bath, 1822.
viii, 400 p.   front.   22 cm.

12608 Hamilton, Frank Hastings, 1813-1886.
Eulogy on the life and character of Theodric
Romeyn Beck, M. D., LL. D., delivered before the
Medical society of the state of New York, by Frank
Hastings Hamilton, M. D. Pub. by order of the Senate.
Albany, Printed by C. Van Benthuysen, 1856.
90 p.   front. (port.)   23 cm.

12609 Hamilton, George, surgeon.
A voyage round the world, in His Majesty's frigate
Pandora. Performed under the direction of Captain

Edwards in the years 1790, 1791, and 1792. With the
discoveries made in the South sea; and the many
distresses experienced by the crew from shipwreck
and famine... By Mr. George Hamilton... Berwick
[Eng.] W. Phorson; London, B. Law and son, 1793.
164 p.   front. (port.)   22 1/2 cm.

12610   Hamilton, James, 1786-1857.
Important correspondence on the subject of state
interposition, between His Excellency Gov. Hamilton,
and Hon. John C. Calhoun... Charleston, Printed by
A. E. Miller, 1832.
27 p.   20 1/2 cm.
Copied from the Pendleton messenger of 15th Sept.,
1832.

12611   Hamilton, James, 1786-1857.
An oration, delivered on the Fourth of July,
1821, before the Cincinnati and Revolution societies.
By James Hamilton, jun. ... And pub. at their joint
request. Charleston, Printed by A. E. Miller, 1821.
32 p.   19 1/2 cm.

12612   Hamilton, James, 1814-1867.
A memoir of Richard Williams, surgeon; catechist to
the Patagonian missionary society in Tierra del
Fuego. By James Hamilton, D. D. London, J. Nisbet
and co. [etc.] 1854.
viii, 255, [1] p.   front. (port.)   19 cm.

12613   Hamilton, James Alexander, 1788-1878.
State sovereignty. Rebellion against the United
States by the people of a state is its political
suicide. By James A. Hamilton. Pub. by the
Emancipation league in the city of New York. New
York, Baker & Godwin, printers, 1862.
32 p.   22 cm.

12614   Hamilton, Pierce Stevens.
Nova Scotia considered as a field for emigration, by
P. S. Hamilton... Published by authority of the
provincial parliament of Nova Scotia. London [etc.]
J. Weale [etc.] 1858.
2 p.l., 91 p.   front. (fold. map)   22 cm.

12615   Hamilton, Schuyler, 1822-1903.
History of the national flag of the United States of
America. By Schuyler Hamilton... Philadelphia,

Lippincott, Grambo, and co., 1852.
    4 p.l., [vii]-viii, [13]-115 p.   col. plates.
18 1/2 cm.

12616 Hamilton, William, 1811-1891.
    An Ioway grammar, illustrating the principles of the
    language used by the Ioway, Otoe, and Missouri Indians.
    Prepared and printed by Rev. Wm. Hamilton and Rev.
    S. M. Irvin. Under the direction of the Presbyterian
    B. F. M. [n. p.] Ioway and Sac mission press, 1848.
    xi (i.e. ix), [3], 9-152 p.   15 1/2 cm.
    Preface dated at end "Ioway and Sac mission: Indian
    Territory. 1848."

12617 Hamilton, William Richard, 1777-1859.
    No mistake: or, A vindication of the negotiators
    of the treaty of 1783, respecting the north eastern
    boundary of the United States. In a conversation
    between John Bull and Jonathan. By W. R. Hamilton...
    London, Printed by W. Nicol, 1842.
    2 p.l., 20 p.   map.   22 1/2 cm.

12618 Hamilton, William T   d. 1842.
    A word for the African. A sermon, for the benefit
    of the American colonization society, delivered in
    the Second Presbyterian church, Newark, July 24, 1825.
    By the Rev. William T. Hamilton... Newark, Printed by
    W. Tuttle & co., 1825.
    27 p.   21 1/2 cm.

12619 Hamilton college, Clinton, N. Y.
    A memorial of the semi-centennial celebration of the
    founding of Hamilton college, Clinton, N. Y.... Utica,
    N. Y., E. H. Roberts, 1862.
    232 p.   8 port.   23 1/2 cm.

12620 Hamilton college, Clinton, N. Y.
    Public exercises at the inauguration of Rev. Samuel
    Ware Fisher, D. D., as the sixth president of
    Hamilton college, at Clinton, N. Y., Thursday,
    November 4, 1858... Utica, Roberts, printer, 1858.
    71 p.   22 cm.

12621 Hamlin, Augustus Choate, 1829-1905.
    Martyria: or, Andersonville prison. By Augustus
    C. Hamlin... Boston, Lee and Shepard, 1866.
    256 p.   front., illus., plates, plans (part fold.)
map.   19 1/2 cm.

12622 Hammond, Charles, 1813-1878.
       A sermon on the life and character of Abraham
Lincoln, preached at Monson, at the united service
of the Congregational and Methodist churches, on the
occasion of the national fast, June 1, 1865. By
Charles Hammond... Springfield [Mass.] S. Bowles and
company, printers, 1865.
       21 p.   23 cm.

12623 [Hammond, Jabez Delano] 1778-1855.
       Letter to the Hon. John C. Calhoun, on the
annexation of Texas. Cooperstown, Printed by
H. & E. Phinney, 1844.
       34 p.   22 cm.

12624 Hammond, Jabez Delano, 1778-1855.
       Life and times of Silas Wright, late governor of
the state of New York. By Jabez D. Hammond.
Syracuse, Hall & Dickson; New York, A. S. Barnes
& co., 1848.
       749 p.   front., 3 port. (incl. front.)
23 1/2 cm.

12625 Hammond, James Henry, 1807-1864.
       Gov. Hammond's letters on southern slavery;
addressed to Thomas Clarkson, the English abolitionist.
[Charleston, Walker & Burke, printers, 1845]
       32 p.   25 1/2 cm.

12626 Hammond, James Henry, 1807-1864.
       An oration on the life, character and services of
John Caldwell Calhoun: delivered on the 21st Nov.,
1850, in Charleston, S. C., at the request of the
City council. By J. H. Hammond. Charleston, S. C.,
Steam power-press of Walker & James, 1850.
       73 p.   22 1/2 cm.

12627 Hammond, John, fl. 1655.
       Leah and Rachel, or, The two fruitfull sisters
Virginia and Mary-land: their present condition,
impartially stated and related. VVith a removall
of such imputations as are scandalously cast on
those countries, whereby many deceived souls,
chose rather to beg, steal, rot in prison, and
come to shamefull deaths, then to better their
being by going thither, wherein is plenty of all
things necessary for humane subsistance. By John
Hammond... London, Printed by T. Mabb, and are

to be sold by N. Bourn, 1656.
   (Reprint. In Force, Peter. Tracts... Washington,
1836-46.   23 1/2 cm.   v. 3 (1844) no. 14.
30 p.)
   On verso of t.-p.: Force's Collection of
historical tracts.
   The part relating to Maryland treats of the
troubles between the proprietor and the Puritans
from the standpoint of an adherent of Lord
Baltimore.

12628 Hammond, Jonathan Pinkney, d. 1884.
   The army chaplain's manual, designed as a help to
chaplains in the discharge of their various duties...
By Rev. J. Pinkney Hammond... Philadelphia, J. B.
Lippincott & co., 1863.
   xii, 13-286 p.   19 cm.

12629 Hammond, Marcus Claudius Marcellus, 1814-1876.
   An oration on the duties and the requirements of
an American officer. Delivered before the Dialectic
society of the United States Military academy at
West Point, N. Y., June 5, 1852. By M. C. M.
Hammond... Pub. by order of the Dialectic society.
New York, Baker, Godwin & co., printers, 1852.
   30 p.   23 cm.

12630 Hammond, Samuel H   1809-1878.
   Hills, lakes, and forest streams: or, A tramp
in the Chateaugay woods. By S. H. Hammond...
New York, J. C. Derby; Boston, Phillips, Sampson
& co. [etc., etc.] 1854.
   xii. [13]-340 p.   front., 2 pl.   19 cm.

12631 Hammond, Samuel H   1809-1878.
   Wild northern scenes; or, Sporting adventures
with the rifle and the rod. By S. H. Hammond...
New York, Derby & Jackson, 1857.
   xvii, 19-341 p.   front., 3 pl.   19 cm.

12632 Hammond, Wells Stoddard.
   Oration, delivered at Cherry Valley, on the fourth
day of July, 1839. By Wells S. Hammond. Published
by and at the request of the Committee of arrangements, for celebrating at Cherry Valley the 63d
anniversary of American independence. Albany,
Printed by J. Munsell, 1839.
   16 p.   22 1/2 cm.

12633 Hammond, William Alexander, 1828-1900.
       A statement of the causes which led to the
       dismissal of Surgeon-General William A. Hammond
       from the army; with a review of the evidence
       adduced before the court. [New York, 1864]
          73 p.   23 cm.

12634 Hamon, Henry.
       New York stock exchange manual, containing its
       principles, rules, and its different modes of
       speculation: also, a review of the stocks dealt
       in on 'change... By Henry Hamon. New York,
       J. F. Trow, 1865.
          iv, [5]-405 p.   19 1/2 cm.
       Cover-title: Trow's manual of the stock exchange.

12635 Hampden, pseud.
       The genuine book of nullification: being a true -
       not an apocryphal - history, chapter and verse, of
       the several examples of the recognition and enforce-
       ment of that sovereign state remedy, by the different
       states of this confederacy, from 1798 down to the
       present day. (As originally pub. in the Charleston
       mercury.) To which are added the opinions of
       distinguished statesmen, on state rights doctrines.
       By Hampden... Pub. at the request of the State
       rights association. Charleston, Printed by E. J.
       Van Brunt, 1831.
          2 p.l., 155 p.   21 1/2 cm.

12636 Hanaford, Jeremiah Lynford, b. 1834.
       History of Princeton, Worcester county,
       Massachusetts; civil and ecclesiastical; from
       its first settlement in 1739, to April 1852. By
       Jeremiah Lynford Hanaford... Worcester, C. B. Webb,
       printer, 1852.
          viii, [9]-204 p.   19 cm.

12637 Hanaford, Mrs. Phebe Ann (Coffin) 1829-1921.
       The captive boy in Terra del Fuego: being an
       authentic narrative of the loss of the ship
       Manchester, and the adventures of the sole white
       survivor. By Mrs, P. A. Hanaford... New York,
       Carlton & Porter [1867]
          231 p. incl. front., plates.   16 1/2 cm.

12638   Hanaford, Mrs. Phebe Ann (Coffin) 1829-1921.
            Our martyred President. By Mrs. P. A. Hanaford...
        Abraham Lincoln: born February 12, 1809; died April
        15, 1865... Boston, B. B. Russell and company, 1865.
            22, [2] p.   front. (port.)   21 1/2 cm.
        In verse.

12639   Hanckel, Thomas M
            Oration delivered on the fifth anniversary of the
        South Carolina historical society, at Hibernian hall,
        in Charleston, on Wednesday evening, May 23, 1860.
        By Thomas M. Hanckel. Pub. at the request of the
        society.   Charleston, Walker, Evans & co., 1860.
            34 p.   22 1/2 cm.

12640   Hancock, John.
            The Constitution and government of the United
        States: with questions and answers... With the
        late amendments, by John Hancock... Philadelphia,
        Printed by King & Baird, 1867.
            xiv, 130 p.   front., illus.   16 cm.

12641   Hancock, John.
            Observations on the climate, soil and productions
        of British Guiana, and on the advantages of
        emigration to, and colonizing the interior of, that
        country: together with incidental remarks on the
        diseases, their treatment and prevention: founded
        on a long experience within the tropics. By John
        Hancock, M. D. 2d ed. London, For the author
        [C. Richards, printer] 1840.
            2 p.l., 92 p.   21 cm.

12642   Hancock, John, 1671-1752.
            Rulers should be benefactors. As it was consider'd
        in a sermon preach'd before His Excellency Samuel
        Shute esq.; His Majesty's Council, and the Represent-
        atives of the Province of the Massachusetts-bay in
        New-England, May 30th. 1722. Being the day for
        election of counsellors. By John Hancock, M. A. and
        pastor of the Church of Christ in Lexington. Boston,
        Printed by B. Green, printer to His Excellency the
        the Governor & Council, 1722.
            2 p.l., 30 p.   19 cm.

12643   Hancock, John, 1702-1744.
        A discourse upon the good work. Delivered at
the monthly Tuesday lecture in Pembrook, September
7th, 1742. And now published at the earnest desire
of the hearers. By John Hancock... Boston, Printed
and sold by Rogers and Fowle in Queen-street below
the prison, near the Town-house, 1743.
        38 p.   19 cm.

12644   Hancock, John, 1702-1744.
        The instability of humane greatness, illustrated
and exemplified in a funeral discourse at Braintree
April 23, 1738. Upon the much lamented death of the
Honourable Edmund Quincy, esq; one of His Majesty's
Council, and of the judges of the circuit, and
agent for the Province of the Massachusetts bay, at
the court of Great Britain. Who died of the small
pox in London the 23, of Febr. 1737, 8. In the 57
year of his age. By John Hancock... Boston, Printed
by S. Kneeland, and T. Green, 1738.
        3 p.l., 31, [1] p.   20 1/2 cm.

12645   Hancock, John, 1824-1893.
        The great question for the people! Essays on the
elective franchise; or, Who has the right to vote?
By John Hancock... Philadelphia, Merrihew & son,
printers, 1865.
        40 p.   22 1/2 cm.

12646   Hancock, William, emigrant.
        An emigrant's five years in the free states of
America. By William Hancock... London, T. C. Newby,
1860.
        3 p.l., 321 p.   front. (fold. map)   19 1/2 cm.

12647   Hand, William M
        The house surgeon and physician; designed to assist
heads of families, travellers, and sea-faring people,
in discerning, distinguishing, and curing diseases;
with concise directions for the preparation and use
of a numerous collection of the best American remedies:
together with many of the most approved, from the
shop of the apothecary. All in plain English. By
Wm. M. Hand. 2d ed., rev. and enl. New Haven,
Printed by S. Converse, for Silas Andrus, Hartford,
1820.
        xii, 288 p.   18 1/2 cm.

12648   Handelmann, Heinrich, 1827-1891.
            Geschichte von Brasilien von Heinrich Handelmann...
        Berlin, J. Springer, 1860.
            xxiv, 989 p.   22 1/2 cm.
            "Litteratur": p. [969]-989.

12649   Handlin, William Wallace, b. 1830.
            American politics, a moral and political work,
        treating of the causes of the civil war, the nature
        of government, and the necessity for reform. By
        W. W. Handlin. New Orleans, I. T. Hinton, 1864.
            108 p.   20 1/2 cm.

12650   Handy, Isaac William Ker, 1815-1878.
            Our national sins. A sermon, delivered in the
        First Presbyterian church, Portsmouth, Va., on the
        day of fasting, humiliation and prayer, January 4,
        1861. By Rev. Isaac W. K. Handy, D. D. Portsmouth,
        Va., Printed at the office of the Daily and weekly
        transcript, 1861.
            20 p.   22 cm.

12651   Hanna, Stewart William, d. 1851.
            Notes of a visit to some parts of Haïti, Jan. Feb.
        1835. By the Rev. S. W. Hanna... [London] R. B.
        Seeley & W. Burnside, & L. & G. Seeley, 1836.
            lxii, 153, [1] p.   4 pl.   16 1/2 cm.

12652   [Hanson, Alexander Contee] 1749-1806.
            Considerations on the proposed removal of the seat
        of government, addressed to the citizens of Maryland,
        by Aristides [pseud.] Annapolis, Printed by F.
        Green [1786]
            62 p.   20 1/2 cm.

12653   [Hanson, Alexander Contee] 1749-1806.
            Remarks on the proposed plan of a federal govern-
        ment, addressed to the citizens of the United States
        on America, and particularly to the people of
        Maryland, by Aristides [pseud.]... Annapolis,
        Printed by F. Green [1788]
            42 p.   19 cm.

12654   Hanson, Alexander Contee, 1786-1819, defendant.
            Trial of Alexander Contee Hanson, esq., a lieu-
        tenant in a company of militia attached to the
        Thirty-ninth regiment, upon a charge "conceived
        to be mutinous and highly reproachful to the President

274

and commander in chief of the militia of the U.
States and in direct opposition to the orders of
the commander in chief of the militia of Maryland."
and founded upon a political piece published in the
Federal republican, disputing the policy of a
measure of government. Baltimore, Printed by J.
Robinson, 1809.
　　1 p.l., 56 p.　　22 cm.

12655　Hanson, Mrs. Elizabeth, fl. 1703-1741.
　　An account of the captivity of Elizabeth Hanson,
late of Kachecky in New-England: who, with four
of her children, and servant-maid, was taken captive
by the Indians, and carried into Canada. Setting
forth the various remarkable occurrences, sore trials,
and wonderful deliverances which befel them after
their departure, to the time of their redemption.　A
new ed.　Taken in substance from her own mouth, by
Samuel Bownas.　London, Printed and sold by J.
Phillips, 1782.
　　26 p.　　15 1/2 cm.
　　Apparently first published, Philadelphia and New
York, 1728, under title: God's mercy surmounting
man's cruelty, exemplified in the captivity... of
Elizabeth Hanson...
　　"The substance of the foregoing account was taken
from her own mouth by Samuel Bownas. And in the
seventh month, called September, 1741, Samuel
Hopwood was with her, and received the relation
much to the same purpose." - Note, p. 26.

12656　Hanson, John Halloway, 1815-1854.
　　Poems of the Rev. John H. Hanson... With a memoir
by his sister, Christian Hanson. New York, Pott &
Amery, 1869.
　　167 p.　　18 1/2 cm.
　　Memoir includes an account of the author's grandfather, Charles, brother of Oliver Goldsmith.

12657　Hanson, John Wesley, 1823-1901.
　　History of the old towns, Norridgewock and Canaan,
comprising Norridgewock, Canaan, Starks, Skowhegan,
and Bloomfield, from their early settlement to the
year 1849; including a sketch of the Abnakis Indians.
By J. W. Hanson... Boston, The author, 1849.
　　371, [1] p.　　front., 1 illus., plates.　　19 1/2 cm.

12658   Hanson, John Wesley, 1823-
            History of the town of Danvers, from its early
        settlement to the year 1848. By J. W. Hanson...
        Danvers, The author, 1848.
            vii, [9]-304 p.   illus. (incl. coat of arms)
        19 1/2 cm.

12659   [Hanway, Jonas] 1712-1786.
            An account of the Society for the encouragement
        of the British troops, in Germany and North America.
        With the motives to the making a present to those
        troops, also to the widows and orphans of such of
        them as have died in defense of their country,
        particularly at the battles of Thornhausen, Quebec,
        &c. With an alphabetical list of the subscribers
        to this benevolent design; and a state of the
        receipts and disbursements of the society. London,
        1760.
            viii, 91, 55 p.   22 cm.

12660   Harbaugh, Henry, 1817-1867.
            The life of Rev. Michael Schlatter; with a full
        account of his travels and labors among the Germans
        in Pennsylvania, New Jersey, Maryland and Virginia;
        including his services as chaplain in the French
        and Indian war, and in the war of the revolution.
        1716 to 1790. By Rev. H. Harbaugh... Philadelphia,
        Lindsay & Blakiston, 1857.
            xxxi, 27-375 p.   front.   18 1/2 cm.
        "A true history of the real condition of the des-
        titute congregations in Pennsylvania, by Michael
        Schlatter" (a translation of Getrouw verhaal van
        den waren toestant der meest herderloze gemeentens
        in Pennsylvanien... Amsterdam, 1751): p. 87-234.

12661   Harbaugh, Henry, 1817-1867.
            A tract for the times. The religious character of
        Washington, by Rev. H. Harbaugh... Pub. by the
        Christian commission for the district of Maryland.
        Chambersburg, Pa., M. Kieffer & co.'s caloric book
        and job printing office, 1863.
            24 p.   19 cm.

12662   Harbaugh, Henry, 1817-1867
            Treason and law. A discourse, delivered at
        Clearspring, Maryland, June 1, 1865, the day of
        national mourning. By H. Harbaugh... Philadelphia,

J. B. Rodgers, pr., 1865.
31 p.   17 cm.
On the death of President Lincoln.

12663   The Harbinger; a May-gift.   Boston, Carter, Hendee
        and co., 1833.
            vi p., 1 l., 96 p.   21 cm.
            A collection of poems in three parts: pt. 1, by
        Park Benjamin, p. 1-30; pt. II, by Oliver Wendell
        Holmes, p. 31-61; pt. III, by John O. Sargent,
        p. 63-96. cf. G. B. Ives, Bibl. of Oliver Wendell
        Holmes, p. 118.

12664   Harbison, Massy (White) "Mrs. J. Harbison," 1770.
            A narrative of the sufferings of Massy Harbison,
        from Indian barbarity, giving an account of her
        captivity, the murder of her two children, her
        escape, with an infant at her breast, communicated
        by herself; together with some account of the
        history, laws, religion, wars, and cruelties of
        the Indians, particularly in this western country...
        Edited by John Winter. 4th ed., enl. Beaver [Pa.]
        Printed by W. Henry, 1836.
            xii, 13-192 p.   18 cm.

12665   Harbor and river convention. Chicago, 1847.
            Proceedings of the Harbor and river convention,
        held at Chicago, July fifth, 1847: together with
        full list of names of delegates in attendance:
        letters read at the convention, and a detailed
        appendix. Published by order of the convention.
        Chicago, Printed by R. L. Wilson, 1847.
            79 p.   20 cm.

12666   Harby, Isaac, 1788-1828.
            A selection from the miscellaneous writings of
        the late Isaac Harby, esq. Arranged and published
        by Henry L. Pinckney and Abraham Moise, for the
        benefit of his family. To which is prefixed, a
        memoir of his life, by Abraham Moise. Charleston
        [S. C.] Printed by J. S. Burges, 1829.
            40, 287, [1] p.   22 cm.
            Contents. - Memoir, by A. Moise. - Alberti, a play.
        - Discourse before the Reformed society of Israelites.
        - Political essays. - Criticisms. - Dramatic
        criticisms.

12667 [Harcourt, Sir William George Granville Venables
Vernon] 1827-1904.
Additional letters by Historicus [pseud.] on
some questions of international law. London and
Cambridge, Macmillan and co., 1863.
xv, [1], 44 p.   21 1/2 cm.
The letters on "Belligerent rights of maritime
capture" appeared first in the London Times.
Contents. - Belligerent rights of maritime capture. -
The doctrine of continuous voyages.

12668 [Harcourt, Sir William George Granville Venables
Vernon] 1827-1904.
American neutrality: by Historicus [pseud.]
Reprinted from the London Times of December 22d,
1864. New York, 1865.
11 p.   22 1/2 cm.

12669 [Harcourt, Sir William George Granville Venables
Vernon] 1827-1904.
Belligerent rights of maritime capture. By
Historicus [pseud.]... Liverpool, Printed by Webb
and Hunt, 1863.
22 p.   20 1/2 cm.
"Re-printed by permission from the Times."
Reissued in the author's "Additional letters...
on some questions of international law," 1863.

12670 [Harden, Edward Jenkins] 1813-1873.
Notes of a short northern tour. For private circulation only. Savannah, Morning news press, 1869.
38 p.   22 cm.
Text in English and Latin.

12671 Harden, Jacob S   1837-1860.
Life, confession and letters of courtship of Rev.
Jacob S. Harden, of the M. E. church, Mount Lebanon,
Hunterdon Co., N. J. Executed for the murder of his
wife, on the 6th of July, 1860. At Belvidere,
Warren Co., N. J. Hackettstown, Warren Co., N. J.,
E. Winton, printer, 1860.
vi, 7-48 p. incl. front. (port.)   24 1/2 cm.

12672 Hardie, James, 1750?-1826?
An account of the malignant fever, lately pre-
valent in the city of New York. Containing I. A
narrative of its rise, progress and decline...

II. The manner in which the poor were relieved...
III. A list of the donations... for the relief
of the sick and indigent. IV. A list of the names
of the dead... V. A comparative view of the fever
of the year 1798, with that of the year 1795. By
James Hardie, A. M. New York, Printed by Hurtin
and M'Farlane, at the Literary printing office,
no. 29 Goldstreet, and sold by the author, no. 1
Rider street - by John Low, at the Shakespeare's
head, no. 332 Water street, the other booksellers,
and the printers, 1799.
    iv, [5]-139, [9] p.   22 cm.

12673 Hardie, James, 1750?-1826?
    The American remembrancer, and universal tablet
of memory: containing a list of the most eminent
men, whether in ancient or modern times, with the
atchievements for which they have been particularly
distinguished: as also the most memorable events
in history, from the earliest period till the year
1795, classed under distinct heads, with their
respective dates. To which is added, a table,
comprehending the periods at which the most remarkable cities and towns were founded, their present
population, latitude, and longitude. The whole
being intended to form a comprehensive abridgement
of history and chronology, particularly of that
part which relates to America. By James Hardie...
Philadelphia, Printed for the author by Thomas
Dobson, at the Stone-house, no. 41, south Second
street, 1795.
    vi p., 1 l., 259 p.   fold. tab.   17 1/2 cm.

12674 Hardie, James, 1750?-1826?
    A census of the new buildings erected in this city,
in the year 1824, arranged in distinct classes,
according to their materials and number of stories.
Also, a number of statistical documents, interesting
to the Christian, the merchant, the man of inquiry
and the public in general. By James Hardie, A. M.
New York, Printed by S. Marks, 1825.
    48 p.   20 x 11 1/2 cm.

12675 Hardie, James, 1750?-1826?
    The history of the tread-mill, containing an
account of its origin, construction, operation,
effects as it respects the health and morals of the

convicts, with their treatment and diet; also, a
general view of the penitentiary system, with
alterations necessary to be introduced into our
criminal code, for its improvement. By James
Hardie, A. M. New York, Printed by S. Marks,
1824.
  viii, [9]-70 p.   front.   17 1/2 cm.

12676 Hardie, James, 1750?-1826?
     The Philadelphia directory and register: con-
taining the names, occupations, and places of abode
of the citizens... a register of the executive,
legislative, and judicial magistrates of the United
States and the state of Pennsylvania... to which
is added a short account of the city; and of the
charitable and literary institutions therein.
2d ed. By James Hardie, A. M. Philadelphia,
Printed for the author, by Jacob Johnson & co.,
1794.
  4 p.l., 232 p.   20 1/2 cm.

12677 Hardin, Benjamin, 1784-1852.
     Speech of Mr. Hardin, of Kentucky, on Mr. Adams's
resolutions concerning the loss of the fortification
bill of the last session: delivered in the House
of representatives, January 28, 1836. Washington,
National intelligencer office, 1836.
  28 p.   24 cm.
  [Markoc pamphlets, v. 18, no. 16]

12678 Harding, Benjamin.
     A tour through the western country, A. D. 1818 &
1819. By Benjamin Harding, surveyor. Published
for the use of emigrants. New London, Printed by
Samuel Green, for the author, 1819.
  2 p.l., [3]-17 p.   22 1/2 cm.

12679 Harding, Stephen S
     Oration, by Hon. S. S. Harding, chief justice of
Colorado, delivered at the Denver theatre, in the
city of Denver, February 22d, 1864. Denver, Col.,
Byers & Dailey, printers, 1864.
  36 p.   20 cm.

12680 [Hardy, John] fl. 1670-1671.
     A description of the last voyage to Bermudas,
in the ship Marygold, S. P. commander. By J. H.

Φιλοχειρηρνεία. Begun November the twelfth, 1670. And
ending May the third, 1671. With allowance.
London, Printed for R. Reynald, 1671.
    4 p.l., 24 p. incl. 3 wdcts.   19 x 14 1/2 cm.
    In verse.
    The text ends abruptly on p. 24, with a comma,
leaving the poem apparently incomplete.

12681   Hardy, William, defendant.
        A sketch of the proceedings and trial of William
    Hardy, on an indictment for the murder of an infant,
    November 27, 1806, before the Supreme judicial
    court, holden at Boston, within and for the counties
    of Suffolk and Nantucket, in the commonwealth of
    Massachusetts, on the second Tuesday of March, in
    the year of Our Lord 1807. Reported from the
    minutes of one of the counsel for the defendant.
    Boston, Printed by Oliver and Munroe, no. 78, State
    street, 1807.
        47 p.   21 1/2 cm.
        Speech of George Blake, senior counsel for the
    defendant: p. 13-46.

12682   Hare, R[obert] 1781-1858.
        Suggestions respecting the reformation of the banking
    system. By R. Hare, M. D. Philadelphia, J. C. Clark,
    1837.
        29 p.   22 1/2 cm.

12683   Harlan, Richard, 1796-1843.
        American herpetology, or Genera of North American
    Reptilia, with a synopsis of the species. By
    Richard Harlan... Philadelphia, 1827.
        1 p.l., 87, [1] p.   23 cm.

12684   Harlan, Richard, 1796-1843.
        Fauna americana: being a description of the
    mammiferous animals inhabiting North America. By
    Richard Harlan... Philadelphia, A. Finley, 1825.
        x, 11-318, [2] p.   21 1/2 cm.

12685   Harlan, Richard, 1796-1843.
        Medical and physical researches: or, Original
    memoirs in medicine, surgery, physiology, geology,
    zoology, and comparative anatomy... By R. Harlan...
    Philadelphia, Printed by Lydia R. Bailey, 1835.

xxxix, [9]-653 p.   39 pl. (4 col., 12 fold.)
fold. tab.   24 1/2 cm.

12686 [Harlan, Richard] 1796-1843.
       Refutation of certain misrepresentations issued
       against the author of the "Fauna americana", in
       the Philadelphia Franklin journal, no. 1, 1826,
       and in the North American review, no. 50. Phila-
       delphia, Printed by W. Staveley, 1826.
           42 p.   21 cm.

12687 Harmar, Josiah, 1753-1813, defendant.
       The proceedings of a Court of enquiry, held at
       the special request of Brigadier General Josiah
       Harmar, to investigate his conduct, as commanding
       officer of the expedition against the Miami Indians,
       1790: the same having been transmitted by Major
       General St. Clair, to the secretary of the United
       States, for the Department of war. Published by
       authority. Philadelphia, Printed by John Fenno,
       1791.
           2 p.l., 31 p.   front. (port.)   34 x 21 1/2 cm.

12688 Harnden, Harvey.
       Narrative of the apprehension in Rindge, N. H.,
       of the Rev. E. K. Avery, charged with the murder
       of Sarah M. Cornell, together with the proceedings
       of the inhabitants of Fall River. By Harvey Harnden.
       2d ed. Providence, W. Marshall & co., printers,
       1833.
           36 p.   20 1/2 cm.
           [Miscellaneous pamphlets, v. 989, no. 1]

12689 Harney, William Selby, 1800-1889.
       Official correspondence of Brig. W. S. Harney,
       U. S. Army, and First Lt. Geo. Ihrie, late U. S.
       Army, with the U. S. War department, and subsequent
       personal correspondence. [Washington? 1861?]
           16 p.   24 cm.
       Including a copy of certain legal proceedings
       against Harney for murder of Hannah, a slave, in
       Missouri in 1834.

12690 Harper, Robert Goodloe, 1765-1825.
       An address from Robert Goodloe Harper, of South
       Carolina, to his constituents: containing his
       reasons for approving of the treaty of amity,

commerce and navigation, with Great Britain.
Boston, Printed by Young and Minns, Mercury Office,
at the Press of Rational Federalism, 1796.
36 p.   18 1/2 cm.

12691 Harper, [Robert Goodloe] 1765-1825.
Gen. Harper's speech to the citizens of Baltimore,
on the expediency of promoting a connexion between
the Ohio, at Pittsburgh, and the waters of the
Chesapeake, at Baltimore, by a canal through the
District of Columbia. With his reply to some of
the objections of Mr. Winchester. Delivered at a
meeting, held at the Exchange, on the 20th day of
December, 1823. Baltimore, E. J. Coale, 1824.
78 p.   fold. map.   22 1/2 cm.

12692 Harper, Robert Goodloe, 1765-1825.
A letter from Gen. Harper of Maryland, to Elias
B. Caldwell, esq., secretary of the American Society
for Colonizing the Free People of Colour, in the
United States, with their own consent. Baltimore,
Printed for E. J. Cole, by R. J. Matchett, corner
of Gay and Water streets, 1818.
32 p.   20 1/2 cm.

12693 Harper, Robert Goodloe, 1765-1825.
A letter from Robert Goodloe Harper, of South
Carolina, to his constituents... Portsmouth, N. H.,
Printed by C. Peirce, 1801.
16 p.   21 cm.

12694 Harper, Robert Goodloe, 1765-1825.
Select works of Robert Goodloe Harper; consisting
of speeches on political and forensic subjects;
with the answer drawn up by him to the articles of
impeachment against Judge Chase, and sundry political
tracts. Collated from the original publications
and carefully rev. Vol. 1. Baltimore, O. H. Neilson,
1814.
iv, 400 p.   21 cm.
No more published.

12695 Harper, William, 1790-1847.
Memoir of the life, character, and public services,
of the late Hon. Henry Wm. De Saussure, prepared and
read on the 15th February, 1841, at the Circular
church, Charleston, by appointment of the South

283

Carolina bar association. By the Hon. William
Harper... Charleston, Printed by W. Riley, 1841.
38 p. 22 1/2 cm.

12696 Harper's New York and Erie rail-road guide book...
With one hundred and thirty-six engravings by
Lossing and Barritt, from original sketches made
expressly for this work by William Macleod. New
York, Harper & brothers [1851]
1 p.l., viii, [9]-173 p., 1 l. incl. illus.,
plates. 19 1/2 cm.
From Piermont on the Hudson, through the southern
tier of counties to Dunkirk on Lake Erie.

12697 Harrington, Timothy, 1715-1795.
A century sermon, preached at the First-parish,
in Lancaster. May 28th 1753. By Timothy Harrington
... Leominster [Mass.] Printed by S. & J. Wilder,
for Mr. Joshua Fletcher, of Lancaster, July 1806.
25 p., 1 l. 22 cm.

12698 Harris, Mrs. Caroline.
History of the captivity and providential release
therefrom of Mrs. Caroline Harris, wife of the late
Mr. Richard Harris, of Franklin county... New York;
who, with Mrs. Clarissa Plummer, wife of Mr. James
Plummer, were, in the spring of 1835 (with their
unfortunate husbands) taken prisoners by the Camanche
tribe of Indians, while emigrating from said
Franklin county (N. Y.) to Texas... New York,
Perry and Cooke, 1838.
23, [1] p. incl. col. front. 22 1/2 cm.

12699 Harris, Charles H   of Buffalo.
History of the Venango oil regions... and other
places of note in the oil regions, by Chas. H.
Harris (Oof T Goof) Titusville, Pa., Printed at
the Titusville morning herald office, 1866.
v, 108 p. illus. 20 cm.

12700 Harris, Edward Doubleday, 1839-1919.
An account of some of the descendants of Capt.
Thomas Brattle. Compiled by Edward-Doubleday Harris.
[Boston, Printed by D. Clapp and son] 1867.
2 p.l., 90 p. illus., geneal. tab. 21 cm.

12701   Harris, Edward Doubleday, 1839-1919.
        A genealogical record of Thomas Bascom and his
        descendants. Boston, W. P. Lunt, 1870.
        79 p.   24 cm.
        ----- Thomas Bascom and his descendants. Supple-
        ment [by Clarinda (Bascom) Safford. Kalamazoo,
        Mich., 1871]
        11 p.   24 cm.
        Bound with the main work.

12702   Harris, Edward Doubleday, 1839-1919.
        The Vassals of New England and their immediate
        descendants. A genealogical and biographical
        sketch comp. from church and town records. By
        Edward Doubleday Harris... Albany, J. Munsell,
        1862.
        26 p.   24 cm.

12703   Harris, George, of Baltimore.
        The economy and policy of a Christian education.
        Adapted as a monitor and directory for all professors
        of Christianity; especially governors and directors
        of children and youth, in families and schools.
        By George Harris... Baltimore, Printed by W. Wooddy,
        1823.
        282 p.   18 cm.

12704   Harris, J   Dennis.
        A summer on the borders of the Caribbean Sea.
        By J. Dennis Harris. With an introduction by George
        William Curtis. New York, A. B. Burdick, 1860.
        xi, [13]-179 p.   18 1/2 cm.
        Contents. - Dominican Republic. - Republic of
        Hayti. - Grand Turk's and Caicos Islands. -
        British Honduras. - Conclusive summary. - Appendix.

12705   Harris, James Morrison, 1818-1898.
        Discourse on the life and character of Sir Walter
        Raleigh, delivered by J. Morrison Harris, before the
        Maryland historical society, May 19, 1846...
        Baltimore, Printed for the Society, 1846.
        71 p.   22 1/2 cm.   [Maryland historical society.
        Publications, v. 1, no. 6]

12706   Harris, Luther Metcalf, 1789-1865.
        Robert Harris and his descendants. With notices
        of the Morey and Metcalf families. Comp. by

Luther M. Harris... Boston, H. W. Dutton & son, 1861.
56 p.   24 cm.

12707   Harris, Samuel, 1814-1899.
Inaugural address delivered by Samuel Harris at his induction into the presidency of Bowdoin college, August 6, 1867. Brunswick, J. Griffin, 1867.
45 p.   23 1/2 cm.
On "the necessity, the idea and the methods of collegiate education."

12708   Harris, Thaddeus Mason, 1768-1842.
An address, delivered before the Washington benevolent society, in Dorchester, February 22d, 1813. By Rev. Thaddeus Mason Harris. Pub. by the particular request of the society. Boston, J. Belcher, printer, 1813.
15 p.   21 cm.
[Waterman pamphlets, v. 11, no. 6]

12709   Harris, Thaddeus Mason, 1768-1842.
Biographical memorials of James Oglethorpe, founder of the colony of Georgia in North America. By Thaddeus Mason Harris... Boston, Printed for the author, 1841.
xxii, 424 p.   front. (port.) pl., fold. map, facsim.   23 cm.

12710   Harris, Thaddeus Mason, 1768-1842.
A discourse, delivered at Dorchester, Dec. 29, 1799. Being the Lord's day after hearing the distressing intelligence of the death of General George Washington, late president of the United States, and commander in chief of the American armies. By Thaddeus Mason Harris, A. M. Charlestown, Printed by Samuel Etheridge, 1800.
16 p.   21 cm.   (In Dorchester, Mass. Public expressions of grief, for the death of General George Washington... [Charlestown, 1800])

12711   Harris, Thomas, 1784-1861.
The life and services of Commodore William Bainbridge, United States navy. By Thomas Harris... Philadelphia, Carey, Lea & Blanchard, 1837.
xvi, [17]-254 p., 1 l.   front. (port.)   21 cm.

12712 Harris, W   A
The record of Fort Sumter, from its occupation
by Major Anderson, to its reduction by South Carolina
troops during the administration of Governor Pickens.
Comp. by W. A. Harris... Columbia, S. C., South
Carolinian steam job printing office, 1862.
50 p.   23 cm.

12713 Harris, William Tell.
Bemerkungen auf einer reise durch die Vereinten
Staaten von Nord-Amerika in den jahren 1817, 1818
und 1819, von William Tell Harris, in einer reihe
von briefen an freunde in England. Aus dem englischen
übersetzt von Dr. C. Fl. Leidenfrost... Weimar,
Im verlage des G. H. S. pr. Landes-industrie-
comptoirs, 1822.
viii (i.e. vi), 236 p.   21 x 12 1/2 cm.
(On cover: Neue bibliothek der wichtigsten reise-
beschreibungen. 30. 1)

12714 Harris, William Thaddeus, 1826-1854.
Epitaphs from the old burying-ground in Cambridge.
With notes, by William Thaddeus Harris... Cambridge,
J. Owen, 1845.
vii, 192 p.   illus.   21 1/2 cm.

12715 Harrison, Henry William.
The battle-fields of the republic; from Lexington
to the city of Mexico. By Henry W. Harrison.
Illustrated by numerous engravings of medals,
portraits, and battle-fields. Philadelphia, H. C.
Baird, 1857.
464 p.   front., illus. (incl. ports.) 14 pl.
23 1/2 cm.

12716 Harrison, William Henry, pres. U. S., 1773-1841.
Remarks of General Harrison, late envoy extraordinary and minister plenipotentiary of the United
States to the Republic of Colombia, on certain
charges made against him by that government. To
which is added, an unofficial letter, from General
Harrison to General Bolivar, on the affairs of
Colombia; with notes, explanatory of his views of
the present state of that country. Washington,
Printed by Gales & Seaton, 1830.
69 p.   22 cm.

12717　[Harriss, Julia Mildred]
　　　　Wild shrubs of Alabama; or, Rhapsodies of
　　　　restless hours. By the Minstrel maiden of Mobile.
　　　　New York, C. B. Norton; Mobile, Carver & Ryland,
　　　　1852.
　　　　　　2 p.l., [iii]-viii, [9]-180 p.　　front. (port.)
　　　　19 cm.
　　　　Verse.

12718　[Harrisse, Henry] 1830-1910.
　　　　Notes pour servir à l'histoire, à la bibliographie
　　　　et à la cartographie de la Nouvelle-France et des
　　　　pays adjacents 1545-1700. Par l'auteur de la
　　　　Bibliotheca americana vetustissima... Paris,
　　　　Tross, 1872.
　　　　　　3 p.l., xxxiii p., 1 l., 367 p., 1 l.　　22 1/2 cm.

12719　Harsha, David Addison, 1827-1895.
　　　　The life of Charles Sumner; with choice specimens
　　　　of his eloquence, a delineation of his oratorical
　　　　character, and his great speech on Kansas. By
　　　　D. A. Harsha... New York, Dayton and Burdick,
　　　　1856.
　　　　　　1 p.l., [5]-329 p.　　front., port.　　19 cm.

12720　Hart, Adolphus M　　　　1813-1879.
　　　　History of the valley of the Mississippi. By
　　　　Adolphus M. Hart... Cincinnati, Moore, Anderson,
　　　　Wilstach & Keys; New York, Newman & Ivison, 1853.
　　　　　　286 p.　　18 1/2 cm.
　　　　An enlargement of his "History of the discovery
　　　　of the valley of the Mississippi" (St. Louis, 1852)
　　　　which extends only to 1748　while the later work
　　　　gives also the subsequent history.

12721　Hart, Alfred A
　　　　The traveler's own book, by Alfred A. Hart.
　　　　A souvenir of overland travel, via the great and
　　　　attractive route, Chicago, Burlington and Quincy
　　　　R. R. to Burlington. Union Pacific railroad to
　　　　Ogden. Central Pacific railroad to Sacramento.
　　　　Burlington & Missouri River R. R. to Omaha. Utah
　　　　central railroad to Salt Lake City. Western Pacific
　　　　railroad to San Francisco... [Chicago, Horton &
　　　　Leonard, printers, 1870]
　　　　　　34, [10] p.　　col. plates, fold. maps.
　　　　11 1/2 x 13 cm.

Chromo-lithographs by C. Shober, from photo-
graphs by A. A. Hart.

12722 Hart, Joseph C   d. 1855.
The romance of yachting: voyage the first.
By Joseph C. Hart... New York, Harper & brothers,
1848.
332 p.   20 1/2 cm.
A discussion of the authenticity of Shakespeare's
plays: p. 208-242.
"Vocabulary of sea terms, or nautical phrases":
p. 306-332.

12723 Hart, Levi, 1738-1808.
Religious improvement of the death of great men.
A discourse, addressed to the congregation in the
North society in Preston, on Lord's day, Dec. 29,
1799, occasioned by the death of Gen. George
Washington... By Levi Hart... Norwich [Conn.]
Printed by Thomas Hubbard, 1800.
26 p.   22 cm.

12724 Hart, Luther, 1783-1834.
A memoir of the life of the Rev. Amos Pettengill,
late pastor of the Congregational church in Water-
bury, (Salem) Con. By Rev. Luther Hart...
Written for the Massachusetts Sabbath school
society, and revised by the Committee of publication.
Boston, Massachusetts Sabbath school society, 1834.
1 p.l., viii, 264 p.   14 1/2 cm.

12725 Hart, Oliver, 1723-1795.
America's remembrancer, with respect to her
blessedness and duty. A sermon, delivered in
Hopewell, New Jersey, on Thanksgiving day, November
26, 1789. By Oliver Hart... Philadelphia, Printed
by T. Dobson, at the Stone-house, no. 41, South
Second street, 1791.
24 p.   20 1/2 cm.
[Hazard pamphlets, v. 80, no. 5]

12726 Hart, Seth, 1763-1832.
A sermon, preached in St. George's church, in
Hempstead, on the 24th June, 1801; before an
assembly of Free and accepted masons, convened for
the purpose of celebrating the festival of St. John
the Baptist. By Seth Hart... Brooklyn, Printed by

Thomas Kirk, 1801.
23 p.   19 1/2 cm.

12727   Hartford. Public library.
Catalogue of the library of the Hartford Young
men's institute. Hartford, The Institute, 1873.
x, 471, [1] p.   25 cm.

12728   Hartford hospital, Hartford.
Addresses delivered on the occasion of the dedication
of the Hartford hospital, in Hartford, Conn., on the
18th of April, 1859. Hartford, Press of Case,
Lockwood and company, 1859.
40 p. incl. front., plans.   23 1/2 cm.

12729   Hartley, Cecil B
Heroes and patriots of the South; comprising lives
of General Francis Marion, General William Moultrie,
General Andrew Pickens, and Governor John Rutledge.
With sketches of other distinguished heroes and
patriots who served in the revolutionary war in
the southern states. By Cecil B. Hartley. With
engravings from original designs, by G. G. White.
Philadelphia, G. G. Evans, 1860.
320 p.   front., plates.   19 1/2 cm.

12730   Hartley, Cecil B
Life and times of Colonel Daniel Boone, comprising
history of the early settlement of Kentucky, by
Cecil B. Hartley. To which is added, Colonel
Boone's autobiography complete, as dictated to
John Filson, and published in 1784. Illustrated
with engravings, from original drawings, by G. G.
White and other eminent artists. Philadelphia,
G. G. Evans, 1860.
2 p.l., 3-351 p.   front., plates.   19 cm.

12731   Hartley, David, 1732-1813.
Letters on the American war. Addressed to the
right worshipful the mayor and corporation, to the
worshipful the wardens and corporation of the
Trinity-house, and to the worthy burgesses of the
town of Kingston-upon-Hull. By David Hartley, esq;
member of Parliament for the town of Kingston-upon-
Hull. 5th ed. London, Printed for Almon [etc.,
etc.] 1779.
1 p.l., ii, 126 p., 1 l.   20 1/2 cm.

12732   Hartley, David, 1732-1813.
        Substance of a speech in Parliament upon the
state of the nation and the present civil war with
America. Upon Monday, April 1, 1776... London,
J. Almon, 1776.
        1 p.l., 24 p.   20 1/2 cm.   [With Whitehead,
William. Variety. London, 1776]

12733   Hartlib, Samuel, d. 1662.
        The reformed common wealth of bees. Presented
in severall letters and observations to Sammuel
Hartlib, esq. With The reformed Viginian silk-worm.
Containing many excellent and choice secrets,
experiments, and discoveries for attaining of
national and private profits and riches. London,
Printed for G. Calvert, 1655.
        2 p.l., 62, [2] p.   illus.   19 cm.

12734   [Hartlib, Samuel] d. 1662.
        The reformed Virginian silk-worm, or, A rare and
new discovery of a speedy way, and easie means,
found out by a young lady in England, she having
made full proof thereof in May, anno 1652. For the
feeding of silk-worms in the woods, on the mulberry-
tree-leaves in Virginia... And also to the good
hopes, that the Indians, seeing and finding that
there is neither art, skill, or pains in the thing:
they will readily set upon it, being by the benefit
thereof inabled to buy of the English (in way of
truck for their silk-bottoms) all those things that
they most desire. London, Printed by J. Streater,
for G. Calvert, 1655.
        2 p.l., 40 p.   19 1/2 cm.
        A reprint, with additions, of "A rare and new dis-
covery of a speedy way [etc.]" London, 1652. Also
reprinted as pt. 2 of the author's "The reformed
commonwealth of bees", London, 1655.
        Includes letters by "V. F., gentleman", Edward
Diggs and John Ferrar and verses by Ferrar and Du
Bartas.

12735   Hartlib, Samuel, d. 1662.
        Samuel Hartlib his legacie: or an enlargement of
the Discourse of husbandry used in Brabant and
Flaunders: wherein are bequeathed to the commonwealth of England more outlandish and domestick experiments and secrets in reference to universall

husbandry... London, Printed by H. Hills, for
R. Wodenothe, 1651.
　4 p.l., 131 p.　　18 cm.
Consists chiefly of letters to Hartlib apparently
written by Cressy Dymock, though the first (p. 1-108)
is attributed by some authorities to Robert Child.
cf. Dircks, Biographical memoir of Samuel Hartlib
[1865] p. 69.

12736　Harvard university.
Orders and regulations of the faculty of Harvard
university. Cambridge, Folsom, Wells, and Thurston,
printers, 1841.
13 p.　　19 cm.　　[With Harvard university.
Laws... relative to undergraduates. Cambridge, 1841]

12737　Harvard university.
Roll of students of Harvard university who served
in the army or navy of the United States during the
war of the rebellion. Prepared by order of the
Corporation, by Francis H. Brown, M. D. Cambridge,
Welch, Bigelow and company, printers, 1866.
47, [1] p.　　23 1/2 cm.

12738　Harvey, Arthur, 1834-
... The reciprocity treaty: its advantages to the
United States and to Canada. By Arthur Harvey...
Quebec, Printed by Hunter, Rose & co., 1865.
29 p.　　20 1/2 cm.
Received first prize from the Montreal trade review,
1865.

12739　Harvey, Henry, missionary to the Shawnee Indians.
History of the Shawnee Indians, from the year 1681
to 1854, inclusive. By Henry Harvey... Cincinnati,
E. Morgan & sons, 1855.
x, 11-316 p.　　front. (port.)　　17 1/2 cm.

12740　Hatboro, Pa. Union library company.
The charter and laws, with a catalogue of books,
of the Union library company of Hatborough. To which
is prefixed a short account of its first establishment.
6th ed. Norristown [Pa.] National defender office,
1858.
116 p.　　17 1/2 cm.

12741   Hatch, William Stanley.
          A chapter of the history of the war of 1812
        in the Northwest. Embracing the surrender of the
        northwestern army and fort, at Detroit, August 16,
        1812; with a description and biographical sketch
        of the celebrated Indian chief Tecumseh. By Colonel
        William Stanley Hatch... Cincinnati, Miami printing
        and publishing company, 1872.
          1 p.l., [7]-156 p.   18 cm.

12742   [Hatfield, Julia]
          The Bryant homestead-book. By the idle scholar...
        New York, G. P. Putnam & son, 1870.
          6 p.l., 224, 4 p. incl. illus., plates.   front.
        (port.)   24 cm.
          Illustrations by Hows, engraved by Linton.

12743   Haupt, Hermann, 1817-1905.
          Military bridges: with suggestions of new expe-
        dients and constructions for crossing streams and
        chasms; including, also, designs for trestle and
        truss bridges for military railroads, adapted espe-
        cially to the wants of the service in the United
        States. By Hermann Haupt... Illustrated by sixty-
        nine lithographic engravings. New York, D. Van
        Nostrand, 1864.
          xix, [5]-310 p.   front., 69 pl. (part fold.)
        23 cm.
          "Appendix: Report to Maj. Gen. Halleck giving
        the results of experiments on blanket-boats":
        p. 303-310.

12744   Hautefeuille, Laurent Basile, 1805-1875.
          Quelques questions de droit international maritime,
        à propos de la guerre d'Amérique. Par L. B. Haute-
        feuille... Leipzig, A. Frank [etc., etc.] 1861.
          2 p.l., 74 p.   22 cm.

12745   Haven, Joseph, 1816-1874.
          An address delivered before the students of
        Amherst college, and the citizens of the town...
        Nov. 17, 1852. By Rev. Joseph Haven... Amherst,
        J. S. & C. Adams, 1853.
          43 p.   22 cm.
          Life and character of Daniel Webster.

12746 Haven, Samuel Foster, 1806-1881.
... Archaeology of the United States. Or, Sketches,
historical and bibliographical, of the progress of
information and opinion regarding vestiges of anti-
quity in the United States. By Samuel F. Haven...
[Washington, Smithsonian institution, 1856]
2 p.l., 168 p.   32 1/2 cm.   (Smithsonian
contributions to knowledge. [Vol. VIII, art. 2])
Smithsonian institution publication 71.

12747 Haven, Samuel Foster, 1806-1881.
History of grants under the great Council for New
England: a lecture of a course by members of the
Massachusetts historical society, delivered before the
Lowell institute, Jan. 15, 1869. By Samuel F. Haven,
A. M. Boston, Press of J. Wilson and son, 1869.
36 p.   24 cm.
Also pub. in the Massachusetts historical society's
"Lectures delivered in a course before the Lowell
institute..." Boston, 1869.

12748 Haven, Samuel Foster, 1806-1881.
Remarks on the Popham celebration of the Maine
historical society. Read before the American
antiquarian society, April 26, 1865. By S. F. Haven.
Boston, Press of J. Wilson and son, 1865.
32 p.   23 1/2 cm.

12749 Haw, William.
Fifteen years in Canada; being a series of letters
on its early history and settlement; its boundaries,
divisions, population, and general routes; its
agricultural progress and wealth compared with the
United States; its religious and educational institutions; and its present political condition and
relations; together with the advantages it affords
as a desirable field of emigration. By the Rev.
William Haw. Edinburgh, C. Ziegler [etc., etc.]
1850.
viii, [9]-120 p.   21 1/2 cm.

12750 Hawes, Barbara.
Tales of the North American Indians, and adventures
of the early settlers in America. By Barbara Hawes.
London, Longman, Brown, Green, and Longmans, 1844.
xii, 362 p.   front.   18 cm.

12751 Hawes, Joel, 1789-1867.
Historical sketches of the First church in
Hartford. A centennial discourse delivered in the
First church, June 26, 1836. By Joel Hawes, D. D.
Hartford, Hudson and Skinner, printers, 1836.
35, [1] p.   illus. (plan)   21 cm.

12752 Hawkins, Benjamin, 1754-1816.
A sketch of the Creek country, in 1798 and 99.
By Col. Benjamin Hawkins... With an introduction
and historic sketch of the Creek confederacy. By
W. B. Hodgson... New York, Bartlett & Welford,
1848.
88 p.   21 cm.   (On cover: Collections of the
Georgia historical society. Vol. III - pt. I)

12753 Hawkins, Christopher, 1764-1837.
The adventures of Christopher Hawkins, containing
details of his captivity, a first and second time
on the high seas, in the revolutionary war, by the
British, and his consequent sufferings, and escape
from the Jersey prison ship... Written by himself.
With an introduction and notes by Charles I. Bushnell.
New York, Privately printed, 1864.
2 p.l., x, [4], [11]-316 p.   front., plates,
ports., plan.   23 cm.

12754 [Hawks, Francis Lister] 1798-1866.
The early history of the southern states: Virginia,
North and South Carolina, and Georgia. Illustrated
by tales, sketches, anecdotes, and adventures. By
Lambert Lilly, schoolmaster [pseud.] Philadelphia,
Key, Mielke and Biddle, 1832.
192 p.   front., illus.   16 1/2 cm.
The pseudonym Lambert Lilly has been attributed also
to Samuel E. Goodrich.

12755 Hawkshaw, Sir John, 1811-1891.
Reminiscences of South America: from two and a
half years' residence in Venezuela. By John Hawkshaw... London, Jackson and Walford, 1838.
xii, 260 p., 1 l., 6 p.   16 1/2 cm.

12756 Hay, George, d. 1830.
An essay on the liberty of the press, shewing,
that the requisition of security for good behaviour
from libellers, is perfectly compatible with the

constitution and laws of Virginia. By George Hay.
Richmond, Printed by Samuel Pleasants, Junior,
1803.
48 p.   21 1/2 cm.
[Miscellaneous pamphlets, v. 960, no. 5]

12757 Haygarth, John, 1740-1827.
A letter to Dr. Percival, on the prevention of
infectious fevers. And An address to the College
of physicians at Philadelphia, on the prevention
of the American pestilence... Read to the Literary
and philosophical society of Bath. By John Haygarth... Bath, Printed by R. Cruttwell; for Cadell
and Davies, London, 1801.
2 p.l., 188 p., 1 l.   22 1/2 cm.

12758 Haynes, Dudley C   1809-1888.
The Baptist denomination: its history, doctrines,
and ordinances; its polity, persecutions, and
martyrs; facts and statistics of its missionary
institutions, schools of learning, etc.; the
indebtedness of the world to Baptists, and their
duty to the world. By D. C. Haynes. With an
introduction by John Dowling... New York, Sheldon,
Blakeman & co., 1857.
356 p.   19 1/2 cm.

12759 Haynes, Gideon.
Pictures from prison life. An historical sketch
of the Massachusetts state prison. With narratives
and incidents, and suggestions on discipline. By
Gideon Haynes... Boston, Lee and Shepard, 1869.
290 p. incl. front.   pl.   17 1/2 cm.

12760 Haynes, J
Poems, by Dr. J. Haynes. Respectfully dedicated
to his friends. Quebec, Hunter, Rose & company,
1864.
152 p.   18 1/2 cm.

12761 Haynes, Lemuel, 1753-1833.
Mystery developed; or, Russell Colvin, (supposed
to be murdered) in full life: and Stephen and Jesse
Boorn, (his convicted murderers) rescued from
ignominious death by wonderful discoveries. Containing, I. A narrative of the whole transaction,
by Rev. Lemuel Haynes, A. M.   II. Rev. Mr. Haynes'

sermon, upon the developement of the mystery.
III. A succinct account of the indictment, trial
and conviction of Stephen and Jesse Boorn.
2d ed. Hartford, Published by William S. Marsh,
R. Storrs, printer, 1820.
    48 p.   22 1/2 cm.
    Part 2 has title: The prisoner released. A
sermon, delivered at Manchester, Vermont, Lords day,
Jan. 9th, 1820, on the remarkable interposition of
divine providence, in the deliverance of Stephen
and Jesse Boorn...
    Part 3 has title: A brief sketch of the indictment,
trial, and conviction of Stephen and Jesse Boorn,
for the murder of Russel Colvin... By S. Putnam
Waldo, esq.

12762 Hayward, James, 1786-1866.
    Report on the proposed rail-road between Boston
and Ogdensburgh. By James Hayward. Boston, Carter,
Hendee and Babcock, 1831.
    46 p.   26 cm.

12763 Hayward, John, 1781-1862.
    The Columbian traveller, and statistical register.
Principally relating to the United States. November,
1833. By John Hayward. [Boston] The author [1833]
    40 p.   4 maps (incl. front.)   27 cm.

12764 Hayward, John, 1781-1862.
    A gazetteer of Massachusetts, containing des-
criptions of all the counties, towns and districts
in the commonwealth; also, of its principal mountains,
rivers, capes, bays, harbors, islands, and fashionable resorts. To which are added, statistical
accounts of its agriculture, commerce and manufactures; with a great variety of other useful
information. By John Hayward... Boston, J. Hayward,
1846.
    444 p. incl. 1 illus., tables.   front., plates.
20 cm.

12765 Hayward, John, 1781-1862.
    A gazetteer of New Hampshire, containing descrip-
tions of all the counties, towns, and districts in
the state; also of its principal mountains, rivers,
waterfalls, harbors, islands, and fashionable resorts.
To which are added, statistical accounts of its

agriculture, commerce and manufactures...
By John Hayward... Boston, J. P. Jewett, 1849.
264 p.   front., 1 illus., plates.   20 cm.

12766 Hayward, John, 1781-1862.
A gazetteer of the United States, comprising a
series of gazetteers of the several states and
territories. Maine. By John Hayward... Portland,
Me., S. H. Colesworthy; Boston, B. B. Mussey [etc.,
etc.] 1843.
92 p.   1 illus.   24 1/2 cm.

12767 Hayward, John, 1781-1862.
A gazetteer of Vermont: containing descriptions
of all the counties, towns, and districts in the
state, and of its principal mountains, rivers,
waterfalls, harbors, islands, and curious places.
To which are added, statistical accounts of its
agriculture, commerce and manufactures; with...
other useful information. By John Hayward...
Boston, Tappan, Whittemore and Mason, 1849.
iv, [5]-216 p.   front. (map)   20 cm.

12768 Hayward, John, 1781-1862.
The Massachusetts directory; being the first
part of the New England directory. By John Hayward.
Boston, J. Hayward, 1835.
iv, [5]-198 p.   15 1/2 cm.

12769 Haywood, John, 1762-1826.
The civil and political history of the state
of Tennessee, from its earliest settlement up to
the year 1796, including the boundaries of the
state. By John Haywood. Knoxville, Tenn.,
Printed for the author by Heiskell & Brown, 1823.
3 p.l., 504 p.   23 cm.

12770 Haywood, John, 1762-1826.
The natural and aboriginal history of Tennessee,
up to the first settlements therein by the white
people, in the year 1768, by John Haywood...
Nashville, Printed by G. Wilson, 1823.
viii, 390, liv p.   21 1/2 cm.

12771 Hazard, Joseph, b. 1751?
The conquest of Quebec. A poem. By Joseph
Hazard... Oxford, Printed for J. Fletcher [etc.,

etc.] 1769.
20 p.   25 1/2 x 20 1/2 cm.
A poem offered in competition for the Earl of
Litchfield prize.

12772 [Hazard, Thomas Robinson] 1797-1886.
A constitutional manual for the national
American party. In which is examined the question
of Negro slavery in connexion with the Constitution
of the United States. By a northern man, with
American principles. Providence, A. C. Greene &
brother, printers, 1856.
30 p.   22 1/2 cm.

12773 Hazeltine, Silas Wood.
The traveller's dream, and other poems. By
Silas Wood Hazeltine. Boston, The author, 1860.
3 p.l., ix-xiii, [15]-150, [2] p.   18 1/2 cm.

12774 Hazlitt, William Carew, 1834-1913.
British Columbia and Vancouver island; comprising
a historical sketch of the British settlements in
the northwest coast of America; and a survey of the
physical character... of that region; comp. from
official and other authentic sources. By William
Carew Hazlitt... London, New York, G. Routledge
& co., 1858.
viii, 247 p.   fold. map.   16 1/2 cm.

12775 Headley, Joel Tyler, 1813-1897.
The chaplains and clergy of the revolution. By
J. T. Headley... New York, C. Scribner, 1864.
xii, [13]-102 p.   19 cm.

12776 Heard, Isaac V   D   b. 1834.
History of the Sioux war and massacres of 1862
and 1863. By Isaac V. D. Heard... New York,
Harper & brothers, 1863.
x p., 1 l., [13]-354 p. incl. front. (port.)
illus., plates.   20 cm.
"An appeal for the red man," by Bishop H. B.
Whipple: p. [343]-351.

12777 Heatherington, Alexander, d. 1878.
... A practical guide for tourists, miners, and
investors, and all persons interested in the
development of the gold fields of Nova Scotia, by

299

A. Heatherington... Montreal, Printed by J.
Lovell [etc., etc.] 1868.
iv p., 1 l., [7]-177 p. incl. fold. tables.
fold. front. (diagr.)   16 1/2 cm.

12778   Hedge, Levi, 1766-1844.
Eulogy on the Rev. Joseph McKean... Boylston
professor of rhetorick and oratory. Delivered before
the University, Cambridge, April 22, 1818. By Levi
Hedge... Cambridge [Mass.] University press -
Hilliard & Metcalf, 1818.
20 p.   24 cm.

12779   Henningsen, Charles Frederick, 1815-1877.
Letter from General C. F. Henningsen in reply to
the letter of Victor Hugo on the Harper's Ferry
invasion; with an extract from the letter of the
Rev. Nathan Lord... and an article from the London
"Times" on slavery. New York, Davies & Kent,
printers, 1860.
32 p.   22 1/2 cm.

12780   Henry, John Joseph, 1758-1811.
An accurate and interesting account of the hardships and sufferings of that band of heroes, who
traversed the wilderness in the campaign against
Quebec in 1775. By John Joseph Henry, esq. ...
Lancaster [Pa.] Printed by William Greer, 1812.
225 (i.e. 221) p.   17 cm.

12781   Hepworth, George Hughes, 1833-1902.
The whip, hoe, and sword; or, The Gulf-department
in '63. By George H. Hepworth. Boston, Walker,
Wise and co., 1864.
vi, [7]-298 p.   18 cm.
Second edition.

12782   Herbert, Sidney, comp.
... Republican campaign melodist and register.
By Sidney Herbert... New York, Dick & Fitzgerald
[1868]
[3]-76 p.   15 cm.

12783   Hersey, John, 1786-1862.
An appeal to Christians, on the subject of slavery.
By John Hersey. 2d ed. Baltimore, Armstrong &

Plaskitt, 1833.
iv, [5]-124 p.   14 1/2 cm.

12784   Heustis, Daniel D   b. 1806.
A narrative of the adventures and sufferings of
Captain Daniel D. Heustis and his companions, in
Canada and Van Dieman's Land, during a long captivity; with travels in California, and voyages at
sea. Boston, Pub. for Redding & co., by S. W. Wilder
& co., 1847.
168 p.   19 1/2 cm.

12785   Hildreth, Hosea, 1782-1835.
A view of the United States; for the use of schools
and families... Boston, Carter and Hendee;
Baltimore, C. Carter, 1830.
162 p.   illus., fold. map.   17 1/2 cm.

12786   Hill, Alonzo, 1800-1871.
In memoriam. A discourse preached in Worcester,
October 5, 1862, on Lieut. Thomas Jefferson Spurr,
Fifteenth Massachusetts volunteers... By Alonzo
Hill... Boston, Printed by J. Wilson and son, 1862.
32 p.   23 cm.

12787   Hill, Hamilton Andrews, 1827-1895.
American shipping: its decline and the remedies.
By Hamilton A. Hill. Boston, J. H. Eastburn,
1869.
31 p.   24 cm.

12788   Hill, Hamilton Andrews, 1827-1895.
Commercial associations; their uses and opportu-
nities. By Hamilton A. Hill... Boston, J. H.
Eastburn's press, 1869.
27 p.   24 cm.

12789   Hillard, Elias Brewster, 1825-1895.
The last men of the revolution. A photograph of
each from life, together with views of their homes
printed in colors. Accompanied by brief biographical
sketches of the men, by Rev. E. B. Hillard. Hartford, N. A. & R. A. Moore, 1864.
64 p.   col. plates, ports.   19 cm.
Facsimile letter from Edward Everett, dated 16
Jan., 1865, inserted.

Contents. – Samuel Downing. – Daniel Waldo. –
Lemuel Cook. – Alexander Milliner. – William
Hutchings. – Adam Link. – James Barham.

12790 Hillard, George Stillman, 1808-1879.
A discourse delivered before the New England
society in the city of New York, December 22, 1851.
By George S. Hillard. Published by the society.
New York, G. F. Nesbitt and co., printers, 1852.
31 p.   21 1/2 cm.

12791 Hillary, William, d. 1763.
Observations on the changes of the air, and the
concomitant epidemical diseases in the island of
Barbadoes. To which is added A treatise on... the
yellow fever, and such other diseases as are indigenous or endemial, in the West India Islands, or
in the torrid zone. By William Hillary, M. D.
2d ed. London, Printed for L. Hawes, W. Clarke,
and R. Collins, 1766.
4 p.l., xiii, [1], [15]-360, [4] p.   21 cm.

12792 Hiller, Joseph.
A charge, delivered at St. Peter's church, in
Salem, to the brethren of the Essex lodge of
ancient, free, and accepted masons, upon the
anniversary of St. John the Evangelist, December
27, 1781. By Brother Joseph Hiller. Salem,
Printed by Samuel Hall, near the court-house
[1781]
14 p.   19 1/2 x 15 1/2 cm.

12793 Hillhouse, James, 1754-1832.
Propositions for amending the Constitution of the
United States, providing for the election of president and vice-president, and guarding against the
undue exercise of executive influence, patronage,
and power. Washington, Printed by Gales & Seaton,
1830.
40 p.   21 1/2 cm.
A revision of his Propositions for amending the
Constitution... 1808.
Appendix: Propositions for amending the Constitution
of the United States: submitted by Mr. Hillhouse to
the Senate, on the twelfth day of April, 1808, with
his explanatory remarks. New Haven. Printed by
O. Steele & co., 1808. p. [7]-40.

12794 Hillhouse, Thomas, 1816-1897.
        The conscription act vindicated, by Thomas Hill-
        house... Albany, Weed, Parsons and company,
        printers, 1863.
        1 p.l., 27 p.   23 cm.

12795 Hinman, Royal Ralph, 1785-1868.
        A catalogue of the names of the first Puritan
        settlers of the colony of Connecticut; with the
        time of their arrival in the colony, and their
        standing in society, together with their place of
        residence, as far as can be discovered by the
        records. Collected from the state and town records,
        by R. R. Hinman... Hartford, Printed by E.
        Gleason, 1846.
        367 p.   front. (port.)   22 1/2 cm.

12796 Hinton, Richard Josiah, 1830-1901.
        Rebel invasion of Missouri and Kansas, and the
        campaign of the army of the border against General
        Sterling Price, in October and November, 1864.
        By Richard J. Hinton...   2d ed. Chicago, Church &
        Goodman; Leavenworth, Kan., F. W. Marshall, 1865.
        2 p.l., ii, [3]-351 p. incl. maps.   front.,
        port.   22 1/2 cm.
        Appendix: List of Union soldiers killed in
        Missouri and Kansas engagements.

12797 Hints to both parties; or, Observations on the pro-
        ceedings in Parliament upon the petitions against
        the Orders in council, and on the conduct of His
        Majesty's ministers in granting licences to import
        the staple commodities of the enemy... New York,
        Printed for E. Sargeant, 1808.
        40, 73-92 p.   23 cm.

12798 Hints to the farmers of Rhode-Island. By a freeman.
        Providence, R. I., Office of the Republican herald,
        J. S. Greene, printer, 1829.
        18 p.   14 cm.

12799 Historical anecdotes, civil and military: in a series
        of letters, written from America, in the years 1777
        and 1778, to different persons in England; containing
        observations on the general management of the war, and
        on the conduct of our principal commanders, in the
        revolted colonies, during that period. London,

Printed for J. Bew, in Paternoster Row, 1779.
2 p.l., 85 p.   20 1/2 cm.
[Miscellaneous pamphlets, v. 58, no. 3]

12800   The history and philosophy of earthquakes, from the
remotest to the present times: collected from the
best writers on the subject. With a particular
account of the phaenomena of the great one of
November 1st, 1755, in various parts of the globe.
By a member of the Royal academy of Berlin...
London, J. Nourse, 1757.
2 p.l., 351 p.   23 cm.
Contents. - A methodical account of earthquakes,
by J. C. Sturmius. - Of the nature of earthquakes,
by M. Lister. - Discourses concerning earthquakes,
by R. Hooke. - Earthquakes caused by some accidental
obstruction of a continual subterranean heat, by J.
Woodward. - A physicochymical explanation of sub-
terraneous fires, earthquakes, etc. by M. Lemery. -
Of the volcanos and earthquakes in Peru, by M.
Bouguer. - The natural history of volcanos and earthquakes, by M. Buffon. - A summary of the causes of
the alterations which have happened to the face of
the earth, by Mr. J. Ray. - Some considerations on
the causes of earthquakes, by the Rev. S. Hales. -
The philosophy of earthquakes, by the Rev. W. Stuke-
ley. - Phaenomena of the great earthquake of November
1, 1755 in various parts of the globe.

12801   A history of French influence in the United States.
To which is added, an exposition of a congressional
caucus. Philadelphia, Printed for the author, 1812.
69 p.   20 1/2 cm.
Signed: Camillus (p. 36)

12802   The history of prime ministers and favourites, in
England; from the conquest down to the present time:
with reflections on the fatal consequences of their
misconduct; and political deductions on the perpe-
tuity of freedom in the English constitution: ascer-
tained and vindicated from the despotism affected
by any of our sovereigns... London, Printed for
G. Kearsly, 1763.
1 p.l., 163 p.   20 1/2 cm.

12803   The history of Prince Lee Boo, to which is added,
the Life of Paul Cuffee, a man of colour, also,

Some account of John Sackhouse, the Esquimaux.
Dublin, Printed by J. Jones, 1822.
    180 p. incl. front. (port.) illus.   14 1/2 cm.
[With Wonderful escapes! Dublin, 1822]

12804 History of the Delaware and Iroquois Indians formerly
       inhabiting the middle states. With various anecdotes,
       illustrating their manners and customs... Written
       for the American Sunday school union, and revised
       by the Committee of publication. Philadelphia,
       American Sunday school union, 1832.
           153 p. incl. front., illus.   fold. map.
       14 1/2 cm.

12805 A history of the New York Kappa lambda conspiracy...
       New York, W. Stuart, 1839.
           32 p.   23 1/2 cm.
       "Essays from the 'Medical examiner'."

12806 The history of the Pilgrims; or, A grandfather's
       story of the first settlers of New England...
       Boston, Printed by J. R. Marvin, for the Massa-
       chusetts Sabbath school union, 1831.
           142 p. incl. front.   15 cm.

12807 Hitchcock, Edward, 1793-1864.
           A catalogue of plants growing without cultivation
       in the vicinity of Amherst college. By Edward
       Hitchcock... Published by the Junior class in that
       institution. Amherst, J. S. and C. Adams, and co.,
       printers, 1829.
           64 p.   22 1/2 cm.

12808 Hitchcock, Enos, 1745-1803.
           A discourse on the causes of national prosperity,
       illustrated by ancient and modern history, exempli-
       fied in the late American revolution. Addressed to
       the Society of the Cincinnati, in the state of Rhode
       Island, at their annual meeting at East Greenwich,
       July 4, 1786. By Enos Hitchcock... Providence,
       Printed by Bennett Wheeler [1786]
           28 p.   20 cm.
       [Hazard pamphlets, v. 51, no. 4]

12809 Hitchcock, Enos, 1745-1803.
           A discourse, on the dignity and excellence of the
       human character; illustrated in the life of General

George Washington, late commander of the armies,
and president of the United States. In commemoration
of the afflictive event of his death. Delivered
February 22, 1800, in the Benevolent Congregational
church in Providence, and published by request of
that society. By Enos Hitchcock... Providence,
Printed by John Carter, jun., 1800.
35 p.   23 1/2 cm.

12810   Hitchcock, Enos, 1745-1803.
An oration, in commemoration of the independence
of the United States of America. Delivered in the
Baptist meeting-house in Providence, July 4th,
1793. By Enos Hitchcock, D. D. [Providence]
Printed by J. Carter [1793]
19 p.   18 1/2 cm.

12811   Hitchcock, Gad, 1718?-1803.
A sermon preached at Plymouth, December 22d, 1774.
Being the anniversary thanksgiving, in commemoration
of the first landing of our New England ancestors
in that place, Anno Dom. 1620. By Gad Hitchcock...
Boston, Printed and sold by Edes and Gill, 1775.
44 p.   21 cm.

12812   Hitchcock, Reuben, 1764-1794.
A funeral oration on the death of Mr. Elizur
Belden, of Wethersfield. A senior sophister, in
Yale-college: who died April 8th, 1786, aetat. 23.
Delivered in the college chapel, June 8th, 1786.
By Reuben Hitchcock, fellow-student of the deceased
... New Haven, Printed by Daniel Bowen, 1786.
22 p.   19 1/2 cm.

12813   Hitchcock, Roswell Dwight, 1817-1887.
A eulogy on Daniel Webster, delivered before the
students of Bowdoin college... Nov. 12th, 1852.
By Roswell D. Hitchcock... Brunswick, J. Griffin,
1852.
44 p.   22 1/2 cm.

12814   Hitchcock, Roswell Dwight, 1817-1887.
Thanksgiving for victories. Discourse by Rev.
R. D. Hitchcock... [n. p., 1864]
7 p.   23 cm.
Delivered in Plymouth church, Brooklyn, Sept. 11th,
1864, and published at the unanimous request of the
congregation.

12815 Hittell, John Shertzer, 1825-1901.
        Yosemite: its wonders and its beauties... By
     John S. Hittell. Illustrated with twenty photo-
     graphic views... and a map... San Francisco,
     H. H. Bancroft & company, 1868.
        vi p., 1 l., [9]-59 p.   front. (fold. map)
     xx mounted phot.   19 1/2 x 11 1/2 cm.

12816 Hobart, Aaron, 1787-1858.
        An historical sketch of Abington, Plymouth
     County, Massachusetts. With an appendix. By Aaron
     Hobart. Boston, Printed by S. N. Dickinson, 1839.
        1 p.l., [5]-176 p.   23 1/2 cm.

12817 Hobart, John Henry, bp., 1775-1830.
        The charter of the corporation of Trinity church
     defended against the attacks of a late pamphlet.
     Believed to be by Bishop Hobart. Reprinted from
     the original, published A. D. 1813. New York,
     J. A. Sparks, 1846.
        21 p.   21 1/2 cm.

12818 Hobart, John Henry, bp., 1775-1830.
        The United States of America compared with some
     European countries, particularly England: in a dis-
     course delivered in Trinity church, and in St. Paul's
     and St. John's chapels, in the city of New York,
     October, 1825. By John Henry Hobart... New York,
     Printed by T. and J. Swords, 1825.
        ix, [5]-48 p.   23 cm.

12819 [Hobart, Noah] 1706-1773.
        A congratulatory letter from a gentleman in the
     West, to his friend in the East; upon the success
     of his letter, entituled, The present state of the
     colony of Connecticut considered. New Haven, Printed
     by J. Parker, 1755.
        1 p.l., 15 p.   20 1/2 cm.

12820 Hobbs, George, 1790-
        Genealogy of the Hobbs family of Massachusetts.
     Compiled by George Hobbs... Boston, Dutton & Went-
     worth, printers, 1855.
        16 p.   22 1/2 cm.

12821 Hobby, William, 1707-1765.
        An inquiry into the itinerancy, and the conduct
     of the Rev. Mr. George Whitefield, an itinerant

preacher: vindicating the former against the charge of
unlawfulness and inexpediency, and the latter against
some aspersions, which have been frequently cast upon
him. By William Hobby, A. M., pastor of the First
church in Reading. In a letter to a minister...
Boston, Printed and Sold by Rogers and Fowle in Queen-
street, next to the Prison. 1745.
28 p.   20 cm.

12822 [Hodge, Charles] 1797-1878.
England and America... 2d ed. Philadelphia, W. S.
& A. Martien, 1862.
cover-title, 31 p.   23 cm.
From the Princeton review for January 1962.

12823 Hodge, Michael.
An oration pronounced before the right worshipful
master & brethren of St. Peter's lodge, at the
Episcopal church in Newburyport, on the festival of
St. John the Baptist, June 24th, 5802. By Brother
Michael Hodge, jun., P. M. From the press of
Brother Angier March, Newburyport, June 28, 5802
[1802]
15 p.   26 1/2 cm.

12824 Hodge, William L
The public debt, the currency, specie payments, and
national banks. By William L. Hodge. Washington,
Intelligencer printing house, 1867.
30 p.   23 cm.
Reprinted from the National intelligencer.

12825 Hodgins, John George, 1821-1912.
The geography and history of British America, and
of the other colonies of the empire; to which is
added a sketch of the various Indian tribes of
Canada, and brief biographical notices of eminent
persons connected with the history of Canada. By
J. George Hodgins... Toronto, Maclear & co., 1857.
viii, [9]-128 p., 1 l. incl. illus., port., maps,
facsim.   18 1/2 x 14 cm.

12826 Hodgins, John George, 1821-1912.
... A school history of Canada, and of the other
British North American provinces. By J. George
Hodgins... Montreal, J. Lovell [etc., etc.] 1865.
iv, [5]-281 p., 1 l. incl. illus., port., maps,

308

tab.   17 1/2 x 10 1/2 cm.   (Lovell's series of
school books)

12827 Hodgkin, Thomas, 1798-1866.
       An inquiry into the merits of the American colon-
       ization society: and a reply to the charges brought
       against it. With an account of the British African
       colonization society. By Thomas Hodgkin... London,
       J. & A. Arch [etc.] 1833.
       62 p.   map.   22 cm.

12828 Hodgkinson, John, 1766-1805.
       A narrative of his connection with the Old
       American company, from the fifth September, 1792,
       to the thirty-first of March, 1797, by John
       Hodgkinson. New-York, Printed by J. Oram, no. 33,
       Liberty-street, 1797.
       28 p., 1 l.   20 cm.
       Concerns chiefly Hodgkinson's difficulties with
       Mr. and Mrs. Lewis Hallam.

12829 Hoffer, Isaac, b. 1820.
       Genealogy of Matthias Hoffer and his descendants
       in the United States of America. By Isaac Hoffer.
       Mount Joy, Pa., J. R. Hoffer, 1868.
       2 p.l., 29, [1] p., 2 l., 31-33, [1] p.
       19 1/2 cm.
       p. 31-33 (with special t.-p.): "Andrew Hofer,
       the Tyrolean patriot. A short sketch of his life,
       character and death, prepared by J. R. Hoffer.
       Mount Joy, Pa., Published by J. R. Hoffer, 1868."

12830 Hoffman, Christian.
       Longevity: being an account of various persons,
       who have lived to an extraordinary age, with several
       curious particulars respecting their lives; the
       whole comprising an abridgement of longevity, as
       far as history extends in every quarter of the world,
       from the creation to the year 1792. Authenticated
       by referential notes from authors of veracity.
       By Christian Hoffman... New-York, Printed and sold
       by Jacob S. Mott, no. 70 Vesey-street, 1798.
       120 p.   17 1/2 cm.

12831 Hoffmeister, Jonathan M
       ... Come to the rescue! An appeal to the people
       of the South. Rev. J. M. Hoffmeister... Raleigh

[N. C.]   Raleigh register steam-power press, 1863.
14 p.   16 1/2 cm.   (Evangelical tract society,
Petersburg, Va. no. 229)

12832 [Hogan, John]
Thoughts about the city of St. Louis, her commerce
and manufactures, railroads, &c. First published in
the Missouri republican. St. Louis, Republican steam
press print, 1854.
77, [3] p.   fold. front., plates.   23 1/2 cm.

12833 Hogan, John Sheridan, 1815?-1859.
Canada. An essay: to which was awarded the first
prize by the Paris exhibition committee of Canada.
By J. Sheridan Hogan... Montreal, B. Dawson [etc.,
etc.] 1855.
iv, [5]-86 p., 1 l.   front. (fold. map)
21 cm.

12834 Hogan, William d. 1848, defendant.
The trial of the Rev. William Hogan, pastor of
St. Mary's church, for an assault and battery on
Mary Connell. Tried before the Mayor's court in
and for the city of Philadelphia, on Monday the
first of April, 1822, and succeeding days.
Including the speeches of counsel on both sides
at length; the examination, cross-examination and
re-examination of the witnesses, verbatim; together with the anonymous correspondence, &c.
To which is added a digested index. The whole
taken in short hand, by Joseph A. Dowling...
Philadelphia, R. Desilver, 1822.
272, 8, [2] p.   21 1/2 cm.

12835 Hoge, Jane Currie (Blaikie) "Mrs. A. H. Hoge."
The boys in blue; or, Heroes of the "rank and file."
Comprising incidents and reminiscences from camp,
battle-field, and hospital, with narratives of the
sacrifice, suffering, and triumphs of the soldiers
of the republic. By Mrs. A. H. Hoge... With an
introduction by Thomas M. Eddy, D. D. With illustrations from original drawings of the most striking
scenes of the war of the rebellion. New York, E. B.
Treat & co.; Chicago, Ill., C. W. Lilley, 1867.
4 p.l., [13]-477 p.   front., plates.
23 cm.

12836   Hoge, William James, 1821-1864.
            A discourse, delivered by the Rev. William J.
        Hoge, D. D., collegiate pastor of the Brick
        Presbyterian church, New York, on the resignation
        of his charge, July 21, 1861. New York, Baker &
        Godwin, printers, 1861.
            26 p., 1 l.   23 cm.

12837   Hoge, William James, 1821-1864.
            Sketch of Dabney Carr Harrison, minister of the
        gospel and captain in the army of the Confederate
        States of America. By William J. Hoge... Richmond,
        Presbyterian committee of publication of the
        Confederate States, 1862.
            55 p.   14 cm.

12838   Hoit, C   W
            Fraudulent Mexican land claims in California,
        and the false location of the Sutter grant. A
        lecture, delivered at Turnverein hall, March 24th,
        and repeated at the State house assembly chamber,
        July 28, 1869. By C. W. Hoit... Sacramento, H. S.
        Crocker & co., printers, 1869.
            cover-title, 26 p.   fold. map.   21 1/2 cm.

12839   Hoit, True Worthy, b. 1815.
            The right of American slavery. By T. W. Hoit,
        of the St. Louis literary and philosophical asso-
        ciation. Southern and western ed.... St. Louis, Mo.,
        L. Bushnell, 1860.
            51 p.   22 cm.

12840   [Holbrook, Charles Warren] 1828-1888.
            Record of the descendants of Silence Holbrook,
        of Weymouth, Mass. Worcester, Printed by H. J.
        Howland [1851]
            19 p.   22 1/2 cm.

12841   Holbrook, Samuel F   b. 1793.
            Threescore years: an autobiography, containing
        incidents of voyages and travels, including six
        years in a man-of-war. Details of the war between
        the United States and the Algerine government,
        bombardment of Algiers by Lord Exmouth, and its
        subjugation by the French. Also, two years in
        California, a visit to the Crimea during the bom-
        bardment and capture of Sebastopol, journey
        through Asia Minor, Syria, Palestine and Egypt...

By Samuel F. Holbrook. Boston, J. French and company,
1857.
vi, [11]-504 p.   illus., pl.   19 1/2 cm.
"I shall resume the narrative... with my journey
through Europe to Sebastopol, Asia Minor [etc.]"-
p. 504.
Capture of the Essex: p. 316-340.

12842   Holcombe, James Philemon, 1820-1873.
Sketches of the political issues and controversies
of the revolution: a discourse delivered before the
Virginia historical society, at their ninth annual
meeting, Jan. 17, 1856... Richmond, The Society, 1856.
63 p.   19 1/2 cm.

12843   Holcombe, William Henry, 1825-1893.
Suggestions as to the spiritual philosophy of
African slavery, addressed to the members and friends
of the Church of the New Jerusalem. By Wm. H.
Holcombe, M. D. New York, Mason brothers, 1861.
24 p.   23 cm.

12844   Hold-fast, Simon, pseud.
Facts are stubborn things, or, Nine plain questions
to the people of Connecticut, with a brief reply to
each. By Simon Hold-fast... Hartford, Printed by
Hudson and Goodwin, 1803.
23 p.   20 1/2 cm.
Ms. note inserted in copy of Sabin ascribes authorship to David Daggett.

12845   Holdich, Joseph, 1804-1893.
The Wesleyan student; or, Memoirs of Aaron Haynes
Hurd, late a member of the Wesleyan university,
Middletown, Conn. By Joseph Holdich... Middletown,
E. Hunt & co.; Boston, D. S. King, 1839.
vii, [9]-281 p.   16 1/2 cm.

12846   Holditch, Robert.
The emigrant's guide to the United States of
America; containing the best advice and directions
respecting the voyage, - preservation of health, -
choice of settlement, &c. Also the latest information concerning the climate, productions... and
other subjects, economical and political, affecting the welfare of persons about to emigrate to
the United States and British America. By Robert

Holditch... London, W. Hone, 1818.
iv, 123, [1] p.   22 1/2 cm.

12847 Holgate, Jerome Bonaparte.
American genealogy, being a history of some of
the early settlers of North America and their descendants, from their first emigration to the
present time... By Jerome B. Holgate... Albany,
Printed by J. Munsell, 1848.
1 p. 1., 244 p., 1 l.   30 cm.

12848 Holland, John.
Memoirs of the life and ministry of the Rev. John
Summerfield, A. M., by John Holland. With an introductory letter by James Montgomery. Abridged, with
additional letters and reminiscences. New York,
American Tract Society [1850]
339 p.   front. (port.)   20 cm.

12849 Holland, William M
The life and political opinions of Martin Van
Buren... By William M. Holland. Hartford, Belknap
& Hamersley, 1835.
1 p. 1., [vii]-xiv p., 1 l., [13]-364 p.
19 1/2 cm.

12850 Holley, Orville Luther, 1791-1861, ed.
A description of the city of New York: with a
brief account of the cities, towns, villages, and
places of resort within thirty miles; designed as
a guide for citizens and strangers... Ed. by O. L.
Holley. New York, J. Disturnell, 1847.
114 p.   front., pl., fold. map, fold. plan.
15 cm.

12851 Holley, Orville Luther, 1791-1861.
The life of Benjamin Franklin. By O. L. Holley.
New York, G. F. Cooledge & brother [c1848]
2 p. 1., [3]-460 p.   front. (port.) 19 pl.
18 1/2 cm.
The engravings are by Alexander Anderson.

12852 Holley, Orville Luther, 1791-1861, ed.
The picturesque tourist; being a guide through
the northern and eastern states and Canada: giving
an accurate description of cities and villages,
celebrated places of resort, etc.... Ed. by O. L.

Holley. New-York, J. Disturnell, 1844.
   3 p. l., vii, [9]-336 p.   front., illus., plates,
maps (2 fold.)   17 cm.

12853 [Hollingsworth, S   ]
   An account of the present state of Nova Scotia...
Edinburgh, Printed for W. Creech; and T. Longman,
London, 1786.
   2 p. l., [vii]-viii, 157 p.   21 1/2 cm.
   In manuscript on verso of t.-p.: Arthur Mackie,
M. D. From the author, Mr. Hollingsworth.
   By S. Hollingsworth. - cf. Rich. Bibl. Amer., v. 1,
p. 335.

12854 [Hollingsworth, S   ]
   The present state of Nova Scotia: With a brief
account of Canada, and the British islands on the
coast of North America. The 2d ed., cor. and enl....
Edinburgh, Printed for W. Creech, Edinburgh; and
sold by T. Cadell, and G. Robinson & co. London,
1787.
   2 p. l., [5]-6, [vii]-xii, 221 p.   front.
(fold. map)   22 1/2 cm.
   First published, 1786, under title: An account
of the present state of Nova Scotia.

12855 Hollingsworth, Samuel L
   Memoir of Moreton Stille, M. D., read before the
College of physicians of Philadephia, April 2, 1856.
By Samuel L. Hollingsworth, M. D. Philadelphia,
T. K. and P. G. Collins, printers, 1856.
   35 p. incl. front.   (port.)   22 cm.

12856 Hollister, Gideon Hiram, 1817-1881.
   Mount Hope; or, Philip, king of the Wampanoags:
an historical romance, by G. H. Hollister... New-
York, Harper & brothers, 1851.
   280 p.   19 1/2 cm.

12857 Hollister, Hiel.
   Pawlet for one hundred years. By Hiel Hollister...
Albany, Printed by J. Munsell, 1867.
   272 p.   19 cm.
   "Family sketches": p. 155-267.

12858 Hollister, Horace, 1822-
   Contributions to the history of the Lackawanna

Valley. By H. Hollister, M. D. New York, W. H.
Tinson, printer, 1857.
  viii, 9-328 p.   front.   (port.)   map.
19 1/2 cm.

12859 Hollister, Ovando James, 1834-1892.
    The mines of Colorado; by Ovando J. Hollister...
Springfield, Mass., S. Bowles & company, 1867.
    vii, 450 p.   front.   (fold. map)   19 cm.

12860 Holloway, William Robeson, 1836-1911.
    Indianapolis. A historical and statistical
sketch of the railroad city, a chronicle of its
social, municipal, commercial and manufacturing
progress, with full statistical tables. By W. R.
Holloway. Indianapolis, Indianapolis journal print,
1870.
    2 p. l., [iii]-vii, [1], [3]-390 p.   front.,
plates, map.   23 1/2 cm.

12861 Holly, James Theodore, 1829-
    A vindication of the capacity of the negro race
for self-government, and civilized progress, as
demonstrated by historical events of the Haytian
revolution; and the subsequent acts of that people
since their national independence. A lecture by
Rev. Jas. Theo. Holly... New Haven, W. H. Stanley,
printer, 1857.
    48 p.   front.   (port.)   22 cm.
Published for the Afric-American printing co.

12862 Holman, Nathan, 1769-1844.
    A funeral oration, delivered in the chapel of
Rhode Island college, on Wednesday, XXIXth of June,
1796, occasioned by the death of Mr. Alva Spalding,
a member of the junior class. By Nathan Holman,
class-mate of the deceased. Published at the request of the students. Printed at Providence, by
Joseph Fry, opposite the market. 1796.
    14 p.   29 1/2 cm.

12863 Holman, William Steele, 1822-1897.
    Right of secession - the impending crisis. Speech
of William S. Holman, of Indiana, on the state of the
the Union, delivered in the House of representatives,
January 16, 1861. Washington, M'Gill & Witherow,
printers, 1861.
    15 p.   22 1/2 cm.

12864   Holmes, Abiel, 1763-1837.
            The history of Cambridge. By Abiel Holmes...
        Printed by Samuel Hall, in Cornhill, Boston, 1801.
        1 p. l., 67 p.   22 cm.

12865   Holmes, Abiel, 1763-1837.
            Two discourses, on the completion of the second
        century from the landing of the forefathers of
        Newengland at Plymouth, 22 Dec. 1620, delivered at
        Cambridge 24 Dec. 1820. By Abiel Holmes... Cambridge,
        Printed by Hilliard and Metcalf, 1821.
        28 p.   24 cm.

12866   Holmes, Arthur.
            Parties and their principles: a manual of political
        intelligence, exhibiting the origin, growth, and char-
        acter of national parties... By Arthur Holmes. New-
        York, D. Appleton and company, 1859.
        394 p.   19 cm.

12867   Holmes, Elias Bellows, 1810?-1866.
            Speech of Mr. Elias B. Holmes, of New York, on the
        subject of the Mexican war, delivered in the House
        of representatives of the United States, June 18,
        1846. Washington, Printed by J. & G. S. Gideon, 1846.
        15 p.   22 1/2 cm.

12868   Holmes, Ezekiel, 1801-1865.
            Report of an exploration and survey of the territory
        on the Aroostook River, during the spring and autumn
        of 1838. By E. Holmes. Augusta, Smith & Robinson,
        printers to the state, 1839.
        78 p., 1 l.   21 cm.

12869   Holmes, Francis Simmons, 1815-1882.
            Phosphate rocks of South Carolina and the "great
        Carolina marl bed", with five colored illustrations.
        A popular and scientific view of their origin, geo-
        logical position and age; also their chemical char-
        acter and agricultural value; together with a history
        of their discovery and development. By Francis S.
        Holmes... Charleston, S. C., Holmes' book house,
        1870.
        87 p.   col. front., 4 col. pl.   23 1/2 cm.

12870   Holmes, John, 1773-1843.
            An oration, pronounced at Alfred, on the 4th of
        July, 1815, being the thirty ninth anniversary of

American independence. By John Holmes esq. Published
by request of a committee appointed by the audience.
Boston, Printed by Rowe and Hooper, at the Yankee
office, 1815.
23 p.   24 cm.

12871 Holmes, John, 1773-1843.
Speech of Mr. Holmes, of Maine, in the Senate of
the United States, on his resolution calling upon the
President of the United States for the reasons of his
removing from office, and filling the vacancies thus
created in the recess of the Senate. Washington,
Printed and published at the office of the National
Journal, 1830.
28 p.   23 cm.

12872 Holmes, Oliver Wendell, 1809-1894.
The benefactors of the Medical school of Harvard
university; with a biographical sketch of the late
Dr. George Parkman. An introductory lecture, delivered at the Massachusetts medical college, November 7, 1850, by Oliver Wendell Holmes... Boston,
Ticknor, Reed, and Fields, 1850.
37 p.   24 cm.

12873 Holt, Joseph, 1807-1894.
Letter from the Hon. Joseph Holt, upon the policy
of the general government, the pending revolution,
its objects, its probable results if successful,
and the duty of Kentucky in the crisis. Washington,
H. Polkinhorn, printer, 1861.
23 p.   22 1/2 cm.

12874 Homer, James Lloyd.
An address delivered before the Massachusetts
charitable mechanic association, at the celebration of their tenth triennial festival, October
6, 1836. By James Lloyd Homer. Boston, Printed
for the Association by Homer & Palmer and J. T.
Adams, 1836.
40 p.   21 1/2 cm.

12875 Homes, Henry Augustus, 1812-1887.
Observations on the design and import of medals.
By Henry A. Homes... Albany, J. Munsell, 1863.
8 p.   22 1/2 cm.

12876   Homes, Henry Augustus, 1812-1887.
        Our knowledge of California and the North-west
        coast one hundred years since. Read before the
        Albany institute, February 15, 1870, by Henry A.
        Homes... Albany, N. Y., J. Munsell, 1870.
        20 p.   22 1/2 cm.

12877   Honduras.
        Documentos justificativos de la conducta obser-
        vada, por el spmo. g. de Honduras. En las negocia-
        ciones de paz con el de Guatemala. Habidas ultima-
        mente bajo la intervencion amistosa del Salvador.
        Comayagua, Imprenta del gobierno, 1855.
        2 p. l., 39 p.   27 1/2 cm.
        Preface signed: Trinidad Cabanas.

12878   Hone, Philip, 1780-1851.
        An address, delivered before the Mercantile
        library association, at the Odeon in Boston,
        October 3, 1843. By Philip Hone... Boston, W. D.
        Ticknor, 1843.
        44 p.   17 1/2 cm.

12879   Hood, George.
        A history of music in New England: with bio-
        graphical sketches of reformers and psalmists.
        By George Hood. Boston, Wilkins, Carter & co.,
        1846.
        vii, [9]-252, [3] p.   17 1/2 cm.
        "List of works published before 1800": p. 170-178.

12880   [Hood, Samuel] 1800?-1875.
        A brief account of the Society of the friendly
        sons of St. Patrick; with biographical notices
        of some of the members, and extracts from the
        minutes. Philadelphia, By order of the Hibernian
        society, 1844.
        112 p.   front. (facsim.)   19 cm.

12881   Hooke, William, 1601-1678.
        Nevv Englands teares, for old Englands feares.
        Preached in a sermon on July 23, 1640, being a day
        of publike humiliation, appointed by the churches,
        in behalfe of our native countrey in time of feared
        dangers. By William Hooke... Sent over to a worthy
        member of the honourable House of commons, who
        desires it may be for publick good. London, Printed

by T. P. for I. Rothwell and H. Overton, 1641.
  2 p. l., 23 p.   18 1/2 cm.

12882 Hooker, Thomas, 1588-1647.
    The danger of desertion: or A farvvell sermon
of Mr. Thomas Hooker, somtimes minister of Gods
Word at Chainsford in Essex; but now of New England.
Preached immediately before his departure out of
old England. Together, with ten particvlar rules
to be practised every day by converted Christians.
London, Printed by G. M. for George Edwards, 1641.
  2 p. l., 29 p.   18 1/2 cm.
On Jeremiah XIV, 9.

12883 Hooker, Sir William Jackson, 1785-1865.
    The botany of Captain Beechey's voyage; compris-
ing an account of the plants collected by Messrs.
Lay and Collie, and other officers of the expedition,
during the voyage to the Pacific and Behring's
Strait, performed in His Majesty's ship Blossom,
under the command of Captain F. W. Beechey... in
the years 1825, 26, 27, and 28. By Sir William
Jackson Hooker... and G. A. Walker Arnott...
London, H. G. Bohn, 1841.
  2 p. l., ii, [3]-485 p.   xcix pl.   29 1/2 cm.

12884 Hooker, Worthington, 1806-1867.
    ... Lessons from the history of medical delusions.
By Worthington Hooker... New York, Baker & Scribner,
1850.
  v, [3]-105 p.   19 1/2 cm.   (Rhode Island
medical society. Fiske fund. Prize dissertation[s].
no. XIII. 1850)

12885 Hooper, Lucy, 1816-1841.
    Poetical remains of the late Lucy Hooper, collected
and arranged; with a memoir, by John Keese...
New-York, S. Colman, 1842.
  291 p.   19 cm.
With tributes to her memory by Whittier and others.

12886 [Hooper, Samuel] 1808-1875.
    Currency or money; its nature and uses, and the
effects of the circulation of bank-notes for
currency. By a merchant of Boston. Boston, Little,
Brown and company, 1855.
  112 p.   22 1/2 cm.

12887   Hooper, William Henry, b. 1813.
        The Utah bill. A plea for religious liberty.
        Speech of Hon. W. H. Hooper, of Utah, delivered in
        the House of representatives, March 23, 1870, to-
        gether with the remonstrance of the citizens of
        Salt Lake City, in mass meeting, held March 31, 1870,
        to the Senate if the United States. Washington,
        D. C., Gibson brothers, printers, 1870.
        40 p.   22 1/2 cm.

12888   Hope, James Barron, 1829-1887.
        A poem: pronounced by James Barron Hope, on
        the two hundred and fiftieth anniversary of the
        English settlement at Jamestown, May 13th, 1857.
        Richmond, C. H. Wynne, printer, 1857.
        16 p.   23 cm.

12889   Hopkins, Gerard T
        A mission to the Indians, from the Indian
        committee of Baltimore yearly meeting, to Fort
        Wayne, in 1804. Written at the time, by Gerard
        T. Hopkins. With an appendix, comp. in 1862, by
        Martha E. Tyson. Philadelphia, T. E. Zell, 1862.
        198 p.   illus.   15 1/2 cm/
        Never offered for sale, but presented to Friends
        and others interested in Indian affairs. cf. Field,
        T. W. An essay towards an Indian bibliography.

12890   Hopkins, James Dean, 1773-1840.
        An address to the members of the Cumberland bar,
        delivered during the sitting of the Court of common
        pleas, at Portland, June term, 1833. By James D.
        Hopkins... Pub. at the request of the bar. Portland
        [Me.] Printed by C. Day and co., 1833.
        79 p.   23 cm.
        Consists of extracts from ancient court records
        of Maine and biography of lawyers of Maine, and
        especially of Cumberland County.

12891   Hopkins, John Baker, 1830-1888.
        The fall of the confederacy. By John Baker
        Hopkins. London, W. Freeman [1867?]
        x, [11]-96 p.   19 1/2 cm.

12892   Hopkins, John Henry, bp., 1792-1868.
        The American citizen: his rights and duties,
        according to the spirit of the Constitution of

the United States. By John Henry Hopkins... New
York, Pudney & Russell, 1857.
1 p. l., [5]-459 p.   19 cm.

12893   Hopkins, Mark, 1802-1887.
A discourse commemorative of Amos Lawrence, deli-
vered by request of the students, in the chapel of
Williams college, February 21, 1853. By Mark Hopkins...
Boston, Press of T. R. Marvin, 1853.
36 p.   22 1/2 cm.

12894   Hopkins, Samuel, 1693-1755.
An address to the people of New-England. Representing the very great importance of attaching the
Indians to their interest; not only by treating
them justly and kindly; but by using proper
endeavours to settle Christianity among them. By
Samuel Hopkins, A. M., pastor of a church in
Springfield... Printed in Boston, 1753. Being a
conclusion to the Historical memoirs relating to
the Housatunnuk Indians, with an account of the
methods used for the propagation of the gospel
amongst the said Indians, by the late Reverend Mr.
John Sergeant. Now recommended to the serious consideration of the inhabitants of Pennsylvania, and
the other colonies. Philadelphia, Reprinted by B.
Franklin, and D. Hall, 1757.
27 p.   18 1/2 cm.

12895   Hopkins, Samuel, 1693-1755.
Historical memoirs, relating to the Housatunnuk
Indians: or, An account of the methods used, and
pains taken, for the propagation of the gospel among
that heathenish-tribe, and the success thereof,
under the ministry of the late Reverend Mr. John
Sergeant: together with the character of that
eminently worthy missionary; and an address to the
people of this country, representing the very great
importance of attaching the Indians to their interest,
not only by treating them justly and kindly, but
by using proper endeavours to settle Christianity
among them. By Samuel Hopkins... Boston, N. E.,
Printed and sold by S. Kneeland, 1753.
1 p. l., iv, 182 p.   21 cm.
An account of the early history of the mission to
the Stockbridge Indians in Stockbridge, Massachusetts.

12896 [Hopkins, Stephen] 1707-1785.
The grievances of the American colonies candidly
examined... Printed by authority, at Providence, in
Rhode-Island. London, Reprinted for J. Almon, 1766.
47 p.   21 cm.

12897 [Hopkins, Stephen] 1707-1785.
The rights of colonies examined. Pub. by authority. Providence, Printed by W. Goddard, 1765.
24 p.   21 x 16 1/2 cm.
[Hazard pamphlets, v. 22, no. 3]
Signed: P------. Providence in New-England, Nov.
30, 1764. An English edition, also anonymous,
appeared under title "The grievances of the American
colonies candidly examined." London, 1766.

12898 [Hopkins, Stephen] 1797-1785.
A true representation of the plan formed at Albany,
for uniting all the British Northern colonies, in
order to their common safety and defence; containing
abstracts of the authorities given by the several
governments to their commissioners; and of several
letters from the secretaries of state, and lords
commissioners for trade and plantations, concerning
such an union: together with a representation of
the state of the English and French colonies in
North-America; and the said plan of union, with the
doings of the commissioners thereon; and some remarks
on the whole. [Newport, Printed by James Franklin,
1755]
14 p.   32 1/2 cm.

12899 Hopkins, T[homas] M
Reminiscences of Col. John Ketcham, of Monroe
County, Indiana, by his pastor, Rev. T. M. Hopkins,
of Bloomington, Indiana. Bloomington, Whitaker &
Walker, printers, 1866.
22 p.   22 cm.

12900 Hopkinson, Francis, 1737-1791, defendant.
An account of the impeachment and trial of the
late Francis Hopkinson, esquire, judge of the
Court of admiralty for the commonwealth of
Pennsylvania. Philadelphia, Printed by Francis
Bailey, at Yorick's head, n⁰. 116, High-street,
1794.

(In [Hogan, Edmund] ed. The Pennsylvania state
trials. Philadelphia, M,DCC,XCIV. 21 1/2 cm.
v. 1, p. [1]-62)

12901 Hopkinson, Francis, 1737-1791.
The old farm and the new farm: a political
allegory. By Francis Hopkinson... With an introduction and historical notes by Benson J. Lossing...
New York, Dana and company, 1857.
76 p. 17 1/2 cm.
Contains reproduction of original t.-p.: A
pretty story. Written in the year of Our Lord 1774
by Peter Grievous, esq., A. B. C. D. E. ...
Philadelphia, Printed and sold by John Dunlap, 1774.

12902 Hopkinson, Francis, 1737-1791.
Science. A poem. By Francis Hopkinson, esq....
Philadelphia, Printed by William Dunlap, in
Market-street, 1762.
iv, [5]-19 p. 25 cm.

12903 Hopkinson, Joseph, 1770-1842.
Eulogium in commemoration of the Hon. Bushrod
Washington, late one of the chief justices of the
Supreme court of the United States. By Joseph
Hopkinson. Philadelphia, T. S. Manning, printer, 1830
1830.
1 p. l., [9]-32 p. 19 1/2 cm.

12904 Hopper, Edward, 1816-1888.
The Dutch pilgrim fathers, and other poems,
humorous and not humorous. By Edward Hopper.
New York, Hurd and Houghton; Boston, E. P. Dutton
and company, 1865.
vi, [7]-216 p. 17 cm.

12905 Horne, Henry.
Essays concerning iron and steel: the first,
containing observations on American sand-iron:
the second, observations, founded on experiments,
on common iron-ore... on the sort of iron proper
to be converted into good steel, and the method of
refining that bar-steel by fusion... With an account
of Mr. Reaumur's method of softening cast iron:
and an appendix discovering a more perfect method
of charring pit-coal... By Henry Horne. London,
T. Caddell, 1773.
iii, 223 p. 17 1/2 x 10 cm.

12906   Horner, G[ustavus] R   B
         Medical topography of Brazil and Uruguay... by
         G. R. B. Horner... Philadelphia, Lindsay & Blakiston,
         1845.
         296 p.   4 pl.   24 cm.

12907   Horsford, Eben Norton, 1818-1893.
         The army ration. How to diminish its weight
         and bulk, secure economy in its administration,
         avoid waste, and increase the comfort, efficiency,
         and mobility of troops. By E. N. Horsford... New
         York, D. Van Nostrand, 1864.
         42 p.   22 cm.

12908   Horsford, Eben Norton, 1818-1893.
         Report on Mystic pond water to the Boston harbor
         commission. By E. N. Horsford... Boston, G. C.
         Rand & Avery, city printers, 1861.
         19 p.   fold. map, fold. diagr.   23 1/2 cm.

12909   Horsford, Eben Norton, 1818-1893.
         Solidification of the coral reefs of Florida,
         and source of lime in the growth of corals. By
         E. N. Horsford... Boston, Traveller job press,
         1853.
         11 p.   23 cm.
         "Read before the American scientific asso-
         ciation at their meeting in Cleveland, Ohio,
         July 29, 1853".

12910   Horsford, Mrs. Mary (Gardiner) 1824-1855.
         Indian legends and other poems. By Mary Gardiner
         Horsford. New York, J. C. Derby; Boston, Phillips,
         Sampson, & co. [etc., etc.] 1855.
         viii, [9]-167 p.   18 cm.

12911   Horsmanden, Daniel, 1694-1778.
         The New-York conspiracy, or A history of the
         Negro plot, with the journal of the proceedings
         against the conspirators at New-York in the years
         1741-2... By Daniel Horsmanden, esq. New-York,
         Printed and published by Southwick & Pelsue,
         no. 3, New-street, 1810.
         385, [7] p. incl tables.   21 cm.

12912   Horton, H   P
         A digest of the militia law of the state of New

York, with copious forms adapted to every case.
By H. P. Horton... Albany, J. Munsell, printer,
1848.
   40 p. incl. forms.   24 cm.

12913 [Horton, Rushmore G   ] 1826-
   A youth's history of the great civil war in the
   United States, from 1861 to 1865... New York,
   Van Evrie, Horton & co., 1866.
      xiv, [15]-384 p.   6 pl. (incl. front.) 11 port.
   18 cm.
   Written by a sympathizer with the southern cause.

12914 Hosack, Alexander.
   History of the yellow fever, as it appeared in the
   city of New York, in 1795. By Alexander Hosack, jun.,
   M. D., of New York. Philadelphia, Printed by Thomas
   Dobson, at the Stone-house, no. 41, South second-
   street, 1797.
      vi, [7]-36 p.   23 cm.
   Issued also as thesis (M. D.) University of
   Pennsylvania.

12915 Hosack, Alexander Eddy, 1805-1871.
   History of the case of the late John Kearny Rodgers,
   M. D. Addressed to the profession. By Alexander E.
   Hosack, M. D. New York, Printed by S. W. Benedict,
   1851.
      47 p.   23 cm.

12916 Hosack, David, 1769 1835.
   Hortus Elginensis; or, A catalogue of plants,
   indigenous and exotic, cultivated in the Elgin botanic
   garden, in the vicinity of the city of New-York.
   Established in 1801, by David Hosack... 2d ed. enl.
   New-York, Printed by T. & J. Swords, printers to the
   Faculty of physic of Columbia college, no. 160 Pearl-
   street, 1811.
      x, [2], 65, [1] p.   front.   20 1/2 cm.

12917 Hosack, David, 1769-1835.
   An inaugural address, delivered before the New-
   York historical society, on the second Tuesday of
   February, 1820. By David Hosack, M. D., president of
   the Society. New-York, Printed by C. S. Van Winkle,
   printer to the University, no. 101 Greenwich Street,
   1820.
      14 p.   22 cm.

12918 Hosack, David, 1769-1835.
    A statement of facts relative to the establishment
and progress of the Elgin botanic garden, and the
subsequent disposal of the same to the state of New-
York. By David Hosack... New-York, Printed by C. S.
Van Winkle, no. 56 Pine-street, 1811.
    56 p.   20 1/2 cm.
    [Wolcott pamphlets, v. 54, no. 18]

12919 Hoskins, Nathan, 1795-1869.
    A history of the state of Vermont, from its
discovery and settlement to the close of the year
1830. By Nathan Hoskins... Vergennes [Vt.] J. Shedd,
1831.
    316 p.   18 cm.

12920 Hosmer, Hezekiah L
    Early history of the Maumee Valley. By H. L.
Hosmer. Toledo [O.] Hosmer & Harris, 1858.
    cover-title, [9]-70 p.   21 1/2 cm.
    From Hosmer and Harris' Toledo directory, p. 9-70.

12921 Hosmer, James Bidwell, 1781-1878.
    Genealogy of the Hosmer family. By James B.
Hosmer. Hartford, Steam press of E. Geer, 1861.
    16 p.   24 cm.

12922 Hosmer, Margaret (Kerr) 1830-1897.
    The child captives. A true tale of life among the
Indians of the West. By Mrs. Margaret Hosmer...
Philadelphia, Presbyterian board of publication [1870]
    230 p. front., plates.   15 cm.

12923 Hotchkiss, Frederick William, 1763?-1844.
    A sermon, delivered at the installation of Pythagorus
lodge of free masons; in Lyme, Connecticut, October
7th, 1800. By Frederick W. Hotchkiss... New-London,
Printed by Samuel Green, 1800.
    35 p.   22 1/2 cm.

12924 Hotchkiss, Jedediah, 1827-1899.
    The battle-fields of Virginia. Chancellorsville;
embracing the operation of the Army of northern
Virginia, from the first battle of Fredericksburg to
the death of Lieutenant-General Jackson. By Jed
Hotchkiss... and William Allan... New York, D. Van
Nostrand [etc., etc.,] 1867.

152 p.   front (port.) fold. maps.   22 cm.
"The last days of Jackson," by H. McGuire:
p. 118-131.

12925   Hough, Franklin Benjamin, 1822-1885.
        Bibliographical list of books and pamphlets
        containing eulogies, orations, poems or other papers,
        relating to the death of General Washington, or to
        the honors paid to his memory. By Franklin B. Hough...
        Albany, Privately printed, 1865.
            1 p. l., 59 p.   front. (port.)   27 1/2 cm.
        "From the [author's] Washingtoniana", p. [219]-277.

12926   Hough, Franklin Benjamin, 1822-1885.
        History of Duryée's brigade, during the campaign
        in Virginia under Gen. Pope, and in Maryland under
        Gen. McClellan, in the summer and autumn of 1862.
        By Franklin B. Hough. Albany, J. Munsell, 1864.
            vi, [9]-200 p.   front. (port.)   25 cm.

12927   Hough, Franklin Benjamin, 1822-1885.
        A history of Lewis County, in the state of New
        York from the beginning of its settlement to the
        present time. By Franklin B. Hough... Albany,
        Munsell & Rowland, 1860.
            iv, 319 p.   front., illus., pl., ports.   22 cm.

12928   Hough, Franklin Benjamin, 1822-1885, ed.
        The northern invasion of October, 1780; a series of
        papers relating to the expeditions from Canada under
        Sir John Johnson and other against the frontiers of
        New York, which were supposed to have connection with
        Arnold's treason; prepared from the originals, with
        an introduction and notes, by Franklin B. Hough. New
        York, 1866.
            xv, [1], [17]-224 p.   front., fold map. 26 1/2 cm.
        [Bradford club series, no. 6]

12929   Hough, Franklin Benjamin, 1822-1885.
        Notices of Peter Penet, and of his operations
        among the Oneida Indians, including a plan prepared
        by him for the government of that tribe, read before
        the Albany institute, January 23d, 1866. By Franklin
        B. Hough. Lowville, N. Y., 1866.
            36 p.   front. (fold. map)   26 cm.

12930   Hough, Franklin Benjamin, 1822-1885.
        Papers relating to Pemaquid and parts adjacent in the

present state of Maine, known as Cornwall County, when under the colony of New-York, comp. from official records in the office of the secretary of state at Albany, N. Y., by Franklin B. Hough. Albany, Weed, Parsons & companie, 1865.
vii, 136 p.   25 cm.

12931 Hough, Franklin Benjamin, 1822-1885.
Papers relating to the island of Nantucket, with documents relating to the original settlement of that island, Martha's Vineyard, and other islands adjacent, known as Dukes county, while under the colony of New York. Comp. from official records in the office of the secretary of state at Albany, New York. By Franklin B. Hough... Albany [J. Munsell] 1856.
xviii, 162 p., 1 l. incl. facsims., coat of arms. fold. map. 22 x 17 cm.

12932 [Hough, Franklin Benjamin] 1822-1885, ed.
The seige of Charleston, by the British fleet and army under the command of Admiral Arbuthnot and Sir Henry Clinton, which terminated with the surrender of that place on the 12th of May, 1780. Albany, J. Munsell, 1867.
224 p. 2 port. (incl. front)   22 x 17 cm.

12933 [Hough, Franklin Benjamin] 1822-1885, ed.
The siege of Savannah, by the combined American and French forces, under the command of Gen. Lincoln and the Count d'Estaing, in the autumn of 1779. Albany, J. Munsell, 1866.
187 p. front. (port.)   22 x 17 1/2 cm.

12934 Houghton, Edwin B
The campaigns of the Seventeenth Maine. By Edwin B. Houghton... Portland, Short & Loring, 1866.
x p., 1 l., 333 p.   19 1/2 cm.

12935 Houghton association.
Constitution and officers of the Houghton association, with the proceedings of the Houghton meeting, held in Worcester, Massachusetts, March 3, 1847. New York, Van Norden & Amerman, printers, 1847.
15 p.   25 1/2 cm.

12936 Houseworth, Henry.
Federurbian, or, United States lessons; intended to

promote learning and a knowledge of republican principles, in the minds of our youth... By Henry
Houseworth... Philomath, Ind., The author, 1839.
iv, [5]-144 p.   17 cm.

12937 Houston, James Alexander.
An address, explanatory of the principles and objects
of the United brothers of temperance; delivered at the
Apollo saloon, New York, on the evening of the 11th of
September, 1844... By James Alexander Houston. Pub.
at the request of the State assembly. 2d ed. [New
York] Herald book and job printing office, 1844.
2 p. l., 10 p.   22 cm.

12938 Houston, Samuel, 1793-1863.
Nebraska bill—Indian tribes. Speech of Hon. Sam
Houston, of Texas, delivered in the Senate of the.
United States, Feb. 14 and 15, 1854, in favor of
maintaining the public faith with the Indian tribes.
Washington, Printed at the Congressional globe office,
1854.
15 p.   23 cm.

12939 Houston, Samuel, 1793-1863.
Speech of Hon. Sam Houston, of Texas, exposing the
malfeasance and corruption of John Charles Watrous,
judge of the federal court in Texas, and of his confederates. Delivered in the Senate of the United States,
Feb. 3, 1859. New York, Pudney & Russell, printers,
1860.
100 p.   front. (port.)   19 cm.

12940 Houston, Samuel, 1793-1863.
Speeches of Sam Houston, of Texas, on the subject
of an increase of the army, and the Indian policy of
the government, delivered in the Senate of the United
States, January 29 and 31, 1855. Washington, Printed
at the Congressional globe office, 1855.
20 p.   25 cm.

12941 Houstoun, James, b. ca. 1690.
The works of James Houstoun, M. D., containing memoirs
of his life and travels in Asia, Africa, America, and
most parts of Europe. From the year 1690 to the present time. Giving a particular account of the Scotch
expedition to Darien in America... the rise, progress,
and fall of the two great trading African and South-
Sea companies; the late expedition to the Spanish

West-Indies; the taking and restitution of Cape-
Breton. Some curious anecdotes of the Spanish
court... London, Printed for the author; and sold
by S. Bladon, 1753.
xviii, 435 p.   20 cm.

12942 Hovey, Ivory, 1714-1803.
A farewell sermon. A sermon preached at Rochester
Second parish, October 15th, 1769. Being the day
immediately preceeding the dismission of the author
from his pastoral relation to the church and people
in said parish. By Ivory Hovey... Boston, Printed
by D. Kneeland, for Thomas Leverett, in Corn-hill,
1770.
32 p.   18 cm.

12943 How, David, 1758-1842.
Diary of David How, a private in Colonel Paul
Dudley Sargent's regiment of the Massachusetts line,
in the army of the American revolution. From the
original manuscript. With a biographical sketch
of the author by George Wingate Chase, and illustrative notes by Henry B. Dawson. Morrisania, N. Y.
[Cambridge, Mass., Printed by H. O. Houghton and
company] 1865.
xv, 51 p.   26 cm.

12944 How, Henry, d. 1879.
The mineralogy of Nova Scotia. A report to the
provincial government. By Henry How... Halifax,
N. S., C. Annand, 1869.
vi p., 1 l., 217 p.   21 1/2 cm.

12945 How, Henry K
The battle of Trenton: by Henry K. How...
New-Brunswick, N. J., Press of J. Terhune, 1856.
15 p.   22 1/2 cm.

12946 Howard, E[dward] d. 1841.
Sir Henry Morgan, the buccaneer. By E. Howard...
Paris, Baudry's European library, 1842.
1 p.l., 351 p.   22 cm.

12947 [Howard, Mark] 1817-1887.
Despotic doctrines declared by the United States
Senate exposed; and Senator Dixon unmasked. Hartford,
Press of Case, Lockwood & company, 1863.
cover-title, 24 p.   21 1/2 cm.

12948　Howard, Middleton, b. 1747?
　　　　The conquest of Quebec: a poem. By Middleton
　　　Howard... Oxford, Printed at the theatre; for J.
　　　Fletcher, 1768.
　　　　2 p.l., 12 p.　　25 1/2 x 21 cm.
　　　Awarded the prize offered by the Earl of
　　　Litchfield.

12949　Howard, Oliver Otis, 1830-1909.
　　　　Major-General Howard's address at the second
　　　anniversary of the United States Christian com-
　　　mission. Philadelphia, Caxton press of C. Sherman,
　　　son & co., 1864.
　　　　23 p.　　18 1/2 cm.

12950　Howe, Eber D　　　b. 1798.
　　　　Mormonism unvailed: or, A faithful account of
　　　that singular imposition and delusion, from its
　　　rise to the present time. With sketches of the
　　　characters of its propagators. By E. D. Howe.
　　　Painesville [O.] Printed and pub. by the author,
　　　1834.
　　　　ix, [11]-290 p.　　front.　　18 1/2 cm.

12951　Howe, Elisha P
　　　　The young citizen's catechism, explaining the
　　　duties of district, town, city, county, state,
　　　and United States officers. Together with rules
　　　for parliamentary and commercial business. De-
　　　signed for schools. By Elisha P. Howe. New-
　　　York, A. S. Barnes & Burr, 1861.
　　　　2 p.l., 7-189 p.　　17 1/2 cm.

12952　Howe, Henry, 1816-1893.
　　　　Memoirs of the most eminent American mechanics:
　　　also, lives of distinguished European mechanics;
　　　together with a collection of anecdotes, descrip-
　　　tions, &c. &c., relating to the mechanic arts.
　　　Illustrated by fifty engravings. By Henry Howe...
　　　New York, Harper & brothers, 1847.
　　　　482 p/ incl. illus., plates, ports., facsim.
　　　front., pl.　　19 cm.

12953　Howe, Henry, 1816-1893.
　　　　The times of the rebellion in the West: a
　　　collection of miscellanies, showing the part
　　　taken in the war by each western state -

notices of eminent officers - descriptions of
prominent battles - conspiracies in the West to
aid the rebellion - incidents of guerrilla and
border warfare - individual adventures - anecdotes illustrating the heroism of western soldiers,
etc... By Henry Howe. Cincinnati, Howe's sub-
scrption book concern, 1867.
  252 p. incl. col. front., illus., plates.
plates.   22 cm.

12954   Howe, Joseph, 1804-1873.
  The reciprocity treaty, its history, general
features, and commercial results; a speech delivered by the Honorable Joseph Howe... on the 14th
day of July, 1865. At the great International
commercial convention, held at the city of Detroit.
Specially rev. for publication by Mr. Howe.
Hamilton, Printed by T. & R. White, 1865.
  15 p.   24 cm.

12955   [Howe, Mrs. Julia (Ward)] 1819-1910.
  Passion-flowers. Boston, Ticknor, Reed, and
Fields, 1854.
  iv, 187 p.   18 1/2 cm.

12956   Howe, Mrs. Julia (Ward) 1819-1910.
  A trip to Cuba. By Mrs. Julia Ward Howe.
Boston, Ticknor and Fields, 1860.
  iv, 251 p.   18 cm.

12957   Howe, Samuel Gridley, 1801-1876.
  An essay on separate and congregate systems of
prison discipline; being a report made to the
Boston prison discipline society, by S. G. Howe.
Boston, W. D. Ticknor and company, 1846.
  xi, 90 p.   22 1/2 cm.
  [Prison discipline pamphlets, v. 5. no. 4]

12958   Howe, Timothy Otis, 1816-1883.
  The authority of the nation supreme and absolute; that of the states subordinate and condition-
al. Speech of Hon. T. O. Howe... in the Senate
of the United States, January 10, 1866.
Washington, H. Polkinhorn & son, 1866.
  20 p.   23 1/2 cm.

12959   Howe, William Bell White, bp., 1823-1894.
  Cast down, but not forsaken! A sermon deliver-

ed in St. Philip's church, Charleston, December
15th, 1861, being the Sunday after the great fire.
By Rev. W. B. W. Howe... Charleston, Steam-power
presses of Evans & Cogswell, 1861.
    15 p.   23 1/2 cm.

12960 Howe, William Howe, 5th viscount, 1729-1814.
        The narrative of Lieut. Gen. Sir William Howe,
    in a committee of the House of commons, on the
    29th of April, 1779, relative to his conduct,
    during his late command of the king's troops in
    North America: to which are added, some obser-
    vations upon a pamphlet, entitled, Letters to a
    nobleman. 2d ed. London, Printed by H. Baldwin,
    1780.
        1 p.l., 110 p.   26 1/2 cm.

12961 Howell, George Rogers, 1833-1899.
        The early history of Southampton, L. I., New
    York, with genealogies. By George Rogers Howell...
    New York, J. N. Hallock, 1866.
        4 p.l., [13]-318 p.   19 cm.

12962 Howes, Frederick.
        An address to the Essex agricultural society,
    in Massachusetts, at Topsfield, Oct. 6, 1823.
    By Frederick Howes, esq. Salem, Printed for the
    Society by W. & S. B. Ives, 1824.
        23 p.   23 cm.   [Transactions of the Essex
    agricultural society, v. 1, no. 6]
        Contains also Premiums offered by the Essex
    agricultural society... 1824 (p. [17]-23)

12963 Howison, John.
        Sketches of upper Canada, domestic, local, and
    characteristic: to which are added, practical
    details for the information of emigrants of every
    class; and some recollections of the United States
    on America. By John Howison... Edinburgh, Oliver
    & Boyd [etc., etc.] 1821.
        xvi, 339, [1] p.   22 1/2 cm.

12964 Howitt, Emanuel.
        Selections from letters written during a tour
    through the United States, in the summer and
    autumn of 1819; illustrative of the character of
    the native Indians, and of their descent from
    the lost ten tribes of Israel; as well as descrip-

tive of the present situation and sufferings of
emigrants, and of the soil and state of agriculture.
By E. Howitt... Nottingham, Printed and sold by J.
Dunn [etc., etc., 1820]
 xxi, [1], 230 p. 18 cm.

12965 Howitt, William, 1792-1879.
  Colonization and Christianity: a popular history
of the treatment of the natives by the Europeans in
all their colonies. Bu William Howitt... London,
Longman, Orme, Brown, Green, & Longmans, 1838.
  3 p.l., [ix]-xi, 508 p. 19 1/2 cm.

12966 Howland, Henry Jenkins, b. 1810.
  The heart of the commonwealth: or, Worcester
as it is; being a correct guide to all the public
buildings and institutions, and to some of the
principal manufactories and shops, and wholesale
and retail stores, in Worcester and vicinity.
With many engravings, and a new map of the city.
Worcester, Mass., H. J. Howland, 1856.
  viii, [9]-131 p. illus., fold. plan.
22 1/2 x 18 1/2 cm.

12967 Howse, Joseph.
  A grammar of the Cree language; with which is
combined an analysis of the Chippeway dialect.
By Joseph Howse... London, J. G. F. & J.
Rivington, 1844.
  xix, [1], 324 p. 22 1/2 cm.

12968 Howson, Henry, sr.
  American jute: paper read at the monthly meet-
ing of the Franklin institute, Philadelphia,
October 16th, 1862, by H. Howson. Philadelphia,
Howson's patent offices, 1862.
  8 p. 22 1/2 cm.

12969 Hoyt, David Webster, 1833-1921.
  Hoyt family. A genealogical history of John
Hoyt of Salisbury, and David Hoyt of Deerfield,
(Massachusetts,) and their descendants: with
some account of the earlier Connecticut Hoyts,
and an appendix, containing the family record
of William Barnes of Salisbury, a list of the
first settlers of Salisbury and Amesbury, &c.
By David W. Hoyt... [1st ed.] Boston, C. B.

Richardson, 1857.
144 p.   front., illus., pl., ports.   23 cm.

12970 Hoyt, Epaphras, 1765-1850.
Antiquarian researches: comprising a history of
the Indian wars in the country bordering Connecticut
river and parts adjacent, and other interesting
events, from the first landing of the Pilgrims, to
the conquest of Canada by the English, in 1760:
with notices of Indian depredations in the neighboring country: and of the first planting and progress of settlements in New England, New York and
Canada. By E. Hoyt, esq. Greenfield, Mass., Printed
by A. Phelps, 1824.
2 p.l., [iii]-xii, xii, [13]-312 p.   fold. pl.
22 cm.

12971 Hoyt, George Henry, 1837-
Kansas and the Osage swindle. A letter to Hon.
Sidney Clarke from Geo. H. Hoyt, attorney-general
of Kansas. Washington, Gibson brothers, printers,
1868.
16 p.   22 cm.

12972 Hoyt, Jesse.
Letters from J. Hoyt, late collector, to the
secretary of the treasury, (including many not
before published,) explanatory of the action of
George Poindexter, and his colleagues, commissioners for the investigation of the affairs of
the Custom house at New York. Embracing the
published correspondence between Messrs.
Poindexter and Kelley, two of such commissioners.
New York, The Evening post [1842?]
139 p.   23 cm.

12973 Hoyt, Joseph Gibson, 1815-1862.
An address at the inauguration of Joseph G.
Hoyt, LL. D., as chancellor of Washington university, Saint Louis, Tuesday evening, October
4, 1859... St. Louis, R. P. Studley & Co.,
printers and binders, 1859.
84 p.   22 cm.
"On the relation of culture and knowledge in
a university education."

12974 Hubbard, Henry, 1784-1857.
Speech of Mr. Hubbard, of New Hampshire, upon

the bill making further provisions for the persons
engaged in the land and naval service of the U.
States, during the revolutionary war. Delivered
in the House of representatives, February 29, 1832.
Washington city, Printed at the Globe office, by
F. P. Blair, 1832.
29 p.   22 cm.

12975   Hubbard, S[amuel] D[ickinson] 1799-1855.
Letter from S. D. Hubbard, of Connecticut, to
his constituents, on the alarming crisis in the
affairs of the country. [Washington] J. & G. S.
Gideon, printers [1846]
8 p.   23 1/2 cm.

12976   Hubbard, William, 1621-1704.
A narrative of the Indian wars in New-England,
from the first planting thereof in the year 1607,
to the 1677. Containing a relation of the occasion,
rise and progress of the war with the Indians, in
the southern, western, eastern and northern parts
of said country. By William Hubbard, A. M. minister of Ipswich... Boston, Printed and sold by
John Boyle, 1775.
viii, [9]-288 p.   17 1/2 x 10 1/2 cm.
Third edition (2d American) considerably abridged
from the author's "Narrative of the troubles with
the Indians in New-England... To which is added
a discourse about the warre with the Pequods in
the year 1637", Boston, 1677. "A supplement concerning the warr with the Pequods", "A table shewing the towns [etc.]" and "A postscript" are
omitted.
"A narrative of the Indian wars in New-England
from Piscataqua to Pemmaquid": p. 195-288.

12977   Hubbard, William B
Annual address at the tenth annual meeting of
the United States agricultural society, at the
Smithsonian institution. William B. Hubbard...
president for 1862-'63... Washington city, United
States agricultural society, 1862.
8 p.   23 cm.

12978   Hubbell, Seth, 1759-1832.
A narrative of the sufferings of Seth Hubbell
& family, in his beginning a settlement in the
town of Wolcott, in the state of Vermont.

Danville, Vt., E. & W. Eaton, printers, 1826.
24 p.   18 1/2 cm.
Third edition.

12979 Hubbell, Stephen, 1802-1884.
A discourse commemorative of the Rev. Joseph
Fish, for fifty years (from 1732 to 1781,) pastor
of the Congregational church in North Stonington,
Conn. Delivered at that place, Lord's day, August
16th, 1863, by Rev. Stephen Hubbell... with an
Appendix. Norwich, Bulletin job office, 1863.
26 p.   23 1/2 cm.

12980 Hubbell, William Wheeler.
The way to secure peace and establish unity as
one nation, by William Wheeler Hubbell...
Philadelphia, A. Winch, 1863.
28 p.   front. (port.)   22 cm.

12981 Huber, B   attaché au Ministère des affaires
étrangères.
Aperçu statistique de l'île de Cuba, précédé de
quelques lettres sur la Havane, et suivi de tab-
leaux synoptiques, d'une carte de l'île, et du
tracé des côtes depuis la Havane jusqu'à Matanzas.
Par B. Huber... Paris, P Dufart, 1826.
331, [1] p.   fold. map, 6 fold. tab.   23 cm.

12982 Hudson, Charles, 1795-1881.
Doubts concerning the battle of Bunker Hill.
Addressed to the Christian public. By Charles
Hudson. Boston and Cambridge, J. Munroe & co.,
1857.
1 p.l., 41 p.   front.   18 1/2 cm.

12983 Hudson, Charles, 1795-1881.
A history of the town of Westminster, from
its first settlement to the present time. By
Charles Hudson. Mendon, Mass., G. W. Stacy,
printer, 1832.
42 p.   25 cm.

12984 Hudson, David.
History of Jemima Wilkinson, a preacheress of
the eighteenth century: containing an authentic
narrative of her life and character, and of the
rise, progress and conclusion of her ministry...
By David Hudson. Geneva, Ontario county, N. Y.

Printed by S. P. Hull, 1821.
x, [11]-208, xx p.   19 cm.

12985   Hudson, Eduard Maco.
        The second war of independence in America, by
        E. M. Hudson... Tr. by the author from the 2d rev.
        and enl. German ed., with an introduction by
        Bolling A. Pope. London, Longman, Green, Longman,
        Roberts, & Green, 1863.
        L, 177 p.   21 1/2 cm.

12986   [Hudson, Henry Norman] 1814-1886.
        A chaplain's campaign with Gen. Butler. New-
        York, Printed for the author, 1865.
        66 p.   23 cm.

12987   The Hudson illustrated with pen and pencil; com-
        prising sketches, local and legendary, of its
        several places of interest, together with the
        route to Niagara Falls; forming a companion for
        the pleasure tourist. New York, T. W. Strong,
        1852.
        cover-title, [3]-32 p.   illus.   28 cm.

12988   Huet, Pierre Daniel, bp., 1630-1721.
        A view of the Dutch trade in all the states,
        empires, and kingdoms in the world... Translated
        from the French of monsieur Huet. The 2d ed.
        London, Printed for J. Walthow, jun. and J. Childe,
        1722.
        1 p.l., xii, [4], 232 p.   18 cm.

12989   Hughes, James, 1823-1873.
        Speech of Hon. James Hughes, of Indiana, on
        the admission of Oregon. Delivered in the House
        of representatives, February 10, 1859. Washington,
        Printed by L. Towers, 1859.
        15 p.   24 cm.

12990   Hughes, John, abp., 1797-1864.
        The Catholic chapter in the history of the United
        States. A lecture: delivered in Metropolitan hall,
        before the Catholic institute, on Monday evening,
        March 8, 1852, for the benefit of the House of pro-
        tection, under the charge of the Sisters of mercy.
        By the Most Rev. John Hughes... New-York, E. Dunigan
        & brother, 1852.
        39 p.   21 1/2 cm.

12991 Hughes, John, abp., 1797-1864.
A letter on the moral causes that have produced
the evil spirit of the times; addressed to the
Honorable James Harper, mayor of New-York. Including a vindication of the author from the in-
famous charges made against him by Jas. Gordon
Bennett, William L. Stone, and others. By the
Right Rev. Dr. Hughes... New-York, J. Winchester
[1844]
23 p.   24 cm.

12992 Hughes, Thomas, 1822-1896.
The cause of freedom: which is its champion in
America, the North or the South? By Thomas Hughes...
(Being a speech delivered by him at Exeter hall on
the 29th of January, 1863.)... [London] The emancipation society [1863]
16 p.   17 1/2 cm.

12993 Hughs, Mrs. Mary (Robson)
The life of William Penn, compiled from the
usual authorities, and also many original manuscripts. By Mrs. Hughs... Philadelphia, Printed
by J. Kay, jun. for Carey, Lea & Carey [etc.];
Boston, Munroe & Francis, 1828.
224 p.   19 cm.
This is largely a new work and not merely a
revision of the author's "Life of William Penn,
abridged and adapted."

12994 Hulbert, Charles, 1778-1857.
Museum Americanum; or, Select antiquities, curiosities, beauties, and varieties, of nature and
art, in America; compiled from eminent authorities...
By Charles Hulbert... London, G. & W. B. Whittaker
[etc.] 1823.
iv, [5]-346 p.   front., pl.   15 1/2 cm.
(His Select museum of the world. v. 3]

12995 [Hulett, T   G   ]
Every man his own guide to the falls of Niagara,
or The whole story in few words... To which is added
a chronological table, containing the principal
events of the late war between the United States
and Great Britain. By T. G. H., a resident at the
falls. 4th ed. Buffalo, Printed by Faxon & co.,
1844.
viii, [9]-128 p.   illus., 4 pl. (incl. front.)

2 maps (1 fold.)
"Recession of the falls of Niagara, from Professor
Lyell's Lectures on geology": p. [107]-124.

12996 Hull, Amos Gerald, 1810-1859.
A tribute to the memory of James A. Powell: by A.
Gerald Hull. Delivered by request of the Delphian
institute, at Union college, July 23d, 1829. [New
York, 1829?]
128 p.   front. (port.) 2 pl., geneal. tables.
22 cm.
Genealogy: p. 79-128.

12997 Hull, Isaac, 1773-1843, defendant.
Minutes of proceedings of the court of enquiry,
into the official conduct of Capt. Isaac Hull,
as commandant of the United States' Navy yard at
Charlestown, in the state of Massachusetts, convened
at the Navy-yard in Charlestown, on the 12th-day
of August, A. D. 1822. Printed by order of the
Navy department, from the official record.
Washington city, Davis and Force, 1822.
244, 64 p.   22 1/2 cm.

12998 Hull, William, 1753-1825.
Defence of Brigadier General W. Hull. Delivered
before the general court martial, of which Major
General Dearborn was president, at Albany, March,
1814. With an Address to the citizens of the
United States. Written by himself. Copied from
the original manuscript, and published by his
authority. To which are prefixed, the charges
against Brigadier General Hull, as specified by
the government. Boston, Published by Wells and
Lilly, Court-street, 1814.
2 p.l., [iii]-xlvi, 215 p.   17 1/2 cm.

12999 Hull, William, 1753-1825.
Memoirs of the campaign of the North western
army of the United States, A. D. 1812. In a
series of letters addressed to the citizens of
the United States. With an appendix, containing
a brief sketch of the revolutionary services of
the author. By William Hull... Boston, True &
Greene, 1824.
229, x p.   21 cm.

13000 Hull, William, 1753-1825.
        Report of the trial of Brig. General William Hull;
commanding the North-western army of the United States.
By a court martial held at Albany on Monday, 3rd
January, 1814, and succeeding days. Taken by Lieut.
Col. Forbes... [And Appendix 1-2] New York,
Published by Eastburn, Kirk, and co. at the Literary
rooms, corner of Wall and Nassau-streets, 1814.
        8 p.l., [3]-156, 119, 29 p.   22 cm.

13001 Humason, William Lawrence.
        From the Atlantic surf to the Golden gate. First
trip on the great Pacific railroad.—Two days and
nights among the Mormons... Hartford, Ct., 1869.
        56 p.   20 cm.

13002 The humble address of the publicans of New-England,
        to which king you please. With some remarks upon it...
London, Printed in the year 1691.
        35 p.   19 1/2 x 15 cm.

13003 Humboldt, Alexander i.e. Friedrich Wilhelm Heinrich
        Alexander, freiherr von, 1769-1859.
        An abridgement of Humboldt's statistical essay on
New Spain, being a geographical, philosophical and
political account of the kingdom of Mexico, or the
vice-royalty of Mexico, and the internal provinces,
subject to the commandant or governor general residing
at Chihuahua. By a citizen of Maryland. Baltimore,
Printed by Wane and O'Reilly, 1813.
        vi, [7]-41. [1] p.   21 cm.
        Pub. Paris, 1811, under title: Essai politique
sur le royaume de la Nouvelle-Espagne.

13004 Humboldt, Alexander i.e. Friedrich Wilhelm Heinrich
        Alexander, freiherr von, 1769-1859.
        Views of nature: or, Contemplations on the
sublime phenomena of creation; with scientific
illustrations. By Alexander von Humboldt. Tr.
from the German by E. C. Otté and Henry G. Bohn...
London, H. G. Bohn, 1850.
        xxx, 452 p. incl. col. front. facsim.   18 1/2 cm.
[Bohn's scientific library]

13005 Hume, George Henry.
        Canada, as it is. Comprising details relating to
the domestic policy, commerce and agriculture, of

the upper and lower provinces... especially intended for the use of settlers and emigrants. By George Henry Hume. New York, W. Stodart, 1832.
xxiv, 173 p.   15 cm.

13006   Hume, Sophia, 1701-1774.
An exhortation to the inhabitants of the province of South-Carolina, to bring their deeds to the light of Christ, in their own consciences. By Sophia Hume. In which is inserted, some account of the author's experience in the important business of religion... London, Printed and sold by L. Hinde, 1752.
152 p.   20 cm.
"Divine love commemorated. The author unknown to me": p. 151-152.

13007   Humphrey, Heman, 1779-1861.
Indian rights & our duties. An address delivered at Amherst, Hartford, etc. December, 1829. By Heman Humphrey, D. D. ... Amherst, J. S. & C. Adams and co.; New York, J. Leavitt [etc., etc.] 1830.
24 p.   17 cm.

13008   Humphreys, David, 1752-1818, comp.
The conduct of General Washington, respecting the confinement of Capt. Asgill, placed in its true point of light, by David Humphreys. With a preface and appendix. New York, Printed for the Holland club, 1859.
x, [11]-35 p.   24 cm.
A collection of documents originally published in the New Haven gazette in 1786. cf. Pref.

13009   Humphreys, David, 1752-1818.
Discours en vers, adressé aux officiers et aux soldats des différentes armées américaines. Por M. David Humphreys, colonel au service des Etats-Unis, & aide-de-camp de son excellence le général Washington. Imprimé pour la premiere fois à New-Haven, dans le Connecticut. Paris, Prault, 1786.
66 p.   21 cm.
The poem, and prose translation into French by the Marquis de Chastellux are on opposite pages.

13010   Humphreys, David, 1752-1818.
         Letters from the Hon. David Humphreys, F. R. S.
         to the Rt. Hon. Sir Joseph Banks... containing some
         account of the serpent of the ocean, frequently seen
         in Gloucester bay. New-York, Published by Kirk &
         Mercein, no. 22 Wall-street, 1817.
         86 p.   18 cm.

13011   Humphreys, David, 1752-1818.
         The life and heroic exploits of Israel Putnam...
         By Colonel David Humphreys... New York, E. Strong,
         1834.
         190 p.   front., illus.   14 cm.
         "The main part is from the pen of Colonel Humphreys;
         but so far as General Putnam was connected with the
         battle of Bunker Hill, the principal portion is
         extracted from an 'Historical and topographical sketch
         of Bunker Hill battle, by Samuel Swett.' The
         anecdotes are by the same hand."—To the reader,
         p. [174]
         The original work by Humphreys was first pub.,
         Hartford, 1788, under title: An essay on the
         life of... Israel Putnam.

13012   Humphreys, David, 1752-1818.
         A poem, on the happiness of America: addressed
         to the citizens of the United States. By D.
         Humphreys. London printed, 1786; Hartford, Re-
         printed by Hudson and Goodwin [1786]
         51 p.   20 1/2 x 15 1/2 cm.
         [Wolcott pamphlets, v. 2, no. 3]

13013   Humphrys-Alexander, Alexander, calling himself Earl
         of Stirling, 1783-1859, defendant.
         Report of the trial of Alexander Humphreys or
         Alexander, claiming the title of Earl of Stirling,
         before the High court of justiciary at Edinburgh,
         for the crime of forgery. With an appendix, con-
         taining the whole documentary evidence. By
         Archibald Swinton... Edinburgh, T. Clark, 1839.
         1 p.l., v. [1], xxiv, 356, cviii p. incl. geneal.
         tab.   fold. facsim.   22 1/2 cm.

13014   Hunt, Benjamin Faneuil, 1792-1857.
         An oration, delivered by their appointment,
         before the Washington society, in Charleston,
         South-Carolina, on the 4th of July, 1839. By

Benjamin Faneuil Hunt... Charleston, Printed by
S. S. Miller, 1839.
45 p.   24 1/2 cm.

13015   Hunt, Daniel, 1806-1869.
History of Pomfret. A discourse delivered on the
day of annual thanksgiving, in the First church in
Pomfret, Nov. 19th, 1840. By D. Hunt... Hartford,
J. Holbrook, printer, 1841.
35 p.   22 cm.

13016   Hunt, Edward Bissell, 1822-1863.
Union foundations: a study of American nationality
as a fact of science. By Capt. E. B. Hunt... New
York, D. Van Nostrand [etc., etc.] 1863.
61 p.   22 1/2 cm.

13017   Hunt, Issac, 1742?-1809.
The political family: or A discourse pointing out
the reciprocal advantages, which flow from an
uninterrupted union between Great Britain and her
American colonies. By Isaac Hunt... Numb. 1.
Philadelphia, Printed by James Humphreys, junior.
1775.
32 p.   21 1/2 cm.

13018   Hunt, Isaac H
Astounding disclosures! Three years in a mad
house. By a victim. Written by himself. A true
account of the barbarous, inhuman and cruel treatment of Isaac H. Hunt, in the Maine insane hospital,
in the years 1844, '45, '46, and '47, by Drs. Isaac
Ray, James Bates, and their assistants and attend-
ants... Printed for Isaac H. Hunt, the author
[Skowhegan, Printed by A. A. Mann] 1851.
84 p.   22 1/2 cm.

13019   Hunt, James, 1833-1869.
The negro's place in nature: a paper read before
the London anthropolgical society, by Dr. James
Hunt... New York, Van Evrie, Horton & co., 1864.
27 p.   22 cm.

13020   Hunt, John Warren, 1826-1859.
Wisconsin gazetteer, containing the names, location
and advantages of the counties, cities, towns, villages,
post offices, and settlements, together with a

description of the lakes, water courses, prairies and
public localities, in the state of Wisconsin. Alphabetically arranged. By John Warren Hunt. Madison,
B. Brown, printer, 1853.
    255, [1] p.   21 1/2 cm.

13021 Hunt, Timothy Dwight, 1821-1895.
    Address delivered before the New England society
of San Francisco, at the American theatre, on the
twenty-second day of December, A. D. 1852, by Rev.
T. Dwight Hunt, pastor of the New England church.
San Francisco, Cooke, Kenny & co., 1853.
    20 p.   23 cm.

13022 Hunt, William, 1825-1896.
    The cabinet of nature and philosophy. Book the
first. The cabinet of shells. By William Hunt...
Boston, Munroe and Francis; New York, C. S. Francis,
1833.
    16 p.   plates.   23 1/2 cm.

13023 Hunt, William Gibbes, 1791?-1833.
    An address on the character and services of De
Witt Clinton, delivered at Nashville, March 11, 1828,
at the request of the Grand chapter of Tennessee.
By William Gibbes Hunt... Nashville, Printed by J. S.
Simpson, 1828.
    20 p.   21 1/2 cm.

13024 Hunter, David, 1802-1886.
    Correspondence, orders, etc., between Major-
General David Hunter, Major-General J. G. Foster,
and Brigadier-General Henry M. Naglee, and others.
February and March, 1863. Philadelphia, J. B.
Lippincott & co., 1863.
    60 p.   22 1/2 cm.

13025 [Hunter, John Dunn] 1798?-1827.
    Reflections on the different states and conditions
of society; with the outlines of a plan to ameliorate
the circumstances of the Indians of North America.
London, J. R. Lake, 1823.
    cover-title, 20 p.   22 1/2 cm.

13026 Hunter, Joseph, 1783-1861.
    Collections concerning the church or congregation
of Protestant Separatists formed at Scrooby in north

Nottinghamshire, in the time of King James I: the
founders of New Plymouth, the parent-colony of New-
England.   By the Rev. Joseph Hunter... London, J. R.
Smith, 1854.
    2 p.l., vii-xiv p., 1 l., 205 p.   22 1/2 cm.

13027   Hunter, Joseph, 1783-1861.
    Collections concerning the early history of the
founders of New Plymouth, the first colonists of
New England.   By Joseph Hunter... London, J. R.
Smith, 1849.
    1 p.l., 70 p.   20 cm.   [Mr. Hunter's Critical
and historical tracts.   no. II]
    Reprinted in abridged form in the Collections of
the Massachusetts historical society, 4th series,
v. 1, p. [52]-85.

13028   Hunter, William, of Memphis, Tenn.
    Sovereignty, allegiance and secession; an essay
on the Constitution and government of the United
States.   By Hon. William Hunter... Memphis,
Printed by J. Dumars, 1868.
    43 p.   21 1/2 cm.

13029   Huntington, Enoch, 1739-1809.
    The happy effects of union, and the fatal
tendency of diversions.   Shewn in a sermon,
preached before the free-men of the town of
Middletown, at their annual meeting, April 8,
1776.   By Enoch Huntington... Hartford, printed
by Eben. Watson, 1776.
    28 p.   18 1/2 cm.

13030   Huntington, Enoch, 1739-1809.
    An oration delivered at Middletown, in the
state of Connecticut, February 22, A.D. 1800.
By Enoch Huntington... Middletown, Printed by
Tertius Dunning, 1800.
    9 p.   20 1/2 cm.
    An account of the proceedings of the inhabitants
of Middletown on February 22, 1800, in honor of the
memory of Washington: p. [2]

13031   Huntington, Frederic Dan, 1819-1904.
    Christian citizenship and honest legislation.   A
sermon delivered before His Excellency Henry J.
Gardner, His Honor Henry W. Benchley, the honorable

Council, and the legislature of Massachusetts, at
the annual election, Wednesday, Jan. 6, 1858.
By F. D. Huntington... Boston, W. White, 1858.
44 p.   23 cm.

13022 [Huntington, Gurdon] 1818-1875.
The guests of Brazil, or The martyrdom of Frederick.
A tragedy. New-York, Burgess, Stringer & co., 1844.
70 p., 1 l.   19 cm.
Dramatic poem.

13033 Huntington, Joseph, 1735-1794.
God ruling the nations for the most glorious
end. A sermon, in presence of His Excellency,
and both houses of assembly. Hartford, May 13th,
1784. By Joseph Huntington... Hartford, Printed
by Hudson & Goodwin, 1784.
42 p.   21 cm.

13034 Huntington, Joshua, 1786-1819.
Memoirs of the life of Mrs. Abigail Waters; who
died in Boston, November 22d, 1816, in the 96th
year of her age. To which is prefixed, the sermon
preached on occasion of her death. By Joshua
Huntington... 2d ed. Boston, Published by Samuel
T. Armstrong, no. 50, Cornhill, 1817.
vi, [7]-144 p.   15 cm.

13035 Huntington, Hon. Lucius Seth, 1827-1886.
The independence of Canada. The annual address
delivered before the Agricultural society of the
county of Missisquoi, at Dedford, Sept. 8, 1869.
By the Hon. L. S. Huntington... Montreal, Herald
steam press, 1869.
14 p.   23 1/2 cm.

13036 Huntoon, Benjamin, 1792-1864.
A eulogy, delivered by the request of the Grand
lodge of Massachusetts, at the funeral services in
commemoration of Rev. and R. W. Thaddeus Mason
Harris, D. D., and R. W. Brother Samuel Thaxter,
at the Masonic temple, May 4th, 1842. By Benjamin
Huntoon... Boston, B. H. Greene, 1842.
15, [1] p.   23 1/2 cm.

13037 Huntt, Henry, 1792-1838.
A visit to the Red Sulphur Spring of Virginia,
during the summer of 1837: with observations on

the waters. By Henry Huntt, M. D. With an introduction, containing notices of routes, &c., by an annual visiter. Boston, Dutton and Wentworth, printers, 1839.

40 p.   front.   24 cm.

13038   Hurd, John Codman, 1816-1892.
Topics of jurisprudence connected with conditions of freedom and bondage. By John C. Hurd... New York, D. Van Nostrand, 1856.

ix, 113 p.   23 1/2 cm.

13039   Hurd, John R
A national bank, or no bank; an appeal to the common sense of the people of the United States, especially of the laboring classes. By John R. Hurd. New York, W. E. Dean, 1842.

104 p.   23 cm.

13040   Hurlbert, Jesse Beaufort.
Britain and her colonies. By J. Beaufort Hurlburt... London, E. Stanford, 1865.

xv, [1], 271 p. incl. tables.   23 cm.

13041   [Hurlbert, William Henry]
Gan-Eden: or, Pictures of Cuba... Boston, John P. Jewett; Cleveland, Jewett, Proctor and Worthington; New York, Sheldon, Lamport and Blakeman, 1854.

xii, 236 p.   illus.   20 cm.

13042   Hurlbut, Elisha P
Essays on human rights and their political guaranties: by E. P. Hurlbut... New-York, Greeley & McElrath, 1845.

v, [7]-219 p.   19 cm.

13043   Hurlbut, Elisha P
A secular view of religion in the state, and the Bible in the public schools. By E. P. Hurlbut... Albany, N. Y., J. Munsell, 1870.

55 p.   22 1/2 cm.

13044   Hurt, John.
The love of our country. A sermon, preached before the Virginia troops in New-Jersey. By John Hurt, chaplain. Philadelphia, Printed and sold by Styner and Cist, 1777.

23 p.   21 cm.

13045 Hurt-Binet, Marc Gabriel.
Neuf mois aux États-Unis d'Amérique. Fragment
des Mémoires de m. Marc-Gabriel Hurt-Binet...
Genève [etc.] J. Cherbuliez, 1862.
184 p. 18 cm.

13046 [Huske, John] 1721/-1773.
The present state of North America, &c. Part I.
London, Printed for, and sold by R. and J. Dodsley,
1755.
2 p.l., 88 p. 26 cm.
Table of contents covers eight chapters, but
pt. 1 contains chapters 1-3 only. No more published.

13047 Hussey, Josiah.
An oration, pronounced before the fraternity of
masons, and a numerous auditory, at Hanover, in the
county of Plymouth, June the 24th, A. L. 5793.
Being the festival of St. John. By Brother Josiah
Hussey... Boston, Printed by Brother Benjamin Russell,
at his office in State-street, 5793 [1793]
12 p. 20 cm.

13048 Huston, J   comp.
Légendes canadiennes, recueillies par J. Huston.
Paris, P. Jannet, 1853.
2 p.l., [7]-303 p. 16 cm. (On cover:
Bibliothèque choisie)
"Ces légendes sont extraites d'un recueil intitulé:
Le répertoire national, ou Recueil de littérature
canadienne, compilé et publié par J. Huston.
Montréal, 1848-1850. 4 vol. in-8."

13049 Hutchinson, Francis, bp. of Down and Connor, 1660-1739.
An historical essay concerning witchcraft.
With observations upon matters of fact; tending to
clear the texts of the sacred Scriptures, and confute
the vulgar errors about that point. And also two
sermons: one in proof of the Christian religion;
the other concerning the good and evil angels.
By Francis Hutchinson... London, Printed for R.
Knaplock [etc.] 1718.
xv, [4], 270 p. 19 1/2 cm.

13050 Hutchinson, John Wallace, 1821-1908, comp.
Hutchinson's Republican songster, for the campaign
of 1860. Edited by John W. Hutchinson. New York, O.

Hutchinson, 1860.
    72 p.   16 cm.
    Without the music; tunes of some of the songs
indicated by title.
    Comprises same text as The bobolink minstrel;
or, Republican songster for 1860.   Edited by G. W.
Bungay.

13051 [Hutchinson, Thomas] 1711-1780.
    The case of the provinces of Massachusetts-bay
and New-York, respecting the boundary lines between
the two provinces.   Boston, New England, Printed by
Green and Russell, by order of His Excellency the
governor, the honorable His Majesty's Council, and
the honorable House of representatives, 1764.
    xxx p., 1 l.   32 cm.   (In Journal of the
honourable House of representatives of His Majesty's
province of the Massachusetts-bay... held at
Boston... the twenty-fifth day of May... 1763.
Appendix)

13052 [Hutchinson, Thomas] 1711-1780.
    Strictures upon the Declaration of the Congress at
Philadelphia; in a letter to a noble lord, &c.
London, Printed in the year 1776.
    32 p.   22 1/2 cm.
    "In a volume of tracts which belonged to Sir
James Wright, this is stated to have been written
by Gov. Hutchinson."—Rich, Bibl. amer. nova.,
v. 1, 1846, p. 468.

13053 Hutchinson, Thomas, 1711-1780.
    The witchcraft delusion of 1692, by Gov. Thomas
Hutchinson.   From an unpublished manuscript (an
early draft of his History of Massachusetts) in the
Massachusetts archives.   With notes by William
Frederick Poole.   Boston, Priv. print., 1870.
    43 p.   23 1/2 x 19 cm.
    "Reprinted from the New-England historical and
genealogical register for October, 1870."

13054 Hutchinson, Thomas Joseph, b. 1820.
    Buenos Ayres and Argentine gleanings: with
extracts from a diary of Salado exploration in 1862
and 1863.   By Thomas J. Hutchinson... London, E.
Stanford, 1865.
    xxi p., 1 l., 321, [1] p.   front. (port.)
illus., plates, 3 fold. maps. 22 1/2 cm.

13055　Hyatt, Thaddeus.
　　　　The prayer of Thaddeus Hyatt to James Buchanan,
　　　president of the United States, in behalf of Kansas,
　　　asking for a postponement of all the land sales in
　　　that territory, and for other relief; together with
　　　correspondence and other documents setting forth
　　　its deplorable destitution from the drought and
　　　famine. Submitted under oath, October 29, 1860.
　　　Washington, H. Polkinhorn, printer, 1860.
　　　　68, [4] p.　　22 1/2 cm.

13056　Hyde, Alvan, 1768-1833.
　　　　The nature and danger of heresy. A sermon,
　　　preached before the convention of the clergy of
　　　Massachusetts, May 29, 1817. By Alvan Hyde...
　　　Boston, Published by Samuel T. Armstrong, no. 50,
　　　Cornhill, 1817.
　　　　22 p.　　23 cm.

13057　Hyde, Mrs. Anna M
　　　　The American boy's life of Washington. By Mrs.
　　　Anna M. Hyde... New York, J. Miller, 1868.
　　　　255 p.　　front., illus., 10 pl.　　18 cm.

13058　Hyde, Ezra, 1774-1849.
　　　　History of the town of Winchendon, from the grant
　　　of the township by the legislature of Massachusetts
　　　in 1735, to the present time. By Ezra Hyde.
　　　Worcester, Printed by H. J. Howland [1849]
　　　　viii, [9]-136 p.　　18 cm.

13059　Hyde, James F
　　　　The Chinese sugar-cane; its history, mode of
　　　culture, manufacture of the sugar, etc. with reports
　　　of its success in different portions of the United
　　　States, and letters from distinguished men. Written
　　　and compiled by James F. C. Hyde... Boston, J. P.
　　　Jewett & company; Cleveland, O., H. P. B. Jewett, 1857.
　　　　iv, [5]-106 p.　　front., illus.　　18 cm.

13060　Hyde, William Lyman, 1819-1896.
　　　　History of the One hundred and twelfth regiment
　　　N. Y. volunteers. By Wm. L. Hyde, chaplain of the
　　　regiment. Fredonia, N. Y., W. McKinstry & co., 1866.
　　　　viii, [9]-214 p.　　front., port.　　20 cm.

13061 [Hyneman, Leon] 1805-1879.
The universal masonic record; or, Links in the
golden chain of brotherhood. Containing, the name,
business, profession and residence of subscribers...
Containing also, a list of masonic lodges in America
and Europe... Philadelphia, L. Hyneman, 1857.
234 p. 23 cm.

13062 Hyneman, Leon, 1805-1879.
World's masonic register: containing the name,
number, location, and time of meeting of every
masonic lodge in the world... with the statistics of
each masonic jurisdiction; also, the name... of each
subscriber... By Leon Hyneman. Philadelphia, Printed
for the author by J. B. Lippincott & co., 1860.
xii, 11-566 p. front. (port.) 24 cm.

I

13063 Ide, George Barton, 1804-1872.
Battle echoes, or, Lessons from the war. By
George B. Ide... Boston, Gould and Lincoln; New York,
Sheldon and company [etc.] 1866.
1 p.l., [v]-viii, 9-325 p. 19 1/2 cm.

13064 Ide, Jacob, 1785-1880.
A pastor's review. A discourse preached in Medway,
Mass., Nov. 2, 1864, on the fiftieth anniversary of
the author's ordination and settlement. By Jacob
Ide... Boston, Congregational board of publication,
1865.
72 p. 23 1/2 cm.

13065 The ides of March; or, Abraham Lincoln, private citizen.
Being a sequel to The end of the irrepressible conflict. By a merchant of Philadelphia. Philadelphia,
King & Baird, printers, 1861.
29 p. 23 cm.

13066 Illinois central railroad company.
The Illinois central railroad company offers for
sale over 1,500,000 acres selected farming and wood
lands, in tracts of forty acres and upwards, to
suit purchasers, on long credits and at low rates
of interest, situated on each side of their railroad,
extending all the way from the extreme north to the
south of the state of Illinois. Boston, G. C. Rand
& Avery, printers, 1857.

80 p. incl. front., illus.   2 maps (1 double)
22 cm.

13067   Illinois in 1837; a sketch descriptive of the situation,
boundaries, face of the country, prominent districts,
prairies, rivers, minerals, animals, agricultural
productions, public lands, plans of internal improvement, manufactures, &c., of the state of Illinois:
also, suggestions to emigrants, sketches of the
counties, cities, and principal towns in the state:
together with a letter on the cultivation of the
prairies, by the Hon. H. L. Ellsworth. To which are
annexed the letters from a rambler in the West...
Philadelphia, S. A. Mitchell [etc.] 1837.
       viii, 9-143 p.   front. (fold. map)   22 cm.
       "The publisher is probably the author. It was got
up mainly to promote the sale of Illinois lands then
owned by John Grigg of Philadelphia." - Sabin, Bibl.
amer., v. 9, no. 34260.

13068   Illustrated description of the Broadway pneumatic
underground railway, with a full description of the
atmospheric machinery, and the great tunneling
machine. New York, S. W. Green, printer, 1870.
       20 p.   illus.   28 cm.
       Running title: Broadway pneumatic underground
railway.

13069   The immigrants' guide to Minnesota in 1856. By an old
resident. St. Anthony [Minn.?] W. W. Wales; New
York, Ivison & Phinney [etc., etc.] 1856.
       viii, [9]-116 p. incl. front., illus. (incl. map)
19 cm.

13070   Impartial observations, to be considered on by the
king, his ministers, and the people of Great Britain.
[London, 1763?]
       27 p.   25 1/2 cm.

13071   An impartial review of the rise and progress of the
controversy between the parties known by the names
of the Federalists & Republicans. Containing an
investigation of the radical cause of division; and
of some of the subordinate or auxiliary causes which
have been instrumental in enlarging the breach, and
inflaming the minds of the partizans. In a series of
letters from a partaker in the American revolution

to a junior citizen. Philadelphia, Printed by John
Ormrod, no. 41, Chesnut-street, 1800.
   50 p.   21 cm.
   Merwin-Clayton auction catalogue no. 429, 1911
(no. 10) lists a copy bearing name of Charles Pettit
as author, written in a contemporary hand.

13072 An impartial statement of the controversy, respecting
the decision of the late committee of canvassers,
containing the opinions of Edmund Randolph, esq.,
attorney general of the United States, and several
other eminent law characters. New York, Printed by
Thomas Greenleaf, 1792.
   46 p.   21 cm.
   Relates to the Otsego County votes.

13073 An impartial view of the conduct of the M-----ry,
in regard to the war in America; the engagements
entered into with Russia, Hesse-Cassel, and Prussia;
the cause of throwing out the Militia bill; and the
affairs of the Mediterranean. In answer to the many
inviduous [!] attacks of pamphleteers, &c.... London,
1756.
   52 p.   20 cm.

13074 Incidents and sketches connected with the early
history and settlement of the West... Cincinnati,
J. A. & U. P. James, 1835.
   72 p. incl. front. (port.) illus., 8 pl.   26 cm.

13075 ...Incidents of American camp life: being events
which have actually transpired during the present
rebellion. 2d ed. New York, T. R. Dawley [c1862]
   vi, 7-104 p. incl. front.   16 1/2 cm. (Dawley's
camp and fireside library—no. 1)

13076 Independency the object of the Congress in America.
Or, An appeal to facts. London, Printed for John,
Francis, and Charles Rivington, (No. 62) St. Paul's
Church-yard, 1776.
   1 p.l., 70 p.   21 1/2 cm.

13077 Indian battles, murders, seiges [!] and forays in the
Southwest. Containing the narratives of Gen. Hall,
Col. Brown, Capt. Carr, John Davis, John Bosley,
Samuel Blair, John Rains, Dr. Shelby, Thomas Everrett.
Including accounts of the Nickojack campaign, attack
on Buchanan's station, the Cold Water expedition,

burning of Sigler's fort, battle of Caney Fork,
attack on Greenfield fort, defence of Bledsoe's
Lick, &c. Nashville, Tenn., Wales & Roberts
[etc., c1853]
    100 p.   22 cm.

13078 Indian narratives: containing a correct and interesting history of the Indian wars, from the landing
of our Pilgrim fathers, 1620, to Gen Wayne's victory,
1794. To which is added a correct account of the
capture and sufferings of Mrs. Johnson, Zadock Steele,
and others; and also a thrilling account of the
burning of Royalton... Claremont, N. H., Tracy
and brothers, 1854.
    276 p.   17 1/2 cm.

13079 The Indian reservation sulphur springs, near Buffalo,
N. Y., with an account of its analysis, medicinal
properties and the diseases for which it is applicable.
Together with directions for its use, and some re-
marks on mineral waters in general. Buffalo, A. F.
Lee, printers, 1848.
    28, [2] p.   13 1/2 cm.

13080 Indiana. Constitution.
    Constitution of the state of Indiana, and the
address of the Constitutional convention. New
Albany, Ia., Kent & Norman, printers, 1851.
    cover-title, 32 p.   23 cm.

13081 Indiana canal company.
    ... Report of the Indiana canal company, on the
improvement of the falls of the Ohio. Cincinnati,
T. Wrightson & co., printers, 1856.
    23 p.   22 1/2 cm.
    At head of title: To the Senate & House of
representatives of the U. S.
    Signed: John S. G. Burt.

13082 [Ingersoll, Charles] 1805-1882.
    A brief view of constitutional powers, showing
that the Union consisted of independent states
united. Philadelphia, 1864.
    76 p.   24 cm.

13083 [Ingersoll, Charles] 1805-1882.
    An undelivered speech on executive arrests.

Philadelphia, 1862.
vi, 98 p.   24 1/2 cm.

13084   Ingersoll, Charles Jared, 1782-1862.
A communication on the improvement of government:
read before the American philosophical society, at
a meeting attended by General La Fayette, October 1st,
1824. By Charles J. Ingersoll, esq. ... Philadelphia,
Printed by A. Small, 1824.
24 p.   20 1/2 cm.

13085   Ingersoll, Charles Jared, 1782-1862.
A discourse concerning the influence of America
on the mind; being the annual oration delivered before
the American philosophical society, at the University
in Philadelphia, on the 18th October, 1823... By C. J.
Ingersoll... Philadelphia, A. Small, 1823.
67 p.   23 cm.

13086   Ingersoll, Charles Jared, 1782-1862.
A discourse delivered before the Society for the
commemoration of the landing of William Penn.   On
the 24th of October, 1825.   By C. J. Ingersoll, esq. ...
Philadelphia, R. H. Small, 1825.
36 p.   21 1/2 cm.
"A brief selection of the most remarkable indications
of Philadelphia."

13087   [Ingersoll, Charles Jared] 1782-1862.
Inchiquin, the Jesuit's letters, during a late
residence in the United States of America: being
a fragment of a private correspondence, accidentally
discovered in Europe; containing a favourable view
of the manners, literature, and state of society, of
the United States, and a refutation of many of the
aspersions cast upon this country, by former residents
and tourists.   By some unknown foreigner... New-York,
Printed and published by I. Riley, 1810.
v, 165 p.   22 cm.

13088   Ingersoll, Charles Jared, 1782-1862.
A view of the rights and wrongs, power and policy,
of the United States of America... By Charles Jared
Ingersoll.   Philadelphia, O. & A. Conrad & co.;
Baltimore, Conrad, Lucas & co., 1808.
157 p.   22 1/2 cm.

13089 Ingersoll, Edward, 1817-1893.
    The history and law of the writ of habeas corpus
    with an essay on the law of grand juries, by E.
    Ingersoll... Philadelphia [T. K. and P. G. Collins,
    printers] 1849.
    1 p.l., 67 p.   26 1/2 cm.

13090 [Ingersoll, Edward] 1817-1893.
    Personal liberty and martial law: a review of
    some pamphlets of the day. Philadelphia, 1862.
    2 p.l., 38 p.   22 1/2 cm.

13091 [Ingersoll, Jared] 1722-1781.
    [Mr. Ingersoll's letters relating to the Stamp-
    act. New Haven, Printed and sold by Samuel Green,
    1766]
    1 p.l., iv, 68 p.   19 x 15 cm.
    Correspondence of the stamp-agent for Connecticut,
    1764-1766.

13092 Ingersoll, Joseph Reed, 1786-1868.
    Eulogy on Gen. Zachary Taylor, late president of
    the United States. Delivered October 2, 1850, by
    the Hon. Joseph R. Ingersoll. Philadelphia, Crissy &
    Markley, printers, 1850.
    57 p.   24 cm.

13093 Ingersoll, Joseph Reed, 1786-1868.
    Memoir of the late Samuel Breck, vice-president
    of the Historical society of Pennsylvania, read
    before the society, by Joseph R. Ingersoll, January
    12th, 1863. Philadelphia, King & Baird, printers,
    1863.
    56 p.   24 cm.
    On cover: 2d edition.
    "The Historical society of Pennsylvania" (historical
    sketch, list of officers and members, and constitution):
    p. [39]-56.

13094 [Ingersoll, Joseph Reed] 1786-1868.
    Secession; a folly and a crime. Philadelphia,
    King & Baird, printers, 1861.
    29 p.   22 1/2 cm.

13095 [Ingersoll, Joseph Reed] 1786-1868.
    Secession resisted. Philadelphia, King & Baird, 1861.
    38 p.   23 cm.

13096   Ingersoll, Lurton Dunham.
             Iowa and the rebellion. A history of the troops
         furnished by the state of Iowa to the volunteer armies
         of the Union, which conquered the great southern
         rebellion of 1861-5. By Lurton Dunham Ingersoll.
         3d ed. Philadelphia, J. B. Lippincott and co.;
         Dubuque, B. M. Harger [etc, etc.] 1867.
             743 p. incl. maps. 23 1/2 cm.

13097   Ingersoll, Samuel Bridge, 1785-1820.
             Sermon, preached at Shrewsbury, June 18, 1820,
         the Sabbath after his ordination, by the late Rev.
         Samuel B. Ingersoll... who died, at Beverly, Nov. 14,
         1820... Worcester, Manning & Trumbull, printers, 1821.
             30 p.   23 1/2 cm.

13098   [Inglis, Charles, bp. of Nova Scotia] 1734-1816.
             A vindication of the Bishop of Landaff's sermon
         from the gross misrepresentations, and abusive
         reflections contained in Mr. William Livingston's
         letter to his lordship: with some additional
         observations on certain passages in Dr. Chauncey's
         Remarks. &c. By a lover of truth and decency...
         New-York, Printed by J. Holt, at the Exchange,
         1768.
             viii, 82 p. 19 1/2 cm.
             [Hazard pamphlets, v. 16, no. 10]

13099   Inglis, James, 1777-1820.
             A discourse delivered in the First Presbyterian
         church, in the city of Baltimore, Lord's day
         morning, October 2, 1814. Before the lieutenant-
         colonel, the officers and soldiers of the First
         regiment of artillery, 3d B. M. M.and published
         at their request. By James Inglis, D. D. Baltimore,
         Printed by J. Robinson, for Neal, Wills and Cole,
         1814.
             22 p.   21 cm.

13100   [Ingraham, Edward Duncan] 1793-1854.
             A sketch of the events which preceded the capture
         of Washington, by the British, on the twenty-fourth
         of August, 1814... Philadelphia, Carey and Hart, 1849.
             iv, 66 p.   front. (map)   23 1/2 cm.

13101   An inquiry into the causes and cost of corrupt state
         legislation. By a citizen of Philadelphia.

358

Philadelphia, 1863.
32 p.   22 cm.

13102   An inquiry into the present state of the foreign
relations of the Union, as affected by the late
measures of administration... Published by Samuel
F. Bradford, Philadelphia; Brisban & Brannan, New
York; William Andrews, Boston, and the principal
booksellers in the United States, 1806.
183 p.   19 1/2 cm.

13103   International commercial convention, Portland, Me.,
1868.
Proceedings of the International commercial convention, held in the city of Portland, Me., August
4th and 5th, 1868. Reported by J. M. W. Yerrinton.
Portland, B. Thurston and company, printers, 1868.
160 p.   21 cm.   [With Portland and Rutland
railroad company. Across the continent... Portland,
1868]

13104   International policy. Essays on the foreign relations
of England... London, Chapman and Hall, 1866.
vii p., 2 l., 603 p.   maps (1 fold.)   22 cm.
Contents.- I. The West. By R. Congreve.- II.
England and France. By F. Harrison.- III. England
and the sea. By E. S. Beesly.   IV. England and
India. By E. H. Pember.—V. England and China.
By J. H. Bridges.- VI. England and Japan. By
C. A. Cookson.- VII. England and the uncivilised
communities. By H. D. Hutton.

13105   Iowa. Laws, statutes, etc.
Education laws of the state of Iowa, passed by
the Board of education at its first and second
sessions, and by the General assembly, at its eighth
regular session. Des Moines, Ia., J. Teesdale,
state printer, 1860.
103 p.   21 1/2 cm.
Oran Faville, president of the Board of education.

13106   Iowa. State Geologist (1866-1870)
First and second annual report of progress by
the State Geologist and assistant and chemist on
the geological survey of the State of Iowa, together with the substance of popular letters
contributed to the newspapers of the State during
the years 1866 and 1867, in accordance with law;

also extracts originally contributed to scientific
journals as a part of the work of the survey. Des
Moines, F. W. Palmer, State Printer, 1868.
   284 p.   23 cm.

13107   Iowa institute of science and arts, Dubuque.
   Celebration of the Humboldt centennial and opening
of the Iowa institute of science and arts, at Dubuque,
Iowa, September 14th, 1869. Dubuque, Daily times
printing house, 1869.
   56 p.   22 1/2 cm.

13108   Irving, Theodore, 1809-1880.
   The conquest of Florida, by Hernando de Soto.   By
Theodore Irvin... New York, G. P. Putnam, 1851.
   1 p.l., [v]-xxii, [23]-457 p.   front. (fold. map)
19 1/2 cm.
   Based upon "La Florida del Inca" of Garcilaso de la
Vega, and the English translation of 1686 of the
anonymous "Relaçam verdadeira".

13109   Irving, Washington, 1783-1859.
   Voyages and discoveries of the companions of
Columbus.   Philadelphia, Carey and Lea, 1831.
   350, [1]p.   23 1/2 cm.

13110   Isert, Paul Erdmann, 1757-1789.
   Voyages en Guinée et dans les îles Caraïbes
en Amérique, par Paul Erdman Isert... Tirés de sa
correspondance avec ses amis.   Tr. de l'allemand.
Paris, Maradan, 1793.
   viii, 343, 48 p.   front, pl.   21 cm.
   "Observations météorologiques":   43 p. at end.

13111   [Iturbide, Agustín de, emperor of Mexico] 1783-1824.
   Breve diseño crítico de la emancipacion y libertad
de la nacion mexicana, y de las causas que influyeron
en sus mas ruidosos sucesos, acaecidos desde el grito
de Iguala hasta la espantosa muerte del libertador en
la villa de Padilla.   México, Impr. de la testamentaría
de Ontiveros, 1827.
   16, xxviii, 205, [1]p.   14 1/2 cm.
   Edited with notes, by "L. L. S. E. I."
   With a Spanish version of the preface to the English
translation (London, 1824) xxviii p.
   Previously published under title: Carrera militar
y política de don Agustín de Itúrbide.

13112 Iturri, Francisco, b. 1738.
Carta crítica sobre la historia de America del
señor Don Juan Bautista Muñoz, escrita de Roma por
el P. Francisco Iturri... Puebla, Impresa en Madrid,
y por su original en la Oficina del gobierno, 1820.
67 p.   20 cm.

13113 Ivernois, Sir Francis d', 1757-1842.
Effects of the continental blockade upon the
commerce, finances, credit and prosperity of the
British Islands... By Sir Francis d'Ivernois. Tr.
from the 3d French ed., rev., cor. and enl. To
which are added, Observations on certain statements
contained in a late work, entitled: "A view of the
natural and commercial circumstances of Ireland,
by Thomas Newenham, esq." 4to. 1809. London,
J. Hatchard [etc.] 1810.
152, xxiii, [1] p.   2 fold. tab.   22 1/2 cm.

13114 Ives, Alfred Eaton, 1809-1892.
Victory turned into mourning. A discourse, on
occasion of the death of Abraham Lincoln...
preached at Castine, by Alfred E. Ives... Bangor,
Wheeler & Lynde, printers, 1865.
14 p.   23 cm.

13115 Ives, Charles, 1815-1880.
Chips from the workshop. Parnassus, The outlaw's
dream, or The old man's counsel, and other poems.
By Charles Ives. New Haven, Hitchcock & Stafford,
printers, 1843.
3 p.l., [5]-180 p.   19 cm.

13116 Ives, Levi Silliman, 1797-1867.
The introductory address of the Historical society
of the University of North Carolina, delivered in
the University chapel, June 5th, 1844, by L. Silliman
Ives... Raleigh, Printed by T. Loring, 1844.
18 p.   21 1/2 cm.

13117 [Izard, Ralph] 1742-1804.
An account of a journey to Niagra, Montreal and
Quebec, in 1765; or, " 'Tis eighty years since."
New-York, Printed by W. Osborn, 1846.
30 p.   23 cm.

13118 Izard, Ralph, 1742-1804.
Correspondence of Mr. Ralph Izard, of South Carolina,

from the year 1774 to 1804; with a short memoir.
Vol. I, New-York, C. S. Francis & co., 1844.
xiv, 389, [1]p., 1 l.   front. (port.)   19 cm.
No more published.
Includes Izard's correspondence from 1774 to 1777,
during his residence in Europe as commissioner to the
court of Tuscany.

13119   Izard, George, 1777-1828.
Official correspondence with the Department of
war, relative to the military operations of the
American army under the command of Major General
Izard, on the northern frontier of the United States
in the years 1814 and 1815.   Philadelphia, Published
by Thomas Dobson, at the Stone house, no. 41 South
Second street, William Fry, printer, 1816.
vii, 152 p.   22 cm.

J

13120   The Jack Morgan songster. Compiled by a capt. in
Gen. Lee's army. Raleigh, Branson & Farrar, 1864.
cover-title, 64 p.   14 cm.

13121   Jackson, Andrew, pres. U. S., 1767-1845.
Correspondence between Major General Jackson,
and Brevet Major General Scott, on the subject of
an order, bearing date the 22d April, 1817; published
by the former, to the troops of his division, and
printed about the same time, in most of the public
papers. [Richmond] 1819.
iv, [5]-16 p.   21 1/2 cm.

13122 Jackson, Andrew, b. 1814.
Narrative and writings of Andrew Jackson, of Kentucky;
containing an account of his birth, and twenty-six
years of his life while a slave; his escape; five
years of freedom, together with anecdotes relating
to slavery; journal of one year's travels; sketches,
etc. Narrated by himself; written by a friend.
Syracuse, Daily and weekly star office, 1847.
vi, [7]-120 p. 18 1/2 cm.

13123   Jackson, Charles, 1775-1855.
An oration, delivered before the right worshipful
master and brethren of St. Peter's lodge, at the

Episcopal church in Newburyport, Massachusetts, on
the festival of St. John the Baptist; celebrated
June 25, 5798. By the Worshipful Brother Charles
Jackson, P. M. Newburyport, Printed by Brother
Angier March, A. L. 5798 [1798]
24 p. 20 1/2 x 15 1/2 cm.

13124 Jackson, Ebenezer.
Address delivered before the Middlesex County
agricultural society, at its annual exhibition,
October 13, 1842. By Hon. Ebenezer Jackson.
Middletown, Conn., W. D. Starr, printer, 1842.
19 p. 21 cm.
[Agricultural pamphlets, v. 6, no. 11]

13125 Jackson, Halliday, 1771-1835.
Civilization of the Indian natives; or, A
brief view of the friendly conduct of William
Penn towards them in the early settlement of
Pennsylvania; the subsequent care of the Society
of Friends in endeavoring to promote peace and
friendship with them by pacific measures; and a
concise narrative of the proceedings of the
Yearly meeting of Friends, of Pennsylvania, New
Jersey, and parts adjacent, since the year 1795,
in promoting their improvement and gradual
civilization. By Halliday Jackson... Philadelphia,
M. T. C. Gould; New York, I. T. Hopper, 1830.
120 p. 22 cm.
"A vocabulary of some of the most familiar words
and phrases in the Seneca language, and the English,
in alphabetical order": p. 114-120.

13126 Jackson, Henry, 1798-1863.
An account of the churches in Rhode-Island.
Presented at an adjourned session of the twenty-
eighth annual meeting of the Rhode-Island Baptist
state convention, Providence, November 8, 1853.
By Henry Jackson... Providence, G. H. Whitney, 1854.
134 p. front. 23 cm.

13127 Jackson, Henry Rootes, 1820-1898.
Eulogy upon the life and character of the
Honorable Charles J. McDonald, pronounced by Henry
R. Jackson, at Marietta, April 20th, 1861. Atlanta,
Ga., Franklin printing house, 1861.
35 p. 21 1/2 cm.

13128   Jackson, H[enry] W   R
Historical register and Confederates assistant to
national independence. Containing a discovery for
the preservation of butter, together with other
valuable recipes, and important information for
the soldier, and the people in general throughout
the Confederate States of America... By H. W. R.
Jackson. Augusta, Ga., Printed at the office of the
Constitutionalist, 1862.
47, [1] p.   18 cm.

13129   Jackson, Isaac Rand, d. 1843.
The life of William Henry Harrison, (of Ohio,)
the people's candidate for the presidency. With a
history of the wars with the British and Indians on
our north-western frontier. By Isaac R. Jackson.
4th ed. Philadelphia, Marshall, Williams & Butler,
1840.
1 p.l., [v]-x, 15-222 p.   15 cm.

13130   Jackson, John, d. 1855.
Reflections on peace and war. By John Jackson.
Philadelphia, T. E. Chapman, 1846.
1 p.l., 78 p.   15 cm.

13131   [Jackson, Jonathan] 1743-1810.
Thoughts upon the political situation of the
United States of America, in which that of
Massachusetts is more particularly considered.
With some observations on the Constitution for
a federal government. Addressed to the people
of the Union. By a native of Boston... Printed
at Worcester, Mass., by I. Thomas, 1788.
209 p.   24 cm.
This work has also been attributed to George
Richards Minot. cf. Sabin, Bibl. amer.

13132   Jackson, Robert, 1750-1827.
A treatise on the fevers of Jamaica, with some
observations on the intermitting fever of America,
and an appendix, containing some hints on the means
of preserving the health of soldiers in hot climates.
By Robert Jackson... Philadelphia, Printed for Robert
Campbell, bookseller, 1795.
xi, 276, 19 p.   17 1/2 cm.

13133   Jackson, Samuel, 1787-1872.
An account of the yellow or malignant fever,

as it occured in the city of Philadelphia in 1820.
By Samuel Jackson... Philadelphia, M. Carey & sons,
1821.
    1 p.l., [5]-116 p.   21 cm.

13134   Jackson, Tatlow.
    Authorities cited antagonistic to Horace Binney's
conclusions on the writ of habeas corpus, by Tatlow
Jackson. Philadelphia, J. Campbell, bookseller,
1862.
    cover-title, 8 p.   22 cm.

13135   Jackson, Tatlow.
    Martial law: what is it? And who can declare
it? By Tatlow Jackson. Philadelphia, J. Campbell,
1862.
    19 p.   30 1/2 cm.
    No. 5 of a volume of pamphlets lettered: Gerritt
Smith to his neighbors [etc.]

13136   Jackson, William, 1759-1828.
    An oration, to commemorate the independence of
the United States of North-America, delivered at
the Reformed Calvinist church, in Philadelphia, July
4th, 1786, and published at the request of the Pennsylvania society of the Cincinnati. By Major W.
Jackson. Philadelphia, Printed by Eleazer Oswald,
at the Coffee-house, 1786.
    2 p.l., 29 p.   20 x 17 cm.

13137   Jackson, William Ayrault, 1832-1861.
    An oration, delivered at Windham Centre, Greene
county, N. Y., July 4, 1859, by the late Col.
William A. Jackson, of the Eighteenth regiment of
New-York volunteers. Albany, C. Van Benthuysen,
printer, 1863.
    24 p.   22 cm.
    "Elegy" and "Letter" by O. B. Hitchcock: p. [22]-24.

13138   [Jacob, John Jeremiah] 1758?-1839.
    A biographical sketch of the life of the late
Capt. Michael Cresap. Cumberland, Md., Printed
for the author, by J. M. Buchanan, 1826.
    123, [1]p.   17 1/2 cm.
    A defense of Capt. Cresap, contradicting the
statements made by Thomas Jefferson, in his "Notes
on the state of Virginia."

13139   Jacobs, Bela, 1786-1836.
        A voice from the West. Rev. Bela Jacob's report
        of his tour in the western states, performed in the
        spring and summer of 1833. Presented to the executive
        committee of the Western Baptist educational asso-
        ciation, Boston, September 9, 1833. Pub. by order
        of the executive committee. Boston, J. Howe,
        printer, 1833.
        27, [1] p.   21 1/2 cm.

13140   Jacobs, Michael, 1808-1871.
        Notes on the Rebel invasion of Maryland and
        Pennsylvania, and the battle of Gettysburg, July 1st,
        2d and 3d, 1863... By M. Jacobs... Philadelphia, J. B.
        Lippincott & co., 1864.
        iv, 5-47 p.   front. (fold. map)   18 cm.

13141   Jacobs, Sarah Sprague, b. 1813.
        Nonantum and Natick. By Sarah S. Jacobs...
        Boston, Massachusetts Sabbath school society, 1853.
        336 p. incl. illus., plates, map.   front.
        19 cm.
        A narrative of the missionary work of John Eliot
        among the Indians, "written for the Massachusetts
        Sabbath school Society, and revised by the Committee
        of publication."
        A later edition, Boston, c1858, appeared under
        title: The white oak and its neighbors.

13142   Jacobs, Thomas Jefferson.
        Scenes, incidents, and adventures in the Pacific
        ocean; or, The islands of the Australasian seas,
        during the cruise of the clipper Margaret Oakley,
        under Capt. Benj. Morrell... By Thomas Jefferson
        Jacobs... New York, Harper & bros., 1844.
        xi, [13]-372 p.   front., illus., fold. pl.
        19 cm.

13143   Jacquemin, [Nicolas] 1736-1819.
        Mémoire sur la Louisiane, contenant la description
        du sol et des productions de cette île, et les moyens
        de la rendre florissante en peu de tems; avec un
        vocabulaire et un abrégé de la grammaire de la
        langue des sauvages. Par M. Jacquemin... Paris,
        Impr. de J. M. Eberhart, an XI—1803.
        2 p.l., 67, [1] p.   17 cm.

13144   Jacques, Amédée Florent, 1813-1865.
         Excursion au Rio-Salado et dans le Chaco,
         Confédération argentine, par Amédée Jacques;
         extrait de la Revue de Paris des 1er et 15 mars.
         Paris, Impr. de Pillet fils ainé, 1857.
         39 p.   fold. map.   24 1/2 cm.

13145   Jamaica. Governor, 1682-1684? (Sir Thomas Lynch)
         A narrative of affairs lately received from
         His Majesties island of Jamaica: viz. I. His
         Excellency the governour Sir Thomas Linch's
         speech to the Assembly met Sept. 21, 1682. II.
         Samuel Bernard, esq; speaker of the said Assembly,
         his speech to the governour. III. An humble
         address from His Majesties Council, and gentlemen
         of the Assembly, to His Most Sacred Majesty. IV.
         The governour's speech at the proroguing the
         Assembly. London, Printed for R. Taylor, 1683.
         1 p.l., 6 p.   31 cm.

13146   Jamaica. Laws, statutes, etc.
         An abridgment of The laws of Jamaica, in
         manner of an index. To which is prefixed, a
         table of the general and marginal titles, under
         which the subject-matter of each act and clause
         is properly digested. London, Printed for C. Brett
         and company, printers, booksellers, and stationers,
         in Jamaica, 1756.
         2 p.l., 43 p.   35 1/2 cm.
         Appended to: Jamaica. Laws, statutes, etc.
         Acts of Assembly, passed in the island of Jamaica,
         from 1681, to 1754, inclusive. London, 1756.

13147   Jamaica. Laws, statutes, etc.
         The new act of Assembly of the island of Jamaica,
         intitled, An act to repeal an act, intitled, "An act
         to repeal several acts, and clauses of acts, re-
         specting slaves, and for the better order and
         government of slaves, and for other purposes:" and
         also to repeal the several acts, and clauses of
         acts, which were repealed by the act intitled as
         aforesaid; and for consolidating and bringing into one
         act the several laws relating to slaves, and for
         giving them further protection and security; for
         altering the mode of trial of slaves charged with
         capital offences; and for other purposes; commonly
         called, the New consolidated act, which was passed
         by the Assembly on the 6th of November—by the

Council on the 5th day of December—and by the
lieutenant governor on the 6th day of December,
1788; being the present Code noir of that island.
Published for the use of both houses of Parliament,
and the satisfaction of the public at large, by
Stephen Fuller, esq., agent for Jamaica. London,
Printed for B. White and son [etc.] 1789.
     vii, 17 p.   24 1/2 cm.
     Half-title: The code of laws for the govern-
ment of the negro slaves in the island of Jamaica.

13148   James, Charles P[inckney] 1818-1899.
          Oration and poem, delivered before the Cincinnati
          literary club, July 4th, 1853. Oration by Charles
          P. James. Poem by C. A. L. Richards. Cincinnati,
          Truman & Spofford, 1853.
            46 p.   21 1/2 cm.

13149   James, Charles Tillinghast, 1804-1862.
          Letters on the culture and manufacture of cotton:
          addressed to Freeman Hunt, esq., editor of Hunt's
          Merchants" magazine, and published in the numbers
          of that journal for February and March, 1850, in
          reply to the communications of A. A. Lawrence, esq.,
          originally published in the Merchants' magazine
          for Dec. 1849 and January, 1850. By Charles T.
          James... New York, Printed by G. W. Wood, 1850.
            35 p.   23 cm.

13150   James, George Payne Rainsford, 1801?-1860.
          A brief history of the United States boundary
          question. Drawn up from official papers. By
          G.P.R.James, esq. London, Saunders and Otley,
          1839.
            32 p.   22 cm.

13151   James, Henry, 1811-1882.
          What constitutes the state? A lecture delivered
          before the Young men's association of the city of
          Albany. By Henry James. New York, J. Allen, 1846.
            iv, [5]-59 p.   22 1/2 cm.

13152   James, Horace, 1818-1875.
          The two great wars of America. An oration
          delivered in Newbern, North Carolina, before
          the Twenty-fifth regiment Massachusetts volunteers,
          July 4, 1862. By Rev. Horace James, chaplain.

Boston, Printed by W. T. Brown & co., 1862.
30 p.   23 1/2 cm.

13153   James, James.
The two epistles. The angel's address, or The
glorious message, commanded to be sent to Abraham
Lincoln, July 21, 1864. By James James... [Albany,
N. Y., J. Nixon, 1864]
7, [1] p.   23 cm.
A poem on the emancipation proclamation.

13154   James, Joseph.
A system of exchange with almost all parts of the
world [by Joseph James and Daniel Moore] To which
is added The India directory for purchasing the
drugs and spices of the East-Indies, &c. New York,
Printed by J. Furman, 1800.
180 p.   tables. 18 cm.

13155   James, William, d. 1827.
An inquiry into the merits of the principal
naval actions, between Great-Britain and the
United States; comprising an account of all
British and American ships of war, reciprocally
captured and destroyed since the 18th of June
1812. By William James... Halifax, N. S., Printed
for the author by A. H. Holland, 1816.
vi, 102 p.   4 fold. tab.   20 1/2 cm.
Enlarged and published in 1817 under title: A
full and correct account of the chief naval occurrences.

13156   James, William, d. 1827.
Warden refuted: being a defence of the British
navy against the misrepresentations of a work recently
published at Edinburgh, entitled, "A statistical,
political, and historical account of the United
States of North America, by D. B. Warden"...
in a letter to the author of that work; by William
James... London, Printed for M. Richardson, 1819.
48 p.   fold. tab.   22 1/2 cm.

13157   James, William Dobein.
A sketch of the life of Brig. Gen. Francis Marion,
and a history of his brigade, from its rise in
June, 1780, until disbanded in December, 1782;
with descriptions of characters and scenes, not

369

heretofore published. Containing also, an appendix, with copies of letters which passed between several of the leading characters of that day; principally from Gen. Greene to Gen. Marion. By William Dobein James... Charleston, S. C., Printed by Gould and Riley, 1821.
vii, [9]-182, 39 p.   22 1/2 cm.

13158   Jamieson, Milton.
Journal and notes of a campaign in Mexico: containing a history of Company C. of the second regiment of Ohio volunteers; with a cursory description of the country, climate, cities, waters, roads and forts along the southern line of the American army in Mexico. Also of the manners and customs, agriculture, &c. of the Mexican people. By Milton Jamieson, an officer of the 2nd Reg. Ohio volunteers. Cincinnati, Ben Franklin printing house, 1849.
iv, [5]-105 p., 1 l.   21 cm.

13159   Janeway, James, 1636?-1674.
A token for children, being an exact account of the conversion, holy and exemplary lives and joyful deaths of several young children. By James Janeway... To which is added, A token for the children of New-England, or, Some examples of children, in whom the fear of God was remarkably budding before they died; in several parts of New England. Preserved and published for the encouragement of piety in other children. With new additions. Boston, Printed and sold by Z. Fowle, in Back-street, near the Mill-bridge, 1771.
156 p.   17 x 9 cm.

13160   Janus, pseud.
The critical moment, on which the salvation or destruction of the British empire depend. Containing the rise, progress, present state, and natural consequences of our American disputes. By Janus... London, Printed for H. Setchell, 1776
ii, [3]-121 p.   19 1/2 cm.

13161   Janvier, Francis De Haes, 1817-1885.
Patriotic poems. By Francis De Haes Janvier... Philadelphia, J. B. Lippincott & co., 1866.
88 p.   19 1/2 cm.

13162   Jaques, John Wesley.
            Three years' campaign of the Ninth, N. Y. S. M.,
        during the southern rebellion, by John W. Jaques...
        New York, Hilton & co., 1865.
            199, [2], 47, [1] p.   19 cm.
            Eighty-third regiment volunteers.

13163   Jardine, L   J
            A letter from Pennsylvania to a friend in England:
        containing valuable information with respect to
        America. By L. J. Jardine, M. D. Bath [Eng.]
        Printed by R. Cruttwell, London, Sold by Dilly
        [etc., etc.] 1795.
            2 p.l., 31 p.   22 cm.

13164   [Jarves, James Jackson] 1820-1888.
            Parisian sights and French principles, seen
        through American spectacles... New York, Harper
        & brothers, 1852.
            2 p.l., [9]-264 p.   illus., 1 pl.   19 cm.
            Second series published 1855, with author's
        name.

13165   Jarves, James J[ackson] 1820-1888.
            Scenes and scenery in the Sandwich Islands, and
        a trip through Central America: being observations
        from my note-book during the years 1837-1842. By
        James J. Jarves... Boston, J. Munroe and company,
        1844.
            xi, [13]-341 p.   19 cm.

13166   Jarvis, Abraham, bp., 1739-1013.
            Bishop Jarvis's charge to the clergy of his
        diocese. Delivered immediately after his conse-
        cration, in Trinity church, New-Haven, on the fest-
        ival of St. Luke, October 18, 1797. Together with
        the address of the convention of the Protestant
        Episcopal church, in Connecticut, to their bishop.
        And the bishop's answer. Printed at Newfield
        [Conn.] by Lazarus Beach, 1798.
            29 p.   19 cm.

13167   Jarvis, Leonard, 1781-1854.
            Speech of Mr. Jarvis, of Maine, on the navy
        appropriation bill. In House of representatives,
        April 4, 1836. Washington, Blair and Rives,
        printers, 1836.
            14 p.   23 cm.

13168   [Jarvis, Russell] 1791-1853.
        Facts and arguments against the election of General
        Cass, respectfully addressed to the Whigs and Demo-
        crats of all free states. By an anti-abolitionist.
        New York, Printed by R. Craighead, 1848.
        cover-title, 64 p.   22 1/2 cm.

13169   Jarvis, Samuel Farmar, 1786-1851.
        A discourse on the religion of the Indian tribes
        of North America. Delivered before the New-York
        historical society, December 20, 1819. By Samuel
        Farmar Jarvis... New-York, C. Wiley & co., 1820.
        111 p. incl. tab.   23 1/2 cm.
        Includes a comparison of the etymology of the
        Onondaga, Mohawk, and Lenape or Delaware languages,
        with that of the Hebrew language (p. 71-88)

13170   [Jarvis, Samuel Farmar] 1786-1851.
        A narrative of events connected with the accept-
        ance, and resignation of the rectorship of St. Paul's
        church, Boston. [Boston, 1825]
        108 p.   23 cm.

13171   Jarvis, Sarah M'Curdy (Hart) petitioner.
        The great divorce case! A full and impartial his-
        tory of the trial of the petition of Sarah M. Jarvis,
        for a divorce from her husband, the Rev. Samuel F.
        Jarvis... before a committee of the legislature of
        the state of Connecticut: comprising the testimony,
        letters, and depositions, produced on said trial;
        with a preliminary statement of such parts as are
        necessary to a clear understanding of the case.
        New-York, 1839.
        60 p.   23 cm.

13172   Jarvis, William Charles, d. 1836.
        An oration, delivered at Pittsfield, before the
        Washington benevolent society of the county of
        Berkshire, on the 4th July, 1812. By William C.
        Jarvis... Pittsfield [Mass.] Printed by Milo Smith
        & co., 1812.
        22 p.   20 cm.

13173   Jarvis, William Charles, d. 1836.
        The Republican; or, A series of essays on the
        principles and policy of free states. Having a
        particular reference to the United States of
        America and the individual states. By William C.

Jarvis... Pittsfield [Mass.], Printed by Phinehas
Allen, 1820.
     368 p., 1 l.   17 1/2 cm.

13174   Jay, Sir James, 1732-1815.
          A letter to the governors of the College of New
     York; respecting the collection that was made in this
     kingdom in 1762 and 1763, for the colleges of
     Philadelphia and New York. To which are added ex-
     planatory notes; and an appendix, containing the
     letters which passed between Mr. Alderman Trecothick
     and the author. By Sir James Jay... London, Printed
     for G. Kearsly [etc.] 1771.
          vi, 42 p.   21 cm.

13175   Jay, John, 1745-1829.
          Letters, being the whole of the correspondence
     between the Hon. John Jay, esquire, and Mr. Lewis
     Littlepage. A young man whom Mr. Jay, when in
     Spain, patronized and took into his family. New-
     York, Printed and sold by Francis Childs, at the
     New-printing-office, no. 189, Water-street, 1786.
          1 p.l., 76 p.   21 cm.

13176   Jay, John, 1817-1894.
          America free, or America slave. An address on
     the state of the country. Delivered by John Jay,
     esq., at Bedford, Westchester county, New York.
     October 8th, 1856. [New York, Office of the New
     York tribune, 1856]
          20 p.   illus. (map)   22 1/2 cm.

13177   Jay, John, 1817-1894.
          The church and the rebellion. Mr. Jay's letter
     to the rector and vestry of St. Matthew's church,
     Bedford, with a preface in reply to the rector's
     speech from the chancel on Sunday, June 21, 1863,
     touching the recent visit of a clergyman of doubt-
     ful loyalty. Bedford, N. Y., 1863.
          15, 37 p.   22 cm.   [His Slavery & the war,
     no. 6]

13178   Jay, John, 1817-1894.
          Correspondence between John Jay and Henry B.
     Dawson, and between James A. Hamilton and Henry
     B. Dawson, concerning the Federalist. New York,
     Printed by J. M. Bradstreet & son, 1864.
          2 p.l., 48 p.   24 cm.   (On cover: Current

fictions tested by uncurrent facts: a series of
tracts, personal, political and historical; de-
claratory, argumentative and documentary. By
Henry B. Dawson)
Reprinted from "The Evening post," Feb. 16-Apr.
29, 1834.

13179 Jay, John, 1817-1894.
Facts connected with the presentment of Bishop
Onderdonk: A reply to parts of the Bishop's
statement. By John Jay, one of the counsel orig-
inally employed by the presenting bishops... New
York, Stanford and Swords; Philadelphia, G. S.
Appleton, 1845.
23 p.   20 1/2 cm.

13180 Jay, John, 1817-1894.
Thoughts on the duty of the Episcopal church,
in relation to slavery: being a speech delivered
in N. Y. A. S. convention, February 12, 1839. By
John Jay. New-York, Piercy & Reed, printers, 1839.
11 p.   17 1/2 cm.

13181 [Jay, John] 1817-1894.
Union league club of New York. Address of the
president. June 23, 1866. [New York, 1866]
66 p.   21 cm.

13182 Jay, John Clarkson, 1808-1891.
A catalogue of the shells, arranged according
to the Lamarckian system; together with descriptions of new or rare species, contained in the
collection of John C. Jay... 3d ed. New York
and London, Wiley & Putnam, 1839.
125, [1] p.   x col. pl.   28 1/2 x 23 1/2 cm.

13183 Jay, William, 1769-1853.
Remarks on the character and narrative of the
Rev. John Clark, by William Jay. Interspersed
with brief sketches from the narrative, by way
of illustration, by another hand... Boston,
Cummings and Hilliard [etc.] 1821.
iv (i.e. viii) 91 p.   22 cm.
"Address delivered at the interment": p. [80]-91.

13184 Jay, William, 1789-1858.
An inquiry into the character and tendency of
the American colonization, and American anti-

slavery societies. By William Jay... New-York,
Leavitt, Lord & co.; Boston, Crocker & Brewster,
1835.
1 p.l., 202 p.   19 cm.

13185   Jay, William, 1789-1858.
A review of the causes and consequences of the
Mexican war. By William Jay. 2d ed. Boston, B. B.
Mussey & co.; Philadelphia, U. Hunt & co. [etc.,
etc.] 1849.
333 p.   19 1/2 cm.

13186   Jay, William, 1789-1858.
A view of the action of the federal government,
in behalf of slavery. By William Jay... Utica, Pub.
by J. C. Jackson, for the N. Y. S. anti-slavery
society, 1844.
112 p.   19 cm.
"Appendix. The Amistad case [by Joshua Leavitt]":
p. 95-112.

13187   Jay, William, 1789-1858.
War and peace: the evils of the first, and a plan
for preserving the last. By William Jay... London,
T. Ward and co. [etc.] 1842.
iv, 48 p.   20 cm.

13188   Jefferds, Charles M   1837-1863? defendant.
Trial of Charles M. Jefferds for murder, at New
York, December, 1861. Charles E. Wilbour, reporter.
New York, Ross & Tousey, 1862.
234 p.   24 cm.
John Walton and John W. Matthews were murdered
June 30, 1860. In July, 1861, Charles M. Jefferds
was tried for the murder of Walton and acquitted.
In December, 1861, he was tried in the Court of
general sessions for the murder of Matthews.

13189   Jefferson college, Washington, Miss.
The charter and statutes of Jefferson college,
Washington, Mississippi, as revised and amended:
together with a historical sketch of the institution
from its establishment to the present time: to
which is prefixed a list of the trustees, officers
and faculty, the acts of Congress and of the
Legislature relating to the institution, and a
catalogue of its library, apparatus, &c. Pub.
by order of the Board of trustees. Natchez, Printed

375

at the book and job office, 1840.
      90 p.   21 1/2 cm.

13190   Jefferson Medical College, Philadelphia.
        Catalogue of graduates.
        [Philadelphia]
              v in   24 cm.   decennial (irregular)

13191   [Jefferys, Thomas] d. 1771.
        The conduct of the French, with regard to Nova
        Scotia; from its first settlement to the present
        time.   In which are exposed the falsehood and ab-
        surdity of their arguments made use of to elude
        the force of the treaty of Utrecht, and support
        their unjust proceedings.   In a letter to a member
        of Parliament.   London, T. Jefferys, 1754.
        1 p.l., 77 p.   22 1/2 cm.

13192   Jeffreys, Thomas, d. 1771.
        A description of the Spanish islands and settle-
        ments on the coast of the West Indies, comp. from
        authentic memoirs, rev. by gentlemen who have re-
        sided many years in the Spanish settlements; and
        illustrated with thirty-two maps and plans, chiefly
        from original drawings taken from the Spaniards in
        the last war, and engraved by Thomas Jefferys...
        London, T. Jefferys, 1762.
        3 p.l., xxiv, 106, [2] p.   32 fold. pl. (incl.
        front., maps, plans)   26 x 21 cm.

13193   Jeffries, John, 1796-1876.
        An account of the last illness of the late Hon.
        Daniel Webster, secretary of state, with a descrip-
        tion of the postmortem appearances, etc., by John
        Jeffries, M. D.... Philadelphia, T. K. and P. G.
        Collins, printers, 1853.
        13 p.   24 1/2 cm.
        "Extracted from the American journal of the med-
        ical sciences, for January, 1853."

13194   Jenings, Edmund.
        A full manifestation of what Mr. Henry Laurens
        falsely denominates candor in himself, and tricks
        in Mr. Edmund Jenings.   London, 1783.
        2 p.l., 80 p.   23 1/2 cm.
        [Miscellaneous pamphlets, v. 26, no. 3]

13195   Jenkins, John Stilwell, 1818-1852.
        History of political parties in the State of New-
York, from the acknowledgment of the independence
of the United States to the close of the presidential
election in eighteen hundred forty-four. Auburn,
N. Y., Alden & Markham, 1846.
        vii, 528 p.   ports.   20 cm.

13196   Jenkins, John Stilwell, 1818-1852.
        History of the war between the United States and
Mexico, from the commencement of hostilities, to
the ratification of the treaty of peace. By John
S. Jenkins... Auburn [N. Y.] Derby, Miller & co.;
Buffalo, Derby & Hewson, 1848.
        xiv, [15]-506 p.   front., plates, ports.   20 cm.

13197   Jenkins, John Stilwell, 1818-1852.
        James Knox Polk, and a history of his administra-
tion; embracing the annexation of Texas, the difficulties with Mexico, the settlement of the Oregon
question, and other important events. By John S.
Jenkins... Auburn and Buffalo, J. E. Beardsley
[1850]
        - 3 p.l., [ix]-xv, 395 p.   18 1/2 cm.

13198   Jenkins, John Stilwell, 1818-1852.
        The life of Silas Wright, late governor of the
state of New York. With an appendix, containing a
selection from his speeches in the Senate of the
United States, and his address read before the New
York state agricultural society. By John S. Jenkins...
Auburn and Buffalo, J. E. Beardsley [c1847]
        xi, [13]-378 p.   19 cm.

13199   Jenkins, John S[tilwell] 1818-1852.
        The lives of patriots and heroes distinguished
in the battles for American freedom, by John S.
Jenkins... Auburn, J. C. Derby & co., 1847.
        viii, 17-293 p.   16 1/2 cm.

13200   Jenkins, John Stilwell, 1818-1852.
        Recent exploring expeditions to the Pacific and
the South Seas, under the American, English, and
French governments. By J. S. Jenkins... London,
T. Nelson and sons, 1853.
        viii, 508 p.   front.   18 cm.

377

13201   Jenkins, Joseph.
        An address delivered before the Massachusetts
        charitable mechanick association, December 17,
        1818, being the anniversary of the choice of offi-
        cers, and fourth triennial celebration of their
        public festival. By Joseph Jenkins. Boston, Printed
        by Munroe & Francis, No. 4, Cornhill, 1819.
            24 p.   23 cm.

13202   [Jenkins, Thornton Alexander] 1811-1893.
        Rear Admiral Goldsborough and the retiring laws
        of the navy. No. 2. Washington, Mohun & Bestor,
        1868.
            19, 38 p.   22 1/2 cm.
        "Paper read by Commodore Thornton A. Jenkins,
        U. S. navy, before the Naval committee of the
        House of representatives January 21, 1868, in
        reply to Rear Admiral Goldsborough's claim to be
        continued on the active list of the navy": p.1-30.

13203   Jenkinson, Isaac.
        The peace party and its policy. Speech of Isaac
        Jenkinson, at Fort Wayne, Indiana, March 16, 1863.
        Fort Wayne, Ind., R. C. F. Rayhouser, printer [1863]
            16 p.   23 cm.

13204   Jenks, William, 1778-1866.
        An address to the members of the American anti-
        quarian society, pronounced in King's Chapel,
        Boston, on their first anniversary, October 23,
        1813. By William Jenks... Boston, I. Thomas, jun.,
        1813.
            28 p.   23 cm.   [Minor publications. no. 2]

13205   [Jennings, Dudley S   ]
        Nine years of Democratic rule in Mississippi:
        being notes upon the political history of the
        state, from the beginning of the year 1838, to
        the present time... Jackson, Mi., T. Palmer, 1847.
            xii, 304 p.   19 cm.

13206   Jennings, Isaac, 1816-1887.
        Memorials of a century. Embracing a record of
        individuals and events, chiefly in the early his-
        tory of Bennington, Vt., and its First church. By
        Isaac Jennings... Boston, Gould and Lincoln, 1869.
            xviii, [19]-408 p.   front. (plan) pl.   20 1/2
        cm.

13207 Jennings, James.
    A practical treatise on the history, medical prop-
    erties, and cultivation of tobacco. By James
    Jennings... London, Sherwood, Gilbert and Piper,
    1830.
        vi p., 1 l., 159 p.   2 fold. col. pl. (incl.
    front.)   17 1/2 cm.

13208 Jennings, Louis John, 1836-1893.
    Eighty years of republican government in the
    United States. By Louis J. Jennings. London,
    J. Murray, 1868.
        xv, 288 p.   19 1/2 cm.

13209 Jennings, Paul, b. 1799.
    A colored man's reminiscences of James Madison.
    By Paul Jennings. Brooklyn, G. C. Beadle, 1865.
        vi, [7]-21 p.   front. (facsim.)   30 cm.
    (Half-title: Bladensburg series, no. 2)

13210 Jennings, Samuel Kennedy, 1771-1854.
    An exposition of the late controversy in the
    Methodist Episcopal church; of the true objects
    of the parties concerned therein, and of the
    proceedings by which reformers were expelled,
    in Baltimore, Cincinnati, and other places; or,
    A review of the Methodist magazine and quarterly
    review, on petitions and memorials. By Samuel
    K. Jennings, M. D. To which are appended, re-
    marks on an article, entitled Asbury's life, which
    appeared in the Methodist magazine, &c. for January,
    1831. By a layman. Baltimore, J. J. Harrod, 1831.
        viii, [5]-247 p.   23 cm.

13211 [Jenyns, Soame] 1704-1787.
    The objections to the taxation of our American
    colonies, by the legislature of Great Britain,
    briefly consider'd. London, Printed for J. Wilkie,
    1765.
        20 p.   21 cm.

13212 Jermon, J   Wagner.
    Abram Lincoln and South Carolina. By J. Wagner
    Jermon, esq. Philadelphia, D. E. Thompson, printer,
    1861.
        15 p.   21 1/2 cm.

13213   Jerningham, Edward, 1737-1812.
      The fall of Mexico, a poem.   By Mr. Jerningham.
London, J. Robson, 1775.
      2 p.l., 59 p.   26 1/2 cm.
      "The Venetian marriage": p. [51]-59.

13214   Jerome, Chauncey.
      History of the American clock business for the
past sixty years, and life of Chauncey Jerome,
written by himself.   Barnum's connection with the
Yankee clock business.   New Haven, F. C. Dayton, jr.,
1860.
      8, [11]-144 p.   front. (port.)   18 1/2 cm.
      ---Index on Chauncey Jerome's autobiography, com-
piled by Lockwood Barr.   Pelham Manor, N. Y., 1947.
      8 l.   20 1/2 cm.

13215   Jervis, John Bloomfield, 1795-1885.
      Description of the Croton aqueduct; by John B.
Jervis, chief engineer.   New-York, Slamm and
Guion, 1842.
      31 p.   21 1/2 cm.

13216   [Jervis, John Bloomfield] 1795-1885.
      Letters addressed to the friends of freedom and
the Union, by "Hampden" [pseud.]   Originally pub.
in the New York "Evening post".   New-York, W. C.
Bryant & co., printers, 1856.
      20 p.   22 1/2 cm.

13217   Jewell, Frederick Swartz, 1821-1903.
      School government: a practical treatise, pre-
senting a thorough discussion of its facts, principles and their applications; with critiques upon
current theories of punishment, and schemes of
administration.   For the use of normal schools,
practical teachers, and parents.   By Frederick S.
Jewell... New York, A. S Barnes & co., 1866.
      viii, [9]-308 p.   19 cm.

13218   Jewell, Wilson, 1800-1867.
      Historical sketches of quarantine.   Address,
delivered before the Philadelphia County medical
society, January 28, 1857... by Wilson Jewell, M. D.
on the close of his official term as president...
Philadelphia, T. K. and P. G. Collins, printers,
1857.
      32 p.   23 1/2 cm.

13219 Jewett, Charles, 1807-1879.
         Speeches, poems, and miscellaneous writings, on
         subjects connected with temperance and the liquor
         traffic. By Charles Jewett, M. D. Boston, J. P.
         Jewett, 1849.
         200 p.   front. (port.)   illus.   19 1/2 cm.

13220 [Jewett, Charles Coffin] 1816-1868.
         The close of the late rebellion, in Rhode-Island.
         An extract from a letter by a Massachusetts man
         resident in Providence. 2d ed. Providence, B.
         Cranston & co., 1842.
         16 p.   23 cm.

13221 Jewett, Charles Coffin, 1816-1868.
         ... Notices of public libraries in the United
         States of America. By Charles C. Jewett... Printed
         by order of Congress as an appendix to the Fourth
         annual report of the Board of regents of the
         Smithsonian institution. Washington, Printed for
         the House of representatives, 1851.
         1 p.l., 207 p.   23 cm.   (Smithsonian reports)
         Added t.p.: Appendix to the Report of the Board
         of regents of the Smithsonian institution... Wash-
         ington, Printed for the Senate, 1850. (31st Cong.,
         1st sess. Senate. Miscellaneous, no. 120)

13222 Jewett, Isaac Appleton, 1808-1853.
         Memorial of Samuel Appleton, of Ipswich, Massa-
         chusetts; with genealogical notices of some of his
         descendants. Comp. by Isaac Appleton Jewett.
         Boston, 1850.
         vi, [7]-183 p.   front., 2 pl. (1 fold.)
         fold. geneal. tab.   26 cm.

13223 Jewett, John L
         Franklin—his genius, life, and character. An
         oration delivered before the New York typographical
         society, on the occasion of the birthday of Franklin,
         at the printers' festival, held January 17, 1849.
         By John L. Jewett... New York, Harper & brothers, 1849.
         37 p.   23 1/2 cm.

13224 Jewett, Paul.
         The New-England farrier: or, A compendium of
         earriery[!] in four parts: wherein most of the
         diseases to which horses, neat cattle, sheep and
         swine are incident, are treated of; with medical

and surgical observations thereon. The remedies,
in general, are such as are easily procured, safely
applied, and happily successful; being the result of
many years experience—and first production of the
kind in New-England. Intended for the use of private gentlemen and farmers. By Paul Jewett...
Newburyport, Printed By William Barrett, at his
Printing-Office Merrimack-Street, 1795.
46 p.   17 cm.

13225   Jewitt, Llewellynn Frederick William, 1816-1886.
Grave-mounds and their contents: a manual of
archaeology, as exemplified in the burials of
Celtic, the Romano-British, and the Anglo-Saxon
periods. By Llewellynn Jewitt... London, Groom-
bridge & sons, 1870.
xxiv, 306 p.   front., illus.   19 1/2 cm.

13226   Jex-Blake, Sophia, 1840-1912.
A visit to some American schools and colleges.
By Sophia Jex Blake. London, Macmillian and co.,
1867.
xii, 250 p.   19 1/2 cm.

13227   Jogues, Isaac, 1607-1646.
Narrative of a captivity among the Mohawk
Indians, and a description of New Netherland in
1642-3, by Father Isaac Jogues... With a memoir
of the holy missionary, by John Gilmary Shea...
New York, Press of the Historical society, 1856.
69 p.   23 cm.
"Captivity and death of Rene Goupil. By Father
Isaac Jogues": p. 61-67.

13228   Johnes, Arthur James, 1809-1871.
Philological proofs of the original unity and
recent origin of the human race. Derived from a
comparison of the languages of Asia, Europe,
Africa, and America. Being an inquiry how far the
differences in the languages of the globe are
referrible to causes now in operation. By Arthur
James Johnes... London, S. Clarke, 1843.
1 p.l., [v]-ix, 172, 103, [1] p. incl. tables.
21 cm.

13229   Johnson, A[lexander] B[ryan] 1786-1867.
The advanced value of gold, suspended specie
payments, legal-tender notes, taxation and national

debt, investigated impartially: by A. B. Johnson.
Utica, N. Y., Curtiss & White, printers, 1862.
   32 p.   22 cm.

13230   Johnson, Andrew, pres. U. S., 1808-1875, defendant.
     The great impeachment and trial of Andrew Johnson,
president of the United States. With the whole of
the preliminary proceedings in the House of representatives, and in the Senate of the United States.
Together with the eleven articles of impeachment,
and the whole of the proceedings in the court of
impeachment, with the verbatim evidence of all the
witnesses, and cross-examinations of them, with
speeches of the managers and the counsel on both
sides, with the decisions of Chief Justice Chase,
and the verdict of the court. With portraits of
Andrew Johnson; Chief Justice Chase, and verdict
of the court. With portraits of Andrew Johnson;
Chief Justice Chase; General U. S. Grant; Hon.
Edwin M. Stanton; Hon. Benjamin F. Wade; Hon.
Benjamin F. Butler; Hon. Thaddeus Stevens; Major-
Gen. Lorenzo Thomas. Philadelphia, T. B. Peterson
& brothers [c1868]
   1 p.l., 11-289 p.   ports.   24 cm.

13231   Johnson, Andrew, pres. U. S., 1808-1875.
     Speech of Hon. Andrew Johnson, of Tennessee,
on the proposed expulsion of **Mr.** Bright; delivered
in the Senate of the United States, January 31, 1862.
Washington, Printed at the Congressional globe
office, 1862.
   15 p.   23 cm.

13232   Johnson, Andrew, pres. U. S., 1808-1875.
     Speeches of Andrew Johnson, president of the
United States. With a biographical introduction by
Frank Moore. Boston, Little, Brown, and company,
1865.
   xlviii, 494 p.   front. (port.)   20 cm.

13233   Johnson, Charles Britten, 1788?-1835.
     Letters from the British settlement in Pennsylvania.
To which are added, the constitutions of the United
States, and of Pennsylvania; and extracts from the
laws respecting aliens and naturalized citizens.
By C. B. Johnson, M. D. Philadelphia, Published
by H. Hall, 209 Chestnut street, and in London,
by John Miller, 1819.

xii, [25]-192 p.   2 fold. maps (incl. front.)
15 1/2 cm.
Published by authority of the British emigrant
society, Susquehanna Co., Pa. cf. Pref.
"Remarks on Birkbeck's letters": p. 128-147.
Attributed to Dr. Rose. cf. Rich. Bibl. amer.
nova, v. 2, p. 119.

13234   Johnson, Cuthbert William, 1799-1878.
The farmer's encyclopedia, and dictionary
of rural affairs; embracing all the most recent
discoveries in agricultural chemistry. Adapted to
the comprehension of unscientific readers... By
Cuthbert W. Johnson... Adapted to the United States
by Gouverneur Emerson. Philadelphia, Carey and
Hart, 1844.
vii, 1165 p.   front., illus., 16 pl.   24 1/2 cm.

13235   Johnson, Edwin F[erry] 1803-1872.
The navigation of the lakes and navigable
communications therefrom to the seaboard, and to
the Mississippi River, and relation of the former
to the lines of railway leading to the Pacific.
By Edwin F. Johnson... Hartford, Case, Lockwood
& company, 1866.
48 p.   23 cm.

13236   Johnson, Edwin Ferry, 1803-1872.
Railroad to the Pacific. Northern route. Its
general character, relative merits, etc. By Edwin
F. Johnson, C. E. 2d ed. New York, Railroad
journal job printing office, 1854.
iv, [5]-166 (i. e. 176) p.   front. (fold. diagr.)
plates, 3 maps (2 fold.)   22 1/2 cm.

13237   Johnson, Ezra R
Emancipation oration, by Dr. Ezra R. Johnson, and
poem, by James M. Whitfield, delivered at Platt's
hall, January 1, 1867, in honor of the fourth
anniversary of President Lincoln's proclamation of
emancipation. 1864. San Francisco, Elevator
office, 1867.
32 p.   28 cm.

13238   Johnson, Frederick H
Guide to Niagara falls and its scenery, including
all the points of interest both on the American and

Canadian side. Geology and recession of the falls,
by Sir Charles Lyell... By F. H. Johnson...
[Buffalo, 1868]
   80 p.   front., plates.   15 cm.

13239   Johnson, Herrick, 1832-1913.
        "God's ways unsearchable." A discourse, on the
        death of President Lincoln, preached before the
        Third Presbyterian congregation, in Mozart hall,
        Pittsburgh, Pa. Sunday, April 23d, 1865. By Rev.
        Herrick Johnson... Pittsburgh, W. G. Johnston & co.,
        printers [1865]
           11 p.   21 1/2 cm.

13240   Johnson, James, 1777-1845.
        The influence of tropical climates on European
        constitutions: being a treatise on the principal
        diseases incidental to Europeans in the East and
        West Indies, Mediterranean, and coast of Africa.
        By James Johnson... From the 3d London ed.,
        greatly enl. New-York, E. Duyckinck, G. Long
        [etc., etc.] 1826.
           vii, [9]-416 p.   22 cm.

13241   Johnson, James, 1780-1811, defendant.
        Murders. Report of the trial of James Johnson,
        a black man, for the murder of Lewis Robinson, a
        black man, on the 23d of October last. Also, the
        trial of John Sinclair, a German, aged seventy-
        seven years, for the murder of David Hill, on the
        eighth day of April last. Had before His Honour,
        Chief Justice Kent, the Hon. Jacob Radcliff, mayor,
        and the Hon. Josiah Ogden Hoffman, recorder of the
        city of New-York, on Wednesday, the 19th, and
        Thursday, the 20th December, 1810. Published
        from the short hand notes of William Sampson...
        New-York, Printed and published by Southwick and
        Pelsue, no. 3, New-street, 1811.
           30 p.   22 cm.

13242   Johnson, John Barent, 1769-1803.
        Eulogy on General George Washington. A sermon,
        delivered February 22d, 1800, in the North Dutch
        church, Albany, before the Legislature of the
        state of New-York, at their request: by John B.
        Johnson, one of the chaplains of the house of

assembly... Albany, Printed by L. Andrews,
printer to the state, 1800.
   3 p.l., [5]-22 p.   20 cm.

13243   Johnson, John Barent, 1769-1803.
        A farewell sermon, delivered September 26th,
        1802, in the North Dutch church, Albany. By John
        B. Johnson... Albany, Printed by Charles R. and George
        Webster, 1802.
           96 p.   20 1/2 cm.

13244   Johnson, John Barent, 1769-1803.
        An oration on union, delivered in the New
        Dutch church in the city of New-York, on the
        twelfth of May, 1794. The anniversary of the
        Tammany society, or Columbian order, by John
        B. Johnson... New-York, Printed by J. Buel, 1794.
           24 p.   22 1/2 cm.

13245   [Johnson, John Graver] 1841-1917.
        A criticism of Mr. Wm. B. Reed's aspersions on
        the character of Dr. Benjamin Rush, with an
        incidental consideration of General Joseph Reed's
        character. By a member of the Philadelphia bar...
        Philadelphia, Collins, printer, 1867.
           61 p.   25 cm.

13246   Johnson, Joseph, 1776-1862.
        Traditions and reminiscences, chiefly of the
        American revolution in the South: including
        biographical sketches, incidents and anecdotes...
        By Joseph Johnson... Charleston, S. C., Walker
        & James, 1851.
           viii, 592 p.   fold. pl., fold. maps, facsims.
        23 1/2 cm.

13247   Johnson, Lorenzo Dow, 1805-1867.
        Chaplains of the general government, with
        objections to their employment considered. Also,
        a list of all the chaplains to Congress, in the
        army and in the navy, from the formation of
        the government to this time. By Lorenzo D. John-
        son... New-York, Sheldon, Blakeman & co., 1856.
           iv, [5]-82 p.   19 cm.

13248   Johnson, Lorenzo Dow, 1805-1867.
        The churches and pastors of Washington, D. C.;
        together with five hundred topics of sermons,

delivered in 1855 and '6. To which is added, a
list of all the church edifices, and their
localities. By Lorenzo D. Johnson... New York,
M. W. Dodd, 1857.
1 p.l., vii-x p., 1 l., 13-171 p.   18 cm.

13249   Johnson, Lorenzo Dow, 1805-1867.
Martha Washingtonianism; or, A history of the
ladies' temperance benevolent societies... By
Lorenzo D. Johnson. New York, Saxton & Miles;
Boston, Saxton, Peirce & co., 1843.
88 p.   15 1/2 cm.

13250   Johnson, Lorenzo Dow, 1805-1867.
Memoir of Mrs. Thomazin Johnson, of Braintree,
Mass., with an account of her pious lineage, from
John Alden, the first pilgrim father who placed
foot on Plymouth rock. By her son L. D. Johnson.
Boston, J. Loring, 1835.
117 p.   15 cm.

13251   Johnson, Lorenzo Dow, 1805-1867.
The spirit of Roger Williams, with a portrait
of one of his descendants... By Lorenzo D. Johnson.
Boston, Pub. for the author, by Cassady and March,
1839.
vi, [7]-94 p.   front. (port.)   16 1/2 cm.

13252   Johnson, Louisa.
Every lady her own flower gardener. By Louisa
Johnson. Containing simple and practical directions
for cultivating plants and flowers, in the northern
and southern states. Also Flora's revealings, and
hints for the management of flowers in rooms, &c.,
with brief botanical descriptions of plants and
flowers; the whole in plain and simple language,
expressly calculated for popular use. New Haven,
S. Babcock, 1842.
vii, [9]-142 p.   16 cm.

13253   Johnson, Reverdy, 1796-1876.
An argument to establish the illegality of
military commissions in the United States, and
especially of the one organized for the trial of
the parties charged with conspiring to assassinate
the late President, and others, presented to that
commission, on Monday, the 19th of June, 1865, and

prepared by Reverdy Johnson; one of the counsel of
Mrs. Surratt. Baltimore, Printed by J. Murphy &
co., 1865.
31 p.   23 cm.

13254 [Johnson, Reverdy] 1796-1876.
The dangerous condition of the country, the
causes which have lead to it, and the duty of
the people. By a Marylander. Baltimore, The
Sun book and job printing establishment, 1867.
24 p.   22 1/2 cm.

13255 [Johnson, Reverdy] 1796-1876.
A further consideration of the dangerous
condition of the country, the causes which
have led to it, and the duty of the people.
By a Marylander. Baltimore, The Sun printing
establishment, 1867.
21 p.   22 1/2 cm.
Continuation of pamphlet entitled: The dangerous condition of the country.

13256 Johnson, Reverdy, 1796-1876.
The memorial of Reverdy Johnson, of the city
of Baltimore, to the legislature of Maryland:
with an appendix. Baltimore, Printed by J.
Murphy, 1840.
20, 46 p.   22 cm.
A reply to attacks made upon the author concerning the affairs of the Bank of Maryland.

13257 Johnson, Robert Gibbon, 1771-1850.
An historical account of the first settlement
of Salem, in West Jersey, by John Fenwick, esq.,
chief proprietor of the same; with many of the
important events that have occured, down to the
present generation, embracing a period of one
hundred and fifty years. By R. G. Johnson.
Philadelphia, O. Rogers, 1839.
173 p.   15 cm.

13258 [Johnson, Samuel] 1709-1784.
Political tracts. Containing, The false alarm.
Falkland's islands. The patriot; and, Taxation no
tyranny... London, Printed for W. Strahan, and
T. Cadell, 1776.
2 p.l., 264 p.   22 1/2 cm.

13259 [Johnson, Samuel] 1709-1784.
Thoughts on the late transactions respecting
Falkland's islands. London, Printed for T. Cadell,
1771.
2 p.l., 75 p. 20 cm.
[Miscellaneous pamphlets, v. 230, no. 1]

13260 Johnson, Samuel, 1322-1882.
The crisis of freedom. A sermon, preached at the
Free church, in Lynn, on Sunday, June 11, 1854. By
Samuel Johnson. Pub. by request of the society.
Boston, Crosby, Nichols & co., 1854.
21 p. 23 1/2 cm.

13261 Johnson, Samuel Roosevelt, 1802-1873.
California: a sermon preached in St. John's
church, Brooklyn, N. Y. on Sunday, February 11,
1849. By Samuel Roosevelt Johnson... New York,
Stanford and Swords, 1849.
19, [1] p. 22 1/2 cm.

13262 Johnson, Samuel Roosevelt, 1802-1873.
A memorial discourse on the life, character and
services of General Jeremiah Johnson, of Brooklyn,
the first president of the St. Nicholas society of
Nassau island, by Samuel Roosevelt Johnson... a
chaplain of the society. Delivered before the
society in Brooklyn, October 20, 1853. Brooklyn,
I. Van Anden's press, 1854.
34 p. front. (port.) 23 cm.

13263 Johnson, Walter Rogers, 1794-1852.
The coal trade of British America, with researches
on the characters and practical values of American
and foreign coals. By Walter R. Johnson...
Washington, Taylor & Maury [etc., etc.] 1850.
179 p. tables (1 fold.) diagrs. 22 1/2 cm.

13264 Johnson, Walter Rogers, 1794-1852.
... A report to the Navy department of the United
States, on American coals applicable to steam
navigation, and to other purposes. By Walter R.
Johnson. Wahington, Printed by Gales and Seaton,
1844.
xii, 607 p. III fold. pl. 25 cm. ([U. S.]
28th Cong., 1st sess. Senate. [Doc. no.] 386)
Appended are letters from the author on the
subject of further experiments on iron, copper, and

coal. [28th Cong., 2d sess. Senate. [Doc. no.] 1, p. 639-644)

Bound with this is a review of Prof. Johnson's report on American coals, extracted from the American journal of science, vol. XLIX, and reprinted with title "A report to the Navy department... on American coals," New Haven, 1845.

13265 Johnson, William, 1771-1834.

Nugae gĕōrgĭcae; an essay, delivered to the Literary and philosophical society of Charleston, South-Carolina, October 14, 1815. By the Honorable William Johnson... Charleston, S. C., Printed for the Society by J. Hoff, No. 117, Broad-street, 1815.

40 p.   25 cm.   [With Elliott, Stephen. An address to the Literary and philosophical society of South-Carolina. Charleston, 1814]

13266 [Johnson, William] 1771-1834.

Remarks, critical and histrical, on an article in the forty-seventh number of the North American review, relating to Count Pulaski. Addressed to the readers of the North American review, by the author of the Sketches of the life of Greene. Charleston, Printed by C. C. Sebring, 1825.

37 p.   front. (port.)   21 cm.

13267 Johnson, William Cost, 1806-1860.

Speech of Mr. Wm. Cost Johnson, of Maryland, on the bill to appropriate the proceeds of the sales of the public lands, and to grant pre-emption rights. Delivered in the House... June 25 and 29, 1841. Washington, Printed at the National intelligencer office, 1841.

22 p.   23 cm.

13268 Johnson, William Cost, 1806-1860.

Speech of William Cost Johnson, of Maryland, on the subject of the rejection of petitions for the abolition of slavery; with supplemental remarks, in reply to certain charges against General Harrison. Delivered in the House of representatives, January 25, 27, and 28, 1840. Washington, Printed by Gales and Seaton, 1840.

63 p.   23 1/2 cm.

13269 Johnson, William D

Lincoln university; or, The nation's first pledge

of emancipation. By William D. Johnson...
Philadelphia, For the author, 1867.
   32 p. incl. front.   23 cm.

13270 Johnson, William Melanchthon, 1834-1910.
       Our martyred President. A discourse on the death
of President Lincoln, preached in Stillwater, N. Y.,
April 16th, 1865, by Rev. William M. Johnson...
Troy, N. Y., Daily and weekly times printing house,
1865.
   14 p.   22 cm.

13271 Johnston, Elias Schellhammer, 1834-1926.
       Sermon delivered on Thursday, June 1st, 1865,
the day of special humiliation and prayer in
consequence of the assassination of Abraham Lincoln;
at the Second English Evangelical Lutheran church,
Harrisburg, Pa. By Rev. E. S. Johnston.
[Harrisburg] T. F. Scheffer, printer, 1865.
   cover-title.   11p.   22 1/2 cm.

13272 Johnston, James.
       A history of the haunted caverns of Magdelama,
an Indian queen of South America, with her likeness.
Written by Dr. James Johnston. During a captivity
of three years, being taken up as a spy... With
the rise and progress of the Indian tribes, and
that of the white inhabitants of South America...
Philadelphia, J. Sharon, 1821.
   206 p.   front.   19 1/2 x 11 cm.

13273 [Johnston, James F   ]
       The suspending power and the writ of haboas
corpus. Philadelphia, J. Campbell, 1862.
   48 p.   23 1/2 cm.

13274 Johnston, James Finlay Weir, 1796-1855.
       Report on the agricultural capabilities of the
province of New Brunswick, by J. F. W. Johnston...
By authority... Fredericton, J. Simpson, printer,
1850.
   1 p.l., 262 p. incl. tables.   2 fold. maps.
23 cm.

13275 Johnston, John, 1778-1855.
       The autobiography and ministerial life of the
Rev. John Johnston, D. D. Edited and compiled
by the Rev. James Carnahan... New York, M. W.

Dodd, 1856.
viii, [9]-225 p.   pl., 2 port. (incl. front.)
19 cm.

13276   Johnston, Josiah Stoddard, 1784-1833.
Letter of Mr. Johnston, of Louisiana, to the
secretary of the Treasury, in reply to his circular
of the 1st July, 1830, relative to the culture of
the sugar cane. Washington, Printed by Gales &
Seaton, 1831.
21 p.   23 cm.

13277   Johnston, Samuel Burr.
Letters written during a residence of three years
in Chili, containing an account of the most
remarkable events in the revolutionary struggles
of that province. With an interesting account
of the loss of a Chilian ship, and brig of war,
by mutiny, and the consequent imprisonment and
sufferings of several citizens of the United
States, for six months, in the dungeons of Callao.
By Samuel B. Johnston... Erie, Pa., R. I. Custis,
1816.
2 p.l., [13]-205 p.   20 cm.

13278   Johnston, William, 1804-1892.
An address on the life and public services of
Hon. Edwin M. Stanton. By William Johnston, of
the Cincinnati bar. Delivered in Pike's music
hall, Cincinnati, January 7, 1870. Pub. by
request. Cincinnati, R. W. Carroll & co., 1870.
16 p.   25 cm.

13279   Johnstone, Walter.
Travels in Prince Edward island, gulf of St.
Lawrence, North-America, in the years 1820-21.
Undertaken with a design to establish Sabbath
schools, and investigate the religious state of
the country... By Walter Johnstone...
Edinburgh, D. Brown [etc., etc.] 1823.
132 p.   front. (fold. map)   18 1/2 cm.

13280   Jollivet, Adolphe, 1799-1848.
Documents américains, annexion du Texas,
émancipation des noirs, politique de
l'Angleterre; par M. Jollivet... Paris, Imprimerie
de Bruneau, 1845.
40 p.   22 1/2 cm.

13281   Joly de Saint Valier,
        Histoire raisonnée des opérations militaires et
        politiques de la dernière guerre, suivie
        d'observations sur la révolution qui est arrivée
        dans les moeurs & sur celle qui est sur le point
        d'arriver dans la constitution d'Angleterre, par
        m. Joly de St. Valier... Liège, 1783.
        xii, 235, [1] p.   22 1/2 cm.

13282   [Jomard, Edme Francois] 1777-1862.
        Note sur les Botecudos, accompagnée d'un
        vocabulaire de leur langue et de quelques remarques.
        [Paris, Impr. de L. Martinet, 1846]
        1 p.l., 13 p.   22 cm.
        With a note on the Cheyenne Indian language, and
        some miscellaneous notes.
        "Extrait du Bulletin de la Société de geographie.
        (Novembre et décembre, 1846)"

13283   Jones, Abner Dumont, 1807-1872.
        Illinois and the West; with a township map,
        containing the latest surveys and improvements.
        By A. D. Jones. Boston, Weeks, Jordan and company;
        Philadelphia, W. Marshall and company, 1838.
        1 p.l., [vii]-xi, [13]-255, [1] p.   front. (fold.
        map)   15 1/2 cm.

13284   [Jones, Absalom]
        A narrative of the proceedings of the black
        people, during the late awful calamity in
        Philadelphia, in the year 1793: and a refutation
        of some censures, thrown upon them in some late
        publications. By A. J. and R. A. Philadelphia,
        Printed for the authors, by William W. Woodward,
        at Franklin's head, no. 41, Chestnut-street, 1794.
        28 p.   18 1/2 cm.

13285   Jones, Alexander, 1802-1863.
        Cuba in 1851; containing authentic statistics of
        the population, agriculture and commerce of the
        island for a series of years, with official and
        other documents in relation to the revolutionary
        movements of 1850 and 1851. By Alexander Jones.
        New York, Stringer & Townsend, 1851.
        vi, [7]-80 p. incl. 2 maps.   14 cm.

13286   Jones, Alexander, 1802-1863.
        The Cymry of '76; or, Welshmen and their

descendants of the American revolution. An address
with an appendix, containing notes, sketches, and
nomenclature of the Cymbri; by Alexander Jones...
To which is added a letter on eminent Welshmen.
By Samuel Jenkins, esq. and a brief sketch of St.
David's benevolent society. New York, Sheldon,
Lamport & co., 1855.
  2 p.l., iii, [5]-132 p.   22 cm.

13287   Jones, Alexander, 1802-1863.
  Historical sketch of the electric telegraph:
including its rise and progress in the United
States. By Alexander Jones... New York, G. P.
Putnam, 1852.
  xiii, [3]-194 p.   illus.   22 1/2 cm.

13288   Jones, Arthur T
  A horse story, by an old gray horse, continued
by Arthur T. Jones, including a narrative of all
the proceedings in the case of the impeachment
of John Orser, high sheriff of the city and county
of New-York, with the decision of the governor of
the state thereon, and the trial and conviction
of deputy sheriff, Thomas Carlin, for a misdemeanor; with the arguments and speeches of
counsel, and all of the correspondence connected
therewith, from November, 1854, to January, 1856...
New-York, G. F. Nesbitt & co., printers, 1856.
  cover-title, 5 p.l., [3]-337 p.   illus.
22 1/2 cm.
  Relates to a horse said to have been stolen
from John Collins, jr., of New Rochelle, owned
by Arthur T. Jones, of New York.

13289   Jones, Cave, 1769-1829.
  A solemn appeal to the church: being a plain
statement of facts in the matters pending between
Dr. Hobart with others. and the author. By the
Rev. Cave Jones, A. M., one of the assistant
ministers of Trinity church, New-York. Together
with an appendix, containing a statement of the
case of the Rev. Mr. Feltus: under his own hand...
New-York, Printed for the author, 1811.
  2 p.l., 104 p.   22 cm.
  "Appendix. A brief statment of the persecutions
and maltreatment experienced by the Rev. Henry J.
Feltus": p. [89]-104.

13290   Jones, Charles Colcock, jr., 1831-1893.
        Monumental remains of Georgia: by Charles C.
        Jones, jr. Part first. Savannah, J. M. Cooper
        and company, 1861.
        119 p.   fold. pl.   25 cm.

13291   Jones, Charles Colcock, jr., 1831-1893.
        Reminiscences of the last days, death and burial
        of General Henry Lee. By Charles C. Jones, jr.
        Albany, N. Y., J. Munsell, 1870.
        43 p.   front. (port.)   23 1/2 cm.

13292   Jones, Charles Colcock, 1804-1863.
        Suggestions on the religious instruction of the
        negroes in the Southern states; together with an
        appendix containing forms of church registers,
        form of a constitution, and plans of different
        denominations of Christians. By Charles Colcock
        Jones, D. D. Philadelphia, Presbyterian board
        of publication, 1847.
        56 p.   23 cm.

13293   Jones, Charles L   S
        American lyrics; comprising The discovery, a
        poem; Sapphic, Pindaric and common ides; songs
        and tales on American and patriotic subjects.
        And also imitations from the Greek, Latin, French
        and Spanish. By Charles L. S. Jones. Mobile,
        [Ala.] Printed by Pollard & Dade, 1834.
        vi, [17]-306 p.   18 cm.

13294   Jones, Charles Lee.
        Supplemental memorial of Charles Lee Jones, in
        reply to the counter-memorial from Jalapa, in
        Mexico, under the signature of certain of the
        volunteers there in garrison, in relation to
        Capt. George W. Hughes, there exercising the
        command of a colonel. Washington, 1848.
        13 p.   22 cm.

13295   Jones, David, 1736-1820.
        Defensive war in a just cause sinless. A
        sermon, preached on the day of the continental
        fast, at Tredyffryn, in Chester County, by the
        Rev. David Jones... Philadelphia, Printed by
        Henry Miller. 1775.
        27 p.   20 1/2 cm.

13296   Jones, David, 1736-1820.
       A journal of two visits made to some nations of
Indians on the west side of the river Ohio, in
the years 1772 and 1773. By the Rev. David Jones...
With a biographical notice of the author, by
Horatio Gates Jones... New York, Reprinted for J.
Sabin, 1865.
       xi p., 1 l., [vii]-ix, 127 p.   22 cm.   (Half-
title: Sabin's reprints. no. II)

13297   Jones, Electa Fidelia, b. 1806.
       Stockbridge, past and present; or, Records of an
old mission station. By Miss Electa F. Jones.
Springfield [Mass.]   S. Bowles & company, 1854.
       275 p.   20 cm.
       "Biographical sketches": P. 255-267.

13298   Jones, George, 1810-1879.
       The history of ancient America, anterior to the
time of Columbus; proving the identity of the
aborigines with the Tyrians and Israelites; and
the introduction of Christianity into the western
hemisphere by the apostle St. Thomas. By George
Jones... [v. 1] The Tyrian æra. London, Longman
Brown, Green, and Longmans; New york, Harper and
brothers [etc., etc.] 1843.
       10 p.1., 461, [1] p.   front. (port.)   25 cm.

13299   Jones, George, 1810-1879.
       Oration on the national independence, Richmond, Va.,
July 4, 1840, before the Franklin society, at the
city-hall. Written and pronounced by George Jones,
tragedian... Richmond, Published at the request of
the Franklin society, by Smith & Palmer, 1840.
       43 pp.   21 cm.

13300   Jones, Horatio Gates, 1822-1893.
       The Levering family; or, A genealogical account
of Wigard Levering and Gerhard Levering, two of
the pioneer settlers of Roxborough township,
Philadelphia county... and their descendants; and
an appendix, containing brief sketches of Roxborough
and Manayunk, by Horatio Gates Jones... Philadelphia,
Printed for the author, by King & Baird, 1858.
       x, 193 p.   front., plates, ports., facsims.
24 cm.

13301   Jones, Hugh, 1669-1760.
       The present state of Virginia. By Hugh Jones,

A. M. New York, Reprinted for J. Sabin, 1865.
4 p.l., viii, 151 p.   22 cm.   (Half-title:
Sabin's reprints, no. 5)

13302 Jones, James.
Practical forms of writs, processes, &c., selected
from the most approved precedents and adapted to the
laws of the state of Illinois now in force; and
with little variation, will apply to those of the
neighboring states and territories with explanatory
notes and references, intended for the use of
judges of probate, clerks of courts, sheriffs,
coroners... and which will be essentially useful
to gentlemen of the bar and private citizens:
together with a variety of useful precedents in
conveyancing; such as deeds for land, deeds of
trust, mortgages, leases, bills of sale, powers
of attorney, &c., to which is added an appendix,
comprising the duties of a justice of the peace,
arising under the laws of the United States; the
mining regulations; with forms of proceedings in
cases of naturalization, military pensions,
fugitives from justice, &c. By James Jones.
Galena, The author, 1830.
164 p., 1 l., 52, 10 p.   18 1/2 cm.

13303 [Jones, James Athearn] 1791-1854.
A letter to an English gentleman, on the libels
and calumnies on America by British writers and
reviewers. Philadelphia, H. C. Carey & I. Lea,
1826.
43 p.   21 cm.

13304 Jones, John, 1729-1791.
Plain concise practical remarks, on the treatment of wounds and fractures; to which is added,
a short appendix on camp and military hospitals:
principally designed for the use of young
military surgeons, in North-America. By John
Jones, M. D., Professor of surgery in King's
college, New York. New-York, Printed by John
Holt, in Water-street, near the Coffee-house,
1775.
1 p.l., 3, viii, 92 p., 1 l.   21 1/2 cm.
Published in 1795 under title: The surgical
works of the late John Jones.

13305   Jones, John G
        A concise history of the introduction of
        Protestantism into Mississippi and the Southwest.
        By Rev. John G. Jones... St. Louis, P. M.
        Pinckard, 1866.
            x, [11]-257 p.   19 1/2 cm.

13306   Jones, John Matthew.
            The naturalist in Bermuda; a sketch of the
        geology, zoology, and botany of that remarkable
        group of islands; together with meteorological
        observations. By John Matthew Jones...
        Assisted by Major J. W. Wedderburn... and J. L.
        Hurdis... London, Reeves & Turner, 1859.
            vi p., 1 l., [vii]-xii, 200 p.   front. (fold.
        map)   illus.   29 1/2 cm.

13307   Jones, Joseph, 1833-1896.
            First report to the Cotton planters' convention
        of Georgia, on the agricultural resources of
        Georgia, by Joseph Jones... Augusta, Ga., Chronicle
        & sentinel, 1860.
            xv, 312 p., 1 l., [4] p., 1 l.   fold. tab.
        23 cm.

13308   Jones, Joseph Seawell, 1811?-1855.
            A defence of the revolutionary history of the
        state of North Carolina from the aspersions of
        Mr. Jefferson. By Jo. Seawell Jones... Boston,
        C. Bowen; Raleigh, Turner and Hughes, 1834.
            xii, 343 p.   18 cm.

13309   Jones, Joseph Seawell, 1811?-1855.
            Memorials of North Carolina. By J. Seawell
        Jones... New-York [Printed by Scatcherd & Adams]
        1838.
            87 p.   23 1/2 cm.

13310   Jones, Lot, d. 1865.
            Memoir of Mrs. Sarah Louisa Taylor; or, An
        illustration of the work of the Holy Spirit,
        in awakening, renewing, and sanctifying the heart.
        By Lot Jones... New York, J. S. Taylor; Boston,
        Weeks, Jordan, and co. [etc., etc.] 1838.
            3 p.l., [v]-xii, [13]-324 p.   front. (port.)
        19 1/2 cm.

13311 [Jones, Morris Charles] 1819-1893.
       Notes respecting the family of Waldo.
       [Edinburgh, Printed by Ballantyne and company,
       1863]
           iv, 35 p.   22 1/2 cm.

13312 Jones, Peter, Chippewa chief, 1802-1856.
           A collection of Chippeway and English hymns, for
       the use of the native Indians. Translated by Peter
       Jones... To which are added a few hymns translated
       by the Rev. James Evans and George Henry... New
       York, Pub. by Lane and Tippett, for the Missionary
       society of the M. E. church, 1847.
           vi, 289 p.   13 cm.
       English and Chippewa on opposite pages.
       "A selection of hymns from the translations
       of the Rev. James Evans and George Henry":
       P. [235]-285.

13313 Jones, Peter, Chippewa chief, 1802-1856.
           History of the Ojebway Indians; with especial
       reference to their conversion to Christianity.
       By Rev. Peter Jones, (Kahkewaquonaby,) Indian
       missionary. With a brief memoir of the writer;
       and introductory notice by the Rev. G. Osborn...
       London, A. W. Bennett [186-?]
           vi p., 1 l., 278 p.   front., pl., port.
       19 cm.
           Second issue. First published in 1861. cf.
       Sabin, Bibl. amer.

13314 Jones, Peter, Chippewa chief, 1802-1856.
           Life and journals of Kah-ke-wa-quo-nã-by: (Rev.
       Peter Jones,) Wesleyan missionary. Published under
       the direction of the Missionary committee, Canada
       conference. Toronto, A. Green, 1860.
           xi, 424 p.   front. (port.)   19 1/2 cm.

13315 Jones, Samuel.
           Pittsburgh in the year eighteen hundred and
       twenty-six, containing sketches topographical,
       historical and statistical; together with a
       Directory of the city... Embellished with an
       engraving of the Episcopal church. By S. Jones.
       Pittsburgh, Printed by Johnston & Stockton, 1826.
           152, [2] p.   front.   18 cm.
           Earlier directories of Pittsburgh appeared in
       1815 and 1820.

13316   Jones, Samuel W
        Memoir of the Hon. James Duane, judge of the
        District court of the U. States for New York. By
        Hon. Samuel W. Jones. [Schenectady] Keyser, printer,
        1852.
        51 p.   22 cm.

13317   Jones, Thomas Laurens, 1819-1887.
        Impeachment of the President. Speech of Hon.
        Thomas Laurens Jones of Kentucky, delivered in
        the House... February 24, 1868. Washington, F & J.
        Rives & G. A. Bailey, printers, 1868.
        8 p.   23 cm.

13318   Jones, Thomas Laurens, 1819-1887.
        Reply of Hon. Thos. L. Jones to Governor Stevenson,
        of Kentucky. Washington, D. C., McGill & Witherow,
        printers [1870]
        cover-title, [3]-40 p.   24 cm.
        Controversy concerning the recommendation to
        President Johnson that Stephen Gano Burbridge be
        appointed commissioner of internal revenue of the
        U. S.

13319   Jones, Uriah James, 1818-1864.
        History of the early settlement of the Juniata
        valley: embracing an account of the early poineers,
        and trials and privations incident to the settle-
        ment of the valley, predatory incursions, massacres,
        and abductions by the Indians during the French and
        Indian wars, and the war of the revolution, &c. By
        U. J. Jones. Philadelphia, H. B. Ashmead, 1856.
        380 p.   front., plates.   23 cm.

13320   Jones, Walter, 1777-1861.
        The case of the battalion stated, with an exposition
        of the grounds upon which Chas. Lee Jones, esq.,
        expected to have had the command of the battalion
        (consisting of three companies raised by himself in
        the District of Columbia, and two to be raised in
        Maryland) conferred upon him, as of right and jus-
        tice due both to him and to the officers and men
        who had volunteered to serve under his command as
        lieutenant colonel: by Walter Jones. Washington,
        Printed by J. & G. S. Gideon, 1847.
        32 p.   23 cm.

13321   See entry on p. 439.

400

13322　Jones, William, 1760-1831.
　　　　　　Remarks on the proposed breakwater at Cape
　　　　Henlopen. Communicated, by request of the secre-
　　　　tary of the Treasury, by William Jones... To which
　　　　are added, the report of the Board of engineers,
　　　　and Captain Bainbridge of the navy; the memorial of
　　　　the Chamber of commerce of Philadelphia, &c. &c.
　　　　Philadelphia, Printed by order of the Chamber of
　　　　commerce of Philadelphia, 1825.
　　　　　　31 p. incl. 2 diagr.　　21 1/2 cm.

13323　Jones, William Alfred, 1817-1900.
　　　　　　Long island. By W. Alfred Jones... Read before
　　　　the Long Island historical society, November 5,
　　　　1863. New York, Baker & Godwin, printers, 1863.
　　　　　　23 p.　　23 cm.

13324　[Jones, William Alfred] 1817-1900.
　　　　　　Memorial of the late Honorable David S. Jones.
　　　　With an appendix, containing notices of the Jones
　　　　family, of Queen's county. New York, Stanford and
　　　　Swords, 1849.
　　　　　　iv, [5]-99 p.　　19 cm.

13325　Jones, William D
　　　　　　Mirror of modern democracy: a history of the
　　　　Democratic party, from its organization in 1825, to
　　　　its last great achievement, the rebellion of 1861.
　　　　To which is prefixed a sketch of the old Federal
　　　　and Republican parties. By William D. Jones. New-
　　　　York, N. C. Miller, 1864.
　　　　　　xii, [13]-270 p., 1 l.　　20 cm.

13326　Jordan, Cornelia Jane (Matthews) 1830-1898.
　　　　　　Richmond: her glory and her graves. A poem.
　　　　In two parts. By Cornelia J. M. Jordan. 1866...
　　　　Richmond, Va., Richmond medical journal print., 1867.
　　　　　　xxxix p.　　22 cm.
　　　　　　Contains other poems.

13327　Jordan, Gibbes Walker.
　　　　　　The claims of the British West India colonists to
　　　　the right of obtaining necessary supplies from
　　　　America, and of employing the necessary means of
　　　　effectually obtaining those supplies under a limited
　　　　and duly regulated intercourse, stated and vindicated
　　　　in answer to Lord Sheffield's Strictures. By G. W.

Jordan, esq., F. R. S., colonial agent for
Barbados. London, Printed for T. Cadell and
W. Davies, 1804.
2 p.l., 119 p.   21 1/2 cm.

13328   Jordan, John, fl. 1826.
Serious actual dangers of foreigners and foreign
commerce, in the Mexican states: useful information
to all travellers in that country, and expecially to
the merchants of the United States; and equally
important to the cabinets of Washington and London,
and to the congress of Tacubaya. By John Jordan...
Philadelphia, Printed by P. M. Lafourcade, 1826.
iv, [5]-52 p.   21 cm.
Relates to the expulsion of Orazio de Attelis
Santangelo from Mexico.

13329   Jordan, Samuel.
The restorer of the union of the United States
to its original purity, and an explanation of the
errors which brought about destruction of life,
liberty and property, and the remedy therefor.
By Samuel Jordan of Abbeville District, South
Carolina. Augusta, Ga., 1866.
v, [7]-171 p.   22 cm.

13330   Joseph, pseud.
New-York aristocracy; or, Gems of japonica-dom.
By "Joseph"... New-York, C. B. Norton; Philadelphia,
W. P. Hazard [etc., etc.] 1851.
152 p.   front., 12 pl.   18 cm.

13331   Joseph, Henry, d. 1834, defendant.
The trial of Henry Joseph and Amos Otis, for
the murder of James Crosby, captain of the brig
Juniper, on the high seas. In the Circuit court
of the United States, district of Massachusetts,
holden at Boston, October term, 1834. Boston,
Light & Horton, 1834.
44 p.   24 1/2 cm.

13332   Josephus, Flavius.
The works of Flavius Josephus... to which are
added, three dissertations, concerning Jesus
Christ, John the Baptist, James the Just, God's
command to Abraham, etc. with an index to the
whole. Tr. by W. Whiston... London, J.

Richardson and co. [etc.] 1822.
4 v.   front (port.) fold. map.   22 cm.

13333   Journal de l'expédition sur le fleuve Saint-Laurent,
        contenant un rapport détaillé des mouvements de la
        flotte et de l'armée anglaises, depuis le moment
        de son embarquement, à Louisbourg, jusqu'à la
        reddition de Québec, en 1759. Extrait du New-
        York Mercury, no. 385, daté de New-York, 31 décembre
        1759. [Québec, Des presses du Journal de Québec, 1855]
        16 p.   20 cm.

13334   Journal de tout ce qui s'est passé à la prise des
        forts de Bocachica, et au siege de Cartagene aux
        Indes Occidentales. Tiré des relations envoyées à
        Sa Majesté par la viceroi de Santa Fé, don Sebastien
        de Eslaba & apportées par don Pedro de Mur, son
        adjutant général. Imprimé à Madrid par ordre de Sa
        Majesté. [n.p.] 1741.
        1 p.l., 14 p.   20 cm.
        Translation of Diario de todo lo occurrido en la
        expugnacion de los fuertes de Bocachica... 1741.

13335   Journal d'un voyage sur les costes d'Afrique et aux
        Indes d'Espagne, avec une description particulière
        de la riviere de la Plata, de Buenosayres, & autres
        lieux; commencé en 1702, & fini en 1706. Amsterdam,
        P. Marret, 1723.
        1 p.l., 372 p.   fold. map.   17 cm.

13336   A journal of an excursion made by the corps of cadets,
        of the American literary, scientific and military
        academy, under Capt. Alden Partridge. June, 1822.
        Concord [N. H.] Printed by Hill and Moore, 1822.
        38 p.   pl.   20 cm.
        The route of the excursion was from Norwich, Vt.,
        to Concord, N. H., by way of Enfield and Salisbury,
        returning through Hopkinton, Hillsborough and Newport.

13337   Journal of an excursion to the United States and
        Canada in the year 1834: with hints to emigrants;
        and a fair and impartial exposition of the advantages
        and disadvantages attending emigration. By a citizen
        of Edinburgh. Edinburgh, J. Anderson, jun., 1835.
        viii, 168 p.   16 cm.
        Relates chiefly to the state of New York.

13338   The Journal of law. Conducted by an association of
        members of the bar... v. 1; July 7, 1830-June 22,
        1831. Philadelphia, S. C. Atkinson, 1833.
           1 p.l., 384 p.   22 cm.
           No more published?

13339   Journal of the expedition to La Guira and Porto
        Cavallos in the West-Indies, under the command of
        Commodore Knowles. In a letter from an officer on
        board the Burford to his friend at London. London,
        Printed for J. Robinson, 1744.
           63 p.   19 1/2 cm.
           Miscellaneous pamphlets, v. 763, no. 51.

13340   Journal of the proceedings of a convention of
        literary and scientific gentlemen, held in the
        Common council chamber of the city of New York,
        October, 1830. New York, J. Leavitt and G. & C. & H.
        Carvill, 1831.
           286 p., 1 l.   26 cm.
           "A meeting of literrary and scientific gentlemen...
        invited by a committee on behalf of the University
        of the city of New York, to confer on the general
        interests of letters and liberal education."—Pref.

13341   [Joy, Benjamin]
           A true statement of facts, in reply to a pamphlet
        lately published by Messrs. Charles Barrell, Henry
        F. Barrell, George Barrell, and Samuel B. Barrell.
        Boston, Printed by J. Eliot, 1816.
           17 p.   23 cm.
           Concerns the settlement of the estate of Mr. Joseph
        Barrell.

13342   Juarros, Domingo, 1752-1820.
           A statistical and commercial history of the kingdom
        of Guatemala, in Spanish America: containing impor-
        tant particulars relative to its productions, manu-
        factures, customs, &c. &c. &c. With an account of
        its conquest by the Spaniards, and a narrative of
        the principal events down to the present time:
        from original records in the archives; actual
        observation; and other authentic sources. By Don
        Domingo Juarros... Translated by J. Baily... London,
        J. Hearne, 1823.
           viii, 520 p.   2 maps (1 fold.)   22 cm.
           Title of Spanish original, "Compendio de la historia
        de la ciudad de Guatemala".

13343   Judd, David Wright, 1838-1888.
        The story of the Thirty-third N. Y. S. vols: or
Two years campaigning in Virginia and Maryland. By
David W. Judd... Illustrations from drawings by
Lieut. L. C. Mix. Rochester, Benton & Andrews, 1864.
        iv, 349, 76 p. incl. illus., pl.   front.
19 1/2 cm.
        With appendix containing biographies of the
officers, general orders, roster, etc.

13344   Judd, Sylvester, 1813-1853.
        A moral review of the revolutionary war, or some
of the evils of that event considered. A discourse
delivered at the Unitarian church, Augusta, Sabbath
evening, March 13th, 1842. With an introductory
address, and notes. By Rev. Sylvester Judd...
Hallowell [Me.] Glazier, Masters & Smith, printers,
1842.
        48 p.   22 1/2 cm.

13345   Judd, Thomas.
        An essay on the improvement in the manufacture of
sugar, adapted for Louisiana. By Thomas Judd. Boston,
Tuttle, Weeks & Dennett, printers, 1836.
        36 p.   illus.   19 cm.

13346   Judd, William, d. 1804.
        William Judd's address to the people of the state
of Connecticut, on the subject of the removal of
himself and four other justices from office, by
the General assembly of said state, at their late
October session, for declaring and publishing their
opinion that the people of this state are at present
without a constitution of civil government... [New
Haven] Printed for the General committee of
Republicans, from Sidney's press, 1804.
        23, [1] p.   22 1/2 cm.

13347   Judson, Levi Carroll.
        A biography of the signers of the Declaration of
independence, and of Washington and Patrick Henry.
With an appendix, containing the Constitution of
the United States and other documents. By L.
Carroll Judson... Philadelphia. J. Dobson, and
Thomas, Cowperthwait & co., 1839.
        ix, [9]-354 p.   21 cm.

13348 Judson, Levi Carroll.
        The probe, or One hundred and two essays on the
nature of men and things. By L. Carroll Judson...
With an appendix, containing the Declaration of
independence, the Constitution of the United States,
Washington's Farewell address, and a miniature
biography of Washington and the signers. Philadelphia,
G. B. Zieber & co., 1846.
        viii, 9-272, 48 p.   20 1/2 cm.
        Published also under title: The moral probe.

13349 Juglar, Clément, 1819-1905.
        Des crises commerciales et de leur retour
périodique en France, en Angletere et aux États-Unis,
par le d^r Clément Juglar... Paris, Guillaumin et cio,
1862.
        2 p.l., xvi, 258 p. incl. tables.   22 1/2 cm.
        "Ouvrage couronné par l'Institut (Académie des
sciences morales et politiques)"

13350 Julian, Antonio, b. 1722.
        La perla de la America, provincia de Santa Maria,
reconocida, observada y expuesta en discursos
historicos, por el sacerdote don Antonio Julian, á
mayor bien de la Católica monarquia, fomento del
comercio de España, y de todo el Nuevo Reyno de
Granada, é incremento de la Christiana religion
entres les naciones barbaras, que subsisten todavia
rebeldes en la provincia. Madrid, A. de Sancha,
1787.
        1 p.l., xxx, 280 p.   fold. map.   21 cm.

13351 Julian, George Washington, 1817-1899.
        The cause and cure of our national troubles.
Speech of Hon. Geo. W. Julian, of Indiana,
delivered in the House of representatives, Tuesday,
January 14, 1862. Washington, D. C., Scammell &
co., printers, 1862.
        15, [1]p.   24 1/2 cm.

13352 Junius, pseud., author of the "Letters."
        The posthumous works of Junius. To which is
prefixed, an inquiry respecting the author: also,
a Sketch of the life of John Horne Tooke... New-
York, G. C. & H. Carvill, 1829.
        xii, [9]-450 p.   port., 2 fold. facsim.   23 cm.
        The "Sketch of the life of John Horne Tooke" is
from the Memoirs of Alexander Stephens.

13353 Junius, jr., pseud.
The vision of judgment; or, A present of the
Whigs of '76 & '37. In ten parts. By Junius, jr. ...
New-York, H. R. Robinson, 1838.
32 p.   10 pl. (incl. front.)   24 cm.
An attack on the Democratic administration and
Andrew Jackson, with caricatures of the leading
Democrats of the period.

13354 Junkin, David Xavier, 1808-1888.
The Christian statesman: a discourse occasioned
by the death of the Hon. James McDowell, late governor
of Virginia: pronounced in the F street Presbyterian
church, Washington city, Sabbath morning, September
14, 1851. By D. X. Junkin... Washington, J. Nourse;
Philadelphia, Daniels & Smith [1851]
20 p.   22 1/2 cm.

13355 Junkin, David Xavier, 1808-1888.
The oath a divine ordinance, and an element in
the social constitution: its origin, nature, ends
efficacy, lawfulness, obligations, interpretation,
form and abuses. By D. X. Junkin... New York,
Wiley and Putnam, 1845.
x, 223 p.   20 cm.

13356 Junkin, George, 1790-1868.
Political fallacies: an examination of the false
assumptions, and refutation of the sophistical
reasonings, which have brought on this civil war.
By George Junkin... New York, C. Scribner, 1863.
332 p.   front. (port.)   18 1/2 cm.

13357 Junkin, George, 1790-1868.
The vindication, containing a history of the
trial of the Rev. Albert Barnes, by the Second
Presbytery, and by the Synod of Philadelphia.
To which are appended, New schoolism in the
seventeeth compared with new schoolism in the
nineteenth century. By Rev. George Junkin, D. D.
Philadelphia, Printed by W. S. Martien, 1836.
2 p.l., [iii]-xxvi, 159 p.   19 cm.

13358 Jusselain, Armand.
Un déporté à Cayenne; souvenirs de la Guyane,
par Armand Jusselain. Paris, M. Lévy frères, 1865.
2 p.l., 326 p.   18 cm.

13359 Justification de la resistance des colonies
américaines aux oppressions du gouvernement
britannique. Dans une lettre ecrite de la
Hollande à M**** a Londres. Leide, Haak et comp.,
1776.
1 p.l., 30 p.   20 1/2 cm.

K

13360 Keating, William Hypolitus, 1799-1840.
Narrative of an expedition to the source of St.
Peter's river, lake Winnepeek, lake of the Woods,
&c. &c. performed in the year 1823, by order of
the Hon. J. C. Calhoun, secretary of war, under
the command of Stephen H. Long, major, U. S. T. E.
Compiled from the notes of Major Long, Messrs.
Say, Keating, and Colhoun, by William H. Keating...
Philadelphia, H. C. Carey & I. Lea, 1824.
2 v.   fronts., 15 pl. (incl. plan, music)
fold. map, tables.   22 cm.

13361 [Kennedy, Archibald] 1685?-1763.
The importance of gaining and preserving the
friendship of the Indians to the British interest
considered. London, Printed for E. Cave, jun.,
1752.
1 p. l., 46 p.   20 cm.

13362 Kennedy, John Pendleton, 1795-1870.
Memoirs of the life of William Wirt, attorney
general of the United States, by John P. Kennedy...
Philadelphia, Lea and Blanchard, 1849.
2 v.   fronts.   (port., facsim.)   23 cm.

13363 Kentucky. Laws, statutes, etc.
A digest of the statute laws of Kentucky, of
a public and permanent nature, from the commencement of the government to the session of the
legislature, ending on the 24th February, 1834.
With references to judicial decisions... By C. S.
Morehead and Mason Brown... Frankfort, Ky.,
Printed by A. G. Hodges, 1834.
2 v.   25 cm.

13364 [Kippis, Andrew] 1725-1795.
Considerations on the provisional treaty with
America, and the preliminary articles of peace

with France and Spain. London, Printed for T.
Cadell, 1783.
    1 p. l., 164 p.   21 1/2 cm.

13365 Knapp, Samuel Lorenzo, 1783-1838.
    The life of Aaron Burr. New-York, Wiley & Long,
1835.

13366 Knight, Mrs. Sarah (Kemble) 1666-1727.
    The journals of Madam Knight and Rev. Mr.
Buckingham. From the original manuscripts,
written in 1704 & 1710. New York, Wilder &
Campbell, 1825.
    129 p.   19 cm.
    "The private jounals kept by Rev. John ⌊i.e.
Thomas⌋ Buckingham of the expedition against
Canada, in the years 1710 & 1711": p. [71]-
129.

13367 Knight, Mrs. Sarah (Kemble) 1666-1727.
    The private journal of a journey from Boston
to New York in the year 1704. Kept by Madam
Knight. Albany, F. H. Little, 1865.
    xii, [13]-92 p. incl. illus., facsim.
21 1/2 x 17 cm.
    Edited by William Law Learned. cf. Allibone's
Dictionary of authors.
    Originally published under title: The journals
of Madam Knight and the Rev. Mr. Buckingham,
from the original manuscripts written in 1704
and 1710. New York, 1825.

13368 [Knox, William] 1732-1810.
    The claim of the colonies to an exemption from
internal taxes imposed by authority of Parliament,
examined: in a letter from a gentleman in London,
to his friend in America. London, 1765.
    48 p.   21 1/2 cm.

13369 [Knox, William] 1732-1810.
    Extra official state papers. Addressed to the
Right Hon. Lord Rawdon and the other members of
... Parliament, associated for the preservation
of the constitution and promoting the prosperity
of the British empire. By a late under secretary
of state. London, Printed for J. Debrett, 1789.
    2 v. in 1.   22 cm.

13370 [Knox, William] 1732-1810.
  A letter to a member of Parliament, wherein the
power of the British legislature, and the case of
the colonists, are briefly and impartially
considered. London, Printed for W. Flexney, 1765.
  1 p. l., 30 p.   20 cm.

L

13371 Lamar, Mirabeau Buonaparte, 1798-1859.
  Letter of Gen. Mirabeau B. Lamar, ex-president
of Texas, on the subject of annexation, addressed
to several citizens of Macon, Geo. Savannah,
Printed by T. Purse, 1844.
  48 p.   22 cm.

13372 [La Peyrère, Isaac de] 1594-1676.
  Relation dv Groenland. Paris, A. Covrbe, 1647.
  8 p. l., 278, [4] p.   fold. pl., fold. map.
16 cm.

13373 Lathrop, John, 1740-1816.
  Innocent blood crying to God from the streets
of Boston. A sermon occasioned by the horrid
murder of Messieurs Samuel Gray, Samuel Maverick,
James Caldwell, and Crispus Attucks, with Patrick
Carr, since dead, and Christopher Monk, judged
irrecoverable, and several others badly wounded,
by a party of troops under the command of
Captain Preston: on the fifth of March, 1770.
And preached the Lord's-day following: By John
Lathrop... London, Printed. Boston, Re-printed
and sold by Edes and Gill, Opposite the New
Court-House in Queen-Street, 1771.
  iv, [5]-21 p.   18 1/2 cm.

13374 Laurens, Henry, 1724-1792.
  Mr. Laurens's true state of the case. By which
his candor to Mr. Edmund Jenings is manifested,
and the tricks of Mr. Jenings are detected.
[London?] 1783.
  77 p.   25 cm.

13375 Lechford, Thomas, 1590?-1644?
  Plain dealing; or, News from New England, by
Thomas Lechford. With an introduction and notes
by J. Hammond Trumbull. Boston, J. K. Wiggin

& W. P. Lunt, 1867.
xl, 211 p. 21 1/2 cm. (Half-title: Library of New-England history, no. IV)

13376 [Lee, Arthur] 1740-1792.
An appeal to the justice and interests of the people of Great Britain, in the present disputes with America. By an old member of Parliament. 2d ed., cor. London, Printed for J. Almon, 1775.
68 p. 20 cm.
[Hazard pamphlets, v. 43, no. 5]

13377 [Lee, Arthur] 1740-1792.
A second appeal to the justice and interests of the people, on the measures respecting America. By the author of the first... London, Printed for J. Almon, 1775.
90 p. 21 1/2 cm.

13378 [Lee, Arthur] 1740-1792.
A speech intended to have been delivered in the House of Commons, in support of the petition from the general Congress at Philadelphia. By the author of An appeal to the justice and interests of Great Britain. London, Printed for J. Almon, 1775.
2 p.l., 67 p. 21 cm.

13379 [Lee, Charles] 1731-1782.
Strictures on a pamphlet, entitled a "Friendly address to all reasonable Americans, on the subject of our political confusions." Addressed to the people of America... Boston, Re-printed and sold by L. Thomas; sold also by the Booksellers in America, 1775.
12 p. 21 cm.
The pamphlet to which this is a reply is by Thomas Bradbury Chandler. cf. Vance, C. H. Myles Cooper. (Columbia university quarterly, Sept., 1930, vol. XXII, no. 3, p. 275-276)

13380 Lee, Henry, 1787-1837.
The campaign of 1781 in the Carolinas; with remarks, historical and critical, on Johnson's Life of Greene. To which is added an appendix of original documents, relating to the history of the revolution. By H. Lee. Philadelphia, E. Littell, 1824.
1 p.l., 511, xlvii p. 21 cm.

411

13381   Lee, Henry, 1787-1837.
        Observations on the writings of Thomas Jefferson,
        with particular reference to the attack they contain
        on the memory of the late Gen. Henry Lee. In a
        series of letters, by H. Lee. 2d ed., with an
        introduction and notes, by Charles Carter Lee.
        Philadelphia, J. Dobson, [etc., etc.] 1839.
        1 p. l., xix, [5]-262 p.   23 cm.

13382   [Lee, Richard Henry] 1732-1794.
        Observations leading to a fair examination of
        the system of government, proposed by the late
        convention; and to several essential and necessary
        alterations in it. In a number of letters from
        the Federal farmer to the Republican. [New-York]
        Printed in the year 1787.
        40 p.   20 x 12 cm.
        Printed by Thomas Greenleaf. cf. Evans'
        American bibl., v. 7, no. 20454.

13383   [Leigh, Sir Egerton, bart.] 1733-1788?
        Considerations on certain political transactions
        of the province of South Carolina: containing
        a view of the colony legislatures (under the
        description of that of Carolina in particular).
        With observations, shewing their resemblance to
        the British model... London, Printed for T. Cadell,
        1774.
        2 p. l., 83 p.   21 1/2 cm.
        [Miscellaneous pamphlets, v. 630, no. 1]

13384   Lewis, Isaac, 1746-1840.
        The divine mission of Jesus Christ evident
        from his life, and from the nature and tendency
        of his doctrines. A sermon preached at Stamford,
        October 11, 1796. before the consociation of
        the western district in Fairfield county. By
        Isaac Lewis, D. D., pastor of a consociated
        church in Greenwich. New-Haven, Printed by T.
        and S. Green, [1796]
        30 p.   22 1/2 cm.

13385   Lewis, Meriwether, 1774-1809.
        History of the expedition under the command
        of Captains Lewis and Clarke, to the sources of
        the Missouri... Performed during the years 1804,
        1805, 1806, by order of the government of the
        United States. Prepared for the press by Paul

Allen, esq. Rev. and abridged by the omission
of unimportant details, with an introduction
and notes, by Archibald M'Vickar... New York,
Harper & brothers, 1842.
    2 v.   front.   (fold. map) pl., plans.
15 cm.   [Harper's family library. v. 154-155]

13386 The Life, trial, and execution of Captain John Brown,
known as "Old Brown of Ossawatomie," with a full
account of the attempted insurrection at Harper's
Ferry. Compiled from official and authentic sources.
Including Cooke's confession, and all the incidents
of the execution. New York, R. M. DeWitt [C1859]
    108 p.   illus., p.   26 cm.
John Brown was tried in the Circuit Court of
Jefferson County for treason, for conspiring with
slaves to produce insurrection, and for murder.

13387 [Lind, John] 1737-1781.
    An answer to the Declaration of the American
Congress... London, Printed for T. Cadell [etc.]
1776.
    132 p.   20 cm.

13388 [Lind, John] 1737-1781.
    An Englishman's answer, to the address, from the
delegates to the people of Great-Britain, in a
letter to the several colonies, which were
represented in the late Continental congress.
New-York, Printed by James Rivington, 1775.
    26 p.   20 1/2 cm.
    [Hazard pamphlets, v. 38, no. 1]

13389 [Lind, John] 1737-1781.
    A letter to the Right Honourable Willoughby
Bertie, by descent earl of Abingdon... In which
His Lordships candid and liberal treatment of the
now Earl of Mansfield, is fully vindicated...
London, Printed for T. Payne & son [etc.] 1778.
    xii, 86 p.   20 1/2 cm.
An answer to certain passages, reflecting on
the Earl of Mansfield, in the Earl of Abingdon's
Thoughts on Mr. Burke's Letter to the sheriffs
of Bristol.

13390 [Lind, John] 1737-1781.
    Three letters to Dr. Price containing remarks
on his Observations on the nature of civil liberty,

the principles of government, and the justice
and policy of the war with America... By a member
of Lincoln's Inn, F. R. S., F. S. A. London,
Printed for T. Payne [etc.] 1776.
1 p. l., xxii, 163 p.   20 cm.

13391 [Lisle, Samuel] bp., 1683-1749.
A sermon preached before the incorporated Society
for Propagation of the Gospel in Foreign Parts; at
their anniversary meeting in the parish-church of
St. Mary-le-Bow, on Friday February 19, 1747. By
the Right Reverend Father in God, Samuel, lord
bishop of St. Asaph. London, Printed by Edward
Owen and sold by J. Roberts [etc.] 1848.
84 p.   21 1/2 x 17 cm.

13392 [Littell, John Stockton] 1806-1875.
The Clay minstrel; or, National songster... New
York, Greeley & M'Elrath; Philadelphia, Thomas,
Cowperthwait and co., 1844.
288 p.   front.   (port.)   illus.
12 1/2 cm.

13393 Livingston, Edward, 1764-1836.
An answer to Mr. Jefferson's justification of
his conduct in the case of the New Orleans
batture. By Edward Livingston... Philadelphia,
Printed by W. Fry, 1813.
xi, 187 p.   2 fold. plans.   22 cm.

13394 [Livingston, Philip] 1716-1778.
The other side of the question: or, A defence
of the liberties of North-America. In answer to
a late Friendly address to all reasonable
Americans, on the subject of our political confusions. By a citizen. New-York: Printed by
James Rivington, fronting Hanover-Square, 1774.
29, [1] p., l l.   20 cm.
[Hazard pamphlets. v. 44, no. 3]
A reply to Thomas Bradbury Chandler's A friendly
address to all reasonable Americans.

13395 [Lloyd, Charles] 1735-1773.
A true history of a late short administration.
London, Printed for J. Almon, 1766.
22 p.   21 cm.

13396 Locke, E   W
       Three years in camp and hospital. By E. W.
       Locke... Boston, G. D. Russell & co. [°1870]
       ix, [10]-408 p.   19 1/2 cm.

13397 Long, John, Indian trader.
       Voyages chez différentes nations sauvages de
       l'Amérique Septentrionale; renfermant des détails
       curieux sur les mœurs, usages, cérémonies religieuses,
       le système militaire, &c. des Cahnuagas, des Indiens
       des Cinq & Six Nations, Mohawks, Connecedagas,
       Iroquois, &c. des Indiens Chippeways, & autres
       sauvages de divers tribus... avec un état exact
       des postes situés sur le fleuve S. Laurent, le lac
       Ontario, &c., &c. Par J. Long, trafiquant, &
       interprète de langues indiennes; traduits de
       l'anglois, avec des notes & additions intéressantes,
       par J. B. L. J. Billecocq... Paris, Chez Prault
       l'aîné, imprimeur, Fuchs, libraire, II. année de
       l'ère républicaine [1794]
       2 p. l., xxxvi, 320 p.   fold. map.   20 1/2 cm.

13398 Loskiel, George Henry, 1740-1814.
       History of the mission of the United Brethren
       among the Indians in North America... By George
       Henry Loskiel. Tr. from the German by Christian
       Ignatius LaTrobe. London, The Brethren's society
       for the furtherance of the gospel, 1794.
       3 pt. in 1 v.   fold. map.   21 cm.

13399 Lossing, Benson John, 1813-1891.
       The home of Washington; or, Mount Vernon and
       its associations, historical, biographical, and
       pictorial. By Benson J. Lossing. Illustrated
       by numerous engravings chiefly from original
       drawings by the author... Pub. by subscription
       only. Hartford, Conn., A. S. Hale & co.;
       Chicago, Ill., G. W. Rogers [etc., etc.] 1870.
       446 p. incl. front., illus., pl., port.
       22 cm.
       First edition, New York, 1859, published under
       title: Mount Vernon and its associations.

13400 Lossing, Benson J[ohn] 1813-1891.
       The pictorial field-book of the revolution;
       or, Illustrations, by pen and pencil, of the
       history, biography, scenery, relics, and
       traditions of the war for independence. By

                          415

Benson J. Lossing. With eleven hundred engravings
on wood, by Lossing and Barritt, chiefly from
original sketches by the author... New York,
Harper & brothers, 1860.
2 v.   front., illus., ports., maps, facsims.
26 1/2 cm.

13401 Louisiana. Citizens.
Memorial presented by the inhabitants of
Louisiana to the Congress of the United States,
in Senate and House of representatives convened.
Tr. from the French. Sole copy acknowledged to
be conformable to the original. Washington,
[D. C.] Printed by Samuel H. Smith, 1804.
21 p.   22 1/2 cm.
A protest against the territorial form of
government, claiming fitness for statehood.

13402 Louisiana. (District) General assembly.
Representation and petition of the representatives
elected by the freemen of the territory of
Louisiana... Washington, Printed by William
Duane & son, 1805.
30 p.   22 1/2 cm.
Dated at St. Louis, September 29, 1804.

13403 [Louvet de Couvrai, Jean Baptiste] 1760-1797.
Interesting history of the Baron de Lovzinski.
With a relation of the most remarkable occurrences
in the life of the celebrated Count Pulaski,
well known as the champion of American liberty,
and, who bravely fell in its defence before
Savannah, 1779. New-York, Printed by H. C.
Sotuhwick [:], No. 2 Wall-street; for Robert
Moore, Book-seller, Pearl-Street; and R. and J.
Moore, Hudson. 1807.
108 p.   14 1/2 cm.
Published anonymously; also published under title:
Love and patriotism.
Taken from the author's "Les amours du chevalier
de Faublas".
"An epitome of the history of Poland, including
Lithuania; taken from Guthrie's Geographical
grammar": p. [99]-108.

13404 [Lowell, John] 1769-1840.
The impartial inquirer; being a candid examination
of the conduct of the President of the United

States, in execution of the powers vested in him, by the act of Congress of May 1, 1810: to which is added, some reflections upon the invasion of the Spanish territory of West-Florida... By a citizen of Massachusetts. [Boston] Russell & Cutler, printers, 1811.
  96 p.   24 cm.
  Originally published in the Columbian centinel of Boston. cf. Introd. remarks.

13405 [Lowrey, Grosvenor Prter]
  English neutrality. Is the Alabama a British pirate? New York, A. D. F. Randolph, 1863.
  32 p.   23 cm.

13406 [Lunan, John, jr.]
  The Jamaica magistrate's and vestryman's assistant, containing a digest of all the laws of the island alphabetically arranged, from 33 Charles II. [1681] to 8 George IV. [1827] With forms of holding quarter-sessions, coroners' inquests, oaths, warrants, summonses, recognizances, &c., &c. Jamaica, Printed at the office of the St. Jago de la Vega gazette, 1828.
  2 p. l., 319, [1] p., 1 l.   21 cm.

13407 Lyman, Joseph, 1749-1828.
  A sermon, preached before His Excellency James Bowdoin, esq., governour; His Honour Thomas Cushing, esq., lieutenant-governour; the honourable the Council, and the honourable the Senate, and House of representatives, of the commonwealth of Massachusetts, May 30, 1787. being the day of general election. By Rev. Joseph Lyman, pastor of the church in Hatfield. Boston, Printed by Adams and Nourse, printers to the honourable the General court [1787]
  61 p.   20 1/2 cm.
  On cover: Mr. Lyman's election sermon. May 30, 1787.

13408 [Lyttelton, George Lyttelton, 1st baron] 1709-1773.
  Considerations upon the present state of our affairs, at home and abroad. In a letter to a member of parliament from a friend in the country. London, T. Cooper, 1739.
  1 p. l., 65 (i.e. 67), [2] p.   22 cm.

13409   Macaulay, Catharine (Sawbridge) 1731-1791.
        An address to the people of England, Scotland,
        and Ireland, on the present important crisis of
        affairs. By Catharine Macaulay. London, Printed
        by R. Cruttwell, in Bath, for E. and C. Dilly, 1775.
        29 p.   21 1/2 cm.

13410   McKeen, Joseph, 1757-1807.
        Two discourses, delivered at Beverly, on the day
        of the national fast, May 9, 1798. By Joseph
        M'Keen... Salem, Printed by Thomas C. Cushing,
        1798.
        31 p.   21 cm.

13411   Mackenzie, Sir Alexander, 1763-1820.
        Voyages d'Alex.^{dre} Mackenzie, dans l'intérieur
        de l'Amérique Septentrionale, faits en 1789, 1792
        et 1793; le Ier, de Montréal au fort Chipiouyan
        et à la mer Glaciale; le 2.me, du fort
        Chipiouyan jusqu'aux bords de l'océan Pacifique.
        Précédés d'un tableau historique et politique
        sur le commerce des pelleteries, dans le Canada.
        Traduites de l'anglais, par J. Castéra, avec des
        notes et un itinéraire, tirés en partie des
        papiers du vice-amiral Bougainville... Paris,
        Dentu, an X-1802.
        3 v.   front.   (port.)   fold. maps.
        20 1/2 cm.

13412   Mackenzie, William L
        The lives and opinions of Benj'n Franklin
        Butler and Jesse Hoyt. By William L.
        Mackenzie... Boston, Cook & co., 1845.
        152 p.   23 1/2 cm.

13413   McMahon, John Van Lear, 1800-1871.
        An historical view of the government of
        Maryland, from its colonization to the present
        day. By John V. L. McMahon. Baltimore, J.
        Lucas & E. K. Deaver, 1831.
        xvi, 539 p.   22 cm.

13414   MacMahon, T   W
        Cause and contrast: an essay on the American

crisis. By T. W. MacMahon. Richmond, Va., West
& Johnston, 1862.
   xv, 192 p.   22 cm.

13415   Marshall, Humphrey, 1760-1841.
      The history of Kentucky. Including an account
   of the discovery - settlement - progressive
   improvement - political and military events - and
   present state of the country. In two volumes...
   vol. I. By Humphrey Marshall. Frankfort,
   Printed by Henry Gore, 1812.
      5, [1], 2, 407 p.   pl.   21 1/2 cm.
      "Of this first edition, vol. I. only was printed."
      - Sabin. Bibl. amer.

13416   Marshall, John, 1755-1835.
      The life of George Washington, commander in
   chief of the American forces, during the war
   which established the independence of his country,
   and first president of the United States.
   Compiled under the inspection of the Honourable
   Bushrod Washington, from original papers... to
   which is prefixed, an introduction, containing a
   compendious view of the colonies planted by the
   English on the continent of North America, from
   their settlement to the commencement of that war
   which terminated in their independence. By John
   Marshall... Philadelphia, Printed and published
   by C. P. Wayne..... 1804-07.
      5 v.   front.   (port.)   21 1/2 cm.   and
   atlas of 10 fold. maps, 22p.   28 x 23 cm.

13417   Martin, Luther, 1748-1826.
      The genuine information, delivered to the
   legislature of the state of Maryland, relative
   to the proceedings of the general convention,
   lately held at Philadelphia; by Luther Martin,
   esquire, attorney-general of Maryland, and
   one of the delegates in the said convention.
   Together with a letter to the Hon. Thomas C.
   Deye, speaker of the House of delegates, an
   address to the citizens of the United States, and
   some remarks relative to a standing army, and a
   bill of rights... Philadelphia, Printed by
   Eleazer Oswald, 1788.
      viii, 93 p.   19 cm.

13418   Massachusetts (Colony) Provincial congress, Feb.May, 1775.
A narrative, of the excursion and ravages of the King's troops under the command of General Gage, on the nineteenth of April, 1775. Together with despositions taken by order of Congress, to support the truth of it. Published by authority. Massachusetts-Bay: Worcester, Printed by Isaiah Thomas, by order of the Provincial congress [1775] [Boston, 1938]
facsim.: 23 p.   23 1/2 cm.   [Photostat Americana. Second series... Photostated at the Massachusetts historical society. no. 49]
"In Provincial congress, Watertown, May 22d, 1775... [Resolution ordering the printing] Attest. Samuel Freeman, sec'y."—p. [2]
The original was the first book printed in Worcester. cf. Church, v. 5, no. 1122.

13419   Mather, Increase.
Remarkable providences illustrative of the earlier days of American colonisation... with introductory preface, by George Offor. London, John Russell Smith, 1856.
xix, 262 p.   front. (port.)   18 1/2 cm.

13420   Mathews, Charles.
The London Mathews; containing an account of this celebrated comedian's trip to America, being an annual lecture on peculiaries, characters, and manners, founded on his own observations and adventures, to which are prefixed several original comic songs, viz., Travellers all, Mrs. Bradish's boarding-house, Opossum up a gum-tree, Militia muster folk, Boston post-office, Ode to General Jackson, Illinois Inventory, the American jester's song, and the Farewell finale... Philadelphia, Morgan & Yeager, 1824.
36 p.   17 cm.

13421   [Mauduit, Israel] 1708-1787.
Remarks upon Gen. Howe's account of his proceedings on Long island, in the extraordinary Gazette of October 10, 1776. London, Printed for Fielding and Walker, 1778.
2 p.l., 54 p.   21 cm.
"The London gazette extraordinary [Octo er 10, 1776"]: p. 35-54.

13422 Mauduit, Israel, 1708-1787.
A short view of the history of the colony of
Massachusetts Bay, with respect to their charters
and constitution. By Israel Mauduit. The 3d ed.,
to which is now added the original charter granted
to that province in the 4th of Charles I. and never
before printed in England. London, J. Wilkie, 1774.
1 p.l., 5-93 p.   21 1/2 cm.

13423 Mellen, John, 1722-1807.
A sermon preached at the west parish in Lancaster,
October 9, 1760. on the general thanksgiving for the
reduction of Montreal and total conquest of Canada.
Containing a brief account of the war, from the
year 1755;—and a review of the first settlement
and several expeditions against (with some of the
reasons for holding) Canada. By John Mellen, pastor
of the second church in Lancaster... Boston, Printed
and sold by B. Mecom [1760]
46 p.l., l.l.   19 1/2 cm.

13424 Mendell, Sarah.
Notes on travel and life. By two young ladies,
Misses Mendel and Hosmer. New-York, Published for
the authors, 1854.
288 p.   21 cm.

13425 [Meredith, Sir William bart.] d. 1790.
Historical remarks on the taxation of free states,
in a series of letters to a friend... London, 1778.
1 p.l., 82 p.   24 x 18 1/2 cm.

13426 Meyen, Franz Julius Ferdinand, 1804-1840.
Outlines of the geography of plants: with
particular enquiries concerning the native country,
the culture, and the uses of the principal cultivated
plants on which the prosperity of nations is based.
By F. J. F. Meyen... Tr. by Margaret Johnston.
London, Printed for the Ray society, 1846.
3 p.l., [v]-x, 422 p.   fold. diagr.   22 cm.
(Added t.p.: The Ray society. [Publications...)
Added t.-p.: Grundriss der pflanzengeographie...
Berlin, Haude und Spener, 1836.

13427 Midgley, R   L
Sights in Boston and suburbs, or Guide to the
stranger. By R. L. Midgley. Illustrated by

Billings, Hill, Barry, and John Andrew. Boston
and Cambridge, James Munroe and company, 1857.
   2 p.l., 2, 5, 225 p.   front., illus., maps
(I fold.) plans (1 fold.)   17 1/2 cm.
   Added t.-p., illus., has title: Boston sights,
and stranger's guide.
   Published later under title: Boston sights: or,
Handbook for visitors.

13428   Miertsching, Johann August.
   Reise tagebuch des missionars John. Aug. Miertsching,
welcher als dolmetscher die Nordpol-expedition
zur aufsuchung Sir John Franklins auf dem schiff
Investigator begleitete. In den jahren 1850 bis
1854. Mit einer charte. Gnadau, Im verlag der
Unitäts-buchhandlung bei H. L. Menz; Leipzig, E.
Kummer, 1855.
   x p., 1 l., 196 p.   II tables, 1 fold. map.
21 1/2 cm.

13429   Milburn, William Henry, 1823-1903.
   Ten years of preacher-life: chapters from an
autobiography. By William Henry Milburn... New
York, Derby & Jackson, 1859.
   x, [2], 13-363 p.   front.   (port.)   19 cm.

13430   Mill, Nicholas.
   The history of Mexico, from the Spanish conquest
to the present æra: containing a condensed and
connected general view of the manners, customs,
religion, commerce, soil, and agriculture -
animal, vegetable, and mineral productions - a
concise political and statistical review of the
changes effected in that country, with its present
form of government, &c. &c. - Also, observations,
speculative and practical, as to the best means of
working the Mexican mines, by a combination of
British talent, capital, and machinery. By
Nicholas Mill... London, Sherwood, Jones and co.,
1824.
   1 p. l., [v]-xii, 300 p.   front.   (fold. map)
22 cm.

13431   Miller, J   R
   The history of Great Britain from the death of
George II to the coronation of George IV.
Designed as a continuation of Hume and Smollett.

By J. R. Miller. Philadelphia, M'Carty & Davis, 1835.
   2 p. l., [iii]-ix, [11]-724 p.   front.   (port.) 23 1/2 cm.

13432   Miller, John, 1666-1724.
   A description of the province and city of New York; with plans of the city and several forts as they existed in the year 1695. By John Miller. A new ed. with an introduction and... notes. By John Gilmary Shea... New York, W. Gowans, 1862.
   127 p. incl. plans.   25 cm.   (Added t.-p.: Gowans' bibliotheca americana. 3)
   Reprint of original London edition of 1843.

13433   Miller, Samuel, 1769-1850.
   An essay on the warrant, nature, and duties of the office of the ruling elder, in the Presbyterian church. By Samuel Miller... Philadelphia, Presbyterian board of publication, [c1832]
   339 p.   15 1/2 cm.

13434   Miller, Stephen Franks, 1810?-1867.
   The bench and bar of Georgia: memoirs and sketches. With an appendix, containing a court roll from 1790 to 1857, etc., by Stephen F. Miller... Philadelphia, J. B. Lippincott & co., 1858.
   2 v.   23 cm.

13435   [Milnor, William, jr.] 1769-1848.
   An authentic historical memoir of the Schuylkill fishing company of the state in Schuylkill. From its establishment on that romantic stream, near Philadelphia, in the year 1732, to the present time. By a member... Philadelphia, J. Dobson, 1830.
   viii, 127 p.   front., 2 port.   23 1/2 cm.

13436   Miner, T   B
   The American bee keeper's manual; being a practical treatise on the history and domestic economy of the honey-bee, embracing a full illustration of the whole subject, with the most approved methods of managing this insect through every branch of its culture, the result of many years' experience. By T. B. Miner. Embellished by thirty-five beautiful engravings. New York,

C. M. Saxton, 1849.
iv, [5]-349 p.   front., illus.   19 cm.

13437 [Mines, John Flavel] 1835-1891.
The heroes of the last lustre. A poem... New
York, D. Dana, jr., 1858.
135 p.   18 1/2 cm.

13438 Minnesota (Ter.) Constitutional convention 1857.
The debates and proceedings of the Minnesota
Constitutional convention including the organic
act of the territory. With the enabling act of
Congress, the act of the territorial legislature
relative to the convention, and the vote of the
people on the constitution. Reported officially
by Francis H. Smith. Saint Paul, E. S. Goodrich,
territorial printer, 1857.
xix p., 1 l., 685 p.   23 1/2 cm.

13439 Minor, John D., et al., plaintiffs.
The Bible in the public schools. Arguments in
the case of John D. Minor et al. versus the Board of
of Education of the City of Cincinnati et al.
Superior Court of Cincinnati. With the opinions
and decision of the court. Cincinnati, R. Clarke,
1870.
420 p.   24 cm.

13440 Minturn, Robert Bowne, 1836-1889.
From New York to Delhi, by way of Rio de Janeiro,
Australia and China. By Robert B Minturn, jr.   2d
ed. New York, London, D. Appleton & co., 1858.
xi, [1], [13]-488 p.   front.   (fold. map)
20 1/2 cm.
" 'Tazu ba tazu, now ba now.'; Persian song of
the nach girls" (with music): p.[485]-488.

13441 Mirabeau, [Honoré Gabriel Riquetti] comte de, 1749-
1791.
Mémoires biographiques, littéraires et politiques
de Mirbeau, écrits par lui-même, par son père, son
oncle et son fils adoptif... Paris, A. Auffray
[etc.] 1834-35.
8 v.   fronts.   (ports., t. 6-8)   fold.
facsims.   20 cm.
Preface signed by Mirabeau's adopted son, Lucas-
Montigny.

13442   Mirick, Benjamin L
         The history of Haverhill, Massachusetts. By B.
         L. Mirick... Haverhill, A. W. Thayer, 1832.
         227 p.   fold. front.   21 cm.
         Probably written in large part by J. G. Whittier,
         who turned his manuscript over to Mirick.

13443   [Mitchell, Donald Grant] 1822-1908.
         Wet days at Edgewood: with old farmers, old
         gardeners, and old pastorals. By the author of
         "My farm of Edgewood". New York, C. Scribner,
         1865.
         vii, 324 p.   illus.   19 1/2 cm.

13444   Moodie, Susanna (Strickland) 1803-1885.
         Roughing it in the bush; or, Life in Canada.
         New York, George P. Putnam, 1852.
         2 v.   illus.   19 cm.

13445   [Munsell, Joel] 1808-1880.
         Cases of personal identity. Albany, J. Munsell,
         1854.
         2 p. l., [3]-102 p.   24 1/2 cm.

                                N

13446   National ship-canal convention, Chicago, 1863.
         Proceedings of the National ship-canal
         convention, held at the city of Chicago, June
         2 and 3, 1863. Chicago, Tribune company's
         book and job printing office, 1863.
         248 p.   21 1/2 cm.

                                O

13447   [Olmsted, Frederic Law] 1822-1903, comp.
         Hospital transports. A memoir of the
         embarkation of the sick and wounded from the
         peninsula of Virginia in the summer of 1862.
         Compiled and published at the request of the
         Sanitary commission. Boston, Ticknor and
         Fields, 1863.
         xiv p., 1 l., [17]-167 p.   18 1/2 cm.

13448   Parker, Thomas V
The Cherokee Indians, with special references to
their relations with the United States Government,
by Thomas V. Parker.   New York, The Grafton press,
1907.
109 p.   20 cm.

13449   Peck, Nathaniel.
Report of Messrs. Peck and Price, who were appointed
at a meeting of the free colored people of Baltimore,
held on the 25th November, 1839, delegates to visit
British Guiana, and the island of Trinidad; for the
purpose of ascertaining the advantages to be derived
by colored people migrating to those places.   Baltimore,
Printed by Woods & Crane; London, Re-printed by
C. Richards, 1840.
25 p.   21 1/2 cm.

13450   The Percy anecdotes, revised edition.   To which is
added, a valuable collection of American anecdotes.
Original and select.   New York, Harper & brothers,
1832.
2 v. in 1.   fronts. (ports.)   24 1/2 cm.
Compiled by Joseph Clinton Robertson and Thomas
Byerley.

13451   Perez, Felipe, 1834–
Jeografia fisica i politica de los Estados Unidos
de Colombia, escrita de orden del gobierno jeneral,
por Felipe Perez...   Bogotá, Imprenta de la Nacion,
1862–63.
2 v.   plates.   21 cm.

13452   Peyton, John Lewis, 1824–1896.
Memoir of William Madison Peyton, of Roanoke,
together with some of his speeches in the House of
delegates of Virginia, and his letters in reference
to secession and the threatened civil war in the
United States, etc., etc.   By John Lewis Peyton...
London, J. Wilson, 1873.
viii, 392 p.   22 cm.

13453   Pfeiffer, Ida (Reyer) 1797–1858.
A lady's second journey round the world: from
London to the cape of Good Hope, Borneo, Java,
Sumatra, Celebes, Ceram, the Moluccas, etc.,

California, Panama, Peru, Ecuador, and the United
States. By Ida Pfeiffer... New York, Harper &
brothers, 1856.
   2 p.l., [vii]-xii, [13]-500 p.   20 cm.

13454 Pfeiffer, Ida (Reyer) 1797-1858.
   A woman's journey round the world, from Vienna
to Brazil, Chile, Tahiti, China, Hindostan, Persia,
and Asia Minor. An unabridged translation from the
German of Ida Pfeiffer. London, Office of the
National Illustrated Library [1850?]
   xii, 338 p.   col. plates.   20 cm.

13455 Philo-Jackson, pseud.
   The presidential election, written for the benefit
of the people of the United States, but particularly
for those of the state of Kentucky; relating, also,
to the constitution of the United States; and to
internal improvements. Sixth series. By Philo-
Jackson. Frankfort, Printed for the author, 1824.
   47 p.   23 cm.

13456 Pickett, Albert James, 1810-1858.
   History of Alabama, and incidentally of Georgia
and Mississippi, from the earliest period. By
Albert James Pickett... Charleston, Walker and
James, 1851.
   2 v.   fronts., plates, maps (1 fold.)   plan.
19 1/2 cm.

13457 Pidgeon, William.
   Traditions of De-Coo-Dah, and antiquarian researches:
comprising extensive explorations, surveys, and
excavations of the wonderful and mysterious earthen
remains of the mound-builders in America; and the
traditions of the last prophet of the Elk Nation
relative to their origin and use; and the evidences
of an ancient population more numerous than the
present aborigines... embellished with seventy
engravings. New York, Published by Horace Thayer,
1858.
   334 p.   fold. front., illus.   23 cm.

13458 Pilsen, John.
   Reply of Lieut.-Col. Pilsen to Emil Schalk's
criticisms of the campaign in the mountain department,
under Maj.-Gen. J. C. Fremont. [New York? 1863?]
   cover-title, 14 p.   21 cm.

13459 Pinckney, Charles, 1758-1824.
Observations on the plan of government submitted
to the Federal convention, in Philadelphia, on the
28th of May, 1787. By Mr. Charles Pinckney, delegate
from the state of South-Carolina. Delivered at
different times in the course of their discussions.
New York, Printed by Francis Childs [1787]
27 p.   19 1/2 cm.

13460 Pitt, William, 1st earl of Chatham, 1708-1778.
Plan offered by the Earl of Chatham, to the House
of lords, entitled, A provisional act, for settling
the troubles in America, and for asserting the
supreme legislative authority and superintending
power of Great Britain over the colonies. Which
was rejected, and not suffered to lie upon the
table. London, Printed for J. Almon, 1775.
14 p.   27 x 23 cm.

13461 Pittman, Philip.
The present state of the European settlements on
the Mississippi; with a geographical description
of that river... By Captain Philip Pittman.
London, Printed for J. Nourse, 1770.
viii, 99 p.   4 fold. maps, 4 fold. plans.
28 x 21 1/2 cm.

13462 A plain state of the argument between Great-Britain and
her colonies. London, Printed for T. Becket, 1775.
19 p.   20 1/2 cm.
"Perhaps by Dr. Johnson." - Sabin, Bibl. amer.,
v. 15, p. 175.

13463 [Preble, William Pitt] 1783-1857.
The decision of the King of the Netherlands
considered in reference to the rights of the United
States, and of the state of Maine. Portland, Printed
by T. Todd, 1831.
35 p.   27 cm.

13464 [Puységur, Antoine Hyacinte Anne de Chastenet]
comte de, 1752-1807.
Detail sur la navigation aux côtes de Saint-
Domingue et dans ses debouquemens. Paris,
Imprimerie royale, 1787.
2 p.l., 81 p.   25 1/2 x 19 cm.
Appended: Détail particulier pour la carte de
la Gonave, ajoutée en 1788 au pilote de l'isle

de Saint-Domingue.   Par m. de Lieudé de Sepmanville.
10 p.

R

13465   Read, Thomas Buchanan, 1822-1872.
        The new pastoral... Philadelphia, Parry &
        M'Millan, 1855.
        252 p.   front.   (port.)   19 cm.

13466   Read, Thomas Buchanan, 1822-1872.
        A summer story, Sheridan's ride and other
        poems. Philadelphia, J. B. Lippincott & co.,
        1865.
        154 p.   20 cm.

13467   [Reichel, Edward H   ] 1820-1877.
        Historical sketch of the church and missions
        of the United brethren, commonly called
        Moravians... Bethlehem, Pa., Printed by J. and
        W. Held, 1848.
        98, [11] p.   17 cm.

13468   Reid, Thomas Mayne, 1818-1883.
        The ocean waifs; a story of adventure on land
        and sea, by Captain Mayne Reid... With illustrations.
        Boston, Ticknor and Fields, 1865.
        v, 366 p.   illus.   19 cm.

13469   Richards, Thomas Addison, 1820-1900.
        The romance of American landscape. By T. Addison
        Richards... illustrated with sixteen engravings
        on steel. New York, Leavitt and Allen [c1854]
        310 p.   front., plates.   23 cm.
        Published also under the title: American
        scenery.

13470   Richmond, James Cook, 1808?-1866.
        Metacomet: a poem, of the North American
        Indians. By James Cook Richmond. 1st American,
        from the London ed.... London, J. Wiley; New York,
        Stanford and Swords, 1851.
        xxiii, [25]-47 p.   17 1/2 cm.
        Canto 1 of an epic poem, written during the
        author's confinement in the McLean asylum for
        the insane at Somerville, Mass.

13471 [Robertson, Rev.   ]
          An enquiry into the methods that are said to
       be now proposed in England to retrieve the sugar
       trade. By the author of the Detection of the state
       and situation of the present sugar planters of
       Barbadoes and the Leward Islands. London, Printed
       for J. Wilford, 1733.
          31 p.   21 cm.

13472 [Robinson, Mrs. Thérèse Albertine Louise (von Jacob)]
       1797-1870.
          Talvi's history of the colonization of America.
       Edited by William Hazlitt... London, T. C. Newby,
       1851.
          2 v.   21 cm.

                            S

13473 Sackville, George Sackville Germain, 1st viscount,
       1716-1785.
          Correspondance du Lord G. Germain avec les
       généraux Clinton, Cornwallis & les amiraux dans
       la station de l'Amérique, avec plusieurs lettres
       interceptées du général Washington, du marquis de
       la Fayette & de m. de Barras, chef d'escadre. Tr.
       de l'anglois sur les originaux publiés par ordre
       de la Chambre des pairs. Berne, La Nouvelle
       société typographique, 1782.
          xvi, 304 p.   fold.   tab.   20 cm.
          Originally published in English in the Parliamentary
       register.

13474 [Sayre, Stephen] 1736-1818.
          The Englishman deceived; a political piece:
       wherein some very important secrets of state are
       briefly recited, and offered to the considerarion
       [!] of the public... London, Printed, New-York,
       re-printed by John Holt, at the Exchange, 1768.
          1 p. l., ii, 40 p.   19 cm.
          [Hazard pamphlets, v. 14, no. 7]

13475 Schomburgk, Sir Robert Hermann, 1804-1865.
          A description of British Guiana, geographical
       and statistical: exhibiting its resources and
       capabilities, together with the present and
       future condition and prospects of the colony.
       By Robert H. Schomburgk, esq. London, Simpkin,

Marshall, and co., 1840.
2 p.l., 155 p.   front.   (fold. map)   21 cm.
[With Hancock, John. Observations on the climate,
soil, and productions of British Guiana... 2d ed.
London, 1840. Copy 2]

13476 Schoolcraft, Henry Rowe, 1793-1864.
Summary narrative of an exploratory expedition
to the sources of the Mississippi River, in 1820:
resumed and completed, by the discovery of its origin
origin in Itasca Lake, in 1832... with appendices,
comprising the original report on the copper mines
of Lake Superior, and observations on the geology
of the lake basins, and the summit of the
Mississippi; together with all the official reports
and scientific papers of both expeditions...
Philadelphia, Lippincott, Grambo, and co., 1855.
xx, 17-596 p.   illus., maps (one fold.),
tables.   24 cm.

13477 [Sheffield, John Baker Holroyd, 1st earl of] 1735-
1821.
Observations on the commerce on the American
states. With an appendix; containing an account
of all rice, indigo, cochineal, tobacco, sugar,
molasses, and rum imported into and exported
from Great-Britain in the last ten years. The
value of all merchandise imported into and
exported from England. The imports and exports
of Philadelphia, New-York, &c. Also, and account
of the shipping employed in America previous the
war. The second edition. London, J. Debrett,
1783.
2 p. l., 122, iv, 9 p., III-XVIII tables
(part fold.)

13478 Sheffield, John Baker Holroyd, 1st earl of, 1735-
1821.
Strictures on the necessity of inviolably
maintaining the navigation and colonial system
of Great Britain. By Lord Sheffield. London,
J. Debrett, 1804.
iv, 65 p.   21 1/2 cm.

13479 [Smith, Sarah Tappan]
History of the establishment and progress of
the Christian religion in the islands of the South
sea; with preliminary notices of the islands and

of their inhabitants... Boston, Tappan & Dennet;
New York, Gould, Newman & Saxton [etc., etc.]
1841.
xxvii, [17]-287 p.   front.   (fold. map)
17 cm.
Ascribed to Sarah Tappan Smith. Cf. Sabin and
Allibone.

13480   Smith, William C
Indiana miscellany: consisting of sketches of
Indian life, the early settlement, customs, and
hardships of the people, and the introduction of
the gospel and of schools. Together with
biographical notices of pioneer Methodist preachers
of the state... Cincinnati, Published by Poe &
Hitchcock, for the author, 1867.
304 p.   20 cm.

13481   Sorenson, Alfred Rasmud.
Early history of Omaha; or, Walks and talks
among the old settlers: a series of sketches
in the shape of a connected narrative of the
events and incidents of early times in Omaha,
together with a brief mention of the most
important events of later years... Illustrated
with numerous engravings, many of them being
from original sketches drawn especially for this
work by Charles S. Huntington. Omaha, Printed
at the office of the Daily Bee, 1879.
248 p.   illus.   23 cm.

13482   Spencer, John W   ,1901-
Reminiscences of pioneer life in the Mississippi
Valley... Published for complimentary distibution,
by his children. Davenport, Griggs, Watson, &
Day, printers, 1872.
73 p.   front.   (port.)   23 cm.

13483   The Spirit of the public journals; or, Beauties of
the American newspapers. 1805. Baltimore,
Printed by G. Dobbin & Murphy.
300 p.   17 cm.
Edited by G. Bourne.

13484   Squier, Ephraim George, 1821-1888.
Notes on Central America; particularly the states
of Honduras and San Salvador: their geography,
topography, climate, population, resources,

productions, etc., etc., and the proposed Honduras inter-oceanic railway. By E. G. Squier... New York, Harper & brothers, 1855.
3 p.l., [v]-xvi, [17]-397 p.   front., illus., plates, fold. maps.   24 cm.

13485   [Squier, Ephraim George] 1821-1888.
Waikna; or, Adventures on the Mosquito shore, by Samuel A. Bard [pseud.]... London, Sampson Low, son, & co., 1855.
366 p.   illus.   21 cm.

13486   Strobel, Philip A
The Salzburgers and their descendants; being the history of a colony of German (Lutheran) protestants, who emigrated to Georgia in 1734, and settled at Ebenezer, twenty-five miles above the city of Savannah... Baltimore, Published by T. Newton Kurtz, 1855.
308 p.   front. (port.)   19 cm.

T

13487   [Taylor, John] 1753-1824.
A definition of parties; or, The political effects of the paper system considered. Philadelphia, Printed by Francis Bailey, no. 116, High-street, 1794.
16 p.   22 cm.
[Duane pamphlets, v. 73, no. 1]
Manuscript note on t.-p.: By Mr. Taylor, of Virginia, formerly senator.

13488   [Taylor, John] 1753-1824.
An enquiry into the principles and tendency of certain public measures. Philadelphia, Printed by T. Dobson, 1794.
iv, 92 p.   23 cm.
On the first Bank of the United States and other financial measures.

13489   Thompson, George, gunner.
Slavery and famine, punishments for sedition; or, An account of New South Wales and of the miserable state of the convicts. With some prelim. remarks by George Dyer. 2d ed. London, J. Ridgway, 1794.
viii, 47, 23 p.   22 cm.

13490 [Thompson, L   ]
     The ethics of American slavery, being a vindication
of the word of God and a pure Christianity in all
ages, from complicity with involuntary servitude;
and a demonstration that American slavery is a crime
in substance and concomitants, by an American citizen.
New York, Ross & Tousey, 1861.
     viii, 146 p.   17 1/2 cm.

13491 [Tucker, Nathaniel]
     The Bermudian. A poem... Williamsburg, Va.,
Printed by Alexander Purdie & John Dixon, 1774.
     4 p.l., 15 p.   22 1/2 x 18 cm.
     [Hazard pamphlets, v. 32, no. 6]

13492 Tudor, William, 1779-1830.
     The life of James Otis, of Massachusetts: containing
also, notices of some contemporary characters and
events, from the year 1760 to 1775. By William
Tudor. Boston, Wells and Lilly, 1823.
     xx, 508 p.   front. (port.) illus., pl., facsim.
22 cm.

13493 Turner, Charles, 1732-1813.
     A sermon preached before His Excellency Thomas
Hutchinson, esq; governor: the honorable His Majesty's
Council, and the honorable House of representatives,
of the province of the Massachusetts-Bay in New-
England, May 26th, 1773. Being the anniversary of
the election of His Majesty's Council for said
province. By Charles Turner, A. M. pastor of the
church in Duxbury. Boston, Printed by Richard
Draper, printer to His Excellency the governor, and
the honorable His Majesty's Council, 1773.
     45 p.   20 1/2 cm.
     [Miscellaneous pamphlets, v. 789, no. 2]

13494 Two papers on the subject of taxing the British colonies
in America. The first entitled, "Some remarks on
the most rational and effectual means that can be
used in the present conjuncture for the future security
and preservation of the trade of Great-Britain, by
protecting and advancing her settlements on the north
continent of America." The other, "A proposal for
establishing by act of Parliament the duties upon
stampt paper and parchment in all the British American
colonies." London, Printed for J. Almon, 1767.
     iv, 5-22 p.   22 cm.

13495 U. S. Dept. of state.
　　　Letter from the secretary of state to Charles C.
Pinckney, esq. in answer to the complaints of the
French minister against the government of the
United States, contained in his notes to the secretary
of state, dated the 27th of October, and 15th of
November, 1796. New York, Printed by Hopkins, Webb
& co., no. 40 Pine street, 1797.
　　　54 p.　　20 1/2 cm.
　　　Signed: Timothy Pickering.
　　　"References in the foregoing letter": p. 54.

13496 U. S. Treasury dept.
　　　Alexander Hamilton's report on the subject of
manufactures, made in his capacity of secretary of
the Treasury, on the fifth of December, 1791.
6th ed.　To which are prefixed, two prefaces by
the editor.　Philadelphia, Printed by W. Brown,
1827.
　　　80 p.　　22 1/2 cm.　　[Miscellaneous pamphlets,
v. 1011, no. 3]
　　　Preface signed: M. C. [i.e. Mathew Carey]

V

13497 [Van Ness, William Peter] 1778-1826.
　　　An examination of the various charges exhibited
against Aaron Burr, esq., vice-president of the
United States; and a development of the characters
and views of his political opponents.　By Aristides
[pseud.] ... New York, Printed by Ward and Gould,
1803.
　　　118 p., 1 l.　　21 cm.
　　　[Duane pamphlets, v. 12, no. 6]
　　　A reply to James Cheetham's "A view of the political
conduct of Aaron Burr," New York, 1802.

13498 [Vaughan, William] 1577-1641.
　　　The golden fleece diuided into three parts, under
which are discouered the errours of religion, the
vices and decayes of the kingdome, and lastly the
wayes to get wealth, and to restore trading so much
complayned of.　Transported from Cambrioll Colchos,
out of the southermost part of the iland, commonly

435

called the Newfovndland, By Orpheus, iunior [pseud.] for the generall and perpeutall good of Great Britaine. London, Printed for Francis Williams, 1626.

 3 pt. in 1.   fold. map.   18 1/2 cm.

An allegory with many interesting references to Vaughan's colony in Newfoundland, and an early map of the island.

The map has title: Insula olim vocata Nova Terra. The island called of olde Newfound Land described by Captaine John Mason an industrious gent: who spent seven yeares in the country.

Latin and English verse interpreted.

13499 A view of the history of Great-Britain, during the administration of Lord North, to the second session of the fifteenth Parliament. In two parts. With statements of the public expenditure of that period... Dublin, Printed by P. Byrne, 1782.

 2 pt. in 1 v.   21 cm.

Part 1 (first published 1781) has title: The history of Lord North's administration, to the dissolution of the thirteenth Parliament of Great-Britain.

13500 Virginia. General assembly, 1799-1800. House of delegates.

Proceedings of the Virginia assembly, on the answers of sundry states to their resolutions, passed in December, 1798. Philadelphia, Printed by James Carey, no. 7, South Front-street, 1800.

 59 p.   21 1/2 cm.

13501 Volney, Constantin François Chasseboeuf, comte de, 1757-1820.

View of the climate and soil of the United States of America: to which are annexed some accounts of Florida, the French colony on the Scioto, certain Canadian colonies, and the savages or natives: tr. from the French of C. F. Volney... London, J. Johnson, 1804.

 xxiv, [iii]-vi, 503, [1] p.   fold. plates, fold. maps.   23 1/2 cm.

13502   Wafer, Lionel, 1660?-1705?
        A new voyage & description of the isthmus of
America, by Lionel Wafer... with Wafer's secret
report (1698) and Davis's expedition to the gold
mines (1704) edited, with introduction, notes and
appendices, by L. E. Elliott Joyce. Oxford,
Printed for the Hakluyt society, 1934.
        lxxi, 221, [1] p.   front. (fold. facsim.)
fold. plates, fold. maps.   22 1/2 cm. (Half-
title: Works issued by the Hakluyt society...
Second series, no. 73)
        First published in 1699.
        Bibliography: p. [203]-206.

13503   [Walker, Fowler]
        The case of Mr. John Gordon, with respect to the
title to certain lands in East Florida, purchased
of His Catholick Majesty's subjects by him and Mr.
Jesse Fish, for themselves and others His Britannick
Majesty's subjects; in conformity to the twentieth
article of the last definitive treaty of peace.
With an appendix. London, Printed in the year 1772.
        32, [42] p.   map.   24 x 19 cm.
        "Appendix. J. M. J. St. Augustine, in the year
1763. Acts and records relative to the property of
a landed estate called Palica, belonging to Francisco
Chrisostomo, a native and inhabitant of this town":
42 p. at end.

13504   Walker, Timothy, b. 1753.
        Two letters addressed to General William Hull on
his conduct as a soldier, in the surrender of Fort
Detroit, to General Brock, without resistance, in
the commencement of the late war with Great Britain.
By Timothy Walker, of Hopkinton, Mass. Boston,
Printed for T. Walker, 1821.
        12 p.   19 cm.

13505   [Walpole, Horatio Walpole, baron] 1678-1757.
        The convention vindicated from the misrepresenta-
tions of the enemies of our peace. London, J. Roberts,
1739.
        1 p.l., 5-29 p.   20 cm.

Referring to the convention between Great Britain
and Spain, concluded at the Pardo, January 14, 1739.

13506   [Webster, Noah]   1758-1843.
    An address to the citizens of Connecticut.
[New Haven]   J. Walter, printer   [1803]
    24 p.   21 cm.
Signed: Chatham.

13507   [West, Beckwith]
    Experience of a Confederate States prisoner,
being an ephemeris regularly kept by an officer of
the Confederate States army.   Richmond, West &
Johnston, 1862.
    64 p.   21 1/2 cm.
The diary extends from May 30 to August 1, 1802.

13508   [Wharton, Samuel]   1732-1800.
    Plain facts: being an examination into the rights
of the Indian nations of America, to their respective
countries; and a vindication of the grant, from the
Six united nations of Indians, to the proprietors of
Indiana, against the decision of the legislature of
Virginia; together with authentic documents, proving
that the territory, westward of the Allegany mountain,
never belonged to Virginia, &c.   Philadelphia,
Printed and sold by R. Aitken, bookseller, in Market-
street three doors above the coffee-house, 1781.
    164 p., 1 l.   20 1/2 cm.
[Wolcott pamphlets, v. 3, no. 1]

13509   [Whately, Thomas]   d. 1772.
    The regulations lately made concerning the colonies,
and the taxes imposed upon them, considered.   London,
Printed for J. Wilkie, 1765.
    114 p.   21 cm.
Authorship revealed in a letter written by Thomas
Whately to John Temple, 14 Aug. 1766.   Cf. Massachusetts Hist. Soc.   Collections, 6th ser., v. 9,
1897, p. 77.
    Erroneously attributed to George Grenville, John
Campbell, and John Dickinson.   Cf. Sabin, Cushing,
and Halkett & Laing.

13510   [White, William, bp.]   1748-1836.
    The case of the Episcopal churches in the United
States considered...   Philadelphia, Printed by
David C. Claypoole, 1782.

iv, [5]-35 p.   19 1/2 cm.
[Miscellaneous pamphlets. v. 757, no. 5]

13511   Wilkinson, James, 1757-1825.
Burr's conspiracy exposed: and General Wilkinson
vindicated against the slanders of his enemies on
that important occasion. [Washington, Printed for
the author] 1811.
3 p.l., 3-18, [3]-99, 136 p.   23 cm.
(Added t.-p.: Memoirs of General Wilkinson. vol. II)

13512   Wilmot-Horton, Sir Robert John, bart., 1784-1841.
Exposition and defence of Earl Bathurst's administration of the affairs of Canada, when colonial
secretary, during the years 1822 to 1827, inclusive.
By the Right Honourable Sir Robert Wilmot Horton,
bart., G. C. H.   London, J. Murray, 1838.
106 p.   20 cm.

13513   Wirt, William, 1772-1834.
The letters of the British spy. 5th ed. with the
last corrections of the author. Baltimore,
Published by Fielding Lucas, Jun., William Fry,
printer, 1813.
186 p.   (4 p. of advertisements at end)
13 1/2 cm.

13321   [Jones, William] 1760-1831.
Reflections upon the perils and difficulties of
the winter navigation of the Delaware. Means by
which these may be meliorated. Plans for the relief
of vessels entangled in the ice. Improvement of the
existing ice-harbours, and for the construction of
intermediate harbours parallel to the direction of
the stream and shore, in order that the force of the
ebb and flow alternately sweeping over the same
ground, may prevent the deposition of alluvion,
and preserve their primitive depth. Philadelphia,
Published by order of the Chamber of commerce, 1822.
15 p.   front.   23 cm.

The correct entry for no. 2857 (The New Sabin, v. II, p. 59)
is given below.

[Burke, Edmund] 1729?-1797.
An account of the European settlements in America.
In six parts. I. A short history of the discovery
of that part of the world. II. The manners and
customs of the original inhabitants. III. Of the
Spanish settlements. IV. Of the Portuguese. V. Of
the French, Dutch, and Danish. VI. Of the English...
London, R. and J. Dodsley, 1765.
2 v.   fronts. (fold. maps)   20 cm.
According to James Boswell this book was compiled
by Edmund Burke's cousin, William Burke (d. 1796).